Roni Mikel-Arieli
Remembering the Holocaust in a Racial State

New Perspectives on Modern Jewish History

Edited by
Cornelia Wilhelm

Volume 10

Roni Mikel-Arieli

Remembering the Holocaust in a Racial State

Holocaust Memory in South Africa from Apartheid to Democracy (1948–1994)

This book was published with the support of **The Alexander Dushkin Foundation** at The Avraham Harman Research Institute of Contemporary Jewry, The Hebrew University of Jerusalem, and with funds granted to the author through a 2019–2020 Phyllis Greenberg Heideman and Richard D. Heideman Fellowship at the **Jack, Joseph and Morton Mandel Center for Advanced Holocaust Studies of the United States Holocaust Memorial Museum**.

The US Holocaust Memorial Museum's Jack, Joseph, and Morton Mandel Center's mission is to ensure the long-term growth and vitality of Holocaust Studies. To do that, it is essential to provide opportunities for new generations of scholars. The vitality and the integrity of Holocaust Studies requires openness, independence, and free inquiry so that new ideas are generated and tested through peer review and public debate. The opinions of scholars expressed before, during the course of, or after their activities with the Mandel Center do not represent and are not endorsed by the Museum or its Mandel Center.

ISBN 978-3-11-152140-4
e-ISBN (PDF) 978-3-11-071554-5
e-ISBN (EPUB) 978-3-11-071563-7
ISSN 2192-9645

Library of Congress Control Number: 2022933840

Bibliographic Information published by the Deutsche Nationalbibliothek
The Deutsche Nationalbibliothek lists this publication in the Deutsche Nationalbibliografie; detailed bibliographic data are available on the Internet at http://dnb.dnb.de.

© 2024 Walter de Gruyter GmbH, Berlin/Boston
This volume is text- and page-identical with the hardback published in 2022.
Cover image: Nelson Mandela at the Opening of the "Anne Frank in the World, 1929–1945" Exhibition, Museum Africa, Johannesburg, Courtesy of Myra Osrin.
Typesetting: Integra Software Services Pvt.

www.degruyter.com

Acknowledgments

Remembering the Holocaust in a Racial State is the first book-length work dedicated entirely to Holocaust memory in the unique context of apartheid South Africa. The book builds on my PhD dissertation titled "Remembering the Holocaust in a Racial State: Cultural and Discursive Aspects of Holocaust Memory in South Africa from Apartheid to Democracy (1948–1994)," written at the Hebrew University of Jerusalem (HUJI) under the supervision of Louise Bethlehem and Amos Goldberg and approved in March 2019. It was my privilege to study and develop under the mentorship of such talented and professional scholars and attentive tutors. Their guidance, insightful suggestions, critical comments, and continuing support made the long journey, which began in 2013, possible.

I am also very grateful for the support of members of my dissertation committee, Manuela Consonni and Jackie Feldman, as well as to the anonymous reviewers of my dissertation, who provided important insights and comments on my research. I would like to acknowledge the editors and anonymous readers of three journals for their helpful advice on several chapters of this book and for permission to reprint them in revised form: *South African Historical Journal* (parts from chapter 6), *Journal of Jewish Identities* (chapter 7), *African Identities* (chapter 7), and *Journal for Genocide Research* (parts from the concluding chapter). At De Gruyter, I was fortunate to work with Cornelia Wilhelm, Editor of New Perspective on Modern Jewish History Series, and Julia Brauch, Acquisitions Editor for Jewish Studies and History, who have helped to shape the manuscript and bring it to publication. I am particularly grateful for the helpful reader's report of Shirli Gilbert as well as for her valuable insights and support throughout the past years.

Working at the intersection of the two fields – Holocaust memory and apartheid South Africa – means that I have incurred many personal and intellectual debts during the years of work on this project. For their valuable insights and endless support, I would like to thank Milton Shain, Gideon Shimoni, Marjorie Feld, and Elliot Ratzman. For their contribution in innumerable ways by reading various drafts, providing advice, discussions, and guidance throughout this journey, I would like to thank Eldad Ben Aharon, Rotem Giladi, Jonathan Alschech, Tal Zalmanovich, Nina Fischer, Ron Levy and Ayala Levin. My special gratitude to Karin Berkman for her important suggestions throughout, for her countless readings and editing suggestions during the final stages of this project, and for her unlimited friendship.

Like many historians, I am much obliged as well to staff in museums, libraries, and archives. For their assistance and insight, I would also like to thank Tali Nates, Director of the Johannesburg Holocaust & Genocide Centre and a very dear friend and colleague; Richard Freedman, Director of the Cape Town Holocaust & Genocide Centre; Mary Kluk, Director of the Durban Holocaust & Genocide Centre; Kier Schuringa, anti-apartheid and southern Africa archivist at the International Institute of Social History in Amsterdam; André Mohammed, Historical Papers Coordinator at the University of Western Cape Robben Island, Mayibuye Archives; Jan Erik Dubbelman, Head of the international department of the Anne Frank House in Amsterdam; Louis Wald of the Herman Wald private collection in London; Neeshan Balton, Director of the Ahmed Kathrada Foundation; and Yasmin Moosa, Archivist at the Ahmed Kathrada Foundation; Naomi Musiker, Archivist at the Rochlin Archive, Johannesburg; David Saks, the South African Jewish Board of Deputies, Johannesburg; Michal Singer, Archivist at the Cape Town Holocaust Centre; Juan-Paul Burke, Librarian at the Kaplan Centre for Jewish Studies, University of Cape Town; and the teams of the Bloomfield Library for the Humanities and Social Sciences, HUJI; the Israeli National Archive, Jerusalem; the Zionist Archive, Jerusalem; the Yad Vashem Archives, Jerusalem; Cape Town and Pretoria National Libraries; the Historical Papers Research Archive, University of the Witwatersrand in Johannesburg; the SABC Radio Archives, Johannesburg; the Johannesburg Public Library; and the South African History Archive, Johannesburg. I would also like to thank the School of Education Ethics in Research Committee at HUJI for providing ethical approval for the personal interviews conducted in the framework of my research (approval number 13902/2016); and to the interviewees who contributed their time and knowledge: Myra Osrin, Jan Erik Dubbelman, Alon Liel, Tali Nates, Richard Freedman, May Kluk, and the late Ahmed Kathrada.

When I first arrived in South Africa, with the help and support of the South African Zionist Federation in Israel (Telfed), I was received by members of the South African Jewish community in Johannesburg, Pretoria, and Durban with open arms. I would like to thank Hillary and Bartie Lubner, who invited me into their home and became my family in South Africa. Sadly, Bartie died in April 2016, and I owe him and Hillary an enormous debt of gratitude for their generosity and support along the way. I would also like to thank Rabbi Fox and his family from Pretoria, and the late Suzanne Edmunds from Durban, for welcoming me into their homes and for their kind hospitality.

Fellowships administered by various foundations enabled me to work on this project: during the years 2014–2018 I was privileged to be a research fellow at the European Research Council under the European Union's Seventh Framework Programme (FP/2007–2013) / ERC Grant Agreement no. 615564. Parts of this book were written within this framework and with the generous support of this fellowship, under the mentorship and professional guidance of Louise Bethlehem. I also benefited from the generosity as well as the stimulating environment provided by the Hoffman Program for Leadership and Social Responsibility, HUJI, between

2014–2017. In my fieldwork journeys, I enjoyed the support of the Christia Maria Foundation in South Africa; the Student Research Authority, HUJI; and the Dinur Center for Jewish History, HUJI. I also received awards from various institutes: the 2015 Research Support Scholarship of the International Institute for Holocaust Studies, Yad Vashem; the 2016 Wiesenthal Award from the Institute for Contemporary Jewry, HUJI; and the 2018 Robert Wistrich prize for outstanding research into Antisemitism, Vidal Sassoon International Center for the Study of Antisemitism, HUJI.

Moreover, I would like to thank The Alexander Dushkin Foundation at The Avraham Harman Research Institute of Contemporary Jewry, HUJI, and the Jack, Joseph and Morton Mandel Center for Advanced Holocaust Studies of the United States Holocaust Memorial Museum, for supporting the publication of this book.

Finally, I would like to acknowledge the support of my partner Guy and my sons Ori and Shaked, as well as the assistance of our extended family. Despite the difficulties involved in multiple fieldwork trips as well as long working hours, you have all joined together to help me carry out my research in the best way possible. This book is the direct outcome of your endless support.

Contents

Acknowledgments —— V

Abbreviations —— XI

List of Figures —— XIII

Introduction: Holocaust Memory in Apartheid South Africa —— 1
    Holocaust Memory: Between the Global and the Local —— 7
    Holocaust Memory in a De-Colonial Age —— 15

Chapter 1
Nazism, Afrikaner Nationalism and the 'Jewish Question' —— 19
    The 'Jewish Question' in South Africa —— 20
    The War Years —— 29

Chapter 2
Memory Engraved in Stone —— 36
    'I am here to stay on earth': Herman Wald's *Kria* —— 43
    The *Six Million* Monument —— 56

Chapter 3
The Holocaust on Trial – Eichmann in Pretoria —— 68
    The Sixties: Years of Anxiety —— 68
    Justice Served by the Victims —— 79
    Cold War Imaginaries —— 87
    Reactions to Capital Punishment —— 94

Chapter 4
Censoring the Holocaust under Apartheid —— 100
    The Apartheid Censorship System —— 108
    Holocaust on Television: *The World at War* —— 113
    Censoring Holocaust Denial under Apartheid —— 121
    Anne Frank: The Diary of a Young Girl in Afrikaans —— 133
    Holocaust Miniseries in South Africa —— 137

Chapter 5
Anne Frank in South Africa – Between the Communal and the National —— 143
    Waiting: South African Jewry during the Transition to Democracy —— 143
    From Amsterdam via London en route to South Africa —— 155
    "Anne Frank in the World Exhibition" in South Africa —— 159

Chapter 6
Holocaust Memory in the Lexicon of the Anti-Apartheid Movement —— 173
    Early Post-War Analogical Connections (1945–1960) —— 173
    The Jewish Genocide in the Anti-Apartheid Lexicon (1960s–1980s) —— 177

Chapter 7
Holocaust Memory in Ahmed Kathrada's Struggle against Apartheid —— 181
    Becoming Communist —— 182
    Reflecting on Apartheid in Post-War Europe —— 186
    The Road to Robben Island —— 193
    Reading Cultures on Robben Island —— 196
    Reading *The Diary of Anne Frank* on Robben Island —— 200

Conclusion: On the Role of Analogies —— 207
    Desmond Tutu and the Evolution of an Analogical Lexicon —— 210
    Desmond Tutu's Pilgrimage to Israel-Palestine (Christmas, 1989) —— 218
    Holocaust Memory in Post-Apartheid South Africa —— 226

Archives —— 231

Bibliography —— 235

Index —— 247

Abbreviations

SAJBD	South African Jewish Board of Deputies
SAZF	South African Zionist Federation
NP	National Party
CP	Conservative Party
ANC	African National Congress
SACP	South African Communist Party
CPSA	Communist Party of South Africa
NF	National Front
UN	United Nations
HNP	Herstigte Nasionale Party
SAIC	South African Indian Congress
SAP	South African Party
UP	United Party
PP	Progressive Party
SJC	Society of Jews and Christians
WCC	Witwatersrand Church Council
PAC	Pan Africanist Congress
YCL	Young Communist League
SABC	South African Broadcasting Corporation
SABC-TV	South African TV Broadcasting Corporation
GK	Gereformeerde Kerk
AFWE	Anne Frank in the World Exhibition
GLC	Greater London Council
EMU	Ethnic Minorities Unit
PLO	Palestinian Liberation Organization
PACT	Performing Art Council of the Transvaal
WFDY	World Federation of Democratic Youth
IUS	International Union of Students
UDF	United Democratic Front
SACC	South African Council of Churches
WCC	World Council of Churches
AWB	Afrikaner Weerstandsbeweging
SHIP	Student Holocaust Interviewing Project
TRC	Truth and Reconciliation Commission
AHF	Anne Frank House

List of Figures

Fig. 1 Herman Wald, *Kria*, Courtesy of Louis Wald —— 47
Fig. 2 The Voortrekker Monument, Mikel-Arieli Private Collection —— 53
Fig. 3 *Six Million* Monument Model, Courtesy of Louis Wald —— 58
Fig. 4 *Six Million* Monument, West Park Jewish Cemetery, Johannesburg, Courtesy of Louis Wald —— 62
Fig. 5 *Six Million* Monument Inscriptions in Yiddish and Hebrew, Mikel-Arieli Private Collection —— 64
Fig. 6 *Six Million* Monument Inscriptions in English and Afrikaans, Mikel-Arieli Private Collection —— 65
Fig. 7 A Model of the Laager at the Voortrekker Monument, Mikel-Arieli Private Collection —— 81

Introduction: Holocaust Memory in Apartheid South Africa

Remembering the Holocaust in a Racial State explores the cultural and discursive aspects of Holocaust memory in South Africa from the early years of apartheid through to the transition to democracy (1948–1994). The book engages with the question: how did the racially managed society of apartheid South Africa perceive, remember, and commemorate the racial persecution and destruction of European Jewry by the Nazis? Relatively few Jewish refugees entered the country during the Second World War due to local immigration legislation, and therefore Holocaust survivors constituted a somewhat small and neglected fraction of South African Jewry. Nevertheless, during the years of apartheid, Jews and non-Jews from all sections of South Africa's political and social spectrum engaged in different ways with the memories of the murder of European Jews by the Nazis.

Throughout the 1940s and 1950s, anti-apartheid activists in South Africa and abroad focused their rhetoric on delineating the parallels between policies of racial discrimination put into practice by the apartheid regime and those adopted by the Nazi regime.[1] The Nazi camps, however, were rarely represented in detail and the Jewish genocide was only cited as a warning of what apartheid might stimulate if left unchallenged.[2] The inflection of Holocaust memory onto the articulation of anti-racist politics in South Africa by way of analogy indeed existed on the margins of South African public discourse. However, as this book demonstrates, Holocaust memory serves first and foremost as a central collective memory for the Jewish community in the country. By providing a rich empirical account of the centrality of Holocaust memorialization to the construction of South African Jewry's collective identity, this book traces the changing responses of the white minority to the Holocaust during the period of apartheid and as South Africa underwent political transition to democratic rule between 1990 and 1994. These responses reflect the white communities' ambivalent attitudes toward Jewish whiteness in South Africa.

Apartheid, a system that legalized racism, was officially introduced in South Africa on 23 May 1948, three years after the end of the Second World War

---

[1] One such example is that of the political activist and journalist Brian Bunting, who systematically compared the Nuremberg Laws and apartheid legislation in his 1964 publication: Brian Bunting, *The Rise of the South African Reich* (Harmondsworth, Middlesex: Penguin Books Ltd, 1964).

[2] Shirli Gilbert, "Anne Frank in South Africa: Remembering the Holocaust During and After the Apartheid," *Holocaust and Genocide Studies* 26.3 (2012): 366–393.

and only nine days after the Israeli Declaration of Independence. Six months later, representatives of the world's nations convened at the Palais de Chaillot in Paris, France, to ratify two historic milestone documents: The Convention on the Prevention and Punishment of the Crime of Genocide and the Universal Declaration of Human Rights. South Africa did not adopt the genocide convention, nor did it sign the human rights declaration due to its potential to disrupt its practice of racial discrimination. Instead, the new nationalistic regime moved to entrench and intensify pre-existing racial segregation.

The apartheid-era 'whiteness' of South African Jews placed them in a much more powerful position than other minorities that belonged to the black, Indian, and Coloured communities. Founded in the early 19th century by British Jews who were joined by Eastern European Jews in the late 19th century, the South African Jewish community quickly assimilated to the English-speaking section of society and enjoyed the economic mobility of the white minority. However, this very integration gave rise to hostility toward Jews on the part of right-wing Afrikaners, culminating in the 1930s.

The rise of Nazism in Germany over the 1930s also inspired an increase in antisemitism in South Africa.[3] At the same time, Afrikaner nationalism and the belief in white supremacy were increasingly taking hold. Chapter 1, *Nazism, Afrikaner Nationalism and the 'Jewish Question'*, examines the historical contexts in which the South African Jewish community was formed and in which the racial definition of Jewishness in South Africa was formulated. The first part of the chapter presents a historiographic overview of the formulation of the "Jewish question" to provide a better understanding of historical perceptions of Jewishness and of Jewish whiteness in South African society. It considers the uncertain situation of Jews living in a racially segregated society – an uncertainty that would continue through to the apartheid era. The second part of the chapter sheds light on an understudied subject, that of the Jewish community's reactions to local antisemitism on the eve of the destruction of Jews in Europe. It provides a glimpse into the relief and rescue enterprises established by the community when the Union's government refused to provide shelter for Jewish refugees.

South African Jewry's ambivalent position was not static but changed significantly across time. The accommodation of Jews within the white minority

---

3 Throughout the book I use the term "antisemitism" instead of the hyphenated spelling (anti-Semitism), following the decision of the International Holocaust Remembrance Alliance in April 2015. See: International Holocaust Remembrance Alliance, "Memo on Spelling of Antisemitism: IHRA Committee on Antisemitism and Holocaust Denial," April 2015, 1–2.

and their assimilation into whiteness was made possible by a relative change in the attitude of the National Party (NP) toward South African Jewry during the 1950s. Events in South Africa did not, however, allay Jewish anxieties: The apparent disproportion of Jewish names on the list of those political opponents of apartheid accused at the Treason Trial (1958–1962) and at the Rivonia Trial (1963–1964) deeply affected the public image of the Jewish community, engendering still more anxiety. Moreover, the strongly Zionist community was deeply affected by the unstable relations between Israel and South Africa.

Israel's anti-apartheid votes at the UN following the Sharpeville massacre of 21 March 1960, as well as its expansion of bilateral diplomatic relations with decolonized African states, brought about an increase in local manifestations of antisemitism and repeated accusations of dual loyalty against the community members. However, the Six-Day War proved to be a turning point in restoring good diplomatic relations between the two countries, and thereafter between the Jewish community and the apartheid regime.[4] During the 1970s and the 1980s, the radicalization of anti-apartheid activism was met by an intensification of violence and oppression orchestrated by the white minority. This led to the appearance of a far more radical right that displayed proto-fascist and sometimes antisemitic elements. From the left, criticism of Israel's close ties with the apartheid regime and of its ill-treatment of the Palestinian people occupied the discourse. For the local Zionist Jewish community, deeply disturbed by what it condemned as Nazi-like antisemitic manifestations from the right and anti-Zionism from the left, Holocaust memory became the prime gauge of the tenuous position of the Jewish community.

As this book demonstrates, during the apartheid years the Jewish community perceived the Holocaust as central to its collective memory. The necessity of contesting the rampant antisemitism that had given rise to the Holocaust was conveyed to local white communities through official national channels. Organized South African Jewry mobilized the lessons of the Holocaust as a bulwark against local antisemitism. However, they perceived these lessons as particular to the Jewish community and did not frame them as universal concerns that might underlie anti-racism in the apartheid context.

As a minority within the privileged white minority, the South African Jewish community, although vulnerable in some sense, was also well-integrated economically. This privilege was central to the work of memory-making in the public

---

[4] For an in-depth examination of the evolving alliance between Israel and the apartheid government in South Africa see Sasha Polakow-Suransky, *The Unspoken Alliance: Israel's Secret Relationship with Apartheid South Africa* (New York: Random House, 2010).

sphere that the community pursued. The affluence and influence of the official community organizations facilitated commemoration projects, legal interventions, and advocacy through the staging of national and international exhibitions in the South African public sphere. Therefore, this book considers the agency of Jewish institutions such as the Jewish Board of Deputies (SAJBD) and the Zionist Federation (SAZF) and carefully explores the interplay between agency and vulnerability within the official Jewish community. In so doing, this book demonstrates how throughout the apartheid years the Jewish community was able to leverage Holocaust memory in order to overcome its ambivalent position in South Africa and aid its assimilation into the white community.

The notion of collective memory has been comprehensively studied in a variety of critical texts. In his seminal work, *On Collective Memory*, Maurice Halbwachs argues that collective memories establish a set of values through which the community affirms its perception of the world, and which thereby define community members versus its external 'other.' Collective memories are thus a socio-political product of cultural practices that express the power relations in society; they constitute a field of cultural negotiation, through which different narratives compete for their place in history.[5] Following Halbwachs, Jan Assmann argues that "the principle of memory follows on from that of 'being chosen' – being chosen means nothing less than a complex network of rigidly fixed obligations not allowing under any circumstances memory to fade away."[6] He distinguishes between two forms of collective memory: communicative memory and cultural memory. While the first is based on day-to-day communication, the second focuses on cultural formations such as ceremonies, traditions, and monuments. Unlike communicative memories, Assmann argues, cultural memory does not develop naturally over time, but is a product of constant and deliberate efforts to restore traditions and customs.[7]

While Assmann focuses on cultural memory and its effects on the formation of collective social identities, Moshe Zuckerman perceives institutionalized instances of collective memory manifest in memorial sites, ceremonies, and official texts as insufficient for revealing local attitudes to a given historical event. Zuck-

---

[5] Maurice Halbwachs, *On Collective Memory* (Chicago: The University of Chicago Press, 1992).
[6] Jan Assmann, *Cultural Memory and Early Civilization* (Cambridge: Cambridge University Press, 2011), 17.
[7] Jan Assmann, "Collective Memory and Cultural Identity," *New German Critique* 65 (1995): 125–126.

erman argues that collective memories are embodied not only in the cultural configurations that represent them but also in the actual discourse about them.[8]

Following Assmann's conception of cultural memory, this book draws on a wide range of primary sources, including speeches and rabbinic sermons, literature, memoirs, plays, films, exhibitions, monuments, oral interviews, and biographic sources, to explore the urgent, ongoing efforts of organized South African Jewry to commemorate the murder of European Jews. At the same time, it adopts Zuckerman's focus on everyday practices and their potential for creating significant modifications to the absorption and interpretation of collective memories. By reading communal and governmental organizations' reports together with reportage in the Jewish and non-Jewish press, this book reveals the role played by those commemorations in the formation of Holocaust consciousness within the non-Jewish white communities in South Africa.

It is important to note that this book utilizes a rich collection of print media both in English and Afrikaans from various areas in South Africa, such as the Gauteng based *Sunday Times, The Star, Beeld, The Citizen, Pretoria News, Die Transvaler, The Rand Daily Mail,* and *The Sunday Star;* the Western Cape based *Cape Times* and *Cape Argus;* the KwaZulu-Natal based the *Daily News, The Witness, The Mercury;* and the Free State based *Volksblad.* The collection also includes political journals such as *Die Kerkblad,* the organ of the Reformist Church of South Africa (Gereformeerde Kerk- GK), *Die Burger,* the organ of the National Party (NP), *Die Suiderstem,* the organ of the United Party (UP), and *Die Afrikaner,* the organ of the Herstigte Nasionale Party (HNP), as well as the ultra-right wing monthly journal, *South African Observer.* This collection includes the collated press clippings of the Rochlin Archive in Johannesburg as well as a selection of original newspapers from the National Libraries in Pretoria and Cape Town.[9] Considering their audiences as well as their relative circulation and influence, the reliance on sources from the contemporary press throughout the book demonstrates the changing attitudes in public discourse regarding Holocaust memory over time.

Many works have addressed the significance and global impact of Holocaust memory.[10] However, despite the growing interest in South Africa and its

---

8 Moshe Zuckerman, השואה בחדר האטום: ה"שואה" בעיתונות הישראלית בתקופת מלחמת המפרץ [*Shoah in the Sealed Room: The "Holocaust" in the Israeli Press during the Gulf War*] (Tel Aviv: Self-published, 1993), 16.

9 In referring to archival materials I have tried to indicate as clearly as possible where they are located. Nevertheless, it should be noted that the Rochlin Archive is not always clearly organized or catalogued, and there is much duplication of material between files.

10 See, among many others, Daniel Levy and Natan Sznaider, *The Holocaust and Memory in the Global Age* (Philadelphia: Temple University Press, 2006); Daniel Levy and Natan Sznaider,

role in the global arena during the Cold War, and despite the existence of a unique Jewish community there, the particularity of the South African memory of the Holocaust have not yet been thoroughly investigated. The history of South African Jewry has been widely researched with a focus on Jewish immigration to South Africa; the establishment of the community and its institutions; the South African Zionist Movement; and its accommodation to the apartheid regime.[11] Another prominent body of literature focuses on antisemitism in South Africa while examining the roots of that phenomenon in the local arena, with a particular interest in the forms of antisemitism that characterized the country in the 1930s and 1940s.[12] Several recent publications have also focused on the few Jewish refugees who came from Europe to South Africa during the Second World War.[13] However, very few publications have addressed the ways in which the Holocaust was remembered and commemorated during the

---

"Memory Unbound: The Holocaust and the Formation of Cosmopolitan Memory," *European Journal of Social History*, 5.1 (2002): 87–106; Amos Goldberg and Haim Hazan, *Marking Evil: Holocaust Memory in the Global Age* (New York and Oxford: Berghahn, 2015).

11 Gideon Shimoni, *Community and Conscience: The Jews in Apartheid South Africa* (Waltham: Brandeis University Press, 2003); Gideon Shimoni, *Jews and Zionism: The South African Experience (1910–1967)* (Cape Town: Oxford University Press, 1980); Richard Mendelson and Milton Shain, *The Jews in South Africa: An Illustrated History* (Johannesburg: Jonathan Ball Publishers, 2008); Claudia Bathsheba Braude, *Contemporary Jewish Writing in South Africa* (Lincoln: University of Nebraska Press, 2001); Oren Baruch Stier, "South Africa's Jewish Complex," *Jewish Social Studies* 10.3 (2004): 123–142; Gustav Saron, *The South African Jewish Board of Deputies, its role and development: an analytical review on its 70th anniversary* (Johannesburg: The South African Jewish Board of Deputies, 1973); Riva Michal Krut, "Building a Home and a Community: Jews in Johannesburg, 1886–1914," (PhD dissertation, University of London, 1985).

12 Milton Shain, "From Undesirable to Unassimilable: The Racialization of the 'Jew' in South Africa," in *Holocaust Memory and Racism in the Postwar World*, ed. Shirli Gilbert and Avril Alba (Detroit: Wayne State University Press, 2019), 72–90; Milton Shain, *The Roots of Anti-Semitism in South Africa* (Charlottesville: University Press of Virginia, 1994); Shain, *A Perfect Storm: Antisemitism in South Africa 1930–1948* (Johannesburg: Jonathan Ball Publishers, 2015); Jocelyn Hellig, *Anti-Semitism in South Africa Today* (Tel Aviv: Tel Aviv University Press, 1996); Patrick Jonathan Furlong, *Between Crown and Swastika: The Impact of the Radical Right on the Afrikaner Nationalist Movement in the Fascist Era* (Johannesburg: Witwatersrand University Press, 1991).

13 Shirli Gilbert, *From things Lost: Forgotten Letters and the Legacy of the Holocaust* (Detroit: Wayne State University Press, 2017); Steven Robins, *Letters of Stone: From Nazi Germany to South Africa* (Cape Town: Penguin Books, 2016); Lotta M. Stone, "Seeking asylum: German Jewish refugees in South Africa, 1933–1948," (PhD dissertation, Clark University, 2010).

apartheid years. Those that do focus mainly on the early post-war years or on the post-apartheid period.[14]

In this context, two innovative studies by Shirli Gilbert stand out: the first focuses on the image of Anne Frank as a symbol that underlies the history and politics of Holocaust memory in South Africa during apartheid and the transition to democracy;[15] the second explores the changing ways in which the Nazi past has featured in curricula and textbooks during the apartheid and post-apartheid years.[16] These two illuminating projects, while important, provide a partial picture of the construction of Holocaust memory in the complex context of apartheid South Africa. This book seeks to further expand the existing literature on the subject by means of a comprehensive synthesis of the dominant discursive and cultural formations of Holocaust memory in South African society during the apartheid period, basing its findings on extensive archival research.

Holocaust Memory: Between the Global and the Local

Since the early 1990s, many historical studies have focused on the different attitudes toward the Jewish genocide in post-war societies. The earliest studies explored Holocaust memory in countries that had direct connections to Nazi Germany during the war. Therefore, the range of national case studies focused initially on the influence of the Holocaust in Nazi occupied countries, as well as

---

[14] For research on Holocaust memory in South Africa during the early post-War years see Juliette Peires. *Ruling by Race: Nazi Germany and Apartheid South Africa* (Cape Town: Century City, 2008); Shirli Gilbert, "Jews and Racial State: Legacies of the Holocaust in Apartheid South Africa," *Jewish Social Studies* 16.3 (2010): 32–64; Michael, A. Green, "South African Jewish Responses to the Holocaust, 1941–1948" (master's thesis, University of South Africa, 1987); Milton Shain, "South Africa," in *The World Reacts to the Holocaust*, ed. David S. Wyman and Charles H. Rosenzveig (Baltimore: The Johns Hopkins University Press, 1996), 670–689. For publications on Holocaust memory in post-apartheid South Africa see Shirli Gilbert, "Remembering the Racial State: Holocaust Memory in Post-Apartheid South Africa," in *Holocaust Memory in a Globalizing World,* ed. J. S. Eder, P. Gassert, and A. Steinweis (Göttingen: Wallstein Verlag: 2016), 199–214; Tali Nates, "'But, apartheid was also genocide . . . What about our suffering?' Teaching the Holocaust in South Africa- opportunities and challenges," *Intercultural Education*, 21.1 (2010): 17–26; Tracey Petersen, "Politics, Policy and Holocaust Education in South Africa," in *Policy and Practice: Pedagogy about the Holocaust and Genocide Papers* 11 (2013).
[15] Gilbert, "Anne Frank in South Africa," 366–393.
[16] Shirli Gilbert, "Nazism and Racism in South African Textbooks," in *Holocaust Memory and Racism in the Post-War World*, ed. Shirli Gilbert and Avril Alba (Detroit: Wayne State University Press, 2019), 350–385.

in Israel (the official representative of the Jewish victims), Germany (the country that perpetuated the Nazi crimes), and the United States of America and Britain (the liberators of the Nazi camps). In these studies, there is a consensus that despite the extensive media coverage around the world following the liberation of Nazi concentration camps during April-May 1945, and in the wake of the Nuremberg Trials of 1946–1945, interest in the Jewish genocide was limited.[17]

Many scholars have also pointed to the effects of early Cold War politics on the construction of counter memories of the Jewish genocide during the postwar period.[18] In the new emergent global struggle between East and West, a shift of alliances occurred: while in the West, the Federal Republic of Germany was newly perceived as an ally and the Soviet Union as an enemy, the East considered the Red Army the only true liberator of Germany and the world from Hitler's fascist hands and saw in America a new aggressive imperialist evil. Nevertheless, in both the East and the West, a somewhat universalist perspective of the Jewish victims was constructed. Emphasis was placed on the victims of fascism as a general entity, without singling out the plight of the Jews.[19]

In Israel too, many historians have argued that during the first decade of Israel's existence the survivors' stories were repressed and silenced and that, as a consequence, the Jewish genocide did not lie at the center of Israel's public discourse; the history of the Holocaust was not integrated into the Israeli education system and, in fact, constituted a marginal element in the formulation of

---

[17] Donald Bloxham, *Genocide on Trial: War Crimes Trials and the Formation of Holocaust History and Memory* (Oxford: Oxford University Press, 2001); David S. Wyman, *The World Reacts to the Holocaust* (Baltimore: The Johns Hopkins University Press, 1996); David Cesarani, "Introduction," in *After the Holocaust: Challenging the Myth of Silence,* ed. David Cesarani and Eric J. Sundquist, (London: Routledge, 2012), 1–15; Judith Miller, *One, By One, By One: Facing the Holocaust* (New York: Simon & Schuster, 1991); Jeffrey Herf, *Divided Memory: The Nazi Past in the Two Germanys* (Cambridge, MA: Harvard University Press, 1997); Hasia R. Diner, *We remember with reverence and love: American Jews and the myth of silence after the Holocaust 1945–1962* (New York: New York University Press, 2010); Peter Novick, *The Holocaust in American Life* (New York: Houghton Mifflin, 1999).
[18] Pieter Lagrou, "Victims of Genocide and National Memory: Belgium, France and the Netherlands, 1945–1966," *Past and Present* 154 (1997): 181–222; Pieter Lagrou, *The Legacy of Nazi Occupation. Patriotic Memory and National Recovery in Western Europe, 1945–1965* (Cambridge: Cambridge University Press, 2000), 7; David Cesarani, "How Post-war Britain Reflected on the Nazi Persecution and Mass Murder of Europe's Jews: A Reassessment of Early Responses," *Jewish Culture and History* 12.1–2 (2010): 95–130, at 96.
[19] On the divide in Holocaust memory during the Cold War period see: Bas Von Benda-Beckmann, *A German Catastrophe? German Histories and The Allied Bombing, 1945–2010* (Amsterdam: Amsterdam University Press, 2010); Herf, *Divided Memory*; Novick, *The Holocaust in American Life.*

Israeli identity.[20] Contesting this position, Dalia Ofer and Anita Shapira argued that during the years 1948–1960 the Holocaust as a political issue was a key element of Israeli public discourse due to the debate over reparations from Germany in 1952 and the Kastner affair, which began in 1953.[21] However, they too concede the dearth of private memories of the Holocaust in the public arena during those years, as a result of the dominance of a national ethos of Jewish heroism, which repressed the stories of 'passive' victims.[22]

Indeed, questions about the passivity of the Jews during the Holocaust who went to their deaths "like sheep to the slaughter," Jewish cooperation with the Nazis, extradition of Jews to their murderers, and other concerns regarding the complex reality of European Jewry under Nazism constituted an exposed nerve in the Jewish world in general and in Israeli society in particular. Roni Stauber claimed that these subjects were viewed during that period through the prism of David Ben-Gurion's ideological stance, which sought to emphasize the ethos and myths associated with the struggle for Israel's independence. The image of the diasporic Jew, the passive victim of Nazi persecution, was repressed.[23] According to Shaul Friedlander, the implication of the passivity of Holocaust victims undergirds the silence of the survivors in Israeli society. After the Eichmann Trial, however, the attitude to the Holocaust and its survivors underwent profound changes.[24]

---

20 Dalia Ofer, "The Strength of Remembrance: Commemorating the Holocaust during the First Decade of Israel," *Jewish Social Studies* 14.1 (2009): 1–35; Tom Segev, *The Seventh Million: The Israeli and the Holocaust* (New York: Picador, 2000).
21 Israel (Rudolf) Kastner was a leader of the Hungarian Jewish community who in 1943 was among the founders of the "Relief and Rescue Committee" which, after the Nazis invasion to Hungary in March 1944, negotiated with Adolf Eichmann in an effort to prevent the destruction of Hungarian Jewry. During the early 1950s, Kastner served as a clerk at the Israeli Ministry of Trade and Industry, and in the summer of 1952, Malchiel Gruenwald, an elderly Hungarian, published booklets accusing Kastner of collaborating with the Nazis. A libel case brought by the Israeli government against Gruenwald ended with the judge's ruling that Kastner had "sold his soul to the Devil." In 1957 Kastner was assassinated in Tel Aviv as part of a right-wing conspiracy. For more information on the Kastner Affair see: Yehiam Weitz, "Changing Conceptions of the Holocaust: The Kasztner Case," in *Reshaping the Past: Jewish History and the Historians*, ed. Jonathan Frankel, (Oxford: Oxford University Press, 1994), 211–230.
22 Anita Shapira, יהודים חדשים: יהודים ישנים [*Yehudim Hadashim: Yehudim Yeshanim*] (Tel Aviv: Am Oved, 1997); Dalia Ofer, "השיח הישראלי על השואה" ["The Israeli Discourse on the Holocaust,"] in *Holocaust in Jewish History*, ed. Dan Michman, (Jerusalem: Yad Vashem, 2005), 328–393.
23 Roni Stauber, *The Holocaust in Israeli Public Debate in the 1950s: Ideology and Memory* (Edgware, UK: Vallentine Mitchell, 2007).
24 Shaul Friedlander, "Opening Lecture: The Shoah between Memory and History," *Jewish Studies* 30 (1990): 11–20.

South Africa, usually considered marginal in the study of diaspora Jews, adopted strategies of public memorialization far earlier than other diasporic Jewish communities. Chapter 2, *Memory Engraved in Stone*, provides an account of the first decade of post-War Holocaust commemoration in South Africa, before the Sharpeville massacre in 1960 decisively reoriented the social fabric of apartheid South Africa at large. During that period, the Jewish community's mnemonic practices took shape as its members mourned the loss of their relatives in Eastern Europe and attempted to commemorate the victims of the Holocaust, all the while confronting antisemitism coming from right wing Afrikaners.

Over the first decade after the war, the organization *She'erith Hapletah* was established to provide a communal home for the few survivors who arrived in the Union; annual Days of Mourning meetings were held throughout the country; monuments were erected; dramatic plays were staged in the national theatre; and the Jewish genocide was prominently featured in the communal press. Moreover, while Jewish communities across the world focused their efforts on communal commemorations, the South African community by contrast mobilized efforts to publicly convey an anti-antisemitic message to local white communities in the country. Holocaust-related publications were translated into Afrikaans, commemoration events were broadcast on national radio, and the national press frequently reported on the traumatic genocide of European Jews.

As Chapter 2 demonstrates, the Jewish community was invested in constructing commemorative monuments in memory of the deceased European Jews. The community conveyed messages embodied in these memorials about the moral crisis of the Holocaust, the intensity of loss that it represented, and the savagery of racism that lay beneath it. However, as these memorials addressed the white communities of South Africa, their message was not made explicitly relevant to the racism of the new regime on the home front.

Many scholars cite the Eichmann trial as triggering increased interest in the Jewish genocide worldwide.[25] For Israelis, the trial provided a first encounter with the stories of the survivors as their horrific testimonies of the catastrophe became the focus of public attention. The trial was the first to implement the Nazis and Nazis Collaborators Punishment Law of 1950, and preparation for the trial included the promotion of Holocaust documentation and commemoration.[26]

---

25 Wyman, *The World Reacts to the Holocaust*; Miller, *One, By One, By One*; Herf, *Divided Memory*; Novick, *The Holocaust in American Life*; Dean, *Aversion and Erasure*; Deborah Lipstadt, *The Eichmann Trial* (New York: Random House, 2011).
26 Hanna Yablonka, *The State of Israel vs. Adolf Eichmann* (New York: Schocken Books, 2004).

The Eichmann trial aroused great interest throughout the world. As countries followed the trial's unfolding from beginning to end, this contributed to the shaping of Holocaust memory in Western culture.[27] While criticism regarding some of the legal aspects of the trial was voiced worldwide, it was still perceived as a turning point in global Holocaust consciousness. It converted Holocaust memory from a collective memory in which the personal experience of the victims was occluded and which focused almost entirely on the heroic ethos of Jewish resistance to a memory that relocated the survivors and their testimonies to the forefront. In addition, it heralded a worldwide recognition of Israel as the representative of the six million Jewish victims of the Holocaust.[28]

In South Africa, too, the Eichmann trial occupied a central role in public discourse. Chapter 3, *The Holocaust on Trial – Eichmann in Pretoria*, focuses on the early 1960s and examines the reception of the Eichmann Trial in different segments of the racially stratified South African society. It reveals how, through this reception, the global arena was brought closer to the local sphere and the Holocaust came increasingly to be placed at the forefront of the public discourse. Eichmann's line of defense, which stressed his inability to defy his superiors' instructions, bore relevance for similar situations in South Africa. Nonetheless, a discourse analysis of the Afrikaans and English national press reveals the marginality of questions regarding moral responsibility in the local matrices of events.

By focusing on the Jewish narrative of the Holocaust while overlooking the broader lessons that could be drawn from it for a local context, the South African Jewish community sought to provide the white public with an alternative narrative with which to identify. However, while there is no doubt that the white population in South Africa perceived the Holocaust as an integral part of the Jewish community's history and identity, criticism of the Jewish claims upon experiences of human suffering occupied the discourse. This overshadowed the community's efforts to use the Eichmann Trial instrumentally to contest antisemitism in the national public sphere. Instead of promoting empathy, the Jewish community's confrontational preoccupation with the affair served mainly to perpetuate its own uncertain status.

---

27 Andy Pearce, *Holocaust Consciousness in Contemporary Britain* (London: Routledge, 2014), 22–23; Idith Zertal, *Israel's Holocaust and the Politics of Nationhood* (Cambridge: Cambridge University Press, 2005), 109–110.
28 For more reading on the Eichmann trial as a turning point in Israeli society, see: Yablonka, *The State of Israel Vs. Adolf Eichmann*; Aharon Appelfeld, *The Story of a Life* (New York: Schocken, 2006); Oz Almog, *The Sabra: The Creation of the New Jew* (Berkeley: University of California Press, 2000).

Although many historians have pointed to the Eichmann trial as a major landmark that placed the Holocaust on the map of historical, educational, legal, and cultural discourse in Israel and the diaspora, some have argued that the Six-Day War was in fact the major turning point in Holocaust memory. Scholars such as Tom Segev, Peter Novick, and others claimed that following the 1967 war, and even more so after the 1973 war, Jewish communities around the world reinforced the sense that Israel and the Jewish people shared a common fate and that the relationship of diaspora Jews to Israel reached a new level of intimacy.[29] During those years, the Holocaust became a symbol for existential threats and the reason for maintaining a strong Israeli military force.[30]

A new perception of the Holocaust emerged around the Jewish world during that period. This perception was based on the claim that the Holocaust must be viewed as a unique event in human history. Any comparison of another event with the Holocaust came to be conceived as an expression of contempt for the memory of the victims.[31] Interestingly, although this perception became more widespread among Jewish and non-Jewish constituencies following the Six-Day War, this book demonstrates how this perception can be detected in South African Jewry's commemoration projects since the early post-Second World War years. This position gathered force in the 1970s when Israeli and Zionist communities worldwide began to focus on the global struggle against antisemitism, on the need to prosecute war criminals, and on contesting widespread Holocaust denial.[32] Contesting the uniqueness of the Holocaust was positioned as "far more insidious than outright denial," since it was seen both to nurture and to be nurtured by Holocaust denial.[33]

In the late 1970s, the American network NBC televised the five-part miniseries *Holocaust: The Story of the Family Weiss*, which was screened in the United States and thereafter in many other countries. The series exposed a variety of audiences to the calculated brutality of the killers, the silent agony of the victims, and the indifference of the outside world. However, such images of the Holocaust, presented on commercial television, instigated a stormy debate regarding

---

29 Segev, *The Seventh Million*, 368; Novick, *The Holocaust in American Life*, 149.
30 Levy and Sznaider, "Memory Unbound," 96.
31 Novick, *The Holocaust in American Life*, 154.
32 Pearce, *Holocaust Consciousness in Contemporary Britain*, 26–27.
33 Deborah Lipstadt, "Holocaust-Denial and the Compelling Force of Reason," *Patterns of Prejudice* 26.1-2 (1992): 64–76, at 72–73.

what many American survivors perceived as the trivialization of the Holocaust.³⁴ Following the screening of *Holocaust* in April 1978, and in response to American Holocaust survivors rejecting what they perceived as a disgraceful representation of their traumatic past, survivors' testimony projects began to emerge, aiming to represent the Holocaust through the voices of actual victims.³⁵ The influence of this discourse increased in the 1980s with the screening of Claude Lanzmann's *Shoah* documentary, the Historikerstreit in West Germany, and the emergence of various oral history projects collecting Holocaust testimonies. The Holocaust was perceived as a formative event in human history, and the survivors as heroes who had stories to tell and lessons to share with future generations.³⁶

Chapter 4, *Censoring the Holocaust under Apartheid*, examines the ways in which the repressive apparatus of state censorship in South Africa was used by official Jewish institutions during the 1970s to counter the racism inherent in discourses of Holocaust denial as these circulated through the print media in South Africa. The chapter addresses the SAJBDs' struggle against the publication *Did Six Million Really Die? The Truth at Last* (1974) by British Holocaust denier Richard Harwood, which appeared in the local ultra-right-wing press. This analysis is set against a countervailing account of the national responses to Holocaust-related content in popular cultural media such as the televised British documentary *The World at War* (1976), the above-mentioned American mini-series *Holocaust* (1978), and the theatrical production of *The Diary of Anne Frank* (1977) in Afrikaans. Through an analysis of popular culture, this chapter examines Jewish leadership's efforts to publicly promote representations of the Holocaust on the one hand, and to confront and censor scripts of Holocaust denial through the local censorship system on the other.

Another important landmark in the global construction of Holocaust memory is the fall of the Iron Curtain in 1989. As Manuela Consonni argues, when the Cold War ended, not only was the East-West political conflict over – the conflict between the two counter interpretations of Nazism, Fascism, and the Holocaust

---

34 Levy and Sznaider, *The Holocaust and Memory in a Global Age*, 116; Tom Dreisbach, "Transatlantic Broadcasts: Holocaust in America and West Germany," *Penn History Review* 16.2 (2009): 76–97, at 76.
35 Michal Givoni, אתיקה של עדות: היסטוריה של בעיה [*The Ethics of Witnessing: A History of a Problem*] (Jerusalem: Van Leer Institute, 2015), 131–132.
36 Givoni, אתיקה של עדות [*The Ethics of Witnessing*]; Wyman, *The World Reacts to the Holocaust*; Alon Confino, *Foundational Pasts: The Holocaust as Historical Understanding* (Cambridge: Cambridge University Press, 2012); David B. MacDonald, *Identity Politics in the Age of Genocide: The Holocaust and Historical Representation* (London: Routledge, 2008), 21–23.

between East and West now drew to a close.[37] Daniel Levy and Natan Szneider also mark the end of the Cold War as providing critical momentum for the creation of a more globalized discourse concerning the Holocaust. They point to the establishment of a global human rights regime in which Holocaust memory plays a central role in restructuring the international arena around a global symbol of evil.[38] A similar stance was adopted by Jeffrey Alexander in his essay "On the Social Construction of Moral Universals," where he argues that following the end of the Cold War, the Holocaust gained "a mythical status that transformed it into the archetypical sacred-evil of our time."[39]

This new global positioning of Holocaust memory in the early 1990s provided a powerful vehicle for promoting national unity during the critical period of transition from apartheid to democracy in South Africa. The political and social instability of the time served as the basis for a new local discourse on the Holocaust. Increasingly, emphasis was placed on the analogies between the events of the Holocaust and the situation in apartheid South Africa. The historical trauma of the holocaust was thus evoked in order to provide a means of examining ongoing trauma under the apartheid regime. The examination of these parallels held potential for mutual understanding and empathy.

Chapter 5, *Anne Frank in South Africa: Between the Communal and the National*, focuses on the exhibition *Anne Frank in the World, 1929–1945*, displayed in South Africa between 1994 and 1996 and described by Gilbert as a pivotal event in the construction of post-apartheid Holocaust memory. It examines challenges and tensions emerging throughout the planning process of the exhibition, mainly around the issue of analogies and the issue of Israel's cooperation with the apartheid regime. This chapter reveals how this exhibition presented a history of Jewish oppression, resistance, and liberation that cast South African Jews as anti-racist heroes and victims of racism at the same time, thus claiming a space for Jews in the new landscape of black democratic rule.

As this book demonstrates, the shaping of Holocaust memory in South Africa intersected with processes occurring throughout the Western world, and especially in the United States, Western Europe, and Israel. However, these shared nodes represent not merely a transfer of Holocaust memory from one national arena to another. This book seeks to tease out the connections, correspondences,

---

37 Manuela Consonni, *1945–1985* רויסטנצה או שואה: זיכרון הגירוש וההשמדה באיטליה [*Resistance or Holocaust: The Memory of the Deportation and the Extermination in Italy, 1945 -1985*] (Jerusalem: Magness Press, 2010), 147.
38 Levy and Szneider, "Memory Unbound," 87–106.
39 Jeffrey Alexander, "On the Social Construction of Moral Universals: The 'Holocaust from War Crime to Trauma Drama," *European Journal of Social Theory* 5.1 (2002): 5–85, at 31.

distinctions, and ramifications of such nodes in the specific context of apartheid-era South Africa.

Holocaust Memory in a De-Colonial Age

This book is located within a growing body of literature which addresses attitudes toward Nazism and the Jewish genocide in the age of de-colonization.[40] It interweaves South African local history with global developments in Holocaust memory and invites a dialogue between what the historian Charles Maier refers to as the two opposing master narratives of the twentieth century: the Holocaust and post-colonialism.[41]

While the Holocaust narrative "focuses on the Holocaust and/or Stalinist Communist political killing as the culminating historical experience of the century," the post-Colonial narrative, conversely, argues that "the domination of the West over the massive societies of what once could be called the Third World established the preeminent historical scaffolding of the century."[42] The Holocaust narrative suggests that modern principles of human rights were formulated in response to the atrocities of the Holocaust. The post-Colonial narrative, by contrast, demonstrates how the very same modern liberal democratic states that espoused such principles were themselves responsible for pervasive human rights violations. Nevertheless, as Maier argues, "both narratives claim current relevance, and they are often intertwined."[43]

In his seminal book, *Multidirectional Memory: Remembering the Holocaust in the Age of Decolonization*, Michael Rothberg argues that "the emergence of collective memory of the Nazi genocide in the 1950s and 1960s takes place in a punctual dialogue with ongoing processes of decolonization and civil rights struggle and their modes of coming to terms with colonialism, slavery, and

---

[40] A recent and very important publication, edited by Shirli Gilbert and Avril Alba, explores Holocaust memory and Racism in the post-War world. It engages with diverse case studies of racial societies in which Holocaust memory has been encountered, including Australia, Israel-Palestine, North America and South Africa. See: Shirli Gilbert and Avril Alba, *Holocaust Memory and Racism in the Post-War World* (Detroit: Wayne State University Press, 2019).
[41] Charles S. Maier. "Consigning the Twentieth Century to History: Alternative Narratives for the Modern Era," *American Historical Review* 165.3 (2000): 807–830.
[42] Maier, "Consigning the Twentieth Century to History," 826.
[43] Maier, "Consigning the Twentieth Century to History," 827.

racism."⁴⁴ While Maier focuses on the divergence of these two counter narratives, Rothberg suggests a paradigm of multidirectional memory, which steers the discussion of memory away from competitive models toward the claim that the dynamics of different historical memories are not necessarily based on zero-sum struggles.⁴⁵ He criticizes the literary critic Walter Benn Michaels's position on "the seemingly incompatible legacies of slavery and the Nazi genocide in the United States." While he agrees with Michaels that "a direct line runs between remembrance of the past and the formation of identity in the present," he does not perceive the competitive framework as inevitable. Instead, Rothberg focuses on the public articulation of collective memory by marginalized and oppositional social groups as carrying the potential to enable other groups to voice their own claims for recognition and justice.⁴⁶

Like Michaels, many memory scholars have argued that the relationship between different collective memories is shaped by a competitive framework. Based on the assumption that memories are a tool to enable people to construct their pasts, and that the collective dimension of memory represents the past as common collective knowledge, the historical narrative is often perceived as a closed narrative representing a zero-sum struggle between contested memories. In such struggles, the rejection of the 'other' and his histories of suffering is affected. Therefore, collective memories serve not only to construct a shared identity; they are also an arena for ideological and identity struggles, closely linked to questions of power and symbolic capital.⁴⁷

Such questions are particularly glaring when examined in the South African context, due to its local histories of colonialism, segregation, and apartheid. Through the prism of Holocaust memory, this book views South African society as an arena of conflict between the interests and identities of different groups. The wide range of attitudes toward Nazism and the Jewish genocide among different sectors in South Africa are not simply responses to the historical event of the Holocaust; instead, they are a function of the distinct identities at play in each of these sectors and a reflection of their positions within the social and political hierarchy in apartheid South Africa.

Most of the chapters in this book focus on white perceptions of the Holocaust and reveal tensions between the white communities in the country regarding the

---

44 Michael Rothberg, *Multidirectional Memory: Remembering the Holocaust in the Age of Decolonization* (Stanford: Stanford University Press, 2009), 22–23.
45 Rothberg, *Multidirectional Memory*, 18.
46 Rothberg, *Multidirectional Memory*, 21.
47 Jeffrey C. Alexander, *Remembering the Holocaust: A Debate* (New York: Oxford University Press, 2009); Novick, *The Holocaust in American Life*.

place of collective memories of suffering in the public arena. However, the book also moves beyond an insular focus on the South African Jewish community in its consideration of state actors and, in a very different modality, it investigates prominent figures in the anti-apartheid struggle and the role of Holocaust memory in their fascinating journeys towards freedom.

This focus draws on Louise Bethlehem's paradigm of "The Restlessness of Apartheid." She argues that the global circulation of anti-apartheid expressive culture is a tool for reading historical contestations of race beyond the borders of South Africa. Through charting the diffusion of anti-apartheid expressive culture beyond South Africa, Bethlehem interprets apartheid as a heuristic through which struggles over race and social justice might be interpreted in a transnational setting.[48]

Inspired by her model, which alerts us to the importance of tracking the itineraries of opponents of apartheid as they operate in the global cultural sphere, this part of the book focuses on the role of Holocaust memory in the struggle against apartheid. Chapter 6, *Holocaust Memory in the Lexicon of the Anti-Apartheid Movement*, provides the larger context of the use of the Nazi analogy in anti-apartheid activism from the 1940s through to the 1980s. Chapter 7, *Holocaust Memory in Ahmed Kathrada's Struggle against Apartheid*, and then the concluding chapter, *On the Role of Analogies*, focus on the transnational journeys of two prominent figures in the anti-apartheid struggle – the Muslim, Indian South African veteran of the anti-apartheid struggle, treason trialist, and long-serving political prisoner Ahmed Mohamad Kathrada and the anti-apartheid activist and Nobel Peace Prize laureate, Archbishop Desmond Mapilo Tutu.[49] Following Rothberg's claim for possible productive interactions between Holocaust memory and other traumatic memories of decolonization, racism, and other legacies of slavery, these chapters explore within a multidirectional model the circulation of cultural formations of Holocaust memory in the form of memorial sites, canonical texts, and exhibitions reflecting the

---

48 Louise Bethlehem, "Apartheid: The Global Itinerary: South African Cultural Formations in Transnational Circulation 1948–1990," ERC research proposal, 2013; Louise Bethlehem, "Restless Itineraries: Antiapartheid Expressive Culture and Transnational Historiography," *Social Text* 36.3 (2018): 47–69.

49 As mentioned in the acknowledgment, parts of chapter 7 and of the concluding chapter were written under the framework and with the generous support of the European Research Council under the European Union's Seventh Framework Programme (FP/2007–2013) / ERC Grant Agreement no. 615564, under the mentorship and professional guidance of Louise Bethlehem.

struggles of anti-apartheid activists. In this way these analyses expose analogical connections drawn between Holocaust memory and apartheid South Africa.

Through focusing on the engagement of black South African leaders with the traumatic memories of the Holocaust, this part of the book provides a companion to the study's overall framework and its concentration on white perceptions and reactions to the Holocaust in South Africa. It explores how the Holocaust functions as a lens through which the political trajectories of both Kathrada and Tutu can be seen to illustrate how processes of negotiation between different practices of commemoration and memory construction can create space for promoting solidarity and justice.

Chapter 1
Nazism, Afrikaner Nationalism and the 'Jewish Question'

Race has been at the heart of South African history since the inception of European colonialism in the area. The Union of South Africa was founded in 1910 by the Afrikaners who settled in the region in 1652 and by the British who conquered the area in the late 18th century.[1] The arrival of the British gave rise to a divide between the Afrikaner settlers and their new colonial masters, as earlier fears of a possible change in the colony's Afrikaner character now merged with fears of dispossession. The great power of the British empire in the region, alongside the economic impoverishment of Afrikaner peasants, eventually led to a mass migration of Afrikaners from the British Cape colony into the interior of southern Africa in search of a place where they could establish their own homeland. This epic journey, known as the Great Trek of 1836, became a formative event for the Afrikaner national movement.[2]

Following the Great Trek, the Afrikaner immigrants established several independent republics inland and in the Natal area. Afrikaner hostility toward the British authorities remained intense and tensions also arose with the indigenous African tribes living within the new Afrikaner republics. These intersocial tensions, along with the increase in the economic power of the republics following the discovery of gold in the last third of the 19th century, led to a violent escalation of tensions between the British and the Afrikaners, culminating in the outbreak of the South African War (1899–1902).[3] In the course of this bloody war, the Afrikaners lost their sovereign independence.

Under the Act of Union, which came into force in 1910, South African society was divided into four racial groups: Europeans, Bantu /Africans, Coloured peoples (people of mix races), and Indians. The Union's constitution established white supremacy by defining the Africans, Coloureds, and Indians as "non-white" as well as separate spheres (physical, cultural, social, and economic) for whites and "non-whites".

---
[1] Nigel Worden, צמיחת המדינות החדשות באפריקה: התהוותה של דרום אפריקה המודרנית [*The Making of Modern South Africa*] (Tel Aviv: The Open University Press, 2002). 25–29.
[2] Richard Elphick and Hermann B. Giliomee, *The Shaping of South African Society* (Cape Town: Maskew Miller Longman, 1989), 472–518.
[3] Worden, צמיחת המדינות החדשות באפריקה: התהוותה של דרום אפריקה המודרנית [*The Making of Modern South Africa*], 45–56.

The 'Jewish Question' in South Africa

Within the white minority Jews occupied an uneasy position. The South African Jewish community was founded by British Jews who arrived on the continent in the early 19th century. These were followed by Jewish immigrants from Eastern Europe in the late 19th century, primarily from Lithuania. It is estimated that between the years 1880–1914 about 40,000 Jews emigrated to South Africa and that another 30,000 entered the country by 1948. Moreover, between the years 1933–1937, 3,600 Jewish refugees from Nazi Germany succeeded in entering South Africa.[4]

The first British Jewish immigrants laid the foundations for a communal institutional structure: the first synagogue was established in Cape Town as early as 1841. Later, in 1898, the South African Zionist Federation (SAZF) was formed; and in 1903 the South African Jewish Board of Deputies (SAJBD) was established, first in the Transvaal area, and a year later in the Cape region. In 1912, these two regional organizations were merged into one national Board, which served as the official community leadership organization.[5] Nevertheless, the community was not a homogenous entity. At the turn of the 20th century, one could describe South African Jewry as a community of immigrants, very heterogenous culturally, ideologically, and socially, and shallowly rooted in the society.[6]

The first British Jewish immigrants quickly assimilated into the English-speaking communities of the country. They settled mainly in city centers and were largely integrated into the economic and commercial sectors: by the mid-19th century, Jews were already established as peddlers, merchants, and warehouse owners.[7] The discovery of gold on the Witwatersrand in 1886 – a foundational moment for the South African economy – was followed by a massive wave of immigrant Jews from Western Russia, and Jewish involvement in the South African economy gained momentum. Most of these Jewish immigrants came from Lithuania, one of the poorest regions in the area. However, their exodus was driven not only by economic causes, but also by local

---

4 Shimoni, *Community and Conscience*, 1–2; Shain, *A Perfect Storm*,110–128.
5 Shimoni, *Community and Conscience*, 2.
6 Richard Mendelsohn, "The Boar War, The Great War, and the Shaping of South African Jewish Loyalties," in *Memories, Realities and Dreams: Aspects of the South African Jewish Experience*, ed. Milton Shein and Richard Mendelsohn (Johannesburg: Jonathan Ball Publications, 2002), 50–59, at 50; Krut, "Building a Home and a Community," 35.
7 Jocelyn Hellig, "The Jewish Community in South Africa," in *Living Faiths in South Africa*, ed. Martin Prozesky and John de Gruchy (New York: St. Martin's Press, 1995), 156.

anti-Jewish legislation and the constant pogroms being undertaken in their homeland.[8]

From the beginning of the 20th century until the end of the Second World War, the South African economy underwent increased industrialization. In the context of the predominance of Afrikaner settlers in rural economies, and the colonial commitment of British colonists, who preferred to import products from Great Britain to meet domestic demands rather than to buy local products, Jewish entrepreneurs recognized the potential of local demand. They turned to local industrial development, focusing initially on the production of textiles and wood. The arrival of Jewish refugees escaping Nazi Germany in the 1930s, many of whom specialized in ceramics, diamond cutting and fashion, contributed to the development of these industries in the country as well. South African Jews were also successful in trade, and many worked as lawyers, doctors, accountants, as well as in advertising and entertainment. Since unskilled jobs and manual labor were undertaken almost exclusively by the black, Indian, and Coloured populations of South Africa, Jewish immigrants tended to take up entrepreneurial positions and thus enjoyed the economic mobility that characterized the white minority.[9]

Long before the establishment of the apartheid regime, alongside the economic mobility enjoyed by members of the Jewish community, Jews were centrally involved in socialist and communist organizations. This included mainly Jewish immigrants that arrived in South Africa from Eastern Europe after 1900, who were "the products of some years of intense political volatility in pre-revolutionary Russia."[10] On 30 July 1921, the Communist Party of South African (CPSA)[11] was founded in the aftermath of a conference held by six organizations, including the Jewish Socialist Society of Cape Town and the Jewish Socialist

---

8 Krut, "Building a Home and a Community," 7–8.
9 Marcus Arkin, *South African Jewry: A Contemporary Survey* (Cape Town: Oxford University Press, 1984), 59–60; Mendel Kaplan, *Jewish Roots in the South African Economy* (Cape Town: C. Struik Publishers, 1986).
10 Krut, "Building a Home and a Community," 38. Lithuania was the center of the Jewish Labour movement, 'the Bund,' and of Zionism, both established in 1897. For the history of Bundism and Zionism in Lithuania, see Jonathan Frankel, *Prophecy and Politics: Socialism, Nationalism & the Russian Jews, 1862–1917* (Cambridge: Cambridge University Press, 1984).
11 The Communist Party of South Africa (CPSA) changed its name to the South African Communist Party (SACP) in 1953, after it had been forced underground following the Suppression of Communism Act of 1950.

Society of Johannesburg (Poale Zion).[12] It was the only political party in South Africa that opened its doors to members of all social and racial groups in the country. Indeed, in the early 1930s most of its members were black. Nevertheless, Jews accounted for a significant percentage of the party's leadership and played a major role in its ideological development and organizational activities. Jews were also prominent in the trade unions and for the most part belonged to the militant "color-blind" section of the union movement, and thus were the main organizers of 'non-white' unions in the 1930s.[13] As Immanuel Suttner argues in his important collection of interviews with South African Jewish activists, *Cutting Through The Mountains*, the combination of the Eastern European experience of marginalization and persecution with proletarian militancy created an openness to radical attitudes and empathy towards oppressed populations among many Jews in South Africa.[14]

Jews were white and therefore superior to the communities that were defined as 'non-white' by the Union's law. However, although color served as the principle racial definer in South African society, Jews were perceived as a separate race in the political atmosphere of the first half of the 20th century.[15] Jewish economic integration gave rise to hostility toward the nascent community from sections of the white minority, particularly from right-wing Afrikaners. This hostility intensified in the 1930s and 1940s following the infiltration of ideas from Nazi Germany and Fascist Italy.[16] However, as Milton Shain argues, although organized antisemitism was not evident in South Africa until the early 1930s, the 'Jewish question' first emerged in the beginning of the 20th century as part of the public discourse on the restriction of immigration into the Union.[17]

From the late 19th century, a variety of Immigration Restriction Acts were enacted in the Natal, Cape and Transvaal areas.[18] Aimed at preventing immigration from Asia and particularly from India, these Acts limited the entry of all

---

[12] Sheridan Johns, "The Comintern, South Africa and the Black Diaspora," *The Review of Politics* 37.2 (1975): 200–234; Mark Israel and Simon Adams, "'That Spell Trouble': Jews and the Communist Party of South Africa," *Journal of Southern African Studies* 26.1 (2000): 145–162.
[13] Gideon Shimoni, "The Jewish Community and the Zionist Movement in South African Society (1910–1948)" (PhD dissertation, The Hebrew University of Jerusalem, 1974), 247–248.
[14] Immanuel Suttner, *Cutting Through the Mountain: Interviews with South African Jewish Activists* (New York: VIKING, 1997), 2.
[15] Shain, "From Undesirable to Unassimilable," 72–90; Hellig, "The Jewish Community in South Africa," 156.
[16] Shain, *The Roots of Anti-Semitism in South Africa*, 3–8.
[17] Shain, *The Roots of Anti-Semitism in South Africa*, 1–5.
[18] To read more about migration regulation in South Africa during the late 19th century and the early 20th century, see Jonathan Klaaren, "Early practices of regulating mobility," in *From*

immigrants who spoke "non-European" languages. The entry of Jews was restricted as well since Yiddish was not defined as a European language. This definition not only cast Eastern European Jews as undesirable 'others' whose accommodation into South African society was questionable, but also threatened the status of Jews who already lived in the country, most of whom spoke Yiddish and had Eastern European origins.[19] In 1903 the SAJBD was established in response to the passing of the Immigration Restriction Act of 1902, to coordinate efforts to prevent legislation aimed at restricting Jewish immigration to South Africa.

In his formative book *A Perfect Storm* (2015), Shain focuses on the phenomenon of antisemitism in the political and cultural context of South Africa during the 1930s and 1940s. Shain points to the centrality of the 'Jewish question' in the white South African political arena and in Afrikaner nationalism in particular. He argues, "From the mid-1920s, nativist and eugenicist concerns with race, miscegenation and the 'Nordic' character of South African 'stock' amplified obsession with the Jew."[20] Stereotypes of a Jewish capitalist takeover of the economy merged with stereotypes of Jewish alliance with the radical left, and these obsessions served as fertile soil for the Quota Act of 1930.

Presented to the South African parliament on 29 January 1930, the Quota Act effectively reduced Jewish immigration from Eastern Europe. While in itself it did not mention the word 'Jew,' the Quota Act imposed a limit of 50 immigrants per year from a list of countries that included Latvia, Lithuania and Poland – at that time the main centers of Jewish immigration into the Union.[21] In contrast with the previous Immigration Acts where Jewish immigrants were not the main target, this legislation was driven by an explicit desire to limit Jewish immigration to South Africa.[22] The governing principle of the Act was the Afrikaner nation's aspiration to preserve its racial base and to prevent the entry of Eastern and Southern European citizens, considered vastly different from and inferior to citizens of Western Europe.[23]

Prohibited Immigration to Citizens: The origins of citizenship and nationality in South Africa (Cape Town: University of Cape Town Press, 2017), 14–46.
19 Hellig, "The Jewish Community in South Africa," 157.
20 Shain, *A Perfect Storm*, 1–6.
21 Shain, *A Perfect Storm*, 12.
22 Klaaren, "Early practices of regulating mobility," 187.
23 The countries from which immigrants could have been absorbed under the 1930 Quota Act were: British Commonwealth countries, Austria, Belgium, Denmark, France, Germany, the Netherlands, Italy, Norway, Portugal, Spain, Sweden, Switzerland, and the United States. For more information see Judah Daniel Elazar and Peter Medding, *Jewish Communities in Frontier Societies: Argentina, Australia, and South Africa* (New York: Holmes & Meier, 1983), 156.

The wide support for the Quota Act, cutting across Party and linguistic lines, fractured the illusion that South African Jewry was well integrated, and the SAJBD organized gatherings across the Union to denounce the new legislation as illiberal, antisemitic and unjust.[24] The SAJBD accused the government of misleading the Jewish community by assuring its leaders that Jewish immigration to South Africa would not be restricted while instituting legislation directly targeting Jews.[25]

Another central factor in the formulation of the 'Jewish question' in South Africa in the 1930s and 1940s was the influence of ideas imported from Nazi Germany. The Nazi party established local branches for German citizens living in the Union from as early as 1932, prior to Adolf Hitler's rise to power in Germany. Initially operating underground, the party rapidly expanded in the second half of 1933 to population centers in Johannesburg, Pretoria, Durban, Port Elizabet, and Bloemfontein.[26] On 1 November 1933, General Jan Christian Smuts, then Minister of Justice, publicly denounced the movement, stating:

> Wild charges are made against the Jews as a community, which are calculated to create ill-feeling and racial prejudice and in the end to lead to breaches of the peace [. . .] what is even more lamentable is that this movement has its origins abroad and is an attempt to import into South Africa the alien hatreds and rancour of the Old World, and this, too, at a time when the people of South Africa are making a supreme effort to get away from the unhappy racial divisions of the past.[27]

Nevertheless, anti-Jewish agitation persisted in South Africa and gained in extent and strength.

About a month after Hitler came to power in Germany, the South African Christian National Socialist Movement, the *Greyshirts*, was established under the leadership of Louis T. Weichardt. This movement was inspired and influenced by Hitler's success, the *Brownshirts* movement, and by Nazi propaganda.[28] In the Transvaal, the Afrikaner nationalist Manie Wessels founded the antisemitic *Blackshirts* movement in December 1933. However, the movement suffered from inner disagreements, eventually leading to the withdrawal

---

[24] Adolph Schauder, *Eastern Province Herald*, 7 February 1930, Press Items of Jewish Interest, Rochlin Archive, Johannesburg.
[25] Gustav Saron and Louis Hotz, *The Jews of South Africa: A History* (Oxford: Oxford University Press, 1955).
[26] Furlong, *Between Crown and Swastika*, 16.
[27] Quoted in SAJBD, *The Anti-Jewish Movements in South Africa: The Need for Action* (Johannesburg: SAJBD, 1936), 3.
[28] Shain, *A Perfect Storm*, 33, 53–62; Shain, "South Africa," 670–689.

of Chris Havemann, who established the nationalist People's Movement (Die Volksbeweging) in Johannesburg.[29]

The emergent pro-Nazi movements gave rise to antisemitic action such as the targeting of Jewish gatherings and the distribution of anti-Jewish booklets. Across the Union, such groups employed Nazi symbols and rhetoric: they wore uniforms with swastikas, gave the Nazi salute, and organized grandiose parades. Antisemitism became increasingly common when its manifestations shifted from the private sphere to the public, as politicians from more moderate and liberal sections of the political spectrum publicly addressed the 'Jewish question,' labelling the Jew as an undesirable 'other' in South African society.[30] The growing influx of German Jewish immigrants to the Union following Hitler's rise to power in 1933 further escalated the essentialist discourse regarding the 'Jewish question' in the public sphere. As Shain argues, "at a time of instability and an escalating (predominantly Afrikaner) 'poor white' problem, the growth of vulgar radical right movements ensured that the 'Jewish question' shifted from the periphery to the centre of South African politics."[31]

This shift was well reflected in the introduction of the Aliens Bill by the United Party (UP) in 1937. Although the word 'Jew' was never mentioned in the wording of the law, it was a direct response to the arrival of 3,600 Jewish refugees from Nazi Germany between the years 1933–1937. The bill stipulated that immigration would only be approved by a committee that would grant entry permits to South Africa based on required characteristics and on the expectation of assimilation into the local European population. Moreover, the bill formally excluded the Yiddish language from the list of European languages and imposed restrictions on foreigners in the fields of employment and property.[32]

Throughout this period, the SAJBD made enormous efforts to oppose Nazi propaganda in the local sphere. In its biannual report to the SAJBD Executive Council in July 1942, the Board stated that "[i]n thus exposing Nazism and all its evil works, the Board has been sustained by the knowledge that it was striking a blow not only for the rights of Jewish citizens, but also for the safeguarding of South Africa's democratic liberties, and the protection of our country against the insidious activities of Hitler's secret agents," thus linking local pro-Nazi tendencies with a world-wide Nazi conspiracy.[33]

---

29 Furlong, *Between Crown and Swastika*, 20–21.
30 Shain, *A Perfect Storm*, 42–44, 48–50.
31 Shain, "From Undesirable to Unassimilable," 74–75.
32 Shain, "From Undesirable to Unassimilable," 74–75.
33 SAJBD Report of the Executive Council, June 1940 to July 1942, 12, SAJBD Reprots, Rochlin Archive, Johannesburg. All SAJBD reports were courteously provided by David Saks.

The SAJBD acknowledged that there was no lawful means to prevent libelous or injurious attacks upon sections of the population of the Union. Therefore, in an effort to fight against local antisemitism, it introduced "a systematic campaign of enlightenment" that included a thorough study of the South African press; the publication of articles containing accurate information on all phases of Jewish life; the distribution of pamphlets and books; and addresses delivered to both Jewish and non-Jewish audiences. One such booklet published by the Board in July 1936 pointed to the urgent need to curb the present pro-Nazi and antisemitic tendencies and described the waves of Nazi propaganda sweeping the Union: "[t]he growth of organizations having as their avowed object to injure the fair name and status of Jews as citizens of the Union has, in our opinion, reached such proportions as to become a serious political problem demanding immediate attention".[34]

Therefore, when the Society of Jews and Christians (SJC) was formed by the Witwatersrand Church Council (WCC) on 19 November 1937, the SAJBD followed its activities with great interest.[35] The SJC came into existence for the purpose of creating better relations between Jews and non-Jews and to combat antisemitism in South Africa through public gatherings, lectures, and the dissemination of various publications.[36] Indeed, in his address at the first annual general meeting of the SJC, the South African politician and intellectual Jan Hendrik Hofmeyr called upon Christians to oppose the spread of antisemitic propaganda as "inimical to the welfare of the country" and "contrary to the spirit of Christ."[37] He described antisemitism in South Africa as "a poisonous infection which wafted here by evil winds from across the sea" and as "something utterly foreign to our spirit, to our tradition, to our characteristics as a nation."[38]

Hofmeyr was a prominent Afrikaner politician who played a significant role in welding the National and South African Parties into the UP in 1934. He became Minister of Education, the Interior and Public Health in 1933 and was known for his liberal attitude towards blacks, Coloureds and Indians, a cause of great concern to his Party members. In 1937, when he made the above

---

[34] SAJBD, *The Ani-Jewish Movements in South Africa*.
[35] Shain., *A Perfect Storm*, 161.
[36] SAJBD Report of EC, June 1940 to July 1942, 12–13, SAJBD Reports, Rochlin Archive, Johannesburg.
[37] "The origins of the Society," in *Some Facts About the Society*, The Society of Jews and Christians, Publication No. 2, 2, Society of Jews and Christians Folder 607.A, Rochlin Archive, Johannesburg.
[38] "An Address by the Hon. Jan H. Hofmeyr, delivered at the First Annual General Meeting on November 19th, 1937," in *Some Facts About the Society*, The Society of Jews and Christians, Publication No. 2, 3, Society of Jews and Christians Folder 607.A, Rochlin Archive, Johannesburg.

statement, he was serving as Minister of Labour and Mines, Education and Social Welfare, a position he held until 1938. His resignation that year was triggered by the appointment of A. P. J. Fourie to the senate as a member specially qualified to speak for the blacks.[39] By then Hofmeyr had abandoned his concept of 'constructive segregation' in favor of a 'new liberalism' that, while it rejected white domination, baulked at full social, political, and economic integration.[40]

Hofmeyr's address was not at all surprising if we consider his liberal stance. It was also consistent with his attitude towards Zionism. In November 1927, speaking on the tenth anniversary of the signing of the Balfour Declaration in Johannesburg, he stated, "it is in the Hebrew prophets that we first get the appeal to the individual moral conscience against oppression, and that has been the real source of liberalism. It is to the Hebrews above all that we owe the first clear and uncompromising statements of the supremacy of spiritual and intellectual over material values."[41] However, in Hofmeyr's maiden speech in Parliament on 10 February 1930, he displayed a much more ambivalent attitude towards Jews when he supported Daniel Francois Malan's Immigration Quota Act.[42] While his speech focused on the Jewish contribution to South African national life, this did not deter him from supporting the Act:

> There is therefore in South Africa today the possibility of disharmony and strife between Jews and non-Jews and if the present tendencies of immigration prevail unchecked then I am very much afraid of the possibility becoming a fact. It is on this basis that I support the principle of this measure and it is on that basis I would make an appeal to our Jewish citizens, not as Jews but as South African citizens.[43]

As detailed earlier, the passage of the Quota Act and its repercussion for Jewish immigration exposed the latent potential for antisemitism within the white communities in South Africa. With Hofmeyr's support, the Act passed almost unanimously, proving that the 'Jewish question' was not simply an issue of importance for the extremists but rather lay at the heart of South African Party politics. However, in his address to the annual meeting of the SJC, Hofmeyr castigated Malan for promoting ideas imported from Nazi Germany and claimed,

---

39 Rodney H. Davenport, *South Africa: A Modern History* (London: MacMillan, 1991), 340.
40 Edna Bradlow, "J. H. Hofmeyr, Liberalism and Jewish Immigration," *South African Historical Journal* 40.1 (1999): 114–129, at 122.
41 Jan Hendrik Hofmeyr, "The Jew in History," in *The Open Horizon: Speeches and Addresses Delivered by Jan H. Hofmeyr Administrator of the Transvaal Province, 1924–1929* (Johannesburg: Central News Agency, 1929).
42 Bradlow, "J. H. Hofmeyr, Liberalism and Jewish Immigration," 118.
43 House of Assembly debates, 29 January 1930 col 590.

"[h]ostility for Jews is a precursor to dictatorship."[44] He pointed to two main causes for antisemitism in South Africa: the "otherness" of the Jews and their success. The source for the first was the Jews' unique history of survival as a separate nation, which marked them as unassimilable. The second was a result of the successful Jewish integration into the South African economic system, which made Jews an object of envy.[45]

The SJC issued five pamphlets both in English and Afrikaans, focusing mainly on Jews in South African society, before establishing its monthly booklet, *Common Sense*, in July 1939.[46] The name *Common Sense* reflected belief in a natural intelligence common to all human beings, with no distinction of nationality, race, color, or class. "We claim, there is a natural common sense of mankind to which sound reasoning appeals, and if that can be brought to bear upon our problems their solution will at least be brought a stage nearer," said the first President of the Society, Rev C. H. S. Runge, in his first editorial statement.[47]

Rev Runge further argued, "[u]neasy relations between Jews and non-Jews form only one of the problems of our time and of our country. There are other equally urgent racial, political, economic. All tend to be confused and obscured by unthinking prejudice and by fastening labels of strong emotional colour to those with whom we disagree."[48] While the initial objectives of the SJC were in no sense obscured, they were combined with the promotion of a more general policy of inter-racial and inter-faith understanding and with an emphasis on the solution of socio-economic problems. This followed on the growing awareness of the deep-seated effects of segregation and racism in South Africa.

Common Sense was one of the leading progressive journals in the country. However, an analysis of the issues' contents reveals that most of its publications focused on Jewish-related subjects. Articles about the Talmud, Jewish literature, and Afrikaner-British-Jewish relations, among others, were presented together with commentaries on Nazism and antisemitism, democracy vs. totalitarianism,

---

44 Shain, *A Perfect Storm*, 184–185.
45 "An Address by the Hon. Jan H. Hofmeyr, delivered at the First Annual General Meeting on 19 November 1937," in *Some Facts About the Society*, The Society of Jews and Christians, Publication No. 2, 5–6, Society of Jews and Christians Folder 607.A, Rochlin Archive, Johannesburg.
46 The Society of Jews and Christians: Report of the Executive Committee for the period 19 November 1937 to 23 November 1938, 1, Society of Jews and Christians Folder 607.A, Rochlin Archive, Johannesburg.
47 C. H. S. Runge, "Common Sense," *Common Sense*, July 1939, 3, Society of Jews and Christians 607.7, Rochlin Archive, Johannesburg.
48 C. H. S. Runge, "Common Sense," *Common Sense*, July 1939, 3, Society of Jews and Christians 607.7, Rochlin Archive, Johannesburg.

the war, and the way toward peace. Only in its February 1940 issue did the subject of race relations in South Africa first appear.[49] Nevertheless, the fight against antisemitism was perceived by the SJC as inseparable from the fight against all forms of racism and intolerance.

The SJC was indeed a rare voice during this dark period. As I will demonstrate in Chapter 6, only during the early post-War years did activists' rhetoric begin to make connections by pointing to parallel policies of racial discrimination on the part of the apartheid and the Nazi regimes.[50] Nevertheless, as Shimoni argues, while the "Nine Point Programme" to combat antisemitism adopted by the SAJBD in May 1945 explicitly framed the fight against antisemitism "as part of the defence of democracy and of freedom," the official Jewish community perceived Nazi-inspired antisemitism in the Union as completely different from the local racism against blacks, Indians, and Coloureds, and restricted its activities "only to the antisemitic aspect of Afrikaner politics."[51]

The War Years

The South African United Government's decision on 6 September 1939 to join Britain and to declare war against Nazi Germany further escalated the antisemitic propaganda in the Union. At that point, the country was led by a coalition of the NP of James Barry Munnik Hertzog and the South African Party (SAP) of Jan Christian Smuts. While Hertzog preferred that South Africa remain neutral in the war, Smuts wanted to fight on the side of the Allies. Hertzog resigned as Prime Minister and was succeeded by Smuts. This led to an intensification of the antisemitic atmosphere in South Africa, along with distinct pro-Nazi support led by Afrikaner Nationalistic movements.[52] As Shain argues, "As war clouds gathered, it would appear that the NP believed they would gain support by identifying Jews as the driving force behind Smuts' pro-British stance."[53]

While the parliament supported Smuts, he was confronted with a lack of broader national support for the war efforts among the white population in the Union. This situation provided a fertile ground for Nazi propaganda, broadcasted

---

49 Ellen Hellman, "Liberalism and Native Policy," *Common Sense*, February 1940, 4; J. D. Dexter Taylor, "Quiet Adventures in Race Relations," *Common Sense*, February 1940, 7, Society of Jews and Christians 607.7, Rochlin Archive, Johannesburg.
50 Gilbert, "Jews and Racial State," 34.
51 Shimoni, *Community and Conscience*, 16–17.
52 Shain, *A Perfect Storm*, 232–237.
53 Shain, *A Perfect Storm*, 232.

by the German-based Zeesen radio in Afrikaans, which throughout the war continued to foster defeatism and to cultivate neutrality, and which was received with enthusiasm in many Afrikaner centers in the country. Smuts' government fought against Nazi propaganda through state propaganda agencies such as the Bureau of Information, the Directorate of Military Intelligence, and the Union Unity Truth Service, which sought to shape public opinion in South Africa throughout the war.[54]

While Smuts was persistent in his anti-Nazi stance, the 'Jewish question' was still at the forefront of the public agenda. At the NP Congress held in November 1939, congress members issued the following statement: "Congress expresses its conviction that the Jewish race are not assimilable with the European population, and the Union asks that all further Jewish immigration to the Union be stopped. Congress also favours legislation that will limit Jewish participation in trades and professions to numbers proportionate with their numerical strength."[55] Moreover, in an earlier public address, Malan said that the Jewish problem was "a shadow hanging over South Africa."[56]

During that year, the Ossewa Brandwag, a prominent pro-Nazi and anti-War movement that focused on the cultivation of Afrikaner nationalism, was formed by right-wing Afrikaner extremists. The movement had direct contact with the Third Reich during the war, and German diplomatic records show that in 1940, when South Africa had already joined the war against the Germans, the leadership of the movement offered to provide the Nazi government with 170,000 volunteers to fight alongside Nazi Germany. In 1942, one of the movement's leaders, Balthazar Johannes Vorster, declared: "we stand for Christian Nationalism which is an ally of National Socialism [. . .] you can call such an anti-democratic system a dictatorship if you like. In Italy it is called Fascism, in Germany National Socialism and in South Africa Christian Nationalism." Vorster's pro-Nazi statements and actions resulted in his incarceration in a government camp for enemies of the Union for the duration of the war.[57]

The local atmosphere drove the Jewish community into believing that if the Nazis won the war, South Africa, like other countries, would become a vassal state and would have to align itself with Nazism. These fears were further intensified by developments in Europe, where the Nazi advance into

---

[54] Fankie L. Monama, "South African Propaganda Agencies and the Battle for Public Opinion during the Second World War, 1939–1940," *Scientia Militaria* 44.1 (2016): 145–167, at 147–148.
[55] I would like to thank Louise Bethlehem for the reference to this source from her private collection: "Jewish Question Discussed at Nationalist Congress," *Zionist Record*, 10 November 1939, 21.
[56] "Jewish Question Discussed at Nationalist Congress," *Zionist Record*, 10 November 1939, 21, Louise Bethlehem private collection.
[57] Polakow-Suransky, *The Unspoken Alliance*, 3–4, 18.

Poland threatened vast Jewish communities: thousands of South African Jews still had relatives in these communities. This situation drove the small Jewish community, located in the Southern Hemisphere of the African continent, to play its part both on the battlefield and in all other aspects of the war effort.[58]

From the beginning of the war, local Jewish organizations launched campaigns to mobilize recruitment to the South African Defence Force. The South African Jewish Ex-League opened a recruitment operation and organized rallies and the SAJBD maintained contact with and placed representatives on multiple war-related committees in the country. According to the official figures of the Union Office of Census and Statistics, by the end of the war the number of South African Jews serving in the Union Defence Forces and other Allied forces exceeded 10,000, out of a total of 211,193 recruits in the South African Army.[59]

On the home front, the SAJBD and the SAZF focused their efforts on raising funds for the relief of European Jewry, for South African Jewish soldiers and their dependents, and for war purposes in Palestine and assistance to refugees there.[60] Discussions regarding the establishment of a relief fund were held by South African Jewish institutions long before the beginning of the war, and there was complete unanimity on the necessity for the establishment of a War Victims' Fund on lines similar to that instituted during the First World War.[61] However, soon a bitter struggle arose between the SAJBD and the SAZF, who disagreed about the fund's objectives. The resolution drafted by the Board defined the objectives as follows: "the relief and reconstruction of Jewish victims of war. The proceeds shall be used for the purposes of relief, economic rehabilitation and reconstruction and kindred objects whenever and wherever such may be practicable."[62] The fact that the resolution did not mention Palestine was the cause for strong resentment on the part of the Zionist Federation, and an amendment was put forward, which included "the upbuilding of Palestine as the only country which can provide the immediate and permanent home for the uprooted Jews of the Diaspora."[63] Therefore, while discussions about a South African Jewish War Appeal started in the late 1930s, it took two and a

---

[58] SAJBD, *South African Jews in World War II* (Johannesburg: SAJBD, 1950), 3–4.
[59] SAJBD, *South African Jews in World War II*, 5–6, 14.
[60] Marcia Gitlin, *The Vision Amazing: The Story of South African Zionism* (Johannesburg: The Menorah Book Club, 1950), 346.
[61] "South African Jewish Board of Deputies- Report for Constituent Bodies on War Victims' Fund," *HASHALOM*, December 1939, 14, Clippings Collection, Durban Holocaust & Genocide Centre Archive.
[62] Quoted in Gitlin, *The Vision Amazing*, 347.
[63] Gitlin, *The Vision Amazing*, 347.

half years before the Appeal was eventually established to render assistance to Jewish victims of Nazism.[64]

Before the war broke out, when reports of distress in Poland reached South Africa in 1937, there was a public appeal for the inauguration of a fund to help Polish Jewry. Following the *Anschluss* – the annexation of Austria into Nazi Germany on 12 March 1938 – the persecution of Austrian Jewry also intensified, spurring the need for the establishment of a local fund for the relief of Austrian and Polish Jews.[65] The Austrian & Polish Jewish Relief Fund was eventually launched under the auspices of the SAJBD on 26 October 1938 in Johannesburg. As this campaign was put into motion, a pogrom against Jews known as "Kristallnacht" was carried out throughout Nazi Germany on 9–10 November 1938. The horror that this event inspired in the Jewish world and among South African Jews in particular was so enormous that even though the Austrian-Polish campaign had just begun, the SAJBD immediately agreed to the request of the Council of German Jewry in London to start a new campaign for the relief of German Jews.[66]

The developments in Europe had prompted a greater exodus of refugees from the continent. While European Jewish refugees were turned away by the South African government due to the 1937 Immigration Quota, some did manage to enter other countries located in the Southern part of the continent. Indeed, in 1938 and 1939 several hundred German Jews fleeing Nazi persecution found their way to Swaziland, Mozambique, and Northern Rhodesia, among other places, as did smaller numbers of Jews from Lithuania and Latvia.[67] While the Jewish institutions in South Africa were helpless in the face of the closing of the gates to Jewish refugees, they made enormous efforts in assisting the refugees arriving in Southern Africa. The SAJBD, together with the Council of German Jewry in London, formed a committee in Johannesburg to render relief to these refugees, and the Council for Refugee Settlement was established. This Council later also included in the sphere of its activities the Island of

---

[64] Gilbert, "Jews and the Racial State," 38.
[65] G. Osrin, "Note on Refugee Funds Raised in the Union: Austrian & Polish Jewish Relief Fund," 1, Austrian and Polish Jewish Relief Fund 1938–1941, SAJBD Archive, Holocaust-Related Records, USHMM.
[66] "Austrian-Polish Jewish Relief Fund," 12 September 1938, SAJBD Johannesburg and Cape Committee Secretary's, Austrian and Polish Jewish Relief Fund 1938–1941, SAJBD Archive, Holocaust-Related Records, USHMM.
[67] Messers J. Meyer and Gustav Saron, "The Refugees in Swaziland: Report of Visit," 16 April 1939, 1, Refugee Settlement: Swaziland 1939–1946, File 1: Swaziland Refugees, Reports 1939, ARCH 210.14; "Notes on Refugee Funds Raised in the Union," 6, Austrian and Polish Relief Fund, Report 1941, ARCH 216.1, File 4, SAJBD Archive, Holocaust-Related Records, USHMM.

Mauritius in the Indian Ocean, where a British detention camp for Jewish 'illegal immigrants' was established in December 1940.[68]

In January 1941, the United South African Jewish War Appeal was finally established by the SAJBD and the SAZF, aiming to help the dependents of Jewish volunteers and "to assist those countless numbers all over the world who, through war conditions, had become refugees."[69] Its first campaign for relief of war victims overseas was launched in March 1942, with the cardinal aim of constructive efforts towards the support of Palestine, "which is the only country providing an immediate and permanent home for uprooted Jews."[70] A few days later, a first meeting was held in Johannesburg to commemorate the tragedy of European Jewry, and a day of mourning was announced on 29 December 1942. The SAJBD, in conjunction with the SAZF, called on all Jewish businesses in the country to close and for all members of the community to refrain from sport and entertainment activities and to engage in prayer in their synagogues.[71] As Gilbert argues, while these were Jewish gatherings, "the SAJBD's intention in convening these meeting was in substantial part to draw the non-Jewish public's attention to the unfolding catastrophe in Europe."[72]

The South African press followed events in Europe with great interest, and from December 1942 reports on the Nazi atrocities against Jews occupied the front pages of all national newspapers.[73] The *Rand Daily Mail*, a Jewish-owned newspaper from Johannesburg, reported, "we are watching the deliberate and cold-blooded annihilation of a nation [. . .] men, women and children are ruthlessly put to death by poison gas, electrocution and by being sent on long journeys to unknown destinations in bitterly cold weather without food or

---

[68] In December 1940, 1,581 Jewish men, women, and children who fled Nazi-controlled Europe and survived a long journey to Haifa were deported by the British Mandatory authorities in Palestine to the British colony of Mauritius. The detainees spent four years and seven months behind iron gates before leaving the island on August 1945. On the establishment of the SAJBD's special committee on Mauritius, see "Notes on Refugee Funds Raised in the Union," 2–3; On the Jewish deportation to Mauritius see Geneviève Pitot, *The Mauritian Shekel: The Story of the Jewish Detainees in Mauritius 1940–1945* (Lanham, MD: Rowman & Littlefield, 1998).
[69] "United Jewish Appeal Launched in South Africa," *Jewish Telegraphic Agency*, 26 January 1941.
[70] "Campaign for Relief of War Victims Overseas Launched by South African Jews," *Jewish Telegraphic Agency*, 31 March 1942.
[71] "Day of Mourning: A Call to Every Jew," File 520.2A: Holocaust Commemoration 1940–1949, Rochlin Archive, Johannesburg.
[72] Gilbert, "Jews and the Racial State," 38.
[73] Among the press reports see: "Hitler's Threat to the Jews," *Friend*, 5 December 1942; "Steady Extermination in Poland," *Cape Argus*, 4 December 1942, File 520. 2A: Holocaust Commemoration 1940–1949, Rochlin Archive, Johannesburg.

drink."[74] The *Jewish Herald* also warned, "persecution of Jews in Poland from the very first day of German occupation has taken extremely acute forms since March 1942, when Himmler ordered the extermination of 50 percent of the Jewish population in the General Government to be carried out by the end of 1942."[75] Such reports intensified in 1943, following the shocking estimation of millions of Jews killed or deported by the Nazis.[76]

In addition to promoting campaigns for the relief of European Jewry and offering assistance to Jews seeking refuge or detained in countries close to South Africa, the tragic reports from Europe drove South African Jewry to increase efforts to convince the government to open its gates to Jewish refugees. On 26 February 1943, a memorandum on the Nazi persecution of the Jews was submitted to the South African government by representatives of the SAJBD and the SAZF. "Atrocities unparalleled in the annals of barbarism are being perpetrated against the victims of Nazism," the memorandum stated, emphasizing that "the Jews have been specially singled out for destruction."[77] Delivered to Prime Minister Smuts in his office at the House of Assembly in Cape Town, the memorandum was accompanied by a short address given by Rabbi Israel Abrahams, who introduced himself as representing "the complete solidarity of the Jewish community."[78]

Rabbi Abrahams condemned the Allied world for its immigration regulations, arguing that "the victims are pitied, but sanctuary is mostly refused them," and further proclaimed, "as South African Jews it grieves us particularly to have to point out that latterly there has been an increase rather than a decrease in the stringency with which the immigration regulations have been applied by the Union." He concluded: "The voice of South Africa, we feel, will be listened to by the United Nations with respect. [. . .] we beg you to do all in your power to bring salvation to our people before it is too late."[79]

---

[74] "Nazi Atrocities of Jews in Europe," *Rand Daily Mail*, 10 December 1942, File 520.2A: Holocaust Commemoration 1940–1949, Rochlin Archive, Johannesburg.

[75] *Jewish Herald*, 4 December 1942, File 520.2A: Holocaust Commemoration 1940–1949, Rochlin Archive, Johannesburg.

[76] "Nazis Have Killed or Deported 5,000,000 Jews," *Rand Daily Mail*, 28 August 1943; "Mass of German People Held Responsible for Nazi Crimes," *Rand Daily Mail*, 18 June 1943; "Concentration Camp Horror," *Natal Daily News*, 26 June 1943, Press Cutting Collection, South African National Library, Cape Town.

[77] "Nazi Persecution of the Jews," Memorandum submitted to the Prime Minister by the SAJBD and the SAZF, 26 February 1943, 1, SAJBD Reports – Reel 1, USHMM.

[78] "Address Given by Prof. Rabbi Israel Abrahams," Special Committee on the Tragedy of European Jewry, 26 February 1943, Annex to Document No. 16, 1, SAJBD Reports – Reel 1, USHMM.

[79] "Address Given by Prof. Rabbi Israel Abrahams," 2–3, Special Committee on the Tragedy of European Jewry, 26 February 1943, Annex to Document No. 16, 1, SAJBD Reports - Reel 1, USHMM.

After commenting favorably on the Memorandum, Smuts stated, "it seemed incredible that such atrocities as the Nazis perpetrated could happen in the 20th century. The Jews, whatever their faults, did not deserve this." He argued that the United Nations should try to defeat Hitler as quickly as possible and called for the intensifying of war efforts as "the best way to save the victims."[80] Responding to the Rabbi's criticism of the South African immigration policy, Smuts argued, "there may be some justice in that criticism of our immigration laws. Some of the 'red tape' should be relaxed or removed." He defined the Jewish question as a world problem, one, he maintained, which Hitler had recognized: "He (Hitler) realised that the Jewish position constituted a problem affecting the whole world. So far, he was right, but there was only one solution: The Jews must have a National Home of their own, where they could live in their own way without interference from anyone."[81]

Smuts did not open the borders for Jewish refugees during the war. However, as evidenced above, he was committed to modern Zionism, which he perceived as a solution to the Jewish problem. He was one of the first to endorse the Balfour Declaration, a public statement issued by the British government in 1917 in support of establishing a national homeland for the Jewish people in Palestine.[82] As Gideon Shimoni argues, with Smuts' support the reality of ethnic segregation which characterized South African society served as fertile ground for "the preservation of Jewish ethnicity that found expression in Zionism."[83]

The Jewish experience in South Africa during the Second World War shaped the community's collective identity for years to come. Jews living in a racially segregated society, where a large number of the privileged white minority was drawn to antisemitic ideologies and still mourning the tragic killing of their relatives in Eastern Europe, found themselves in a tenuous position – one that would evolve throughout the apartheid era.

---

80 "Memorandum of Deputation of the Prime Minister: The Prime Minister's reply," Special Committee on the Tragedy of European Jewry, 26 February 1943, Document No. 16, 1–2, SAJBD Reports – Reel 1, USHMM.
81 "Memorandum of Deputation of the Prime Minister: The Prime Minister's reply," Special Committee on the Tragedy of European Jewry, 26 February 1943, Document No. 16, 2, SAJBD Reports - Reel 1, USHMM.
82 David W. Schmidt, *Partners Together in This Great Enterprise: The Role of Christian Zionism in the Foreign Polices of Britain and American in the 20th Century* (Jerusalem: Xulon Press, 2011), 56–59.
83 Shimoni, *Community and Conscience*, 4.

Chapter 2
Memory Engraved in Stone

On 19 April 1948, a monument was unveiled in Warsaw on the site of the obliterated Jewish Quarter to commemorate the battle of the Warsaw ghetto of 1943. Designed by the Polish Jewish sculptor Nathan Rapoport, it was the first memorial erected during the post-war years to mark both the heroism of Jewish resistance to the Nazis and the destruction of Warsaw Jewry.[1] Earlier that year, the SAJBD had been informed by the Swedish section of the World Jewish Congress that they had succeeded in buying granite which had been ordered by Hitler and which they would use for a "Victory Monument," and they suggested that the Board join them in presenting the granite for use in the erection of the monument in Warsaw. A committee was appointed to collect the South African Jewish community's contribution to the cost of the granite.[2]

At that time, the South African community felt that the annual Days of Mourning held to commemorate the recent Jewish genocide were not enough, yet it did not reach a consensus regarding the proper ways to commemorate this tragedy on South African soil.[3] Contributing to a monument located on the site of the heroic battle of the Warsaw ghetto, though, was an easier enterprise to agree upon. Nonetheless, when the SAJBD issued a public appeal in April 1948 urging Jewish institutions as well as individuals to contribute to the Warsaw ghetto memorial, the response was rather sparse.[4]

At the SAJBD Executive Council meeting of 5 April 1948, the comparatively poor response to the appeal was attributed to feelings on the part of the Jewish public that a "living memorial should be devised in place of the erection of a stone monument."[5] President of the SAJBD, Bernard Arthur Ettlinger, added: "the establishment of the State of Israel places on those who have looked forward

---

[1] James E. Young. "The Biography of a Memorial Icon: Nathan Rapoport's Warsaw Ghetto Monument," *Representations* 26 (1989): 69–106.
[2] SAJBD Report of the Executive Council August 1947 to May 1949, Johannesburg 1949, 7, SAJBD Reprots, Rochlin Archive, Johannesburg.
[3] SAJBD, Meeting of Deputies, 21 March 1948, 1467a–1467b, SAJBD Reports, Rochlin Archive, Johannesburg.
[4] Quoted in a letter from SAJBD Secretary to the Editor of *Jewish Affairs* on the Warsaw Ghetto Memorial Board's Appeal, 5 April 1948, File 520 A: Holocaust Commemoration 1940s, Rochlin Archive, Johannesburg.
[5] "Battle of Warsaw Ghetto," *South African Jewish Times*, 2 July 1948, File 520 A: Holocaust Commemoration 1940s, Rochlin Archive, Johannesburg.

to it so eagerly and welcomed it with such joy, new and greater obligations. The nascent State must be accorded the fullest moral and material support."[6]

Calls for advancing "a living memorial" rather than an inanimate monument were somewhat abstract and unclear. However, when read together with Ettlinger's address, the call for a living memorial is directly linked to the epic developments unfolding in the Middle East. Less than a month after Rapoport's monument was erected in Warsaw, the last British forces left Palestine and the State of Israel was established. South African Jewry had played its part in what was defined as the most important struggle of the Jewish people yet: that is, the struggle for the establishment of statehood in its ancestral home. Israel was perceived as the ultimate home for many tens of thousands of displaced persons and as providing an end to the most tragic chapter in Jewish history. In fact, soon after the UN's decision of 29 November 1947 that recommended the creation of independent Arab and Jewish States, the SAJBD together with the SAZF established the Israeli United Appeal, which achieved the proud distinction of collecting the largest sum of money ever contributed to a single enterprise from South African Jewry.[7] Therefore, the call for "a living memorial" can be interpreted as an appeal to invest all material efforts in the new Jewish homeland for the living, instead of investing in stone monuments to commemorate the dead.

The declaration of the establishment of the State of Israel was welcomed by most of the South African public, and the connection between the creation of the Jewish State and the recent destruction of European Jewry received special attention in many national newspapers. On the eve of the most dramatic general elections in the history of the Union of South Africa, Smuts, in one of his last diplomatic actions as the union's Prime Minister, recognized *de facto* the new State in a telegram to the Israeli Foreign Minister, Moshe Shertok. Referring to the recent tragedy of European Jewry, Smuts wrote, "The Union Government expresses its cordial good wishes to the State of Israel as the fulfillment of the policy of the Jewish national home in Palestine, and as a contribution to historic justice and to world peace."[8] The recent tragedy of European Jewry was also favorably covered by prominent Afrikaner newspapers: The Cape Town Afrikaner afternoon paper and mouthpiece of the UP, *Die Suiderstem,* observed that "[n]ow that the Jews have their own State they can at least save a portion of persecuted

---

[6] SAJBD Report of the Executive Council August 1947 to May 1949, Johannesburg 1949, 7, SAJBD Reports, Rochlin Archive, Johannesburg.
[7] SAJBD Report of the Executive Council August 1947 to May 1949, Johannesburg 1949, 5–6, SAJBD Reports, Rochlin Archive, Johannesburg.
[8] "Telegram from Gen. Smuts to Mr. Moshe Shertok," May 1948, 141–142, Items of Jewish Interest, Rochlin Archive, Johannesburg.

Jewry in Europe and accord them a new home;"[9] and the Bloemfontein Afrikaner-language daily newspaper *Die Volksblad*, which had a wide distribution area and influence in the Free State and Northern Cape provinces, reported: "A great historical ideal was finally fulfilled when the Jews established their own State."[10]

Indications of the connection drawn between the establishment of the State of Israel and the recent tragedy of European Jewry can be traced in the SAJBD's discussions during the meeting described above regarding the failure of the Warsaw Ghetto Monument appeal. At the meeting, members of the Board argued that "apart from that [the Warsaw ghetto Monument], the only other country in which it was necessary to build a monument to the Jewish martyrs of Europe was Israel."[11] This stand is not surprising considering that in the postwar non-European arena, no statues or markers on public space were erected in cities with substantial and influential Jewish communities. Although Jewish communities in Europe built memorials to commemorate the recent Jewish tragedy, all were in places where Jewish life had once flourished, and which were then destroyed by Nazi brutality. As many of these locations came under communist control during the post-war years, most of the memorials established in Central and Eastern Europe from the 1950s to the 1980s were confined either to the actual killing sites or to Jewish communal spaces such as cemeteries or synagogues.[12]

The two monuments of the Warsaw ghetto uprising of 1943 are the most prominent examples of the first attempts at commemorating the murdered Jews in Europe. Established on the ruins of the ghetto, the first monument was designed by the architect Leon Suzin and was unveiled in 1946 to mark the third anniversary of the outbreak of the uprising. The second monument was the abovementioned monument to the ghetto heroes, created by Rapoport and unveiled in 1948.[13] Another remarkable example is that of the Jewish monument in Auschwitz-Birkenau, erected by the ruins of a gas chamber and crematorium in the former Birkenau part of the camp in 1948.[14]

---

9 *Die Suiderstem*, 27 May 1948, Press Digest 1940s, 142, Rochlin Archive, Johannesburg (a translated collection).
10 *Die Volksblad*, 26 May 1948, 142–143, Press Digest 1940s, Rochlin Archive, Johannesburg (a translated collection).
11 "Battle of Warsaw Ghetto," *South African Jewish Times*, 2 July 1948, File 520. 2, Rochlin Archive, Johannesburg.
12 Marek Kucia, "Holocaust Memorials in Central and Eastern Europe: Communist Legacies, Transnational Influences and National Developments," *Remembrance and Solidarity* 5 (2016): 159–184.
13 Kucia, "Holocaust Memorials in Central and Eastern Europe: Communist Legacies," 162–163.
14 To read more about the Jewish monument in Auschwitz-Birkenau, see Jonathan Huener, *Auschwitz, Poland, and the politics of commemoration, 1945–1979* (Athens: Ohio University Press, 2003).

Outside Europe, however, Jewish communities had no need to be rebuilt, nor did any require that new communal structures be linked to the past by a monument. American Jewry, for example, was only involved in the building of monuments outside of the US, such as the Paris memorial. However, all attempts to establish a monument in the American public space to the millions of European Jews who had been martyred by the Nazis ended in failure.[15] Yad Vashem in Jerusalem, which was officially declared as an Israeli national monument in 1953, provided the one exception. Despite being geographically distant from the atrocities conducted by the Nazis, Israel positioned itself as the spiritual and practical representative of all Holocaust victims. Moreover, unlike other countries in the world, Israel did not contain a Jewish minority, and therefore the question of whether to commemorate Jewish victims of the Holocaust in the common public space of a non-Jewish majority did not arise.

Two days after Smuts' *de facto* recognition of the State of Israel, the UP, which had led the government from its establishment in 1933, was ousted by the reunited NP, led by Malan. Promising white supremacy and racial boundaries at all costs, Malan became the new Prime Minister of South Africa and the Minister of Foreign Affairs. The new Cabinet was announced as the first all-Afrikaans Cabinet.[16] While the election results came as a shock to all of the Union's citizens, the fact that the Pro-Zionist Smuts and his UP were replaced by Malan and the Nationalists, who had closely associated themselves with the policies of the Nazis during the war, was particularly harrowing for the Jews of the country.

As described in detail in the previous chapter, institutional racial segregation had been government policy since the creation of the Union of South Africa in 1910. As Claudia BraudeBraude, Claudia argues, throughout the first half of the 20th century, "Jews did not automatically fit into 'European' and 'white' social and legal frameworks. Nor were they ever completely marginalized as 'non-European,' 'colored,' or 'black.' This ambivalent racial in-betweenness produced anxieties about Jewish racial status and belonging within the white power base."[17] Indeed, the peculiar position of South African Jewry during that period was characterized

---

15 In October 1947 a memorial cornerstone was laid at 84th Street and Riverside Drive in New York in memory of the martyred European Jews. However, all attempts to erect the memorial above the cornerstone ground-level ended in failure. To read more about American Jewry's attempts to establish monuments, see Hasia Diner, "Fitting Memorials," in *We remember with reverence and love: American Jews and the Myth of Silence after the Holocaust, 1945–1962* (New York: New York University Press, 2009), 16–84.
16 Saul Dubow, *Apartheid, 1948–1994* (Oxford: Oxford University Press, 2014), 12–15.
17 Braude, *Contemporary Jewish Writing in South Africa*, ix–x.

by its relations with the Nationalist government. As many members of the NP had been outspokenly pro-Nazi during the War and had made no bones about their intentions should they come to power, the position of Jews under the Nationalist government was more than uncertain.

In a pre-election interview to the national press, Malan was asked whether the NP was "anti-Jewish." He replied that as far as "our stated Party policy" is concerned, the answer is "no," adding that while there were anti-Jewish individuals in the Party, there was less covert anti-Jewishness than in the UP. As for the Party's policy on Jewish immigration, Malan stated that this policy was not born out of antipathy towards Jews. "As soon as Jews in any land exceed a certain percentage, it creates a race problem there," he argued, "and in South Africa we reached this limit a considerable time ago."[18] While the interview was for the most part reassuring to the Jewish community, it concluded with a warning that "if their [the Jews] chosen leaders are going to call upon the Jews, as Jews, as now appears to be the case, to fight the Nationalist Party, it certainly will not be the best way to further the interests of their race. The Jews need friends today and not political enemies."[19]

In response to Malan's warning, an official statement was issued by the SAJBD to both the communal and national presses stating: "The Board of Deputies takes no part whatever in the party-political struggle. Party politics are entirely beyond its province. The Board is concerned only to protect the Jewish community against discrimination or any interference with their rights as citizens."[20] This policy of non-involvement in politics except where Jewish interests were implicated was adopted by the Board and the Zionist Federation and was reformulated in various formal resolutions during the 1950s and 1960s.[21] However, as seen in the previous chapter, the origins of this policy go back to the 1930s and 1940s, when Jewish institutions had to respond to the various legislation restricting Jewish immigration into the Union, while not addressing the similar restrictions aimed at other social groups.

The Jewish community was only partially reassured by Malan's pre-election statements. While immediately after the elections the NP declared that its policy would be one of equality and non-discrimination as far as the Jews of the

---

[18] "Dr. D. F. Malan on H. P. Policy towards Jews," SAJBD Report of the Executive Council, August 1947 to May 1949, 9–10, SAJBD Reports, Rochlin Archive, Johannesburg.
[19] "Dr. D. F. Malan on H. P. Policy towards Jews," SAJBD Report of the Executive Council, August 1947 to May 1949, 11, SAJBD Reports, Rochlin Archive, Johannesburg.
[20] "The Board and Party Politics," SAJBD Report of the Executive Council, August 1947 to May 1949, 15, SAJBD Reports, Rochlin Archive, Johannesburg.
[21] Shimoni, *Community and Conscience*, 30.

country were concerned, there was no evidence of any radical change in the policy of discrimination against Jews which the Party had adopted some years earlier. Nevertheless, the community welcomed the assertion that antisemitism was not the declared policy of the new government.[22]

A relative change in the attitude of the NP toward South African Jewry took shape when Smuts' *de facto* recognition of Israel became Malan's *de jure* recognition on 14 May 1949. This was followed by the declaration of the opening of an Israeli Consulate General in Johannesburg, which was added to the Israeli legation already active in Pretoria. Edward David Gottein became Israel's first Minister to South Africa and the foundations for diplomatic communication were laid.[23]

The most meaningful exchange of visitors took place in 1953, when Malan became the first head of government in the world to visit Israel.[24] While Malan declared the visit to be religious and not political in nature, he did meet with David Ben-Gurion, the Israeli Prime Minister, in Jerusalem, and proclaimed, "I was impressed by the most sacred places in the country and most of all by what was done by you [the Israelis] in the field of agriculture and the development of the Holy Land."[25] Upon his return, Malan voiced his appreciation for the Jews' ability to maintain their national identity despite centuries of adversity and described the establishment of the Jewish homeland in Palestine as a weighty historical event.[26]

This was indeed a relief for South African Jewry, who found themselves having to balance the joy at the foundation of the Jewish homeland with their apprehension regarding the new political reality at home. Israel's diplomatic actions in the international sphere, however, soon became a new source of concern for the local community. Israel was admitted to the UN on 2 May 1949 and just three days later it supported a General Assembly Resolution on "The Treatment of People of Indian Origin in the Union of South Africa."[27] In fact, during the years 1949–1952, Israel's diplomats developed a formula to relate to apartheid in international forums. As

---

[22] The ban against Jewish membership in the NP in the Transvaal remained in force during the first three years of Malan's premiership and was only lifted in 1951. To read more about the Jewish response to the new NP government, see Shimoni, *Community and Conscience*, 12.

[23] David Fachler, "The Jewish Factor in Israeli Foreign Policy: The Case of South Africa (1948–1994)" (M.A. Thesis, The Hebrew University of Jerusalem, Israel, 2012), 18–19.

[24] "מלאן הגיע ויצא לירושלים" ["Malan arrived and left for Jerusalem",] *Maariv*, 15 June 1953, Historical Jewish Press, The National Library of Israel and Tel-Aviv University.

[25] "מלאן נפרד בשלום" ["Malan says Goodbye,"] *Shearim*, 18 June 1953, Historical Jewish Press, The National Library of Israel and Tel-Aviv University.

[26] Gilbert, "Jews and Racial State," 52–53.

[27] This resolution was part of India's campaign against South African race policies towards its Indian population, which had been put in place in 1946.

Rotem Giladi, Rotem argues, during that period, "Israel approached apartheid with equivocation, which was reflected in its voting praxis; its diplomats devised and acted on a formula that, in their own words, enabled them 'to have our cake and eat it.'"[28] While the Israeli formula was rooted in *realpolitik*, the conflict between Israel's commitment to the struggle against racism and the necessity of maintaining good relations with South Africa in order to protect the South African Jewish community was evident.[29]

It was under the framework of this formula that on 2 December 1950 Israel joined thirty-three other countries in supporting a UN resolution stating that the South African policy of racial segregation was based on doctrines of racial discrimination and which called on South Africa to delay implementation of the Group Areas Act.[30] In November 1955, Israel further supported the condemnation of that same Act in the UN General Assembly, while aligning itself with the then newly established Afro-Asian international bloc.[31] This decision had immediate repercussions for South African Jewry: The Jewish community was accused of having dual loyalties, and the newspaper *Die Burger* warned that the Israeli anti-apartheid vote would cause "great distress" to the Jewish community, who were trying to collect funds for armaments for Israel.[32] Posing such an explicit threat by one of the most prominent and widely circulated national newspapers, which served as the mouthpiece of the NP, was a cause for a great concern for the Zionist Jewish community that was reputedly the most financially supportive of Israel among diaspora Jewry per capita.

These developments profoundly affected the community's political, cultural, and social behavior throughout the first decade of apartheid and shaped its collective identity. As a minority within the privileged white minority, the South African Jewish community was vulnerable in some senses, but also self-organized and economically integrated. This privilege was central to the work of memory-making in the public sphere that the community pursued. It enabled

---

28 Rotem Giladi, "Negotiating Identity: Israel, Apartheid, and the United Nations, 1949–1952," *The English Historical Review* 132.559 (2017): 1440–1472, at 1445.
29 Giladi, "Negotiating Identity," 1456–1457.
30 The Group Area Act of 1950 aimed at eliminating mixed neighborhoods in favor of racially segregated ones to enable South Africans to develop separately. On UN resolution on the matter see "Treatment of people of Indian origin in the Union of South Africa: resolution / adopted by the General Assembly," A/RES/395(V), Voting Record Search, UN Library Home.
31 The Afro-Asian bloc was established at the 1955 Bandung Conference – a meeting of leaders from Asian and African states, most of which were newly independent. To read more about the Bandung Conference see Ryan M. Irwin, *Gordian Knot: Apartheid and the Unmaking of the Liberal World Order* (Oxford: Oxford University Press, 2012), 3–6.
32 Fachler, "The Jewish Factor in Israeli Foreign Policy," 19.

the community to invest in relief work during the war period and well into the post-war years, as described in the previous chapter. During the post-war period, it also maintained a vital interest in commemorating the tragedy of European Jewry in the South African public sphere.

In many ways, the new regime of 1948 marked the establishment of a homogenous identity and culture for South African Jewry in the face of a reality of increasing institutional racial segregation. In a country where cultural segregation between all social groups became institutionalized, apartheid's "separate development" paradigm encouraged the Jewish community, like every other ethnic group in the country, to invest in the construction of a distinct ethnic identity.[33] This separation was reflected not only in community institutions, schools, synagogues, and cultural centers, but also in the community's mnemonic practices.

'I am here to stay on earth': Herman Wald's *Kria*

Despite disputes over the proper form of commemorating the Jewish genocide, South African Jewry, usually considered marginal in the study of diaspora Jewry, adopted strategies of public memorialization far earlier than other diasporic communities. Concrete discussions regarding the possibility of erecting a communal monument in memory of the Jews murdered by the Nazis began in 1946 with the appearance of the Jewish South African sculptor Herman Wald's statue *Kria*.

Herman Wald was born in Cluj, then part of Hungary, in 1906 to an orthodox Jewish family. He was one of eight children who grew up in the atmosphere of the Chassidic tradition, one which left a deep impression on his life and work. When he became interested in carving shapes and figures, he came into conflict with his father, Rabbi Jacob Wald, for whom the religious injunction against graven images was quite serious. Nonetheless, young Wald secretly continued to sculpt, and it was the carving of Theodor Herzl's likeness that gained him his father's approval. When young Wald announced his intention of taking up art studies in Budapest, he received his father's blessing. He graduated from the Budapest Academy in 1928 and went to Vienna to join the studio of Anton Hanock, one of the best-known Austrian sculptors of the early 20th century. Soon after, Wald moved to Berlin to continue his studies. However, the rise of Nazism in Germany in 1933 forced him to move to Paris and then to London.[34]

---

33 Hellig, "The Jewish Community in South Africa," 156.
34 Herman Wald, *Craved Thoughts* (Johannesburg: unpublished, 1944), 1–8.

Herman Wald immigrated to South Africa in 1937 after his brother, Marcus Wald, settled there and was appointed minister to the Kimberley Jewish community. Herman himself settled in Johannesburg, where he established a studio.[35] One of his first works to be exhibited in South Africa was *The Refugees,* a sculpture dedicated to the figure of the Jewish refugee mother, presented in 1937 at the Jewish Refugees Aid Exhibition held at the Lidchi Art Gallery in Johannesburg.[36] Portraying a woman attempting to save her child and herself from her persecutors, the sculpture was donated by Wald to this event, organized by the SAZF, as part of the United South African Jewish War Appeal to raise funds for Jewish refugees trying to flee Nazi-controlled Europe.[37]

As Wald began to establish his career in South Africa, the Second World War broke out. Like many members of the local Jewish community, he volunteered for the South African Forces and served in the Engineers' Camouflage Unit. Wald explains the reason behind his decision to enlist in an unpublished book of aphorisms called *Carved Thoughts,* which he produced during the war years. He writes, "With the outbreak of the Second World War, my vagabond life was interrupted. The shocking news of the cold-blooded murder of my co-vagabond poet induced me to sign the dotted line, and I became an active member of the South African army."[38] He was discharged from the Army in 1944 and re-opened his studio in Johannesburg, often expressing his war experiences in his art.

In his country of birth, Hungary, the local government expressed its antisemitic sentiments long before German invasion took place. Therefore, following the German occupation of Hungary on 19 March 1944, the Germans enjoyed full cooperation from the local authorities in the deportation of Hungarian Jews. Wald once wrote, "[a]fter the war, in 1946, as soon as I was demobilized, I had found out for certain that, like so many others, almost my entire family had been wiped out."[39] This tragic loss, especially of his mother Pearl Wald who numbered among the dead, had an enormous impact on his work.

Kria, one of his first artistic works from the post-war period, was a monumental statue of a man rending his garments in mourning. He sculpted it in

---

35 Wald, *Craved Thoughts,* 9.
36 "Monument to Mother," *South African Zionist Record,* 24 March 1944, Newspaper Articles and Other Writing, Herman Wald Private Collection.
37 Joseph Sachs, "Herman Wald," *South African Jewish Affairs,* April 1947, 22, File Wald Herman 199, Rochlin Archive, Johannesburg.
38 Wald, *Craved Thoughts,* 9.
39 Herman Wald, Undated document, quoted in Ute Ben Yosef, "The South African years: part 2," The Life and Art of Herman Wald (1906–1970), http://www.lifeandartofhermanwald.co.za/ [Accessed on 7 July 2020].

1946 in memory of European Jewry murdered by the Nazis. Wald described the sculpture as follows:

> 'Kria', meaning the rending of garments, is a symbol of Jewish mourning, originating from biblical days and still practiced today. The figure represents the present-day Jewish people in defiance of its enemies, yet with dignified hope and feet firmly planted on the ground saying, 'I am here to stay on earth', which is the birthright of any man, Jew or any other race.[40]

Created two years before the establishment of the State of Israel, *Kria* can be interpreted as representing an early connection between the recent annihilation of European Jewry and the future rebirth of Israel, highlighting the contrast between the sorrow of the past and hope for the future.

Wald's *Kria* employs an explicitly Jewish mythology: by exaggerating the Jewish motif of the rending of a garment as a signifier of mourning, Wald suggests the enormity of the tragedy of the annihilation of European Jewry. At the same times he marks Jewish empowerment by representing the muscles of the figure, exposed by the torn garment.

In many ways, Wald's muscular figure reflects Max Nordau's notion of Muscular Judaism. In his speech at the Second Zionist Congress held in Basel on 28 August 1898, Nordau spoke of the need to form a new Jew endowed with mental and physical strength to achieve the goals of Zionism. He coined the term "Muscular Judaism" in answer to Jewish vulnerability. The characteristics of the muscular Jew were positioned as the antithesis of the diasporic Jew represented in antisemitic literature, which depicts Jews as a weak, helpless, and poor people, and as a counterpoint to the rabbinic or Haskalah Jew, perceived as a man of letters.[41] Nordau promoted the physical education of the Jews as an antidote to eighteen centuries of persecution which had plagued the Jewish people in exile. He bound muscular Judaism to the image of Simeon Bar-Kokhba, who he believed embodied the strength of Judaism. "Let us once again become deep-chest, sturdy, sharp-eyed men," he proclaimed.[42]

The perception of the "Muscular Jew" was prominent in different forms of commemoration centered on the Warsaw ghetto uprising. The ghetto fighters

---

[40] Quoted from "Herman Wald Public Works," http://www.hermanwald.com/pages/Public_Work.aspx [Accessed on 26 July 2020].

[41] Moshe Zimmermann, "Muscle Jews versus Nervous Jews," in *Emancipation Through Muscles: Jews and Sports in Europe*, ed. Michael Brenner and Gideon Reuveni, (Lincoln: University of Nebraska Press, 2006), 13.

[42] Paul Breines, *Tough Jews: Political Fantasies and the Moral Dilemma of American Jewry* (New York: Basic Books, 1990), 142–143.

who fought against their oppressors linked the memory of the Jewish genocide to the creation of the State of Israel, suggesting the rebirth not only of a new homeland for the Jewish people but also of a new and powerful Jew.[43] This was an expression of a traditional Jewish meta-narrative adopted by Zionism, reformulated after the war from its first iteration – "from destruction to redemption" – into "from Holocaust to revival." Above all, this "Muscular Jew" was an expression of "Holocaust and Heroism," termed by Mooli Brog as Israel's "memorial label for the national tragedy," which combines two complementary elements – the destruction and the Zionist uprising in the ghettos.[44]

This perception was amply represented in an address made by the founder of the first progressive congregation in Johannesburg, Rabbi Moses Cyrus Weiler, at the Johannesburg gathering to commemorate the sixth anniversary of the battle of the Warsaw ghetto, where he stated:

> The new Jew that was born in the Battle of the Warsaw Ghetto helped to forge the State of Israel and the new spirit that has become part and parcel of the Jewish nation [. . .] these Jews had won the battle of Israel – a battle that began in Warsaw. This spirit we need here in South Africa in order to strengthen our ranks against reaction both internal and external.[45]

In an interview to *South African Jewish Affairs* from April 1947, Wald testified that in creating *Kria* his ambition was that it would be erected somewhere in Palestine "as a monument to the past and a beacon to the future."[46] When read together with Wald's attraction to Zionism from childhood, this interview serves as indication of

---

[43] This perception was particularly prominent in the monuments erected in Israel during the first decade of its establishment. One distinct example is that of the Mordechai Anilevich memorial monument. Located on a hill overlooking kibbutz Yad Mordechai, the bronze monument was sculpted by Nathan Rapoport and erected in 1951 as a memorial to the leader of the Warsaw ghetto uprising. Like the man in Wald's *Kria*, Rapoport's monument shows a strong young man with a look of determination on his face and a grenade in his hand. By depicting Anielewicz as a strong man, and by positioning the sculpture in front of the war-damaged water tower, Rapoport connects the heroism of the Warsaw ghetto uprising with the members of Kibbutz Yad Mordechai, who fought the Egyptian army during the War of Independence in 1948. To read more on the Mordechai Anilevich memorial monument see Dalia Ofer, "We Israelis Remember, But How? The Memory of the Holocaust and the Israeli Experience," *Israel Studies* 18.2 (2014): 70–85.
[44] Mooli Brog, "Victims and Victors: Holocaust and Military Commemoration in Israel Collective Memory," *Israel Studies* 8.3 (2003): 69–99.
[45] Quoted in "Heroes of the Warsaw Ghetto Recalled," *South Africa Jewish Times*, 6 May 1949, File 520.2A: Holocaust Commemoration 1940–1949, Rochlin Archive, Johannesburg.
[46] Joseph Sachs, "Herman Wald," *South African Jewish Affairs*, April 1947, 25, File Wald Herman 199, Rochlin Archive, Johannesburg.

the influence of Zionism on his work. While the battle of the Warsaw ghetto was indeed central to post-war Jewish discourse in 1946, *Kria* was a very early manifestation of its significance. Its figurative and monumental nature dealt explicitly with the dichotomy between the destruction and suffering of the Jewish people on the one hand and their heroism and empowerment on the other.

Fig. 1: Herman Wald, *Kria*, Courtesy of Louis Wald.

In the South African press, the new sculpture was reviewed long before it was formally acquired as a monument by the Jewish community. Under the title "Symbol of Chaos and Hope," the weekly Johannesburg based newspaper *Sunday Express* published an article on 16 June 1946 stating that *Kria* symbolized the quotation from the Bible, "Rend your heart and not your garments," and expressed the chaotic state of the contemporary world, as well as hopes for the future.[47] A day later, the daily newspaper *The Star* reported on Wald's latest creation as a memorial to the suffering of the Jewish people and as a monument to remind mankind of the tragedy in Europe that must never be repeated.[48]

A similar impression of *Kria* was recorded in the local Jewish newspaper, the *South African Jewish Times*, on 28 June 1946. It reported on honorary treasurer of the South African Jewish War Appeal Leo Feit's interpretation of the biblical meaning of *Kria*, which "has left the same tear on the Jewish soul because of the same old unsolved problem of the Jewish race." As in Wald's own words, the article also described the dichotomy expressed in the sculpture between suffering and resistance. It related to Wald's ambition to see the memorial erected as a monument to remind mankind of the tragedy which was never to occur again, stating that "Johannesburg Jewry might well consider the purchasing of *Kria* as a memorial to fallen Jewry."[49]

Three and a half years later, on 9 December 1949, the *Jewish Times* reported, "The great piece of work has not yet been cast and may be lost because, collectively, the community is not interested, and some have suddenly discovered that a piece of sculpture is an image and opposed to Jewish religion."[50] The *Jewish Times* also published a letter in its Open Forum urging that *Kria* be acquired as a memorial by the Jewish community: "*Kria* is a monument not to our dead but to the survivors, a declaration that we live, an expression of sorrow at our bereavement, yet full of defiance. 'Am Yisrael Chai' is the message of *Kria*."[51] This letter clearly expresses the desire of members of the Jewish community to establish a memorial not only for their relatives who had perished, but chiefly for those who had survived.

As mentioned in the previous chapter, during the post-war period practical relief for the surviving Jews in Europe was a primary concern for South African Jewry. However, there was a widespread belief among the leaders of the community that the survivors in Europe could only be successfully rehabilitated if they were permitted to enter Palestine. Moreover, at a meeting of the Aliens and Refugees Committee of the Board held in June 1945, it was reported that South

---

[47] "Symbol of Chaos and Hope," *Sunday Express*, 16 June 1946, Newspaper Articles and Other Writing, Herman Wald Private Collection.
[48] "'Kria': Herman Wald's Latest Creation," *The Star*, 20 June 1946, Newspaper Articles and Other Writing, Herman Wald Private Collection.
[49] "'KRIA', Herman Wald's Latest Work," *South African Jewish Times*, 28 June 1946, Newspaper Articles and Other Writing, Herman Wald Private Collection.
[50] "On Transvaal Soil – J.M. Sherman's Stories and Poems," *South African Jewish Times*, 9 December 1949, Newspaper Articles and Other Writing, Herman Wald Private Collection.
[51] "Herman Wald's Kria," *South African Jewish Times*, 30 December 1949, File Wald Herman 199, Rochlin Archive, Johannesburg.

Africa's policy regarding Jewish immigration remained rigid.[52] Therefore, despite thousands of applications from Jews who wished to bring relatives to South Africa, only 1,512 refugees were eventually permitted to enter the Union between 1946 and 1948.[53] In 1951 the SAJBD decided that an organization should be established to provide aid for those few survivors who eventually were admitted into the Union. The organization was named *She'erith Hapletah– Jewish Survivors Association in South Africa* – and its main purpose was to provide a communal home for the survivors and to promote social and cultural ties between the survivors and the community.[54] The survivors were defined by the Jewish institutions as the living reminder of a great people and the new organization as one with a special national significance.[55]

By the end of January 1950, a committee was finally formed in Johannesburg to acquire *Kria* for the Jewish community. The community's intention was that *Kria* be given its permanent home in the Communal Building in Johannesburg, and the SAJBD issued an appeal to members of the community to contribute to this communal effort.[56] While the sculpture was indeed acquired as a memorial by public subscription in 1950, it was placed at the disposal of the Board for its eventual display in a suitable site. Addressing a gathering of Jewish communal leaders in Wald's studio in Johannesburg in late 1950, the famous South African Jewish writer Sarah Gertrude Millin stated, "We need memorials because people forget. Memorials are not for the dead, but for the living. Every time we are in danger of forgetting the six million dead, this figure will remind us."[57] Looking up at the figure of *Kria*, Millin added,

> He is tearing his garment in mourning, yet through his grief there is also sullen defiance and pride on his face. The head is uplifted with determination. This is a figure not only of mourning, but the determination to carry on. Here is a breast bared to the world. Do what

---

52 Green, "South African Jewish Responses to the Holocaust, 1941–1948," 146–147.
53 Shain, "South Africa," 670–689.
54 Xavier Piat-ka, "She'erith Hapletah," in *In Sacred Memory: Recollections of the Holocaust by Survivors Living in Cape Town*, ed. Gwynne Schrire (Cape Town: Holocaust Memorial Council, 1995), 194–198.
55 "She'erith Hapletah: What it Stands For," She'erith Hapletah Annual Commemoration Issue, April 1965, Cape Town Holocaust & Genocide Center Archive.
56 "Jewish Community to Acquire Kria - Imposing Sculpture by Herman Wald," *South African Jewish Times*, 27 June 1950, File Wald Herman 199, Rochlin Archive, Johannesburg.
57 Edgar Bernstein, "The Art of Herman Wald," *Jewish Guild New Year Annual* 19, 109 (October 1951), File Wald Herman 199, Rochlin Archive, Johannesburg.

you will, it seems to say: here I am and here I shall stand. It is a figure of Jewish endurance which Mr. Wald has created, and we owe him our gratitude for putting these thoughts into concrete form.[58]

Despite the great desire on the part of members of the community to purchase *Kria* as a communal monument, the question of a permanent site was yet to be resolved.

Meanwhile, on the sunny morning of 3 October 1954, in the peaceful gardens of Pinelands Jewish Cemetery in Cape Town, located at the foot of Table Mountain, thousands gathered to participate in the consecration ceremony of the first communal memorial in memory of the six million Jews to be erected on South African soil.[59] This monument was a polished black granite stone, quarried from Table Mountain sandstone and designed as a gravestone with no mortal remains.[60] The inscriptions on the monument, which appeared in Hebrew and English, stated:

> The stone shall cry out of the wall. In loving and sacred remembrance of our martyred kinsfolk who died during the Nazi terror 1933–45. These things I remember and pour out my soul within me. Many waters cannot quench love, neither can the floods drown it. Thy dead shall live . . . for thy dew is as the dew of light."[61]

Initial discussions regarding the possibility of erecting a memorial to the six million martyred Jews in Cape Town were held in July 1953 by several local synagogues. It was decided that the memorial project would be a joint effort involving all Cape Jewry, and arrangements for the erection were put in the hands of a committee consisting of representatives of the Chevra Kaddisha of Cape Town and Wynberg. While the Cemeteries Board granted the site for the memorial free of charge, all local congregations were asked to contribute to the costs of the monument. A few days after the event, there was much talk about the conspicuous absence from the official proceedings of representatives of the Reform movement in the Cape. In fact, Simon Roy, President of the local Reform movement, argued that his congregation was deliberately ignored in the arrangements for the erection of the monument, although it included the

---

[58] Edgar Bernstein, "The Art of Herman Wald," *Jewish Guild New Year Annual* 19, 109 (October 1951), File Wald Herman 199, Rochlin Archive, Johannesburg.

[59] "Consecration of Memorial to Memory of the 6,000,000 Jews who Perished During the Nazi Persecutions," *South African Jewish Chronicle*, 8 October 1954, File 520.2A: Holocaust Commemoration 1950s, Rochlin Archive, Johannesburg.

[60] "Cape Town Jewry Say Kaddish," *South African Jewish Times*, 8 October 1954, File 520.2A: Holocaust Commemoration 1950s, Rochlin Archive, Johannesburg.

[61] "Monument to Six Million Consecrated," *Zionist Record*, 8 October 1954, File 520.2A: Holocaust Commemoration 1950s, Rochlin Archive, Johannesburg.

largest group of survivors in Cape Town.⁶² Nevertheless, the ceremony was described as one of the finest communal occasions in the history of the city.

Like the Cape Town community, the Durban community also chose to commemorate the tragedy of European Jewry with a memorial designed as a gravestone, erected on Yom Kippur eve, 11 October 1959, at the Stellawood Cemetery.⁶³ As noted earlier, during the post-war years, Jewish communities outside Europe avoided the establishment of public monuments and focused primarily on private Jewish commemoration efforts outside the national sphere. Therefore, memorials were placed in many Jewish cemeteries around the world in the form of empty graves without human remains. Unlike monuments, which are usually defined as artwork aimed at meeting a particular social need among the living, tombstone memorials lack visual characteristics and focus only on the deceased.

A few weeks after the erection of the monument in Cape Town, an urgent meeting was held in Johannesburg. At the meeting, Leo Feit, Chairman of the Building Fund for the new Jewish Home for the Aged, informed the Board that his Executive Committee was keen to have *Kria* suitably placed in the Garden of Remembrance, created in front of the new Home, in memory of the six million Jews.⁶⁴ The erection of the monument was finally announced to the public on 19 April 1955.⁶⁵ However, the opening ceremony of the vast new building was not held until 1 December 1957.

Kria's massive figure was positioned at the entrance of the building carrying the inscription: "To the sacred and undying memory of Europe's Martyred Jews, 1939–1945," in Hebrew, English, and Afrikaans.⁶⁶ The reason for including modern Hebrew inscriptions is clear in this context: it was the official language of the State of Israel and was used for prayer or study in Jewish communities around the world, including in South Africa. The use of the English inscriptions also reflects the use of English as the spoken language of most of the members of the local Jewish community. However, the use of Afrikaans here points to the community's recognition of the status of Afrikaans

---

62 "Unfortunate Incident Surrounding Cape Town Monument to Martyrs," *South African Jewish Times*, 22 October 1954, File 520.2A: Holocaust Commemoration 1940–1949, Rochlin Archive, Johannesburg.
63 "Memorial to 6,000,000," *South African Jewish Times*, 12 October 1959, File Wald Herman 199, Rochlin Archive, Johannesburg.
64 "Herman Wald's 'KERIAH'," SAJBD Executive Council, 15 November 1954, 2, SAJBD Reports, Rochlin Archive, Johannesburg.
65 "Johannesburg Memorial to the Jewish Martyrs of Europe," (8238), SAJBD Executive Council, 19 April 1955, 1, SAJBD Reports, Rochlin Archive, Johannesburg.
66 "Monument to The Jews," *The Star*, 10 December 1957; "Home for the Jewish Aged," *Rand Daily Mail*, 2 December 1957, Newspaper Articles and Other Writing, Herman Wald Private Collection.

as one of the official languages of the country. Thus, placing Wald's sculpture as a memorial to the recent tragedy of European Jewry in a Jewish Home for the Aged, while using inscriptions in Afrikaans, indicates Jewish efforts to accommodate the new regime.

It is important to situate *Kria* within the context of South African memorialization of that period. Dana Arieli-Horowitz claims that art and politics are not to be conceived as distinct realms but as dynamics in constant interaction. She argues that many political movements and leaders are well aware of this fact, and deliberately put art to instrumental use.[67] Focusing on art in totalitarian countries, she claims that dictators in the period between the two World Wars were drawn to the style of realism which they saw as a means of reducing the ambiguity they identified in modern art. While abstract art was seen as a subversive, self-directed, and uncontrolled channel of communication, realism, by contrast, would convey continuity and dialogue with the past.[68]

In South Africa, the local implementation of the realist style can be detected in the Great Trek Monument (Voortrekker Monument), one of the greatest Afrikaner commemorative efforts of the twentieth century. This monument was designed by architect Gerard Moerdijk during the mid-1930s on a hill outside Pretoria to commemorate the epic of the Great Trek of 1836, in which Afrikaner men, women, and children, dissatisfied with British rule in the Cape colony, set off in a convoy of ox wagons from Cape Town on a journey to form independent republics in what were to become the Transvaal and the Orange Free State.[69] The monument is a vast granite temple visible for miles with broad steps leading through an ox-wagon *laager* into the main hall. The *laager*, a famous battlefield strategy developed in the late eighteenth century, was adopted by the Afrikaner warriors during the Great Trek: their wagons were placed in a circle overnight with their weapons turned outwards, with the women and children confined within the circle. The *Laager* became a symbol for Afrikaner survival and was often used to express the importance of the preservation of white supremacy in a country with a black majority.[70] The monument itself was a

---

[67] Dana Arieli-Horowitz, "The Politics of Culture in Nazi Germany: Between Degeneration and Volkism" *The European Legacy* 6.6 (2001): 751–762.

[68] Dana Arieli-Horowitz, אמנות ורודנות: אוואנגרד ואמנות מגויסת במשטרים טוטליטריים [*Creators and Dictators: Avantgarde and Mobilized Art in Totalitarian Regimes*] (Tel Aviv: Tel Aviv University Press, 2008), 266.

[69] Annie E. Coombes, *History After Apartheid: Visual Culture and Public Memory in a Democratic South Africa* (Durham, NC: Duke University Press, 2003), 26.

[70] Uriel Abulof, *The Mortality and Morality of Nations: Jews, Afrikaners, and French-Canadians* (New York: Cambridge University Press, 2015), 288.

Fig. 2: The Voortrekker Monument, Mikel-Arieli Private Collection.

symbol of the Boers' victory over the Zulu in the 1836 Battle of Ncome River, also known as Battle of Blood River. It represented the inferiority of blacks in South Africa and the superiority of the Boers to their colonial predecessors.[71]

On 16 December 1938, the foundation stone of this central monument was laid during a reconstruction of the Great Trek marking its one-hundred-year anniversary.[72] Officially inaugurated in 1949, the monument reflects the national strategies of commemoration that characterized Afrikaner nationalism at a time when the apartheid state's resources were being channeled to assert the

---

[71] Rebecca Weaver-Hightower, "This is the Place Salt Lake City, Utah and the Voortrekker Monument Pretoria: monuments to settler constructions of history, race, and religion," *Safundi: The Journal of South African and American Studies* 22.2 (2021): 105–129, at 107.
[72] Abulof, *The Mortality and Morality of Nations*, 288.

Afrikaners' cultural, political, and economic dominance over the black majority. Admittedly, the design of the monument preceded the establishment of the apartheid regime; however, its initiation a year after the critical elections of 1948 and the establishment of white supremacy in the country gave ceremonial expression to Afrikaner nationalism. As T. Dunbar Moodie argues, the memory of this commemorative festival "would constitute a potent political force during the next decade."[73]

One can interpret the decision to erect *Kria* as an official monument in memory of the perished European Jews as a duplication of this monumentalization within Afrikaner nationalism. In a country where the white hegemonic minority invested tremendous resources in constructing its national identity through monuments, the local Jewish community sought to embrace a similar memorial strategy within the accepted boundaries of apartheid policy.

In the South African national press, *Kria* was defined as a site of mourning dedicated to the undying memory of Europe's Jews martyred between 1939 and 1945, an indication of the reception of the Jewish tragedy by the South African white society.[74] However, in the world press, Kria was defined as "a remarkable war study."[75] A connection can be drawn between the divergent opinions of the local and that of the larger western world and early Cold War politics. As mentioned in the introductory chapter, during the post-war period Western countries perceived Stalingrad and the resistance to Nazism as the Soviet Union did.[76] This perception consisted of universalist perspectives that focused on victims of fascism as a general entity without singling out the Jews as the victims of the Nazis. However, while the West saw the Federal Republic of Germany as the ally and the Soviet Union as the new enemy, the East positioned the Red Army as the only true liberator of Germany and the world from Hitler's fascist hands, and America as the new aggressive imperialist evil.[77]

Descriptions of the monument as a war memorial in the Western world press highlight Western countries' perception of the Jewish genocide as immediately linked to other atrocities of the war and the ethnic and historical conflicts that accompanied it. Within the Western narrative, the systematic policy

---

[73] Dunbar Moodie, *The Rise of Afrikanerdom: Power, Apartheid, and the Afrikaner Civil Religion* (Berkeley: University of California Press, 1975), 180.
[74] "Monument to the Jews," *The Star*, 10 December 1957, Newspaper Articles and Other Writing, Herman Wald Private Collection.
[75] "Sculpture from South Africa," *Tatler and Bystander*, 12 November 1947, Newspaper Articles and Other Writing, Herman Wald Private Collection.
[76] Joel Kotek, *Students and the Cold War* (London: Palgrave Macmillan, 1996), 62–63.
[77] Benda-Beckmann, *A German Catastrophe?* 35–36.

of discrimination, persecution, and mass violence against the Jews marked just another example of Nazi cruelty. In South Africa, however, the destruction of European Jews was presented as a uniquely anti-Jewish persecution. The explanation for this divergence lies in the political context of the 1950s, when South Africa was moving towards increased segregation and racial repression. Yet, the Jewish community was indeed a distinct social group, and given the centrality of memory to the construction of group identity and racial definition, the Jewish tragedy informed much of Jewish national existence in South Africa.

Another indication of the South African perception of the Jewish genocide as a uniquely antisemitic event can be located almost a year prior to the erection of *Kria* in two local stage adaptations of *The Diary of Anne Frank* in January 1957. The first performance was produced by the Jewish South African theatrical director and producer Leonard Schach in Cape Town, and the production then toured across Southern Africa for eight months. The second performance was staged by another Jewish producer, Minna Schneier, for the Johannesburg Repertory Theatre. Both productions enjoyed enormous success among Jewish audiences as well as among non-Jewish white viewers.[78]

The Diary was first adapted for the stage in 1955, based on a script by the husband-and-wife American screenwriters Frances Goodrich and Albert Hackett. This was the first time that mainstream American theater staged a play whose plot dealt with the persecution of the Jews by the Nazis.[79] However, in the process of adapting the content of the diary for an American audience, Anne Frank's Jewishness and Jewish suffering were diminished, and the play's content was presented as universalist in nature.[80]

The South African stage dramatization of *The Diary* was quite different in that it was far more Jewish than the American one. Schach's production portrayed Anne Frank's story as an exclusively Jewish narrative, emphasizing its relevance for confronting local antisemitism. As Gilbert puts it, Schach was "far more willing to assert Jewish distinctiveness than [his] American counterparts."[81] While the South African stage version focused on the individual story of Anne Frank as a Jewish victim in a specific historical setting, it had no explicit reference to inhumane Nazi acts. The white community in South Africa

---

[78] Gilbert, "Anne Frank in South Africa," 371.
[79] Edna Nahshon, "Anne Frank from Page to Stage," in *Anne Frank Unbound: Media, Imagination, Memory*, ed. Barbara Kirshenblatt-Gimblett and Jeffrey Shandler (Bloomington, IN: Indiana University Press 2012), 59–92, at 61.
[80] Judith E. Doneson, "The American history of Anne Frank's diary," *Holocaust and Genocide Studies* 2.1 (1987): 149–160, at 153–154.
[81] Gilbert, "Anne Frank in South Africa," 371.

would have been particularly sensitive to these kinds of references considering the pro-Nazi past of many right-wing Afrikaners. Moreover, the play did not deal with the bystanders at all and, in general, dealt very little with the Jewish genocide and its causes. As in the case of *Kria*, the play addressed the Jewish narrative while avoiding the broader implications of the Jewish tragedy for a South African local context.

The *Six Million* Monument

While *Kria's* permanent home was still under discussion, the Club of Polish Jews in Johannesburg began to promote the building of another official monument in memory of the six million Jews.[82] A Provisional Committee was appointed to consider the commemoration project and, on 15 March 1955, Abel Shaban, the Committee Chairman, invited the SAJBD to send a representative to a Committee meeting with the aim of considering the nature of the monument and its possible location. In his invitation, Shaban explained that the project was still in the exploratory stage. He suggested that a monument should be erected in the Jewish cemetery, as was the case in Cape Town and many cities overseas. In addition to the Board's representative, the Provisional Committee included delegates of practically all the states represented within the Landsmanschaften,[83] as well as from the South African Yiddish Cultural Federation and the Histadruth Ivrit.[84]

Members of the Committee suggested the West Park Jewish cemetery as a suitable place for a monument because "all members of the Jewish community, young and old, Yiddish- or English-speaking, visited it on some occasion during their life-time."[85] However, when the Board discussed the matter at a meeting held on 5 April, some members argued that it should instead be placed more centrally in the city. Again, as in the discussions regarding the erection of *Kria*, members of the Board voiced a strong preference for the creation of a

---

[82] "Monument to Martyred Jews to be Built in Johannesburg," *South African Jewish Times*, 6 May 1955, File 520.2A: Holocaust Commemoration 1950s, Rochlin Archive, Johannesburg.
[83] The Landsmanschaften was an immigrant benevolent organization formed and named after members' birthplaces or East European residence, for mutual aid, hometown aid, and social purposes.
[84] "Johannesburg Monument to Jewish Victims of the Nazis," SAJBD Executive Council Meeting, 21 March 1955, 4, SAJBD Reports, Rochlin Archive, Johannesburg.
[85] "Johannesburg Memorial to the Jewish Martyrs of Europe," SAJBD Executive Council Meeting, 5 April 1955, 2, SAJBD Reports, Rochlin Archive, Johannesburg.

"living memorial" rather than a tombstone. This memorial could take the form of the establishment of educational bursaries instead of a physical monument, some suggested. Another suggestion was made that the museum containing the silver liturgical objects salvaged from the Nazis should constitute a memorial. Shaban defended the project to build a monument, claiming that it did not preclude the consideration of other forms of commemoration. Gustav Saron, General Secretary of the Board, agreed with Shaban and stated, "a monument at the entrance to the cemetery would be seen by a very considerable proportion of the Jewish community."[86] However, the issues of the nature and place of the monument were yet to be resolved.

In a later discussion held by the Board on 19 April, Adolph Schauder, Vice President of the Eastern Province Board, strongly favoring the suggestion of a "living memorial," argued that there would come a time when the cemetery would be filled. Jack Hersov, then Chairman of the South African Jewish Appeal, joined Schauder, stating, "when the ground for the West Park Cemetery had been secured by the Chevra Kadisha from the Johannesburg City Council, it was calculated that it would suffice for the requirements of the Jewish community for 100 years." He further reminded the Board that the new Jewish Home for the Aged would be a "living memorial" to the martyrs, where *Kria* was to be erected.[87] Nevertheless, the President of the Board, Israel Maisels, concluded that "as the Landsmannschaft, who were a representative section of the Jewish community, wanted the monument, the Board should give the project its blessing," and on this basis the project for a monument at the West Park Cemetery was approved in principle.[88]

In March 1956, the Beth Din and the Jewish Helping Hand and Burial Society of Johannesburg agreed that a plot should be set aside at the West Park Cemetery for the memorial. In the meantime, designs were submitted, and one, by Herman Wald, was approved by the Monument Committee.[89] In May of that year, a model of the monument was first presented to the Jewish press.[90] Soon after, an appeal to all Jewish organizations and individuals to contribute to the erection of South

---

86 "Johannesburg Memorial to the Jewish Martyrs of Europe," SAJBD Executive Council Meeting, 5 April 1955, 2–3, SAJBD Reports, Rochlin Archive, Johannesburg.
87 "Johannesburg Memorial to the Jewish Martyrs of Europe," SAJBD Executive Council Meeting, 19 April 1955, 1, SAJBD Reports, Rochlin Archive, Johannesburg.
88 "Johannesburg Memorial to the Jewish Martyrs of Europe," SAJBD Executive Council Meeting, 19 April 1955, 1–2, SAJBD Reports, Rochlin Archive, Johannesburg.
89 "Martyrs Memorial," SAJBD Executive Council Meeting, 19 March 1956, 5, SAJBD Reports, Rochlin Archive, Johannesburg.
90 "Rand Memorial to Jewish Martyrs," *Jewish Herald*, 19 May 1956, File Wald Herman 199, Rochline Archive, Johannesburg.

African Jewry's monument was initiated. The committee defined the monument as "a truly representative effort," implying that the memorial project was an effort to represent the community's traumatic collective memory to the national public, and not merely a community memorial site.[91]

Fig. 3: *Six Million* Monument Model, Courtesy of Louis Wald.

This definition provides an answer to the question of what drove the Johannesburg community to erect an additional monument in memory of the perished European Jews. It is safe to assume that the erection of the Cape Town monument a year earlier and the long and ongoing postponement of the *Kria* erection were direct triggers for the new project. At that time, it had already been decided that *Kria* would be erected at the new Jewish Home for the Aged. However, for the memorial to serve as "a truly representative effort," it was critical to choose a location that was central to all members of the Jewish community.

---

[91] "Monument Committee Appeals to community," *South African Jewish Times*, 25 January 1957; "Let us honour the memory of the six million who perished by restoring the spiritual values for which they died," South African Jewish Times, 3 May 1957, File Wald Herman 199, Rochlin Archive, Johannesburg.

While antisemitism in South Africa was in decline, the recent memories of pro-Nazi and anti-Jewish manifestations in the South African public sphere also dictated a need to represent the anti-antisemitic message to the white minority.

With the model of the monument in hand, the monument committee decided to increase its size, a decision that doubled its costs from £6,000 to £12,000. While the committee members felt confident that the funds could be raised, Shaban disagreed, as did some of the members of the Board. At an Executive meeting held on 23 July 1956, it was clear that the Board had concerns regarding the funding of the project. While Shaban gave categorical assurance that the Board would not be called upon to cover some of the costs, some members expressed the view that the Committee should not proceed with its plans until they were certain they would be able to collect the full funding required for the project.[92] Two weeks later, A.L. Meyer announced his resignation as one of the Board's representatives on the Committee, claiming that he was "in disagreement with the decision to increase the size, and consequently, the expense, of the monument."[93] This dramatic announcement was followed by a stormy discussion with a clear division of opinion as to whether the fact that the Monument Committee was under the auspices of the Board meant that the Board had thereby assumed any responsibility for its activities.[94]

Eventually, the Committee decided to reduce slightly the size of the monument.[95] However, it still seemed that it would not be able to collect the necessary funds. Therefore, at an Executive Council meeting on 18 March 1957, a suggestion was made to publicize the need for funds for the erection of the monument at the upcoming gatherings concerning the Day of Mourning. This suggestion was the source of another heated discussion and the Executive Council expressed its opposition to any collection of funds at such meetings. However, the Council left it to the Honorary Officers to decide whether the Committee should be allowed to place leaflets on the seats at the Day of Mourning meetings in Johannesburg. Eventually, in line with Shaban's request to the Board, it was decided that while the speakers at the Day of Mourning would not

---

[92] "Communal Relations Committee- Report," SAJBD Executive Council Meeting, 23 July 1956, 3–4, SAJBD Reports, Rochlin Archive, Johannesburg.
[93] "Johannesburg Memorial to the Jewish Martyrs of the Nazis," SAJBD Executive Council Meeting, 8 August 1956, 1, SAJBD Reports, Rochlin Archive, Johannesburg.
[94] "Johannesburg Memorial to the Jewish Martyrs of the Nazis," SAJBD Executive Council Meeting, 8 August 1956, 1, SAJBD Reports, Rochlin Archive, Johannesburg.
[95] "Communal Relations Committee-Report," SAJBD Executive Council Meeting, 20 August 1956, 5, SAJBD Reports, Rochlin Archive, Johannesburg

be permitted to make an appeal for funds for the monument, they would be allowed to mention the monument in their addresses at the gatherings.[96]

Although there is no doubt that the monument was intended as a piece of Jewish communal memorial, it received the attention of the national press from its planning stages. The *Rand Daily Mail* published an article on 17 July 1956 under the headline, "Rand Man Creates Memorial to Mark Death of 6m. Jews," describing the memorial model in detail.[97] This article was discussed in the July 1956 meeting of the Communal Relations Committee of the Board, which was troubled by the fact that the paper also stated that the Johannesburg memorial was to be unveiled on 19 April 1957, "the day on which world Jewry commemorate the rising of the Warsaw Ghetto against the Nazis." The scheduled date for the Day of Mourning in South Africa accorded with the date fixed by the Israeli authorities, namely the 27th of Nissan in the Hebrew calendar. Shaban quickly tried to mitigate the situation and referred to the *Rand Daily Mail* report as unauthorized and inaccurate.[98]

While the date of the erection of the Six Million monument was still pending, the *South African Engineer* magazine devoted a major article in its September 1957 issue to Wald's design, declaring that it was "a reminder to more than the Jewish community of the crime of genocide on a scale unmatched since the time of Genghis Khan."[99] This description of the monument inscribes the destruction of European Jewry as the most traumatic and destructive event of modern times. This was not another attempt to position Nazism as the ultimate evil while subsuming Jewish fatalities within the totality of war victims, as had happened repeatedly in the East and West during the post-war period. Instead, the statement was a recognition of the antisemitism that had led to the Jewish genocide, and it placed the destruction of European Jewry, rather than the war, at the center. The magazine described in detail the symbolic Jewish elements of the design, portraying how it includes "six hands clasping six ram's horns, traditionally used to summon the faithful at New Year and the Day of Atonement." It described the appearance of the initial Hebrew letters from the words of the commandment "Thou shalt not

---

[96] "Day of Mourning," (8690), SAJBD Executive Council Meeting, 23 April 1957, 7–8, SAJBD Reports, Rochlin Archive, Johannesburg.

[97] "Rand Man Creates Memorial to Mark Death of 6m Jews," *Rand Daily Mail*, 19 July 1956, File Wald Herman 199, Rochlin Archive, Johannesburg.

[98] "Communal Relations Committee- Report," (8536), SAJBD Executive Council Meeting, 23 July 1956, 4, SAJBD Reports, Rochlin Archive, Johannesburg.

[99] "Foundry Drama Has Happy Ending – CO2 Process used for Bronze Monument Casting," *South African Engineer*, September 1957, Newspaper Articles and Other Writing, Herman Wald Private Collection.

kill," placed one on top of the other; the article also elaborated on the enormous size of each of the six bronze hands.[100]

The South African Engineer emphasized that "the Jewish religion does not permit the inclusion of human figures in the design." This explanation points to an aesthetic difference evident in the *Six Million* monument and very much absent from *Kria*. As described earlier, *Kria* had invoked a heated debate within the Jewish community regarding whether or not to purchase the sculpture as a communal monument, partly due to the religious injunction against graven images. In the *Six Million* monument, the dilemma was solved since Wald adopted elements of the abstract style while still retaining clear figurative motifs. The powerful and enormous hands of the *Six Million* monument are reminiscent of the muscular Jewish figure in *Kria*. Likewise, the ram's horns that they hold are a clear symbolic Jewish element, much like the distinctly Jewish custom of the tearing of garments in *Kria*. Wald described the *Six Million* monument as follows:

> This monument depicts six mighty bronze fists, each five feet high, bursting out of the ground as a protest of the dead, each fist representing one million Jews who perished under Hitler, and each gripping a ram's horn, the Jewish ritual trumpet standing twenty feet high. In pairs they create three arches; the arches of trials and tribulations that the Jewish people have all gone through during all the generations of persecution. In the centre there is a flame shaped Eternal Light, spiraling fifteen feet up. Through the ram's horns the dead are blasting out the Sixth Commandment: "Though shalt not kill," while the centre eternal light is stylized through the medium of the Hebrew lettering, to form a flame which spells in Hebrew "Lo Tirtzach" (thou Shalt Not Kill).[101]

From Wald's description it is evident that one cannot ignore the presence of the monument when entering the Jewish cemetery. The size of the various elements indicates the desire to perpetuate this memory in the landscape. The hands emanate from the ground and their location at the Jewish cemetery simulates their emergence from graves, reflecting the verse from the Book of Genesis (4:10), "the voice of thy brother's blood cries unto me from the ground."[102] In addition, the rupture between each pair of ram's horns creates an image of three broken arches, which signify the inability to represent the traumatic and tragic events of the destruction of European Jews. In the center the eternal light, forming a

---

[100] "Foundry Drama Has Happy Ending – CO2 Process used for Bronze Monument Casting," *South African Engineer*, September 1957, Newspaper Articles and Other Writing, Herman Wald Private Collection.
[101] "Herman Wald Public Works," Herman Wald Site, http://www.hermanwald.com/pages/Public_Work.aspx [Accessed on 2 January 2016].
[102] This verse represents the first murder, and thus is representative of the Jewish (and Christian) understanding of what murder is.

Fig. 4: *Six Million* Monument, West Park Jewish Cemetery, Johannesburg, Courtesy of Louis Wald.

flame, spells in Hebrew the imperative, "do not forget." A unique symbolism was given to the number six in the monument: the use of the sixth commandment in its center; the six Hebrew letters in the commandment; the six hands clasping six rams' horns coming out of the earth, each six meters high and representing one million of the six million Jews murdered during the Holocaust.

On 31 August 1958, the foundation stone for the memorial was laid at the West Park Cemetery in Johannesburg. The event was covered by both the Jewish and the national presses in South Africa. The *Rand Daily Mail* on 1 September 1958 published an article under the headline, "A Monument to Six million Jews – Tears at Ceremony." The description of the ceremony stated that groups of survivors of the

Nazi concentration camps were "standing amid the rough casts of several sections of the monument." The article also described the future structure of the monument, highlighting the fact that the inscription on the foundation stones would be in English, Afrikaans, Yiddish, and Hebrew.[103] Those inscriptions would reflect the audience for which the monument was intended, indicating that although it was a Jewish symbolic commemorative statue, it was also directed at the country's white community as a whole. As in the case of *Kria*, here too the inscriptions on the monument reflected the institutional awareness of the Jewish community regarding the status of English and Afrikaans as official languages in South Africa. However, unlike *Kria* where the inscriptions were translated into three languages, the *Six Million* monument contained inscriptions with different wording in each language.

The monument was officially unveiled at the West Park Cemetery in Johannesburg on 10 May 1959.[104] The four inscriptions mentioned above were imprinted at the bottom of the plinth where the monument was laid. The Hebrew text included phrases from the Book of Lamentations, which focuses on the destruction of Jerusalem and the exile of its inhabitants, as a way to reflect the terrible mourning represented by the memorial and to draw a direct line from Jewish ancient history to modern times. In so doing, it also alluded to the analogical connections between the Jewish genocide and the destruction of the Jerusalem Temple by the Babylonians in 586 BCE. The Yiddish inscription, on the other hand, contained no biblical elements but rather described the killing sites, including the names of the death camps where European Jews were murdered.

The decision to include Yiddish inscriptions on the monument is not surprising since the main initiators of the monument project were part of the Polish-Jewish Club, together with the Yiddish Cultural Federation. But at the same time, in the local Jewish community, while there was a relatively large number of Yiddish speakers, the Eastern European language was constantly undermined in favor of Hebrew culture and Zionism. While Hebrew was considered the language of the Bible and was adopted as the language of the Zionist movement in the late 19th century, Yiddish was perceived as the representative of the opposing ideology in Jewish life, the language of the Eastern European, secular Jewish socialist movement known as the Bund.[105] As South Africa attracted a sufficiently large

---

103 "A Monument to Six Million Jews – Tears at Ceremony," *Rand Daily Mail*, 1 September 1958, File 520.2: Holocaust Commemoration 1956-1959, Rochlin Archive, Johannesburg.
104 "Johannesburg Jewish Communal Monument," SAJBD Report, April 1958 to August 1960, 48, SAJBD Reports, Rochlin Archive, Johannesburg.
105 The Bund was a secular Jewish socialist party that was formed in the Russian empire in 1897 and later merged into the Communist Party of the Soviet Union.

Fig. 5: *Six Million* Monument Inscriptions in Yiddish and Hebrew, Mikel-Arieli Private Collection.

community of Eastern European Jews, a Yiddish culture inevitably developed. Nonetheless, Yiddish in South Africa was, as Veronica Belling , Veronica argues, "a language under siege." It posed a challenge for the South African Jewish communal institutions that were by and large strongly committed to Zionism. It was also rejected by the South African government, which was at that time fearful of the spread of Communism.[106] Nevertheless, during the immediate post-war years, Yiddish culture flowered in South Africa, and during the late 1950s a quarter of the Jewish population were Yiddish speakers. As *Six Million* was a communal monument, this Yiddish-speaking part of the population had to be represented.

---

106 Veronica Belling, "Yiddish," in *The Social and Political History of Southern Africa's Languages*, ed. Tomasz Kamusella and Finex Ndhlovu (London: Palgrave Macmillan, 2018), 331–339.

Fig. 6: *Six Million* Monument Inscriptions in English and Afrikaans, Mikel-Arieli Private Collection.

The inscriptions in English and Afrikaans were identical but differed in significant ways from the Hebrew and Yiddish texts. The text stated: "In everlasting memory of the six million Jews. Victims of man's inhumanity to man who perished in the death camps of Europe 1939–1945. 'Thou shalt not forget.'" Presumably, Jewish religious references like the ones that appeared in the Hebrew text were excluded from the texts in English and Afrikaans as being distinctly Jewish. In an effort to mediate the destruction of European Jews to the white population, the Jewish community chose to present to the non-Jewish visitors a text with which they could identify. This does not mean that in the above texts the victim's Jewish identity was not emphasized. The monument was erected on a Jewish site, the design had distinctive Jewish symbolic elements, and the inscriptions explicitly stated that this was a monument in the memory of the six million Jews killed during the Holocaust. However, the English and Afrikaans texts emphasize the universal aspect, portraying the Jewish genocide as the ultimate expression of man's inhumanity to man, a message to which a non-Jewish visitor could relate.

The monument was unveiled on 10 May 1959 and the ceremony was broadcast on the national radio station by the South African Broadcasting Corporation (SABC) in both English and Afrikaans.[107] The decision to broadcast the event was another indication that the monument was aimed not only at the Jewish community but also at the entire white community.

The memorial was consecrated by Rabbi Mordechai Nurock of the Israeli Knesset, who came to South Africa especially for the ceremony.[108] Nurock, himself a Holocaust survivor originally from Latvia who lost his wife and two children during the tragic events in Europe, was at the time a member of the third Knesset as the representative of the National Religious Party. During his visit, Rabbi Nurock met the then Prime Minister, Hendrik Frensch Verwoerd, and expressed his gratitude for the Union's good faith towards the State of Israel. He emphasized the shared destiny of the two nations, stating, "Both South Africa and Israel share a strong desire for freedom, independence and sovereignty. Both are democracies and have good parliamentary regimes." He then mobilized Afrikaner anti-British sentiments and proclaimed, "even in the days of the Boar War, the sympathy of the Jewish people was on the side of the Afrikaner people and against the British."[109]

The sympathy Rabbi Nurock referred to was actually more an anti-British sentiment then a pro-Afrikaner one. This stand historically stems from opposition to British rule and policies during the period of British Mandate Palestine, particularly following the 1939 British White Paper, which enforced a strict immigration quota for Jews entering Palestine. An anti-British armed uprising was led by Jewish underground movements such as the *Lehi* and the *Irgun*, which focused efforts on acts of assassination against British policemen and high-ranked persons, and on acts of sabotage against government offices, police officers, and other British installations respectively.[110] While there were disagreements within the Jewish *Yishuv* institutions regarding some of the movements' methods, from the establishment of the state of Israel the dominant national narrative depicted

---

[107] "Unveiling on 5/10 – SABC to Broadcast Proceedings," *Jewish Herald*, 1 May 1959, File Wald Herman 199, Rochlin Archive, Johannesburg.
[108] "The Six Million Martyrs," *Jewish Affairs*, June 1959, File 520.2: Holocaust Commemoration 1956-1959, Rochlin Archive, Johannesburg.
[109] "הרב ד"ר מ. נורוק אצל ראש ממשלת דרום אפריקה" ["Rabbi M. Nurock meets the South African Prime Minister,"] HaTzofe, 15 May 1959, Historical Jewish Press, the National Library of Israel and Tel-Aviv University.
[110] Abraham Malamat and Hayim Tadmor, *A History of the Jewish People* (Cambridge, MA: Harvard University Press, 1976), 1044.

the Jewish struggle against the British Mandate as a struggle for national liberation and Jewish underground movements as national liberation efforts.

The ceremony for the *Six Million* monument was featured throughout the non-Jewish and Jewish press in South Africa. *The Star* and the *Rand Daily Mail* published articles describing the unveiling of the monument, accompanied by photographs. According to *The Star*, "Survivors of concentration camps formed a guard of honor as an eternal flame in the centre of the monument was kindled."[111] The *Rand Daily Mail* reported that "Serious-faced men and weeping women – many of whom lost relatives in the gas chambers of Auschwitz and Belsen – streamed into the cemetery from buses and from about 3,000 cars."[112] Those descriptions in two highly circulated newspapers nationwide also reflect the national interest in the Jewish community at the time and the recognition of its tragedy.

The event was also featured in *The New York Times* on 11 May 1959, under the headline "Victims of Hitler Honored in Africa." The reporter emphasized that the theme of the monument, "Thou shall not forget," was inscribed on the base of the memorial in Hebrew, Yiddish, Afrikaans, and English. The article also pointed out that some of the speakers dwelt on a theme that had a wholly unintended relevance to the surrounding context of South African race relations.[113] *The New York Times*' criticism of the Jewish community's failure to acknowledge the universal message of the Jewish genocide and its blindness to the monument's pertinence to South African racism was not addressed by the Jewish community, still anxious to placate the apartheid regime.

The white minority in South Africa found it difficult to identify with the universal implications of the Jewish genocide and their relevance to the fight against racism. By using official national channels, and in the context of the close ties forged between Israel and South Africa, South African Jewry chose to frame the tragedy of European Jewry as an essential pillar in its collective identity and to mediate it to South Africa's white population as part of an anti-antisemitic campaign. Thus, while focusing on the Jewish tragedy as a means to combat local antisemitic and pro-Nazi sentiments, the community ignored the universal message of the condemnation of racism in all its manifestations.

---

110 Abraham Malamat and Hayim Tadmor, *A History of the Jewish People* (Cambridge, MA: Harvard University Press, 1976), 1044.
111 "Jewish Memorial Unveiled," *The Star*, 11 May 1959, File Wald Herman 199, Rochlin Archive, Johannesburg.
112 "Jewish Community Remembers," *Rand Daily Mail*, 11 May 1959, File Wald Herman 199, Rochlin Archive.
113 "Victims of Hitler Honored in Africa," *New York Times*, 1 May 1959, Flie Wald Herman 199, Rochlin Archive, Johannesburg.

Chapter 3
The Holocaust on Trial – Eichmann in Pretoria

On 30 August 1962, a periodical report of the SAJBD was submitted to the delegates to the 23rd Congress of the Board in Johannesburg. Reviewing the antisemitic activities in the country, the report stated,

> Relations between the Jewish community and the rest of the population have been influenced, not only by many significant domestic developments within the Republic of South Africa, but also by the historic events connected with the capture, trial and execution of Adolf Eichmann [. . .] There can be no doubt that it did much to enlighten the moderate sections of the populace on the real implications of Nazism. However, it also stimulated a measure of activity among the professed supporters of Nazism in this country.[1]

As the report suggests, the historic events associated with the capture, trial, and execution of Adolf Eichmann aroused great interest in South Africa. An examination of the Jewish communal newspapers reveals the efforts made by the community to expose the general public to the horrors of the Jewish genocide through its comprehensive coverage of the trial. Moreover, the Jewish institutions were quick to respond to the publication of critical reports, letters, and commentaries regarding the trial. An in-depth analysis of reports in the national press reveals the extent and scope of criticism voiced by sections of the white society regarding the affair and holds up a mirror to the existing tensions between the Jewish community and the white communities in South Africa. However, before exploring the South African reactions to the Eichmann trial, we must address the prevailing atmosphere in the country in the period leading up to it.

The Sixties: Years of Anxiety

The South African general election, held on 16 April 1958, led to a victory for the NP, under the leadership of Johannes Gerhardus Strijdom. However, four months later, Strijdom died from illness and his successor, Hendrik Frensch Verwoerd, became Prime Minister. During his Ministry, Verwoerd promoted major legislative acts implementing his vision of 'separate development.'[2] He was also notorious for

---

[1] SAJBD Report, September 1960–August 1962, 15–16, SAJBD Reports, Rochlin Archive, Johannesburg.
[2] Kenny Henry, *Architect of Apartheid: H. F. Verwoerd, an Appraisal* (Johannesburg: John Ball, 1980).

his antisemitic and pro-Nazi activities during the 1930s.³ In 1936 he served as a Professor of Applied Psychology at Stellenbosch University and vocally protested against the admission of 3,000 German Jewish refugees into South Africa; from 1937 onward, he continued to express his antisemitic propaganda as the editor of the new nationalist daily newspaper in Johannesburg, *Die Transvaler*.⁴

For these reasons, when Verwoerd became Prime Minister two decades later, newspapers both in South Africa and overseas pointed to his past association with controversial policies affecting the Jewish community.⁵ Nonetheless, the SAJBD conveyed the community's good wishes to Verwoerd on his appointment and a formal meeting was held in October 1958 where the Prime Minister ensured the community's leaders that "he had fully identified himself with the policy of his predecessors in office [. . .] towards the South African Jewish community and the State of Israel."⁶

While Verwoerd's statement was indeed reassuring for the Jews of the country, six months later the community received a reminder of the past when an outburst of antisemitism in parliament arose from radical sections of the NP. In May 1959, two Jewish parliamentarians, Helen Suzman and Boris Wilson, then members of the liberal segment of the UP which a few months later would break away to form the Progressive Party (PP), criticized the abuse of the South African labor system whereby black citizens under arrest were forced to work as farm labor. Suzman and Wilson soon found themselves under attack from NP members, who emphasized their Jewishness and accused them of being communists while invoking antisemitic stereotypes.⁷

---

3 Roberta Balstad Miller, "Science and Society in the Early Career of H. F. Verwoerd," *Journal of Southern African Studies*, 19.4 (1993): 634–661, at 660.
4 Stanley Uys, "Dr. Hendrik Frensch Verwoerd, Prime Minister of South Africa," *Africa South*, January 1959, Clippings Collection, UWC-Robben Island Mayibuye Archives.
5 SAJBD Report, April 1958 to August 1960, 8, SAJBD Reports, Rochlin Archive, Johannesburg; The Israeli Newspaper *Davar* expressed the fear that South Africa's new Prime Minister would pursue an anti-Israeli policy in international affairs and an antisemitic policy in domestic affairs. See: "ישראל ודרום אפריקה באו״ם," ["Israel and South Africa in the UN,"] Davar, 22 December 1958, Historical Jewish Press, The National Library of Israel and Tel-Aviv University.
6 SAJBD Report, April 1958 to August 1960, 8, SAJBD Reports, Rochlin Archive, Johannesburg. See also: "South Africa's Premier Pledges Friendly Policy Toward Jewry in Press," *Bnai Brith Messenger*, 3 October 1948, Rochlin Archive, Johannesburg.
7 "Ben Woolfson was te bang om te gaan veg," ["Ben Woolfson was too scard to fight,"] Die Vaderland, 18 June 1959; "Anti-Semitic Uproar in Assembly," *Daily Dispatch*, 19 June 1959; "Nationalist M.P.s in Anti-Jewish Outburst," *Daily News*, 18 June 1959; "Anti-Semitism Comes Out," *Natal Mercury*, 18 June 1959, Items of Jewish Interest, Jewish Studies Library and Research Resources, Kaplan Centre for Jewish Studies, University of Cape Town.

As mentioned in the previous chapter, the SAJBD policy of noninvolvement in domestic politics except where Jewish interests were implicated was adopted as soon as the apartheid regime was established.[8] As the antisemitic remarks on Parliament were certainly a case of 'Jewish interest,' the SAJBD were obliged to react. Stressing the friendly relations of the government with Israel, the Zionist movement, and the South African Jewish community, the SAJBD maintained that the Jewish members of parliament spoke as representatives of their party, and not of the community. However, the Board avoided addressing the issue as an antisemitic incident.[9]

The public debate surrounding the antisemitic remarks in Parliament reflect one of the main issues that occupied the Board during the Verwoerd era: the preponderance of Jews in liberal segments of the white society and involved in activities opposing apartheid, which raised the question of the Board's responsibility for the actions of individual members of the community. While the great majority of members of the community were not hostile to the Nationalist government, the prominence of Jews in liberal, left-wing, and labor union politics contributed to the public image of Jews as radicals and as therefore inimical to the Union and its policies.[10]

While the SAJBD tried to disassociate the community from such activists, it was from time to time challenged by Jewish politicians from the opposition, and on some occasions by religious leaders, mainly from within Reform Judaism. Such was the case of Rabbi Andre Ungar. Born in Budapest, Hungary, Ungar was appointed Rabbi to the West London Synagogue in 1952 and arrived in South Africa in December 1954 to become minister of Temple Israel, the Jewish Reform congregation in Port Elizabeth.[11] Soon after his arrival in the Union, Ungar became an active member of the South African Institute of Race Relations, one of the oldest liberal institutions in the country, and on several occasions spoke out in criticism of the apartheid policy.[12]

Ungar's most renowned action was taken in November 1956, when he spoke publicly against the plan to zone the city of Port Elizabeth under the Group Areas Act of 1950, stating that "racial hatred is an evil and the Group Areas Act is a despicable evil." He compared the removal of communities from their homes into group areas with what had happened in Hungary during his childhood, where

---

8 Shimoni, *Community and Conscience*, 29–33.
9 SAJBD Report, April 1958 to August 1960, 8, SAJBD Reports, Rochlin Archive, Johannesburg; "Jews and Farm Labour- Comment," *Zionist Record*, 26 June 1959, Clippings Collection, Jacob Gitlin Jewish Library, Cape Town.
10 Shimoni, *Community and Conscience*, 82–84.
11 "New Minister for Temple Israel Port Elizabeth," *Zionist Record*, 22 October 1954, Ungar Biographical File, Rochlin Archive, Johannesburg.
12 Shimoni, *Community and Conscience*, 36.

the Nazis displaced Jews from their homes and forced their transfer into ghettos. He warned, "Hitler is again on the march in the Transvaal in Natal, in the Cape and ironically enough in the province that calls itself the Free State."[13]

Ungar's critical views were not overlooked by the South African government and after his two-year residency period had expired, he was declared as an "undesirable immigrant" and his permit to stay in the country not renewed. While Ungar had no intention of staying in South Africa and had already accepted an appointment in London, the government's decision was intended to intimidate others who did not agree with the government's policy but who nevertheless would have liked to remain in the Union.[14] Some press reports on the matter were indeed critical of the government's decision. However, most of the Afrikaner papers, as well as the Jewish communal press, were quick to support it and to deny any attempt at intimidation aimed at South African Jewry.[15]

On 7 January 1957 Ungar left the Union wearing an African National Congress (ANC) badge on his coat lapel: his departure was met with a sigh of relief on the part of the majority of the community.[16] As the SAJBD's general-secretary, Gustav Saron, stated, "I know that the people of the Board and others were perfectly happy to see Ungar go because they thought that young fellow, who

---

13 "No Critics Allowed," *Evening Post*, 10 December 1956; "A Pride to be Paid: Warning to P. E. Whites," *Evening Post*, 13 October 1956; "Groepsgebiedewet is 'N Gruwel, Se Rabbyn," ["Group Areas Act is an Abomination, Says the Rabbi,"] *Die Volksblad*, 14 November 1956, Ungar Biographical Collection, Rochlin Archive, Johannesburg (translated by the author).
14 The Port Elizabeth daily press as well as national newspapers featured the government decision as front-page news: "Rabbi told to leave Union by Jan. 15," *Cape Argus*, 11 December 1956; "The Case of Dr. Ungar," *The Star*, 10 December 1956; "Rabbi is Ordered From S. A." *Cape Times*, 10 December 1956; "Foreign busybodies' not wanted in S. Africa," *Evening Post*, 11 December 1956; "Expulsion not attempt to frighten Jews," *Evening Post*, 14 December 1956; "Rabbi Ordered by Donges to Quit S. Africa," *Rand Daily Mail*, 8 December 1956, Ungar Biographical File, Rochlin Archive, Johannesburg.
15 "The Case of Rabbi Ungar- Board's E. P. Committee Denies Alleged Intimidation of S.A. Jews," *Zionist Record*, 28 December 1956; "Minister of the Interior and Rabbi Ungar," *Jewish Affairs*, January 1957; "Rabbi Ungar Ordered to Leave Union," *South African Jewish Times*, 19 December 1956; "Rabbyn is Bekend Vir Kwaai Toesprake," ["Rabii known for Angry Speeches"] *Die Oosterlig*, 11 December 1956; "Intimidasie Van S.A. Se Jode," ["Intimidation of S.A. Jews"] *Die Oosterlig*, 18 December 1956, Ungar Biographical Collection, Rochlin Archive, Johannesburg (translated by the author).
16 "Expelled Rabbi Wears ANC Badge," *Natal Witness*, 8 January 1957; "Rabbyn Kry ANC Wapen," ["Rabbi Gets ANC Weapon"] *Die Burger*, 7 January 1957; extract from the "Jewish Review" (Organ of Eastern Province Jewry), December 1956, Ungar Biographical Collection, Rochlin Archive, Johannesburg (translated the author).

doesn't know South Africa, is speaking in a language and in a tone which is not compatible with what the situation calls for."[17]

This sense of relief, however, was short-lived: in December 1956 the infamous Treason Trial began. One hundred fifty-six anti-apartheid activists were arrested by the apartheid police; of these, twenty-three were whites, more than half of them Jews, all of whom had been associated with the Communist Party of South Africa, which was outlawed in 1950.[18] The trial was conducted in a building known as "The Old Synagogue" of Pretoria, which was purchased by the government in 1952. Furthermore, the defense team was led by Israel Maisels, a prominent Jewish leader who served at the time as the president of the SAJBD, while the prosecution was led by Oswald Pirow, an ex-Nazi supporter and an extreme Afrikaner nationalist.[19] Local press reports portrayed the Jewish defender as yet another pro-communist Jew representing the anti-apartheid communists, while the Afrikaner prosecutor was portrayed as the defender of the whites against the danger of communism.[20]

Two months before the Eichmann affair erupted into public consciousness, South African society was shaken by the Sharpeville massacre of 21 March 1960, in which local police officers opened fire on a crowd of black protesters, killing 69 people.[21] The massacre was reported worldwide, evoking widespread dismay and fueling anti-apartheid sentiment.[22] The UN Security Council and governments worldwide, including Israel, condemned the apartheid policies that prompted this violent assault.[23]

---

[17] Interview with Gus Saron by Simon Herman and Geoffrey Wigoder, 4–5 August 1961, Oral Records Center, Institute of Contemporary Jewry, Hebrew University of Jerusalem, 42.
[18] The Treason trial lasted until 29 March 1961, when all the defendants were acquitted. The trial and resulting periods of detention of anti-apartheid activists strengthened connections between the various opposition movements in the country and set the foundations for the struggle against apartheid. It was also crucial for the transformation of the anti-apartheid movement abroad where the Treason Trial Defence Fund, which would later become the Defence and Aid Fund for South Africa, was launched in order to pay the legal costs of the accused. to read more about the trial see Rob Skinner, *The Foundations of Anti-Apartheid: Liberal Humanitarians and Transnational Activists in Britain and The United States, c. 1919–1964* (New York: Palgrave Macmillan, 2010), 147–150.
[19] For further information about Oswald Pirow see Alex Mouton, "'Fascist or opportunist?:' The political career of Oswald Pirow, 1915–1943," *Historia* 63.2 (2018): 93–111.
[20] Shimoni, *Community and Conscience*, 60–62.
[21] Skinner, *The Foundations of Anti-Apartheid*, 63.
[22] Polakow-Suransky, *The Unspoken Alliance*, 30.
[23] A resolution deploring the policies and actions of the government of the Union of South Africa was adopted at the urgent request of a group of 29 African and Asian members. The

While there was no official statement regarding the massacre on the part of Jewish institutions, their position can be discerned between the lines of the periodic report of the SAJBD. The report stated, "For many years now it has been the accepted policy of the community that neither the Board of Deputies, as its representative organization, nor the Jewish community as a collective entity, can or should take up an explicit attitude in regard to specific policies in the political field."[24] The Board did call upon every Jew "to play his part in his own sphere in furthering inter-racial and inter-group goodwill and harmony."[25] However, it did not challenge the racist policy or explicitly call for action against apartheid.

While the Sharpeville massacre achieved global resonance, Jewish organizations such as the World Jewish Congress and the American Jewish Congress remained silent.[26] Nevertheless, questions as to whether Jewish solidarity prevented Western Jews from speaking out against apartheid were raised throughout the Jewish world, forcing South African Jewish leaders to provide explanations and clarifications regarding the community's position on apartheid policy. Responding to such demands, the Board stated, "it is not easy, especially for people outside South Africa, to understand the full complexity of our problems" and stressed that the Board did not express views on the racial problems in South Africa, not out of indifference but "because it is not its function to enter the political arena other than in matters of specific Jewish concern."[27]

This viewpoint was further explained in a report written by Edgar Bernstein, a representative of the Jewish Telegraphic Agency in Johannesburg, which was published in the Jewish presses worldwide. Bernstein stressed that "the suggestion that the Jews in South Africa are 'afraid to talk' is devoid of all truth. South Africa's 100,000 Jews have no reprisals to fear and such fear is not the reason why they as a group adopt no point of view regarding apartheid." Furthermore, he argued, "in the first place the South African Jews know that the present leaders of the Union are not Nazis and Jew-haters. They accept the Jews as full and equal citizens of South Africa. The Jews feel offended when

---

Security Council considered the issue at six meetings between 30 March 30 and 1 April 1960. See 1960 U.N.Y.B. 142–143, U.N. Sales No. 61.1.1.
24 SAJBD Report, April 1958 to August 1960, 9, SAJBD Reports, Rochlin Archive, Johannesburg.
25 SAJBD Report, April 1958 to August 1960, 9, SAJBD Reports, Rochlin Archive, Johannesburg.
26 Marjorie N. Feld. *Nations Divided: American Jews and the Struggle over Apartheid* (New York: Palgrave Macmillan, 2014), 29–30.
27 SAJBD Report, April 1958 to August 1960, 9, SAJBD Reports, Rochlin Archive, Johannesburg.

they are accused of cowardice by Jewish publications issued seven thousand miles away from the Union."[28]

After dismissing the possibility of antisemitic tendencies within the South African government, Bernstein further claimed that "it must be remembered that the policy of separation between white and black was part of the policy of every South African government since [the] Union – including that of Gen. Smuts." While he correctly argued that South African Jewry "took up no group attitude to segregation under previous regimes," he also proclaimed that South Africa was not a colony where a handful of white imperialists oppressed non-white nations, but rather an independent state where "three million whites who have no other home have been confronted with the problem of making fair provision for ten million black people belonging to dozens of different tribes and who are on a different level of civilization to the whites. Apartheid is an attempt to solve this problem by segregation."[29] This line of defense, erasing South Africa's colonial past as if the ancestors of the three million white citizens of South Africa had not reached a country already inhabited by indigenous peoples and predicated upon the assumption of black inferiority, enabled Bernstein to mediate apartheid for the Jewish world as a solution rather than a problem. Bernstein's position thereby transformed the seemingly neutral position of the Jewish community to one which actively explained and justified apartheid policy.

While the Jewish community made enormous efforts to maintain its status quo with the apartheid government, by the late 1950s Israel had adopted a somewhat critical approach towards the Union's racial policy.[30] Whenever Israel voted against South Africa in the UN forums, the SAJBD representatives emphasized that the community had no right to try to influence Israel's foreign policy: "it must be realized that in numerous countries there are Jewish minorities and in regard to matters of 'human rights,' Israel considers it necessary to take up an attitude of principle. Otherwise, how would Israel be able to make its voice heard in any case where there was persecution against Jews?" To some extent, in addressing this question the SAJBD drew connections between antisemitism and other forms of prejudice and racial persecution. However, such a

---

28 "Suid-Afrikaanse Jode Antwoord Apartheidskritici," ["South African Jews Answer Apartheid Critics"] *Dagbreek*, 22 May 1960, Items of Jewish Interest, Rochlin Archive, Johannesburg (a translated collection).
29 "Suid-Afrikaanse Jode Antwoord Apartheidskritici," ["South African Jews Answer Apartheid Critics"] *Dagbreek*, 22 May 1960, Items of Jewish Interest, Rochlin Archive, Johannesburg (a translated collection).
30 SAJBD Report, April 1958 to August 1960, 17–18, SAJBD Reports, Rochlin Archive, Johannesburg.

moral stand was not explicitly adopted by the community institutions until the mid-1980s. Michael Comay, the South African-born acting director-general of Israel's Department of Foreign Affairs, claimed in December 1958: "Israel had a feeling of friendship towards South Africa and is conscious of the historic bonds which bind the two lands . . . [however] the reasons which affect Israel's attitude spring from its own unique position and it has no bearing on any lack of goodwill towards South Africa."[31] Reading the SAJBD statements together with Comay's explanation of Israel's "unique position" invites a re-examination of Israel's actions, which did not necessarily stem from explicit opposition to apartheid or sincere feelings of solidarity towards black South Africans, but rather from Israel's Jewish identity and desire to gain legitimacy for its struggle against antisemitism.

Israel's UN votes against apartheid were also linked to its decision to expand its diplomatic relations with the newly independent African countries. When Maurice Yaméogo, President of the Republic of Upper Volta, visited Israel in July 1961, a joint communique was issued with Ben-Gurion stating that the two countries "considered the apartheid policy of South Africa detrimental to the interests of the African majority in that country."[32] This statement evoked a sharp editorial comment in the NP organ of the Transvaal area, *Die Transvaler*, which described the communique as "an unfriendly act" and wondered, "what has the racial policy which is followed by the Republic to do with the visit of a foreign head of state to Israel? What would the government of Israel think if the government of the Republic had gratuitously concerned itself with the fact that now for thirteen years Arab refugees are living in the most deplorable circumstances upon their original homes?"[33]

Similar analogies were drawn in an article published in the English newspaper *The Star* by Senator Jan Grobler, one-time member of the Nazi-like "New Order" movement. He wondered:

> If Mr. Ben-Gurion 'deplores' apartheid and does not subscribe to 'separate development' between white and black in South Africa, why does he insist on maintaining Israel as a separate geographical entity? [. . .] why does he not abolish the boundaries between

---

31 SAJBD Report, April 1958 to August 1960, 18, SAJBD Reports, Rochlin Archive, Johannesburg.
32 Maurice Yaméogo and David Ben-Gurion's Joint Communique, 11 July 1961, Israel-South Africa Relations 1961–1967 File, ISA-PMO-StateDocumentsDep-0012tfj, Israel State Archive, Jerusalem.
33 "'N Onvriendelike Wet," ["An Unfriendly Act"] *Die Transvaler*, 13 July 1961, Items of Jewish Interest, Jewish Studies Library and Research Resources, Kaplan Centre for Jewish Studies, University of Cape Town (a translated collection).

Israel and the surrounding Arab states and allow the Jews in Israel to be integrated with the Arab communities in the Middle East and Egypt?³⁴

Grobler did not leave his own questions unanswered but argued that Ben-Gurion should realize that Israel "would be swamped by millions of Arabs if integration should be allowed." He stressed that the South African government, for the very same reasons, could never subscribe to integration between the blacks and whites in the country.³⁵ Such commentary can be interpreted as a very early manifestation of the Israel-apartheid analogy, emerging, ironically, from white segments of South African society, which framed the Israeli government's condemnation of apartheid as a hypocritical act considering Israel's own segregationist practices toward the Palestinians.

In this atmosphere, Israel's decision on 11 October 1961 to join sixty-seven delegations in voting in favor of a resolution of censure upon South Africa's Foreign Minister, Eric Louw, at the UN General Assembly only further fueled public discourse.³⁶ Louw, a well-known antisemite from the pre-1948 period, defended South Africa's apartheid policy against African criticism, and on the same day the Assembly adopted a Liberian censure motion with the support of the Afro-Asian bloc. While all the Western nations, apart from Holland and Israel, abstained or absented themselves, only South Africa voted against the motion.³⁷

A week after the motion was adopted, Verwoerd publicly announced that South Africa and the Afrikaner people in particular were deeply shocked at the stand taken by the Holland and the Israeli governments at the UN. Moreover, in a radio broadcast from New York on 20 October 1961, Louw himself accused Israel of hostility and ingratitude in supporting the censure motion against South Africa. He mentioned the efforts made by the South African government and members of the Cabinet to foster good relations with Israel in the past and referred particularly to the special facilities granted by the South African Minister of Finance for the transfer of large sums of money to Israel by South African Jews.³⁸

---

34 "Israel Attack on Apartheid," *The Star*, 24 July 1961, Items of Jewish Interest, Jewish Studies Library and Research Resources, Kaplan Centre for Jewish Studies, University of Cape Town.
35 "Israel Attack on Apartheid," *The Star*, 24 July 1961, Items of Jewish Interest, Jewish Studies Library and Research Resources, Kaplan Centre for Jewish Studies, University of Cape Town.
36 SAJBD Report, September 1960 to August 1962, 10–12, SAJBD Reports, Rochlin Archive, Johannesburg.
37 UNGAOR, 16ᵗʰ Session., Plenary Meeting, Verbatim Record, I, 387–395, 11 October 1961 (Louw's speech), and I, 395–406 (discussion of motions to expunge and to censure).
38 "U.N.O. Censure Motion," *Cape Argus*, 20 October 1961, Items of Jewish Interest, Jewish Studies Library and Research Resources, Kaplan Centre for Jewish Studies, University of Cape Town.

Again, the SAJBD was forced to respond, stating: "Israel's vote of censure on Mr. Louw's speech had given rise to strong criticism among many South African Jews. It is recognised that Israel, in determining her international policies, must take into account delicate and complex factors upon which she alone is competent to judge." However, the Board stressed that this specific case was a simple one: "the question of freedom of speech in the international forum. In these circumstances, Israel should have joined the Western Nations in abstaining from voting on the Afro-Asian motion of censure."[39]

The official institutes of the community had hitherto refrained from such a clear declaration of support for South Africa and had not voiced such open criticism of Israel before. Instead, they had constantly stressed the principle of noninvolvement in domestic political issues and of Israel's sovereign right to make its own foreign affairs decisions. At the same time, the use of the term "many South African Jews" in the statement indicates a state of mind rather than an official position on the part of the community, thus allowing the SAJBD to maintain a semblance of neutrality. Moreover, the explanation given by the Board for its condemnation was based on the claim that the Israeli vote was an infringement of South Africa's right to freedom of speech in the international arena and was therefore different from other Israeli votes in the UN, which dealt directly with the apartheid policy.

The controversy relating to Israel's vote took a new and unexpected turn on 19 November 1961, when Johannesburg's *Sunday Times* published a private letter addressed by Prime Minister Verwoerd two weeks earlier to former Cape Town city councilor and Jewish resident of Cape Town, Sidney East. In this letter, Verwoerd stated, inter alia, that Israel's attitude was "a tragedy for South African Jewry."[40] He recounted the earlier pro-Israel feelings in South Africa which, he said, were now changing as a result of Israel's vote at UN. However, his most controversial claim was that the support given by "so many Jews" to the PP and by "so few" to the NP "did not pass unnoticed."[41]

---

39 The SAJBD's official statement on the Israeli vote appeared at the SAJBD Report, September 1960 to August 1962, 19–20, SAJBD Reports, Rochlin Archive, Johannesburg. The statement was also published in *The Star*, 24 October 1961; *Die Vaderland*, 24 October 1961. A similar statement made by the SAZF appeared in *Zionist record*, 24 October 1961, Items of Jewish Interest, Jewish Studies Library and Research Resources, Kaplan Centre for Jewish Studies, University of Cape Town.
40 "The Verwoerd Letter," *Sunday Times*, 26 November 1961, File 131.1: Jewish Community 1952–1975, Historical Papers Research Archive, University of the Witwatersrand, Johannesburg.
41 "The Verwoerd Letter," *Sunday Times*, 26 November 1961, File 131.1: Jewish Community 1952–1975, Historical Papers Research Archive, University of the Witwatersrand, Johannesburg.

The publication of this letter sparked an extensive debate in the national press. Most of the English press condemned Verwoerd's letter for what it perceived as a veiled threat toward the Jewish community,[42] while the Afrikaner press defended the Prime Minister and further attacked the Jews of the Union for its dual loyalty and ungratefulness.[43] Eventually, Verwoerd issued a public statement denying the allegations that he had threatened the Jewish community. He reaffirmed that Jews had the same democratic right as other (white) citizens of the Republic to support what parties they might individually choose and added that he did not associate his criticism of Israel's vote against South Africa with his position vis-à-vis South African Jewry.[44] However, this episode was yet another indication of the government's new line of thought regarding the Jewish community and its relations with Israel.

The combination of Jewish visibility in opposition to apartheid and Israeli anti-apartheid votes at the UN gave rise to manifestations of antisemitism across the country. The SAJBD had to deal with the circulation from time to time of antisemitic material as well as some deliberate provocative anti-Jewish demonstrations, such as antisemitic leaflets placed in stores in Durban in April 1960;[45] Swastikas painted on synagogues doors around the country in December of that year; the explosion at the Great Synagogue in Johannesburg in January 1961; and the bombing of the *Six Million* monument in the Johannesburg Jewish cemetery in proximity to Eichmann's execution in June 1962.[46] It was in this explosive atmosphere that the Eichmann affair erupted into public consciousness in South Africa, shifting some of the focus of public attention away from the domestic sphere to the developments in the small Jewish State in the Middle East.

---

[42] "Veiled Threat In Letter: Verwoerd's Astonishing Statement on Jews," *Cape Times*, 26 November 1961; "Jewish Newspaper's Criticism," *Cape Times*, 24 November 1961; "Dr. Verwoerd and Israel," *Cape Argus*, 24 November 1961; "Verwoerd Denies he Tried to Threaten S.A. Jews in 'East Letter'," *Cape Argus*, 25 November 1961; "He's the Same Old Dr. Verwoerd," *Sunday Times*, 26 November 1961, File 131: Jewish Community 1937–1965, Historical Papers Research Archive, University of the Witwatersrand, Johannesburg.

[43] Such arguments appeared in the following Afrikaner presses: *Die Transvaler*, 1 December 1961; *Die Vaderland*, 1 December 1961; *Die Vaderland*, 4 December 1961; *Die Oosterlig*, 29 November 1961, Items of Jewish Interest, Jewish Studies Library and Research Resources, Kaplan Centre for Jewish Studies, University of Cape Town (a translated collection).

[44] "Prime Minister dispels misgivings aroused by his private letter," *Southern African Jewish Times*, 1 December 1961, Clippings Collection, Jacob Gitlin Jewish Library, Cape Town.

[45] "Anti-Semitic Pamphlets," *Natal Mercury*, 26 April 1960, Items of Jewish Interest, Jewish Studies Library and Research Resources, Kaplan Centre for Jewish Studies, University of Cape Town.

[46] "Swastikas on the Rand," *Sunday Express*, 4 December 1960, Items of Jewish Interest, Jewish Studies Library and Research Resources, Kaplan Centre for Jewish Studies, University of Cape Town.

Justice Served by the Victims

On 23 May 1960, David Ben-Gurion made a dramatic announcement in the Israeli Knesset. In his statement, Ben-Gurion informed the Knesset that Adolf Eichmann, one of the most notorious Nazi war criminals, had been discovered by the Israeli security services in Argentina and was now under arrest in Israel.[47] He also stated that Eichmann was to be interrogated by the Israeli police and later tried in Israel under the Nazis and Nazis Collaborators (Punishment) Law of 1 August 1950.[48]

This announcement was received with much excitement on the Israeli street. The historian Tom Segev has compared the reaction of the Israeli public to its reactions to the Declaration of Independence twelve years earlier.[49] The pride in Eichmann's capture, and the fact that he was to be tried by Jewish judges at the theater of Beit Ha'am ("The People's House"), embodied the statehood and sovereignty of the new Israeli state – a clear expression of the fulfillment of Zionism.[50] The trial provided a first encounter for Israeli society with the stories of the survivors, who were summoned as witnesses to narrate their traumatic experiences of the Holocaust.[51]

Eichmann's capture by Israeli Mossad agents in Argentina in May 1960, and his detention in an Israeli prison, was a major topic of discussion in the world press and was featured prominently and extensively.[52] In South Africa too, these issues were widely discussed. On 5 July 1960, an article published in *The Star* argued that if Eichmann was still a German subject, he should be tried and punished in West Germany, and that since he had become a citizen of Argentina, those who tracked him down could have asked the West German authorities to request his extradition, which Argentina would most likely have granted. It further noted that "[The] UN has confirmed that Eichmann's abduction to and trial in Israel is a breach of international law," and condemned Israel's actions, which defied international law "for the sake of vengeance."[53]

---

[47] Prime Minister David Ben-Gurion announcement, Article 349: Capture of Eichmann, Government Meeting Protocol, 23 May 1960, File Stenograms of Government meetings, 1960, ISA-PMO-GovernmentMeeting-0002eel, Israel State Archive, Jerusalem.
[48] Nazis and Nazi Collaborators (Punishment) Law, 5710–1950, Ministry of Foreign Affairs Archive, Israel.
[49] Segev, *The Seventh Million*, 326.
[50] Szymon Pietrzykowski, "Holocaust, Israeli Statehood and Jewish Identity: International Reception of the Eichmann Trial (1961–1962)," *Humanistic Scripts* XIV (2016): 117–157, at 118.
[51] Yablonka, *The State of Israel vs. Adolf Eichmann*, 165–166.
[52] Lipstadt, *The Eichmann Trial*, 38–40.
[53] "The Eichmann Case," *The Star*, 5 July 1960, Eichmann A. File 527, Rochlin Archive, Johannesburg.

The Afrikaner daily newspaper *Die Volksblad* also published an editorial wondering what gave Israel the right to try a man for alleged crimes committed in another country against a people, which only afterwards established its own state. It called for an international court to be assembled instead. However, it mentioned that Israel was determined to proceed with the trial and had invoked the Allied statement of 1943 that Nazi criminals might be tried and punished by the peoples against whom they committed crimes. The article then turned to the issue of Israel's violation of Argentina's sovereignty by capturing Eichmann in its territory. It stated that observers believe that the vote in the UN will be against Israel and wondered if Israel will remain the only state which 'steals' a man it is seeking from another country if it believes that the other countries will not agree to surrender him.[54]

While similar claims did surface in places outside of South Africa, an intriguing line of argument was expressed in the Afrikaner daily afternoon newspaper *Die Vaderland*. It stated that while Jews undoubtedly had a right to feel dissatisfied about the fact that Eichmann was alive and had found shelter in Argentina, Israel had no right to smuggle him in such a way: "One is sometimes amazed at the inhabitants of Israel. As people who make such a fuss about violation of their frontiers by Arabs and Egyptians, they sometime do fantastic things."[55] This claim compared Israel's fear of a possible invasion of Arab armies against Israel's own violation of Argentine's sovereignty in the act of abducting Eichmann. As will be discussed in the next chapter, from the late 1960s, particularly during the period between the Six Days War and the Yom Kippur War, the Afrikaner press constantly pointed to a "common lot" by using Israel's positioning of a possible Arab armies' invasion of its borders as a real existential threat, as an analogy to the South African white minority's situation in the country. Afrikaner nationalism drew on the ethos of the *laager* mentioned in the previous chapter, which served as a survival strategy of the Afrikaner trekkers against Africans' invasion of their camps, during the Great Trek of 1836.[56] The *laager* became a symbol of the Afrikaner fighting spirit and was frequently compared to the Zionist enterprise of *Tower and Stockade* (Homa UMigdal), which aimed at defending Jewish settlements during the Arab revolt of

---

54 "Eichmann," *Die Volksblad*, 16 June 1960, Items of Jewish Interest, Jewish Studies Library and Research Resources, Kaplan Centre for Jewish Studies, University of Cape Town (a translated collection).
55 "Eichmann," *Die Volksblad*, 16 June 1960, Items of Jewish Interest, Jewish Studies Library and Research Resources, Kaplan Centre for Jewish Studies, University of Cape Town (a translated collection).
56 Abulof, *The Mortality and Morality of Nations*, 288.

Fig. 7: A Model of the Laager at the Voortrekker Monument, Mikel-Arieli Private Collection.

1936–1939 in British Mandatory Palestine.[57] Furthermore, the ethos of the Blood River Battle, in which 464 Voortrekkers fought against an estimated 10,000 Zulu fighters on the bank of the Ncome River on 16 December 1838, was of a battle of few against many, which repeatedly served as a parallel to Israel's situation as a small state, surrounded by many enemies. However, Eichmann's abduction by the Israelis a decade earlier prompted a different position on the threats against Israel. Instead of local solidarity with Israel's existential vulnerability, criticism of Israel's hypocrisy in invading Argentina's borders became manifest.

While criticism regarding the Israeli action in Argentina was prominent in the public discourse, sympathy towards the Jewish people was constantly expressed, and emphasis was placed on the centuries-old suffering of the Jews. The *Natal Witness,* a daily newspaper with a provincial focus, even addressed the local manifestations of antisemitism as vivid proof of the importance of the trial as an instrument to educate the public. It stated "here, in South Africa, a certain political philosophy is in the ascendant which has certain

---

57 Abulof, *The Mortality and Morality of Nations*, 288.

affiliations, so far at least as some of its spokesmen and supporters are concerned – and that fact cannot fail to cause acute fear and uneasiness among the Jewish people in our midst."[58] The political philosophy the paper refers to is apartheid, the philosophy of the NP. The reference to its members' pro-Nazism during the Second World War, evoked in close proximity to recent antisemitic statements in parliament, suggest that the uneasiness felt by the local Jewish community was understandable.

Nevertheless, the report above provided a rare voice, while most of the local coverage of the affair continued to express criticism towards Israel actions in Argentina. A letter written by a citizen under the pseudonym *Belakun*, published in *The Star* newspaper stated, "About the Eichmann affair, I wonder what the reaction of the Israeli government would be if a group of 'volunteers' from, say England, were to arrive in Israel charged with the capture of the leaders of the Jewish terrorists responsible for the murder of so many British soldiers." It further emphasized that "the Jews would do well to remember that they were not the only people to have suffered as the result of man's folly towards his fellow-man."[59]

The use of the term "volunteers" in this context was not at all coincidental. As soon as the news of Eichmann's capture became public, Argentina demanded details. In response, Israel issued what has been described as one of the most undiplomatic notes in diplomatic history.[60] The Israeli statement, presented by Arieh Levavi, then Israeli ambassador in Buenos Aires, to the Argentinian government, asserted that a "group of volunteers who happened to be Israeli had established contact with Eichmann and inquired whether he would come to Israel for trial. After he spontaneously agreed, they brought him to Israel and turned him over to the authorities." It further emphasized, "Israel had been ignorant of these details until Argentina demanded an explanation and an investigation was conducted" and observed that Argentina was known to provide a "home to numerous Nazis."[61]

Israel's statement is directly related to the tenets of general international law under which, if a state exercises powers in the territory of another state without the latter's consent, it commits an international tort. This means that if

---

[58] "The Eichmann Case," *Natal Witness*, 11 June 1960, Items of Jewish Interest, Jewish Studies Library and Research Resources, Kaplan Centre for Jewish Studies, University of Cape Town.
[59] "The Eichmann Case- Letters in the Press," *The Star*, 29 June 1960, 6, Eichmann A. File 527, Rochlin Archive, Johannesburg.
[60] Lipstadt, *The Eichmann Trial*, 21.
[61] Ministry of Foreign Affairs to the Israel Missions Abroad; Jerusalem, 7 June 1960, ISA/RG 93.43/MFA/293/13, Israel State Archive, Jerusalem.

Eichmann was forcibly abducted from Argentina by Israeli agents and with the Israeli government's consent, this constitutes a violation of international law. However, if he was abducted by private individuals acting independently without the previous knowledge or consent of the Israeli government, as averred in the Israeli statement above, their actions would not relate to Israel's international responsibility towards Argentina.[62] *Belakun* saw through the Israeli effort and criticized Israel's response for its lack of reliability. Moreover, by defining members of the Jewish underground movements in the Jewish *Yishuv* in Palestine during the British Mandate as Jewish terrorists, *Belakun* undermined the Jewish-Zionist narrative which perceived the struggle against the British Mandate as a struggle for national liberation and Jewish underground movements as national liberation efforts.

The Jewish community issued an official response to the above letter, stating that, "To place, even by analogy, in the same category events occurring in a conflict between two nations [presumably Britain and Israel] and those of the most brutal and wicked act of genocide in human history is incongruous and irrelevant." It further argued that while it is true that the Jews were not the only ones to have suffered at the hands of the Nazis, they were the only nation against whom a deliberate act of genocide was planned and implemented.[63]

While the statement defined "the murder of British soldiers by Jewish terrorists" as "events in a conflict between two nations," it did not challenge the words "murder" and "Jewish terrorists" as a description of the Jewish underground army during the British Mandate in Palestine. Instead, it focused on *Belakun*'s view of the Holocaust as "the result of man's folly towards his fellow-man," criticizing it as a position that obscured the uniqueness of the destruction of European Jewry. It argued that such misconceptions regarding the Holocaust are "one more proof that only through Eichmann being tried in Israel will the nature and scope of the atrocities committed by Nazi Germany against the Jewish people be given proper prominence in humanity's consciousness for all time, so that mankind might be shielded from their recurrence."[64]

The Jewish reaction above properly reflects the perception of the uniqueness of the Holocaust – a perception based on the claim that the Holocaust is completely different from any other event in human history, and therefore that

---

62 Hans, W. Baade, "The Eichmann Trial: Some Legal Aspects," *World Law* (1961): 400–420, at 405.
63 "Questions about the Eichmann Affair," *The Star*, 29 June 1960, 6, Eichmann A. File 527, Rochlin Archive, Johannesburg.
64 "Questions about the Eichmann Affair," *The Star*, 29 June 1960, 6, Eichmann A. File 527, Rochlin Archive, Johannesburg.

any association of the Holocaust with another event is "as a reductive, tasteless, or even morally and politically questionable banalization of the topic."[65] This position was adopted by many Jewish communities around the world during the first decades after the war.[66] As historian Daniel Blatman argues, "what became fixed in the collective awareness, mainly among Jews, was the message, conveyed by the survivors, that it was a 'different planet' – the phrase coined by writer Yehiel Dinur with regard to Auschwitz during his testimony at the Eichmann trial."[67] This perception became even more widespread among other Jewish and non-Jewish constituencies worldwide following the 1967 War, particularly in America, where the Holocaust became an effective weapon for defending Israel in local political forums.[68]

Holocaust uniqueness was the source of frequent criticism in several letters to the South African press throughout the trial, which accused the Jews of claiming ownership over human suffering. These letters repeatedly compared Jewish suffering during the Holocaust to the suffering of others in human history, pitting different traumatic memories against each other in a zero-sum struggle. For the most part, these letters contained no claims of Holocaust denial, although some argued for Jewish exaggeration and hypersensitivity about their trauma. Nonetheless, they reveal tensions between the various white communities in the country regarding the place of collective memories of suffering in the public arena.

Interestingly, the memories of suffering that were invoked in most of the letters to the South African press during the trial were not memories of marginal groups who drew analogies between their suffering under the apartheid regime and the suffering of Jews under Nazism, as frequently seen in the anti-

---

65 Bashir Bashir and Amos Goldberg, *The Holocaust and the Nakba: A New Syntax of History, Memory, and Political Thought* (New York: Colombia University Press, 2019), 6.
66 The debate over the uniqueness of the Holocaust as a historical event has been central to Holocaust studies since its inception. However, in the above context, I am referring to the perception of uniqueness as it appears in mainstream collective cultures of Jewish communities around the world. To read more about the scholarly considerations of the question of uniqueness see Daniel Blatman, "Holocaust Scholarship: towards a post-uniqueness era," *Journal of Genocide Research*, 17.1 (2015): 21–43; Alan Rosenberg, "Was the Holocaust Unique?: A Peculiar Question?," in *Genocide and the Modern Age*, ed. Isidor Wallimann and Michael N. Dobkowoski (Syracuse, NY: Syracuse University Press, 2000), 145–161.
67 Blatman, "Holocaust Scholarship: towards a post-uniqueness era," 21.
68 During the late 1960s, the Holocaust was foregrounded in the American Jewish consciousness and its uniqueness became the main marker of its collective identity. To read more about the perception of the uniqueness of the Holocaust in America, see Novick, *The Holocaust in American Life*.

apartheid rhetoric during those years. Instead, the memories invoked were of the Afrikaner community – memories that constitute the core of the Afrikaner civil religion.

The concept of civil religion was first defined by Robert Bellah as "a set of beliefs, symbols, rituals, and assumptions by means of which a country interprets its secular history."[69] In the South African context, T. Dunbar Moodie argues that Afrikaner nationalism is a kind of civil religion that combines the history of the Afrikaners, the formalized language of Afrikaans, and Afrikaner Calvinism as key symbols.[70] He stresses that civil religion provides justification for power: "it serves as a symbolic universe, within the boundaries of which articulation may take place for a body politic, however defined."[71] Central to the Afrikaner civil religion, Moodie argues, is the idea that the Afrikaners are God's chosen people of Africa.[72] Similarly, John de Gruchy defines Afrikaner nationalism as "a civil religion based on a doctrine of creation, history, culture and calling, designed to uphold the Afrikaner people in their struggle for identity, survival, and power, against all odds."[73]

As mentioned earlier, Afrikaner nationalists based their collective identity on the cycles of suffering and death following the Great Trek, the Blood River Battle, their victory over the British in the first Boer War, and their suffering in the second Boer war.[74] These cycles of suffering were amply represented in a letter to *Die Volksblad*, written by a Cape Town citizen under the pseudonym *Regverdig* ("Righteous" in Afrikaans):

> It amazes me that Germany, which was and still is a highly civilized nation, produced so many "war criminals" during the Second World War, while the Allies emerged from the fight with so much honor [...] one wonders what the following are called: (1) the British who threw 30,000 women and children into camps in the English War of whom about 25,000 perished of cold, hunger and maltreatment. (2) the wiping out of the German city of Dresden when women and children were chased onto an open square and put under the annihilating petrol bombs there and about 50,000 of them were exterminated. (3) when the Americans burnt to death half a million Japanese women and children with their "experimental atom bomb" so that today there are still thousands of them who have to drag themselves along malformed [...] what are all these and numerous other cruelties? Bravery? Heroic deeds? Western achievement? Or what? Are not

---

69 Robert N. Bellah, "Bibical Religion and Civil Religion in America," *Daedalus, Journal of the American \ Academy of Arts and Sciences*, 96.1 (1967): 1–21.
70 Moodie, *The Rise of Afrikanerdom*, 19.
71 Moodie, *The Rise of Afrikanerdom*, 298.
72 Moodie, *The Rise of Afrikanerdom*, 296.
73 John W. de Gruchy, *The Church Struggle in South Africa* (Minneapolis: Fortress Press, 2005), 32.
74 Abulof, *The Mortality and Morality of Nations*, 274.

those who made themselves guilty of these cruelties also war criminals? Why are they not also summoned before a court like Eichmann and the Germans at Nuremberg? Is this how our Western Justice looks?[75]

The writer did not deny the killing of European Jews by the Nazis, nor did he defend Eichmann. He did, however, express his displeasure at the fact that under the shadows of the Holocaust, crimes committed by the Allies were disguised. Moreover, the writer singled out victims who had so far been perceived as perpetrators (the Afrikaners, the Japanese and the Germans). While there is no doubt that in all these cases innocent civilians were killed in bloody wars, the writer chose to ignore the difference between victims of racist Nazi persecution and victims of war. The positioning of the Holocaust as equivalent to other war crimes completely disregards the differences between the range of historical events described and thus undermines the possibility of creating empathy and solidarity.

The official Jewish community rushed to denounce the letter's content; however, a fascinating response came from a Holocaust survivor living in Cape Town, who wrote,

> I have seen at various times that certain people doubt stories about the Nazis' cruelties irrespective of the great mass of proofs, but immediately quote the stories of the British camps in order to explain what true cruelties are. Two wrongs do not make a right; therefore, the gassing of millions of innocent people cannot be condoned by the memory of 26,000 Boer women and children who died in camps. Their suffering, like that of the inhabitants of Dresden and Japan, was the ordinary fate of people in war-plagued regions.[76]

This letter attempts to answer the question of how one should think about the relationship between different social groups' histories of victimization and respective claims that the remembrance of one history does not necessarily erase others from view. The survivor's letter expresses the rejection of the assumption made by many memory scholars, that the public sphere in which collective memories are articulated is an arena of scarcity and that the interaction of different collective memories within that sphere can only take the form of a competition. While he acknowledges the existence of traumatic histories and a variety of innocent victims, the writer still draws a distinction between the

---

[75] "Die Eichmann-Saak-Briewe in Die Pers," ["The Eichmann Case - Letters to The Press"] *Die Volksblad*, 1 July 1960, Eichmann A. File 527, Rochlin Archive, Johannesburg (translated by the author).

[76] "Die Eichmann Saak," ["The Eichmann Case"] *Die Volksblad*, 15 July 1960, Eichmann A. File 527, Rochlin Archive, Johannesburg (translated by the author).

Jewish victims of the Holocaust and the Afrikaners, Germans, and Japanese, whom he perceives as victim of wars.

During that period, the communal leadership was disturbed by a growing indifference among segments of South African Jewry to the events of the Holocaust. After the Day of Remembrance of April 1960, reports on the poor attendances at the various public commemoration gatherings occupied Jewish communal discourse. "The younger generation were particularly conspicuous by their absence, even at special youth functions," the *Jewish Herald* reported.[77] Solly Yellin, chairman of the South African Jewish Board of Education, condemned members of the community who did not close their clubs and businesses during the communal day of mourning. He stated, "the community had become so smug and complacent that many of its members were no longer willing to remember the past."[78]

The extensive reports on the Eichmann trial in the communal press were designed to combat the growing indifference among the younger generation. However, they were also part of the community's effort to frame the Eichmann trial as the ultimate answer to Holocaust denial at a time when local and international publications were widely distributed around the world and especially in South Africa. Thus, as explicitly stated in an official invitation to an exhibition of photographs of Nazi atrocities presented at the Jewish Guild in Johannesburg in August 1960, the trial was perceived as potentially instrumental for informing the public of the horrors of the Holocaust and as the most effective tool in the struggle against local antisemitism: "The recent antisemitic outbursts have once again brought to the minds of people the horrors of Nazi brutalities which took place during the Second World War. The forthcoming Eichmann trial which will take place in Israel shortly will further cast light on these crimes and make the world realize that such crimes cannot be allowed to be repeated."[79]

Cold War Imaginaries

The Eichmann trial opened on 11 April 1961, a day before the *Vostok* spacecraft completed its trip around the planet and safely returned the Soviet cosmonaut Yuri Gagarin to the Soviet Union, making him the first man to travel to space.

---

[77] "A Distressing Picture," *Jewish Herald*, 6 May 1960, Items of Jewish Interest, Jewish Studies Library and Research Resources, Kaplan Centre for Jewish Studies, University of Cape Town.
[78] "Jews! Do Not Forget," *Zionist Record*, 27 April 1960, Items of Jewish Interest, Jewish Studies Library and Research Resources, Kaplan Centre for Jewish Studies, University of Cape Town.
[79] "Exhibition of Photographs of Nazi Atrocities," 9 August 1960, Eichmann A. File 527, Rochlin Archive, Johannesburg.

Gagarin became a member of the Communist Party of the Soviet Union in 1960, and his accomplishment was perceived as an unparalleled victory of man over the forces of nature, an immense achievement of science and technology, and a triumph of the human mind. At the same time, it was perceived as the greatest achievement of "the country of victorious socialism."[80]

At the beginning of the trial's proceedings, an article published in *Die Kerkblad*, the organ of the Reformist Church of South Africa (Gereformeerde Kerk- GK), paired Gagarin and Eichmann under the heading: "Mankind at Peak and in the Depths."[81] The GK was established in 1859, when Paul Kruger, who served as President of the South African Republic between 1881 and 1900, retired from the Dutch Reformed Churches in Africa (Nederduitsch Hervormde Kerk Van Afrika – NHK), an organization based in South Africa. In response to the NHK's decision to endorse modern hymns in all its communities, Kruger, together with the conservative Dutch priest Dirk Postma, established the Reformed Churches in South Africa.[82] The members of the new church, called "Doppers," were Afrikaners from the countryside who perceived themselves as representatives of Calvinism in Southern Africa and as the true pioneers of the divine mission.[83] They were considered the most conservative congregation among the Dutch reformist churches in South Africa and the backbone of the Afrikaner civil religion.[84]

Die Kerkblad article stated, "Mankind that can travel into space is also capable of murdering millions of people. These two figures underline the fact that man, no matter how high he climbs, will certainly also act as an antichrist: he is a fallen creature." The solution, it stated, lays in Jerusalem but not in Eichmann:

> Eichmann committed the most horrible sin known to mankind, the sin in which Gagarin is infected along with all of us. But Jesus was crucified outside Jerusalem after not finding

---

[80] Yuri Gagarin, *Soviet Man in Space* (Honolulu, HI: University Press of the Pacific, 2001), 12–13.

[81] "Die Eichmann -verhoor," ["The Eichmann Trial"] *Die Kerkblad*, 31 May 1961, Eichmann A. File 527, Rochlin Archive, Johannesburg (translated by the author).

[82] Irvin Hexham and Karla Poewe, "The Spread of Christianity among Whites and Blacks in Transorangia," in *Christianity in South Africa: A Political, Social, and Cultural History*, ed. Richard Elphick and Rodney Davenport (Berkeley: University of California Press, 1997), 126.

[83] Marjorie Hope and James Young, *The South African Churches in a Revolutionary Situation* (Maryknoll, NY: Orbis, 1981), 18–19.

[84] Hermann Giliomee, *The Afrikaner: Biography of a People* (London: Hurst & Co., 2003), 177–179; Moodie, *The Rise of Afrikanerdom*, 60.

refuge in a glass cell and was left unprotected. This was the lowest point of human creation. It opened the way to the brilliant heights of eternal redemption and glory.[85]

The image of the martyr stood at the core of Afrikaner civil religion. Afrikaner Calvinism invoked connections between the suffering of Jesus crucified by his own people and the Afrikaners' suffering following the Great Trek and the South African War.[86] The use of the crucifixion as the ultimate and primary sin in human history is evident in the article above, which reflects a Christian-Calvinist hierarchy of human suffering. Such a hierarchy considers the Jewish tragedy as less terrible than the crucifixion of Jesus. In arguing that "Jesus was crucified outside Jerusalem after not finding refuge in a glass cell," the article censures the Jews who took extensive measures to protect Eichmann during the legal hearings, while Jesus was not afforded such protection by the Jews and was crucified outside the city walls. The Holocaust is framed within Christian paradigms: the Jewish identity of Eichmann's victims remained unmentioned, a fact that obscures the antisemitic motivations of Eichmann's crimes.

While Eichmann is defined as "a poor man," the Soviet astronaut is defined in the article as an anarchist despite his success. This criticism leveled against Gagarin stems from his Soviet identity and is closely related to the place South Africa assumed in the inter-bloc conflict that began after the Second World War. As mentioned in the previous chapter, the pro-Nazi voices of the Afrikaner right in the 1930s and 1940s were almost completely silenced on the eve of the establishment of the apartheid regime in 1948, and most of the architects of apartheid who supported Hitler during the war shunned their pro-Nazi past and joined the Western world in condemning fascism.[87] In 1950, the South African Communist Party, which had stood alongside the government in its fight against fascism during the war, was outlawed, and communism was framed as the new enemy of the country under the framework of the Suppression of Communism Act of 1950.[88]

Within the Cold War global matrix, the South African government had to decide whether to support the Western bloc and thus denounce communism or to support the Eastern bloc, embracing communism and denouncing the Western imperialism. Apartheid ideology stood in complete contrast to Soviet communism, which sought to unite the world's workers without reference to differences of

---

85 "Die Eichmann -verhoor," ["The Eichmann Trial"] *Die Kerkblad*, 31 May 1961, Eichmann A. File 527, Rochlin Archive, Johannesburg (translated by the author).
86 Giliomee, *The Afrikaner*, 151.
87 Sandwith, "Yours for Socialism," 5.
88 Allison Drew, *South Africa's Radical Tradition: A Documentary History, Volume One 1907–1950* (Cape Town: University of Cape Town Press, 1996), 34–35.

religion, race, and gender. Since many of the opposition voices against segregation, and later apartheid, came from local communist movements, the apartheid government targeted communism as a dangerous evil. In so doing, South Africa gained the support of the West, which in return came to see the country as a buffer against Africa's communist forces.

The Afrikaner Calvinistic anti-communist position was also reflected in an article published in the daily Afrikaner-language newspaper *Die Burger*, which was at that time the mouthpiece of the NP. On 17 June 1961, linking Gagarin and Eichmann as symbols of human triumph and human failure respectively, the newspaper reported: "Gagarin's honor is Russia's honor and Eichmann's disgrace is Germany's disgrace. But it goes further, it is world-wide; Gagarin's honor is the honor of mankind and Eichmann's disgrace is the disgrace of mankind, regardless of the people to whom he belongs. Both are people like us – people whose association with us we cannot deny." The article concluded by defining both Gagarin and Eichmann as "sinners who must learn to know God in our God-forgetting triumphs as in our God-dishonoring crimes."[89] While the sin attributed to Eichmann is clear, interestingly, the sin attributed to Gagarin is the forgetting of God. This reflects a distinctly anti-Soviet and anti-communist Calvinist position that characterized the apartheid government.

As a mirror of the Afrikaner Calvinist viewpoint, an account of the Eichmann trial by a Soviet journalist appeared in the leftist newspaper *New Age*. It claimed that Eichmann was a nonentity "in the ultimate sense of the word; an ordinary Prussian policeman, only instead of recording cases of theft, he gave orders to kill millions of people." It argued, "Not only were the Jews killed but all mankind was threatened by Fascism. Sitting with Eichmann in the dock were his successors, the present-day neo-Fascists, revenge-mongers and militarists [. . .] The new, potential Eichmanns are more dangerous to the world than the old."[90]

New Age was founded in 1953 by Ruth First, Govan Mbeki, and Brian and Sonia Bunting, all unionists, academics, and editors with distinctly left-wing socialist tendencies. Its articles sought to reflect on the situation of blacks, Indians, and Coloureds in South Africa and to present the reality of apartheid, focusing on the sociopolitical and economic situation.[91] The above article provides a glimpse into the communist narrative of the Second World War, which

---

89 "Eichmann verhoor," *Die Burger*, 17 June 1961, Eichmann A. File 527, Rochlin Archive, Johannesburg (translated by the author).
90 "Russian Report," *New Age*, 10 August 1961, Items of Jewish Interest, Jewish Studies Library and Research Resources, Kaplan Centre for Jewish Studies, University of Cape Town.
91 Adler Taffy, "Lithuania's Diaspora: The Johannesburg Jewish Workers' Club, 1928–1948," *Journal of Southern African Studies* 6.1 (1979): 70–92, at 92.

diverted attention from the persecution and murder of European Jews while placing at the forefront the suffering of the citizens of the communist countries, as well as their heroic liberation by the Red Army. This narrative unified all victims of the war as victims of the resistance to fascism and thus, in effect, erased the specific ideological motives of Nazism as the motivation for the killing of the Jews: the victims were murdered by the Nazis not because they were Jews but because of their opposition to fascism.

The narrative presented by the Soviet journalist in the *New Age* was radically different from the narrative of the Holocaust perpetuated by the official Jewish community in South Africa. It was also different from the Afrikaner Calvinist narrative, which ignored the specificity of the Holocaust and drew together Jews and other victims of the war against fascism, thus actively transforming the enemy from Nazism into communism. This stance, reflecting the religious-public atmosphere of Afrikaner society, was clearly expressed in the domestic and foreign policies of the apartheid regime, which aimed to suppress atheistic communism at home and abroad. While in both cases the identity of the Jewish victims was blurred, the Soviet narrative marked the neo-fascist capitalist West as the new enemy replacing Nazi fascism. This variety of opposing voices, although marginal, constituted a microcosm of the perceptions of the Second World War and the Holocaust among the Eastern and Western blocs.

Although neither the Afrikaner Calvinist position nor the communist position placed the narrative of the annihilation of European Jews at the center of the discourse, this was not a manifestation of Holocaust denial. Unfortunately, Holocaust denialism did emerge during the trial. The most prominent Holocaust denial publication on the matter was published by Johan Schoeman of Broederstroom, Transvaal, a well-known antisemitic personality in South Africa.[92]

Titled "Eichmann is not Guilty," Schoeman's booklet opened with the antisemitic claim that "behind communism stands world Jewry," directly connecting Jews to the Bolshevik revolution. He praised Eichmann for "serving his country, Germany, the target of a misled, deliberately misinformed humanity" and argued that Eichmann served his homeland "as a patriot and as a man of honour." Schoeman claimed that it was not the Germans who were mass-murderers, but rather the Allies who had bombed Dresden and "brutally maimed bodies of half a million innocent totally defenseless women and children."[93] These mixed arguments blamed the Jews for being communists on the one hand, but on the other adopted a communist

---

92 Shimoni, *Community and Conscience*, 71.
93 Johan Schoeman, "Eichmann is not Guilty," Broederstroom, Transvall, 4–13, Eichmann A. File 527, Rochlin Archive, Johannesburg.

narrative, which viewed the bombing of German cities during the war as an act of terror committed by the Western Allies against innocent German citizens.

Following the distribution of Schoeman's booklet, and in light of other antisemitic incidents described earlier, the Jewish community defined its primary task as remaining "vigilant in respect of manifestations of an anti-Jewish nature."[94] While the Board stated that it was difficult to assess the overall significance of these manifestations, it called for the constant alertness of members of the community while emphasizing, "we believe that the authorities view these anti-Jewish manifestations with disfavor."[95]

However, antisemitic letters to the press kept on appearing, demonstrating a variety of anti-Jewish positions. A letter written to the East London newspaper the *Daily Dispatch* from 20 June 1961 stated, "In these times when stories of the German concentration camps are being presented to us by hysterical and biased witnesses testifying before an incompetent court, the communists are dishing up Sharpeville-type tales for the edification of our detractors."[96] East London was a port town in the East Cape Province with an active Jewish communal life. The letter therefore received several replies from Jewish citizens who condemned the writer and claimed that the Israeli government wanted to try Eichmann in order to let the world know what had happened in the concentration camps. They concluded that, judging by its careful and thorough investigation of the evidence, it would be more accurate to label the Israeli court as "over-competent" rather than "incompetent."[97]

A similar response came from Abraham Addleson, then chairman of the East London and Regional Council of the SAJBD, who also served as East London's mayor between 1957–1959. Addleson attacked the writer for his cynical detachment from the unspeakable horrors perpetrated by Eichmann and his masters, stating that it was unpardonable that anyone should still be able to talk about "hysterical and biased witnesses" in the face of the facts, which Eichmann did not deny, choosing instead to place the responsibility on his superiors.[98]

---

[94] SAJBD Report, September 1960 to August 1962, 15, SAJBD Reports, Rochlin Archive, Johannesburg.
[95] SAJBD Report, September 1960 to August 1962, 16, SAJBD Reports, Rochlin Archive, Johannesburg.
[96] "The Eichmann Trial," *Daily Dispatch*, 20 June 1961, Items of Jewish Interest, Jewish Studies Library and Research Resources, Kaplan Centre for Jewish Studies, University of Cape Town.
[97] "The Eichmann Trial," *Daily Dispatch*, 20 June 1961, Items of Jewish Interest, Jewish Studies Library and Research Resources, Kaplan Centre for Jewish Studies, University of Cape Town.
[98] "The Eichmann Trial," *Daily Dispatch*, 20 June 1961, Items of Jewish Interest, Jewish Studies Library and Research Resources, Kaplan Centre for Jewish Studies, University of Cape Town.

In her dramatic account of the trial from 1963, political philosopher Hannah Arendt defined Eichmann's actions as "banal," arguing that in an extreme political situation, normal people may be involved in terribly evil crimes without understanding their significance. While she did not argue for Eichmann's innocence, Arendt claimed that "it is important to the political and social sciences that the essence of totalitarian government, and perhaps the nature of every bureaucracy, is to make functionaries and mere cogs in the administrative machinery out of men, and thus to dehumanize them."[99]

Eichmann's line of defense, which stressed his inability to defy his superior's instructions, was not a prominent theme in the South African public discourse, and its relevance for situations in South Africa, where the question of moral responsibility was similar, rarely appeared above the surface. Nevertheless, in December 1961, the *Cape Times* reported that Eichmann admitted moral guilt but denied legal responsibility for the Jewish tragedy. Evoking this defense, the article states,

> It is easy to gasp with horror at the extreme effect of this outlook in the case of an official like Eichmann [. . .] When the relevant officials are, for instance, ordered to turn a dozen families out of their homes in the middle of a cold and wet spell, knowing that whatever the legal rights or wrongs, many babies and old people will be cold and probably wet for the night, where does moral responsibility begin or end?[100]

This article was exceptional in the local discourse. It pointed to similarities between Nazism and apartheid by linking the legal and moral responsibility of the aggressors, the SS officers, and South African police. Moreover, its reference to the similarities between the deportation of Jews to concentration camps, and the expulsion of black families from their homes under the Group Areas Act (1950) confirms the essence of Michael Rothberg's conception of multidirectional memory: the disparate histories of black, Indian and Coloured South Africans and European Jews are blended together while simultaneously allowing for the re-articulation of their specific conditions.

Similar analogies between Nazi Germany and apartheid South Africa were articulated by the writer and journalist Mary Benson in her novel *At the Still Point*, which appeared in the US in 1969 and in Britain in 1971. As Louise Bethlehem argues, Benson's novel "aspires to document social history at a time when South Africa was undergoing the transition from an authoritarian into a

---

[99] Hannah Arendt, *Eichmann in Jerusalem: A Report on the Banality of Evil* (New York: Penguin Books, 1963), 289.
[100] "Division of Guilt," *Cape Times*, 12 July 1961, Eichmann A. File 527, Rochlin Archive, Johannesburg.

police state."[101] As Bethlehem points out, in Benson's novel an analogy is drawn between Eichmann's line of defense and questions of responsibility and the implication of sections of the white minority in South Africa. Benson exhorts "To be indifferent is to condone. Worse! It is to collaborate." She criticized the white citizens of South Africa for their indifference, wondering, "where draw the line between Jews here who gave a gold medal to the Prime Minister and the farmer who beats a laborer to death?"[102]

Reactions to Capital Punishment

The debate over the imposition of the death sentence on Eichmann raged from the day his capture was announced until the day he was executed. In Israel there was almost complete agreement on its necessity.[103] Hanging Eichmann was perceived not only as the embodiment of human justice, but also as additional proof of the "victory" of Israel over the fate of Diaspora Jewry – only in their sovereign state were the Jewish people able to capture Eichmann, put him on trial before Israeli judges in full accordance with the law, and execute him.

Outside Israel, however, public opinion was divided. Even before the sentence was announced, voices against imposing the death penalty in the Eichmann trial were heard. On 7 June 1961, Michael Arnon, then Counsellor for Press and Information at the Israel Embassy in Washington, wrote to the legal advisor to the Ministry of Foreign Affairs, Shabtai Rosenne, that some American Jewish organizations had already requested that Eichmann not be sentenced to death for multiple reasons, including their fears of antisemitic reprisals, their own liberality, or their revulsion to the death penalty.[104] After the verdict was given, a petition in the name of a group of eminent intellectuals, artists, and writers against the execution of Adolf Eichmann was delivered to Izhak Ben-Zvi, then

---

[101] Louise Bethlehem, "Stenographic fictions: Mary Benson's *At the Still Point* and the South African political trial," *Safundi: The Journal of South African and American Studies* 20.2 (2019): 193–212, at 195.
[102] Bethlehem, "Stenographic fictions," 206.
[103] Israeli citizens whose relatives were murdered in Poland wrote a letter to Ben-Gurion expressing their satisfaction on hearing that Eichmann had been captured and offering to execute him. See: Letter to Prime Minister David Ben-Gurion, 26 May 1960, ISA/RG55/G/3930/4; Sarah Shafir to the Members of the Knesset; Ashkelon, 19 June 1960, ISA/RG 60/K/592/2 Israel National Archive, Jerusalem.
[104] Michael Arnon, Counsellor for Press and Information at the Israel Embassy in Washington, to Shabtai Rosenne, Legal Adviser to the Ministry of Foreign Affairs; Washington, 7 June 1961, ISA/RG 130.23/MFA/3352/7, Israel National Archive, Jerusalem.

President of Israel. Among the signatories were the philosophers Nathan Rotenstreich, Martin Buber, Hugo Bergmann, and Akiva Ernst Simon.[105]

In South Africa too, articles about Eichmann's fate began to appear in the national press as the trial progressed, urging the Jewish people to choose an act of mercy and not of revenge.[106] Following Eichmann's execution on 1 June 1962, reports of the hanging were generally featured on the front pages of the national press, and world-wide reactions were recorded. Commentaries appeared in the editorial sections of virtually all newspapers, most of which focused on the question of whether Eichmann should have been executed or not. While most of the newspapers agreed on the fairness of the trial, they were ambivalent as to the implementation of the death penalty. The English press mainly used the case to attack capital punishment, while taking cognizance of the feelings of the Jews. *The Star* wondered "what shall it profit the Jews today that this one man should be hanged?" The *Rand Daily Mail* said in an editorial comment: "Inevitably there will be those who will say that it might have been better for the State of Israel to have avoided exacting the death penalty. But the only alternative would have been life imprisonment, and it is difficult to see how Eichmann could have been kept in confinement without making him appear as an exhibit."[107]

The Afrikaans press, on the other hand, was much more critical and less sympathetic toward Israel and the Jews. *Die Burger* reported, "the death of this poor little man in his puny clerk's uniform will certainly not make up for the terrible crimes of which he was found guilty." The paper further asked: "would it not perhaps have been a great act of mercy to have spared his life and in so doing break the ring of hate and recrimination that surrounds the case," and argued that the decision to hang Eichmann was ultimately a political one, intended to show the world and the Arabs that Israel is not 'soft.'[108] *Dagbreek en Sondagnuus,* the Transvaal's major Afrikaans language Sunday paper also published a critical editorial stating, "we trust that the sentence of Adolf Eichmann means the end of the search for (Nazi) scapegoats," and argued that "another

---

105 Yablonka, *The State of Israel vs. Adolf Eichmann*, 154.
106 "Eichmann's Fate," *Pretoria News*, 23 August 1961; Eichmann's Sentence," *Eastern Province Herald*, 13 December 1961, Eichmann A. File 527, Rochlin Archive, Johannesburg.
107 "Reaction of the S.A. Press," *Jewish Herald*, 12 June 1962, Eichmann A. File 527, Rochlin Archive, Johannesburg.
108 "Die Nadraai Van Eichmann," ["The Aftermath of Eichmann"] *Die Burger,* 5 June 1962, Items of Jewish Interest, Jewish Studies Library and Research Resources, Kaplan Centre for Jewish Studies, University of Cape Town (a translated collection).

justified search into the past will make things uncomfortable for some of Mr. Ben-Gurion's Western friends."[109]

Opposition to the execution was also heard in Parliament, mainly by NP members. A survey conducted by *Die Burger* among certain Cape Town dignitaries cited two NP members on the matter: Dr. L. I. Coertze condemned Eichmann's execution, saying that he did not wish to justify Hitler, but he was against the way individuals were trapped by circumstances; and J. H. Visser, also a Nationalist member of Parliament, argued: "the matter was unnecessary. After all the war is over."[110]

It is important to note that between 1900 and 1950, South Africa was the only country in the world with a rising rate of death sentences handed down by the courts. Robert Turrell wrote, "Hanging was a symbolic expression of political power,"[111] and claimed that the death penalty was used as a weapon for social discipline.[112] As part of its repressive strategy, the apartheid regime was quick to use the death penalty against its political opponents. In 1958, the legislation was amended to extend the range of offences considered as 'capital crimes.' In the wake of the outlawing of the ANC and the Pan Africanist Congress (PAC) after the Sharpeville Massacre and the liberation movement's turn away from nonviolence, the apartheid government began to define both violent and non-violent political acts as such.[113] A survey conducted in Cape Town among white middle-class citizens revealed that public opinion among white South Africans was leaning in favor of such practices: while 56.7 percent of those interviewed favored the retention of the death penalty, only 40.4 percent favored its abolition.[114] Nonetheless, in the case of Eichmann's trial, opposition to capital punishment was loudly voiced in the Afrikaner press, as well as in Parliament, and Israel was criticized for what some perceived as a politically motivated show trial, while ethical issues related to the death penalty in general were ignored.

---

109 "Reaction of the S.A. Press," *Jewish Herald*, 12 June 1962, Eichmann A. File 527, Rochlin Archive, Johannesburg.
110 "Reaction of the S.A. Press," *Jewish Herald*, 12 June 1962, Eichmann A. File 527, Rochlin Archive, Johannesburg.
111 Robert Turrell, *White Mercy: A Study of the Death Penalty in South Africa* (Westport: Praeger, 2004), 7.
112 Turrell, *White Mercy*, 46.
113 Sangim Bae, "The right to life vs. the state's ultimate sanction: abolition of capital punishment in post-apartheid," *The International Journal of Human Rights* 9.1 (2005): 49–68, at 51.
114 James Midgley, "Public Opinion and the Death Penalty in South Africa," *The British Journal of Criminology* 14, 4 (1974): 345–358.

An extreme reaction to Eichmann's verdict came two weeks after the execution, when an explosion at the *Six Million* memorial at West Park cemetery in Johannesburg damaged the sculpture surrounding the symbolic eternal flame. *The Star* reported that on the day before the explosion, an anonymous telephone call was made to the newspaper editorial system directly connecting the explosion to Eichmann's execution. The anonymous caller stated: "I am Adolf Eichmann. Come and see me at West Park Cemetery."[115] A statement by a spokesman of the SAJBD said: "anything of this nature can be regarded as an atrocity. The Memorial, which commemorates the 6,000,000 Jews exterminated by the Nazis, has sacred connotations for all members of the Jewish community."[116]

In view of the critical reception of Eichmann's execution in Afrikaner circles, this incident was given prominence from an unexpected direction when the Minister of Justice, Balthazar Johannes Vorster, referred to the explosion in a debate in the Senate on the General Law Amendment Bill. As mentioned in chapter 1, Vorster was known for his anti-British and pro-Nazi tendencies from the late 1930s, when he was a member of Ossewa Brandwag's militant organization, which had strongly opposed South Africa's intervention on the side of the Allies in the Second World War.[117] In the Senate debate, Vorster argued that the explosion at the memorial was the sort of incident against which he wished to act and stressed that the communists as he knew them would do just this sort of thing to incite race feeling in the country.[118] In so doing, Vorster used the antisemitic incident at the memorial to illustrate how wide the scope of his Bill was: "it is aimed at dealing with attempts to destroy not only State property but any property." Thus, he suggested that the legislation was aimed not only at those responsible for communist-motivated sabotage, but also at those motivated by Nazi ideology.[119]

Vorster's decision was made at a critical moment, when antisemitism and communism were both condemned all over the Western world. However, while in

---

[115] "Explosion at West Park Memorial," *The Star*, 14 June 1962, Items of Jewish Interest, Jewish Studies Library and Research Resources, Kaplan Centre for Jewish Studies, University of Cape Town.
[116] "Explosion at West Park Memorial," *The Star,* 14 June 1962, Items of Jewish Interest, Jewish Studies Library and Research Resources, Kaplan Centre for Jewish Studies, University of Cape Town.
[117] Shimoni, *Community and Conscience*, 25.
[118] "Verklaring deur Vorster," ["Statement by Vorster"] *Die Transvaler*, 15 June 1962, Items of Jewish Interest, Jewish Studies Library and Research Resources, Kaplan Centre for Jewish Studies, University of Cape Town (a translated collection).
[119] "Statement by Mr. Vorster," *Cape Argus*, 15 June 1962, Items of Jewish Interest, Jewish Studies Library and Research Resources, Kaplan Centre for Jewish Studies, University of Cape Town.

the US of that period it simultaneously became unpatriotic to be antisemitic or to discriminate against African Americans, South Africa had no intention of retreating from its racial politics.[120] Thus, despite the critical reception of Eichmann's verdict and execution in South Africa, Vorster's statement reflects an acceptance of the anti-antisemitic message within white South African society.

Such acceptance resonates with a marginal anecdote, possibly apocryphal, that appeared in the national press during the trial. Under the heading "Pretoria Man Offers to Hang Eichmann," the *Sunday Times* reported that an Afrikaner citizen, Louis Erasmus, from Pretoria had approached the Israeli Council in South Africa, offering his services as Adolf Eichmann's executioner. "It is not for the possible remuneration that I want to do it," Erasmus told the reporter, "if the Israeli government pays my airfare there and back, I shall be happy." He told the paper that he had decided to offer his help after reading reports of atrocities perpetrated by Nazis such as Eichmann in the death camps and mentioned that in the past, he had been employed by the Pretoria Municipality to gas dogs. "I thought about it and decided that Eichmann had to pay for the suffering he caused so many people. I gassed only dogs, but their suffering preyed so much in my mind that I gave it up."[121]

This anecdote becomes more feasible when read together with another report in *The Star* after Eichmann's indictment of "rumors that Israel had made tentative inquiries about borrowing from South Africa a hangman to execute Adolf Eichmann." Vorster denied that such a request was made to the Ministry of Justice. Given the deteriorating relationship between Israel and South Africa, it is unlikely that the Israeli government would have been eager to seek South Africa's help on such a sensitive issue. However, no official statement was made on the matter from the Israeli side.[122]

The historical and cultural manifestations of rumors, Hans-Joachim Neubauer argues, reveal their cultural power in shaping collective consciousness, particularly at times of a real or imagined threat. Under these conditions, the truth of a rumor is less relevant than its effect in a given public arena.[123] While there is no evidence of Erasmus's offer nor of the Israeli government's alleged appeal to the South African government on the matter, press reports indicate that such

---

120 Doneson, "The American history of Anne Frank's diary," 149–160.
121 "Pretoria Man Offers to Hang Eichmann," *Sunday Times*, 24 December 1961, Eichmann A. File 527, Rochlin Archive, Johannesburg.
122 "Eichmann Hangman Reply," The Star, 23 March 1962, Eichmann A. File 527, Rochlin Archive, Johannesburg.
123 Hans-Joachim Neubauer, *The Rumor: A Cultural History* (London: Free Association Books, 1999), 3.

inquiries, in one form or another, surfaced in the public arena during the trial. Moreover, whether the reports are true or false, their appearance in the national press indicates a slightly less critical attitude toward Israel as far as the trial was concerned. At the same time, there is a manifest irony in imagining a scenario in which the racist apartheid state would be recruited by the Jewish State, established after the Holocaust, to execute one of the most prominent Nazi leaders, tried in Jerusalem for his racist crimes against Jews.

Read against the background of Vorster's Amendment Bill, which condemned antisemitism as well as communism, these rumors underscore governmental perception of antisemitism as distinct from racism. The apartheid government perceived antisemitism as a forbidden prejudice. However, instead of linking antisemitic manifestations with other forms of prejudice and racism inherent to apartheid ideology, the Nationalists mobilized the world struggle against antisemitism for its own ends by representing antisemitism and what it perceived as communist anti-apartheid sentiments as two dangerous phenomena to be condemned.

Chapter 4
Censoring the Holocaust under Apartheid

In July 1975, the famous Jewish writer and Holocaust survivor Elie Wiesel visited South Africa at the invitation of the SAZF. In a compelling piece written during his visit, Wiesel admitted that his response to the encounter with apartheid in South Africa was one of shame. While his hosts expected an uplifting speaking tour focusing on Wiesel's traumatic experiences during the Holocaust, he saw it as an opportunity to condemn apartheid. He was asked by his hosts not to be hasty in passing judgment on the situation in South Africa and to consider South Africa's friendly relations with Israel. However, he later wrote in his diary: "Only when you go inside Soweto, outside of Johannesburg, you are confronted by concentrated poverty and humiliation without parallel. You see men and women barely able to keep body and soul together. You see children without a future. You see a hopeless world. And logic is no longer important."[1]

In his speeches in Cape Town, Johannesburg, Durban, and other Jewish centers throughout the country, Wiesel stated, "I came because I wanted to see your Jewish community, but I was afraid of what I would find here." Referring to local discrimination and apartheid he declared: "I am not a political scientist, but on a purely moral basis my reaction to what I have found here is one of great sadness. I feel very sad at the way the communities are divided."[2] Despite the community's plea for pragmatism, Wiesel called for protest, stating, "one cannot be a Jew and continue in silence about an ideology based solely on the colour of one's skin." He asserted that the people of Soweto must take precedence over the whites of Johannesburg, and that Jews, because of their tradition and their own traumatic past, should stand against all forms of racism wherever it is found.[3]

At the time of Wiesel's visit, relations between Israel and South Africa were flourishing compared to the deterioration of diplomatic relations between the two countries following the Sharpeville massacre. The Six-Day War proved to be a turning point in restoring good diplomatic relations between Israel and South Africa, and the new bond was largely shaped by the mutual self-perception of the two countries within a framework of Cold War politics. This perception is

---

[1] Elie Wiesel, *A Jew Today* (New York: Random House, 1978), 52–55.
[2] "Israel's Problems Greater than those of South Africa," *Cape Times*, 26 July 1975, Items of Jewish Interest, Jewish Studies Library and Research Resources, Kaplan Centre for Jewish Studies, University of Cape Town.
[3] Frederick L. Downing, *Eli Wiesel: A Religious Biography* (Macon, GA: Mercer University Press, 2008), 222–223.

well reflected in a column published by the official organ of the NP in the Cape area, *Die Burger*, on 24 June 1968:

> Israel and South Africa have a common lot. Both are engaged in a struggle for existence, and both are in constant clash with the decisive majorities in the United Nations. Both are reliable forces of strength within the region, which would, without them, fall into anti-Western anarchy [. . .] The anti-Western powers have driven Israel and South Africa into a community of interests which had better be utilized than denied.[4]

The common lot paradigm was further promoted in South Africa following the 1973 events in the Middle East. When the Yom Kippur War broke out, South African defence minister Peter William Botha declared his solidarity with Israel in its struggle against "communistic militarism"[5] and described Israel and South Africa as two vital "gateways between East and West," both sharing a strong opposition to communism.[6]

This remark was endorsed by the local Jewish community that donated resources to the war effort in the Middle East and which was keen to transfer funds to Israel.[7] Harry Hurwitz, then vice-chairman of the SAZF, stated that South Africa and the United States were "the only two nations that had broken the world's silence in support of Israel."[8] Indeed, when the SAZF officially launched an emergency appeal to help meet Israel's 'humanitarian needs,' the spontaneous response to Israel's plight came from Jews and non-Jews alike.[9] In early 1974, another important step was made when Israel decided to upgrade her consulate to the status of embassy;[10] and on 29 December 1975, South Africa reciprocated by formally elevating its diplomatic representation to an embassy as well.[11]

---

4 Quoted in: Bernard Magubane, "Israel and South Africa: the nature of the unholy alliance," First UN Seminar on the Palestine Question, Arusha, Tanzania: 14-8 July 1980, available at: https://www.un.org/unispal/document/auto-insert-193667/ [Accessed on 10 July 2020].
5 Polakow-Suransky, *The Unspoken Alliance*, 70.
6 Shimoni, *Community and Conscience*, 156.
7 See letter from A. Siton to Europe B reporting that the Government had allowed the contents of the emergency Funds to be immediately transferred, 18 October 1973 [ISA /RG130/MFA/5308/31].
8 "Speeches by Prime Minister and Minister of Defence," *The Star*, 15 October 1973, Items of Jewish Interest, Jewish Studies Library and Research Resources, Kaplan Centre for Jewish Studies, University of Cape Town.
9 "Nie-Jode," ["Non-Jews"] *Die Vaderland*, 13 October 1973, Items of Jewish Interest, Jewish Studies Library and Research Resources, Kaplan Centre for Jewish Studies, University of Cape Town (a translated collection).
10 Naomi Chazan, "The Fallacies of Pragmatism: Israeli Foreign Policy towards South Africa," *African Affairs* 82.327 (1983): 169–199, at 173.
11 *The Star*, 30 December 1975, Items of Jewish Interest, Jewish Studies Library and Research Resources, Kaplan Centre for Jewish Studies, University of Cape Town.

These developments were perceived by the Jewish community as particularly encouraging considering the emergence of a radical right accompanied by proto-fascist and sometimes antisemitic elements during that period. The SAJBD executive council report from 1976 stated, "South Africa had a lunatic fringe propagating bizarre theories of 'international Jewish conspiracies' and the 'power of Jewish money,'"[12] referring to Holocaust denial propaganda material that emanated mainly from the US, Canada, and the UK during the 1970s.[13]

While the Jewish community acknowledged that such manifestations were in most cases actions of individuals, their concerns increased dramatically in July 1973 when the neo-Nazi separatist organization, the Afrikaner Resistance Movement (The Afrikaner Weerstandsbeweging – AWB), was established. This political organization adopted a Nazi-like rhetoric, used symbols that resembled the swastika, and made it clear that Jews were not entitled to equal rights in the South African Christian state.[14] A rise in antisemitism was also detected within the the Herstigte Nasionale Party (HNP) of Albert Hertzog, formerly cabinet minister in the NP government until his breakaway formed the HNP in 1968. Through its organ, *Die Afrikaner,* the party had repeatedly attacked Jews, Jewish institutions, Zionism, and the State of Israel.[15]

During that period, much publicity was also given to the UN General Assembly resolution 3379, passed on 11 November 1975, which defined Zionism as a form of racism and racial discrimination. This resolution marked an achievement for the cooperation between the Arab and Soviet countries and was supported by seventy-two states. Thirty-five countries voted against the resolution, including the Western countries, most of Central America, and several African countries; thirty-two countries abstained. South Africa, which was suspended by the General Assembly in November 1974 due to international opposition to apartheid, was counted among the abstainers.[16] Despite South Africa's *de facto*

---

12 "Report of the Cape Committee of the Cape Council 1974–1976," Report to South African Jewry 1974–1976, 51, SAJBD Reports, Rochlin Archive, Johannesburg.
13 One example of such imported antisemitic literature was Arthur R. Butz's publication *The Hoax of the Twentieth Century*, which was positively reviewed by right-wing newspapers in both English and Afrikaans. This book symbolized a new style of Holocaust denial emerging from the West, which focused on the Jewish and Zionist role in what he and his fellow deniers perceived as a world conspiracy.
14 Leonard Weinberg and Peter H. Merkl, *The Revival of Right-Wing Extremism in the Nineties* (New York: Routledge, 2014), 255.
15 Denis Diamond, "South Africa," *American Jewish Yearbook* 78 (1978): 500–516.
16 The United Nations, UN against Apartheid, "The United Nations: Partner in the Struggle against Apartheid," http://www.un.org/en/events/mandeladay/apartheid.shtml [Accessed on 1 September 2017].

abstention, the apartheid government's support for Israel was prominent in public discourse.[17]

Newspapers nationwide reported on the SAJBD condemnation of the UN's "insidious attack" on Zionism as "a fatal blow at the objectivity and integrity of the world body"[18] and covered the SAZF mass rallies organized throughout the country against the resolution with great interest.[19] Afrikaans language newspapers used the UN decision to draw parallels between Israel and South Africa. *Die Burger* argued: "The remarkable parallelism between the old and recent history of Israel and that of South African whites, in particular the Afrikaners, has lately again been extended in the area of UNO politics."[20] The article contemplated not only the historical similarities between Zionist and Afrikaner nationalist movements, but also compared Israel's immediate danger from Arab neighboring countries with South Africa's constant threat from within.

Another source for the condemnation of the UN resolution evident in the Afrikaner press was South Africa's own animosity towards UN institutions. As chapter 6 will demonstrate, from the mid-1950s, the struggle against apartheid became the concrete issue through which postcolonial states, together with the eastern bloc, sought to shape the international order. Until 1966, the UN General Assembly condemned apartheid as violating the principles and spirit of the Charter of the UN and the Universal Declaration of Human Rights, as well as addressing the danger posed to international peace and security due to the tensions this policy created in South Africa.[21] However, the 16 December 1966 condemnation of apartheid as a crime against humanity by the UN General Assembly was a turning point in the international struggle against

---

17 "S.A. Jewry Condemns UN Resolution: Comment," *Rand Daily Mail*, 15 November 1975, Items of Jewish Interest, Jewish Studies Library and Research Resources, Kaplan Centre for Jewish Studies, University of Cape Town.

18 "Board of Deputies Statement," *Natal Mercury*, 12 November 1975, Items of Jewish Interest, Jewish Studies Library and Research Resources, Kaplan Centre for Jewish Studies, University of Cape Town.

19 "S.A. Jewry Condemns UN Resolution: Comment," *Rand Daily Mail*, 15 November 1975; *The Star*, 17 November 1975, Items of Jewish Interest, Jewish Studies Library and Research Resources, Kaplan Centre for Jewish Studies, University of Cape Town.

20 *Die Burger*, November 1975, Press Items of Jewish Interest No. 23 (20 November 1975), Rochlin Archive, Johannesburg (a translated collection).

21 Jonathan Alschech, "פרדיגמת האפרטהייד: היסטוריה, פוליטיקה ואסטרטגיה," ["The Apartheid Paradigm: History, Politics and Strategy"] in Law, Minority and National Conflict, ed. Raif Zarik and Ilan Saban (Tel Aviv: Tel Aviv University Press, 2017), 168.

apartheid.[22] UN podiums became a central stage for the anti-apartheid cause, and the apartheid regime interpreted these aggressive steps as proof that the international fight against apartheid was merely a communist plot with the liberal left in the West its victim. These developments paved the way for the 1973 UN International Convention on the Suppression and Punishment of the Crime of Apartheid.[23]

The diplomatic alliance between Israel and South Africa was immediately evident in Israel's voting on anti-apartheid resolutions at the UN and reports on the increasing closeness of relations between the two countries occupied the press worldwide.[24] Although South African sources vigorously denied the claims made abroad of military aid by Israel to the apartheid regime, a special report prepared by the UN Special Committee Against Apartheid was adopted on 8 September 1976, focusing on the intensification of relations between Jerusalem and Pretoria while condemning "the unholy alliance between South African racism and Israeli imperialism."[25]

The report emerged at a critical time for both Israel and South Africa in the UN arena. It was only two months after the 1973 Apartheid Convention had come into force. By defining the crimes of apartheid in general terms as "inhuman acts committed for the purpose of establishing and maintaining domination by one racial group of persons over any other racial group of persons and systematically oppressing them," the convention made these crimes relevant to other cases of racial persecution.[26] In many ways, this general definition set the ground for the November 1975 resolution 3379, which determined that "Zionism is a form of racism and racial discrimination."[27] The two separate resolutions

---

[22] UN General Assembly, The policies of apartheid of the Government of the Republic of South Africa, 13 December 1967, A/RES/2307, available at: https://www.refworld.org/docid/3b00f1d524.html [accessed 12 April 2022].
[23] UN General Assembly, International Convention on the Suppression and Punishment of the Crime of Apartheid, 30 November 1973, A/RES/3068(XXVIII), available at: https://www.refworld.org/docid/3ae6b3c00.html [Accessed on 10 May 2020].
[24] UN General Assembly and Security Council, Special Committee against Apartheid, Report of the Special Committee Against Apartheid, Supplement No. 22 (A/10022), 13 September 1976, 9.
[25] UN General Assembly and Security Council, Special Committee against Apartheid, Report of the Special Committee Against Apartheid, Supplement No. 22 (A/10022), 13 September 1976, 3.
[26] UN General Assembly, International Convention on the Suppression and Punishment of the Crime of Apartheid, 30 November 1973, A/RES/3068(XXVIII), available at: https://www.refworld.org/docid/3ae6b3c00.html [Accessed on 10 May 2020].
[27] UN General Assembly, Elimination of racism and racial discrimination: resolution adopted by the General Assembly, 16 December 1991, A/RES/46/86, available at: https://www.refworld.org/docid/3b00efab8.html [accessed 12 April 2022].

created two major trajectories of public discourse, providing a strong basis for drawing similarities between the two countries' racist tendencies.[28]

The wording of resolution 3379 also affirmed this with references to apartheid in South Africa. The resolution recalled the General Assembly's condemnation of "the unholy alliance between South African racism and Zionism" from 14 December 1973 and quoted from the Declaration of Mexico on the Equality of Women and their Contribution to Development and Peace from 1975, which stated that "international cooperation and peace require the achievement of national liberation and independence, the elimination of colonialism and neo-colonialism, foreign occupation, Zionism, apartheid and racial discrimination in all its forms."[29]

Such similarities were also deployed with particular intensity in Muslim circles in South Africa. Inspired by the student uprising in Soweto on 16 June 1976, where black school children protested the introduction of Afrikaans as the medium of instruction in local schools, radical Muslim youth movements emerged with a distinct emphasis on anti-Zionism.[30] The Muslim weekly *Muslim News* regularly addressed the Zionist enterprise, accusing Israeli Jews of supporting the apartheid state and several of its publications on the subject were banned by the state censorship system.[31] While such anti-Zionist Muslim expressions rarely appeared in the national (white) public sphere, on the ground Palestine Islamic solidarity movements gained prominence, positioning Zionism as a central threat.[32]

Indeed, the overwhelming support South African Jewry received by the apartheid government over the course of the UN resolution against Zionism was another sign of the close ties established between Jerusalem and Pretoria. Yet, the official indication of the tightening relations came a few months later, on 8 April 1976, when Vorster became the first South African prime minister to visit Israel for almost twenty-five years.

---

28 Alschech, "The Apartheid Paradigm," 173–174.
29 UN General Assembly, Elimination of racism and racial discrimination : resolution adopted by the General Assembly, 16 December 1991, A/RES/46/86, available at: https://www.refworld.org/docid/3b00efab8.html [accessed 12 April 2022].
30 Abdulkader Tayob, *Islamic Resurgence in South Africa* (Cape Town: University of Cape Town, 1995), 122.
31 Muhammed Haron, "The Muslim News (1960–1986): Expression of an Islamic identity in South Africa," in *Muslim Identity and Social Change in Sub-Saharan Africa*, ed. Louis Brenner (London: Hurst, 1993), 222–223.
32 For further reading on the history of Muslim anti-Zionism in South Africa see Milton Shain and Margo Bastos, "Muslim Antisemitism and Anti-Zionism in Postwar South Africa," in *Holocaust Denial*, ed. Robert S. Wistrich (Berlin: De Gruyter, 2012), 137–156.

Trained as a lawyer at Stellenbosch University in the mid-1930s, Vorster was an active student and served as the chairman of the debating society, deputy chairman of the student council and leader of the junior NP. As mentioned in chapter 1, Vorster graduated in 1938 and, after the outbreak of the Second World War, he became a vocal member of the pro-Nazi cultural movement *Ossewa Brandwag*, which focused on the cultivation of Afrikaner nationalism. He rose rapidly through the ranks, becoming a general in its paramilitary wing.[33] In 1966 Vorster became prime minister of South Africa. He considered different initiatives to deflect the mounting international pressure on South Africa, particularly after the 1973 UN apartheid convention, and his visit to Israel was certainly intended to promote this aim.[34]

Vorster's visit opened with a tour of the Yad Vashem Memorial in Jerusalem, where, accompanied by senior Israeli officials and several of his aides, he laid a wreath and inspected an exhibition of photographs from concentration camps. Later he and his foreign minister, Hilgard Muller, conferred with Israel's prime minister Yitzhak Rabin, foreign minister Yigal Allon, and defense minister Shimon Peres, who received the South African delegation with great respect, and cooperation agreements were signed between the two countries.[35] While the South African national press covered the visit with great interest, mainly focusing on its economic, military and strategic implications, only marginal attention was given to Vorster's Yad Vashem visit.

Nevertheless, a leading article devoted to the visit appeared in the May 1976 issue of the ultra-right newspaper *South African Observer*:

> One wonders whether in his wildest dreams in the early 1940s – when he was interned in Koffiefontein, and he inveighed bitterly against Communism, Democracy, the British, and Jewish Bolshevism, and prayed for a German victory – Balthazar Johannes Vorster ever imagined that thirty-five years later, he would desert the conservative principles of his forebears to accept Zionist-Communist equality doctrine [. . .] become a crusader for Zionism; turn his country into an ally of Israel; and find himself solemnly laying a memorial wreath on the shrine in Jerusalem of the 'Six Million Jews murdered by the Nazis.'[36]

---

33 Brian J. Barker, et all., *Illustrated History of South Africa: The Real Story* (Cape Town: The Reader's Digest Association South Africa, 1988), 348–349; Shimoni, *Community and Conscience*, 15.
34 Hermann Giliomee, *The Last Afrikaner Leaders: A Supreme Test of Power* (Charlottesville: University of Virginia Press, 2013).
35 Shimoni, *Community and Conscience*, 157.
36 "Prime Minister's Visit to Israel," *South African Observer*, May 1976, Press Items of Jewish Interest No. 12, Rochlin Archive, Johannesburg.

The writer of the above article was the chief editor of the *Observer*, Sydney Eustace Denys Brown, notorious for his antisemitic views. While his argument clearly reflected right-wing antisemitic propaganda based on Holocaust denialism, his observation of the hypocrisy inherent in the visit to the national Holocaust commemorative site in Jerusalem by the past Nazi supporter was quite accurate. Vorster's visit to Yad Vashem was also criticized by activists from the left side of the political map, who focused on the pragmatic turn taken by the Israeli government during the diplomatic visit: "the idealism of Israel's early years had been replaced by hardened self-interest."[37] Nevertheless, the official Jewish institutions in South Africa made no reference to the Yad Vashem visit in view of Vorster's pro-Nazi past; instead, a month after the visit, the SAZF and the SAJBD gave a banquet in Cape Town in his honor and to celebrate the growing diplomatic ties between Israel and South Africa.[38]

As mentioned earlier, less than two months after Vorster's visit, on 16 June 1976, black South African high school students in Soweto protested the Afrikaans Medium Decree of 1974, which forced all black schools to use Afrikaans and English in the classroom. Twenty thousand students took part in the protests and were met with fierce police brutality.[39] The Soweto uprising did not emerge from nowhere; the riots erupted in response to more than a decade of state-sponsored oppressive legislation, political persecution of opposition organizations, political arrests, and show trials. The government's police reaction incited waves of student protests during the late 1960s as well as worker strikes during the early 1970s in many South African cities.[40] At the same time, black protest movements began to form in the townships, and the government in turn increased its efforts to contest the legitimacy of public protests.

The Soweto uprising was a trigger for further resistance activities countrywide, which continued until the end of the apartheid years. On the home-front, there was a rapid awakening to the frightening reality of the South African situation and the result was a polarization of public opinion. There were those who saw apartheid legislation as the cause of the problems, likely to lead to a cataclysm; others saw apartheid policies as the only means of saving themselves from such a fate. Although relations between Pretoria and Jerusalem continued

---

37 Polakow-Suransky, *The Unspoken Alliance*, 3.
38 "Praise from South African Jews," *The Star*, 13 April 1976; *Die Beeld*, 11 May 1976; *Die Transvaler*, 11 May 1976; *Rand Daily Mail*, 12 May 1976, Press Items of Jewish Interest, Jewish Studies Library and Research Resources, Kaplan Centre for Jewish Studies, University of Cape Town (a translated collection).
39 Shimoni, *Community and Conscience*, 122.
40 Julian Brown, *The Road to Soweto: Resistance and the Uprising of 16 June 1976* (Johannesburg: Jacana Media, 2016).

to tighten, the violent atmosphere of the 1970s raised concerns among local Jewry, manifested in high emigration rates among community members. While large waves of Jewish emigration began in the early 1970s, the three years following the Soweto uprising saw a sharp increase in the number of Jews leaving the country.[41]

The Apartheid Censorship System

It was during these pressing times that the South African Parliament passed the highly controversial Publication Act No. 42 of 1974, which gave the apartheid government the power to censor movies, plays, books, and other entertainment programs. While this development set a new record for level of governmental control, the establishment of a censorship system in South Africa began long before the apartheid era, during the period of the Union of South Africa, under the Entertainments (Censorship) Act of 1931. The first Board of Censors was a governmental body that initially focused on the relatively new medium of cinema, as well as other forms of visual media. In 1934, the board's authority expanded to supervise imported books and magazines, deepening government control over the distribution of printed materials throughout the country.[42]

Until the early 1960s, customs officers controlled all foreign publications, and local publications were banned under the provisions of various laws, especially the Suppression of Communism Act of 1950.[43] However, the foundations for the apartheid censorship system were laid in 1954, when the apartheid government, headed by Malan, announced the establishment of a committee of inquiry to examine undesirable publications. This committee was set up in response to a legal case in 1953 that dealt with an article on prostitution published in two popular Afrikaner newspapers.[44] By the early 1960s, under a state of emergency declared following the Sharpeville massacre, the apartheid government decided

---

41 Shain and Medelsohn, *The Jews in South Africa*, 175.
42 Peter D. McDonald, *The Literature Police: Apartheid Censorship and its Cultural Consequences* (Oxford: Oxford University Press, 2010), 21.
43 Margreet de Lange, *The Muzzled Muse: Literature and Censorship in South Africa* (Amsterdam: John Benjamins Publishing Co., 1997), 7.
44 This episode sparked a storm in official circles and among various church groups. The committee, which was established to raise the political capital of the NP, aimed at examining the regulation of local and imported books and was one of the central expressions of the expansion of the state's power and its takeover of public space in a period when the parliamentary opposition could still openly criticize the new order. For more information on the 1953 episode and the committee that followed see McDonald, *The Literature Police*, 22.

to selectively implement some of the 1954 committee's recommendations. While they completely ignored the committee's suggestions for progressive measures to promote literature, they chose to adopt its regressive recommendations and to establish a new centralized and authoritarian censorship system.[45]

In 1963, the parliament passed the Publication and Entertainments Act, which declared that all publications and objects could be put up for review and banned if they were found harmful or offensive to the interests of the state and its citizens. The declared purpose of the law was "to uphold a Christian view of life in South Africa," and it stated that the publication and distribution of undesirable materials, whether domestic or imported, constituted a statutory offense that might result in high fines and even imprisonment.[46]

The Act defined six categories of undesirable material, ostensibly, in order to protect all social groups in South Africa in an egalitarian manner: in practice, it was another instance of the implementation of the logic of racial segregation and of white supremacy. Evidence of this can be found in the section of the Act that defined the establishment of the Directorate of Publications, whose task was to appoint committees to evaluate any material submitted for examination. According to the Act, members of the committee were to be chosen from a list compiled by the Directorate and approved by the Minister of Home Affairs; as a result, the nominations were more political then professional, enabling the government to gain full control over the new censorship system. Moreover, the Act determined that all citizens would be able to provide materials for examination. It further stated that it would be possible to apply for a judicial reexamination by a state court, a proviso that mostly benefitted the white public due to the high costs of applications to the court at that time.[47]

In 1974, the Publication Act was passed in parliament with the same categories for undesirability as the 1963 Act contained. This new act instituted a Publication Appeal Board, which practically abolished all judicial reviews of the censorship process. In the new act, the pseudo-judicial structure of the censorship apparatus served to enhance the appearance of judicial impartiality, but in reality censorship was controlled by the government. The new institution was run by the Minister of Home Affairs, who not only had the power to appoint the members of the Directorate and designate members of Directorate-appointed committees, but could also instruct the Appeal Board to reconsider the decision

---

45 McDonald, *The Literature Police*, 32.
46 De Lange, *The Muzzled Muse*, 8.
47 De Lange, *The Muzzled Muse*, 8.

of a committee when the Directorate had not done so itself.[48] Moreover, the Minister was responsible for appointing fourteen of the board's members, an authority that also deepened the government's control over the censorship system. The Act applied to most existing cultural media such as books, movies, records, stage performances, artwork, and even amateur photography, determining that possession of any material deemed undesirable was an offense.[49]

Opposition to the new act was loudly voiced when the report of the commission of inquiry into the Publication and Entertainments Amendment Bill was first presented in the House of Assembly. Helen Suzman from the PP criticized the proposed act and particularly the recommendation to abolish the right of appeal to the courts in the case of publications, objects, and public entertainments, and to replace the existing mechanisms by recourse to a special Board of Appeal.[50] Opposition in Parliament was supported by prominent authors, artists and lecturers, who expressed apprehension and disapproval at the proposed changes to South Africa's censorship machinery. Among these was author and Liberal Party member Alan Paton, who claimed that while South Africans should accept that censorship would continue to exist for the foreseeable future, they should demand wide representation on any censorship board and a final right of appeal to the courts.[51]

Nonetheless, Publications Act No. 42 of 1974 came into force. The Directorate of Publications' first chair was Judge Lammie Snyman, who was appointed in 1975 and held the office for five years. Snyman was noted for his conservative views, and his worldview shaped apartheid censorship during this period. In a statement he made at the Johannesburg Film Society's presentation of the Neil Smith Award for Best Film in 1979, he said: "The duty of the Publications Bodies is they must ask the question 'what does the average man in the street with a standard seven education think?' [. . .] The Publications Bodies, the adjudicators, must decide what the moral standards are of the general community, the bulk of which is not sophisticated."[52]

The official reasons offered in defense of censorship, such as Snyman's comments above, hide deeper, insidious objectives: to reinforce the dominant ideology

---

[48] Republic of South Africa, Government Gazette, *Publication Act No.42 of 1974*, Cape Town, 9 October 1974, No. 4426.
[49] De Lange, *The Muzzled Muse*, 9.
[50] "Censorship Proposals Under Fire," *Cape Argus*, 2 January 1974, AD1912 59.2 Censorship 1974, Historical Papers Research Archive, University of the Witwatersrand, Johannesburg.
[51] "Paton's Fears on SA Censors," *Cape Argus*, 5 April 1974, AD1912 59.2 Censorship 1974, Historical Papers Research Archive, University of the Witwatersrand, Johannesburg.
[52] Derek Jones, *Censorship: A World Encyclopedia* (New York: Routledge, 2001), 2297.

and to control reflections upon and interpretations of social experience. The interest of the Directorate of Publications was primarily to benefit those in political power, and when Snyman referred to "the average man in the street," he was not referring to the black, Indian, and Coloured communities, who constituted the majority of South Africa's population, but to citizens from the white minority.[53] The Publication Appeal Board itself was also not representative of the South African population – although Coloured and Indian representatives could advise the appointed committees, blacks were completely overlooked.[54] In fact, in 1981, seven of the eleven board members were over 60 years old, only two were English, and all were white and Christian. The Board was therefore not even representative of white communities in South Africa.[55]

In 1976, television broadcasts began in South Africa, providing new challenges for the country's censorship system. The 1949 Broadcast Amendment Act established control of television under the South African Broadcasting Corporation. However, due to the NP's staunch opposition to the introduction of the new medium, the Act was effectively denied.[56] In 1960, Hendrik Verwoerd, then Prime Minister, compared the dangers inherent in introducing the new medium into South Africa to those of using toxic gas or atomic bombs. Verwoerd was not alone in his campaign against television. The NP feared that it would serve to import foreign ideas from the east as well as from the west, claiming that television is a medium that simultaneously promotes communist ideas alongside American-style capitalist monopoly.[57]

The Nationalists' objection to television stemmed also from inter-state motives. Television was depicted as an agent of cultural fusion during a time when the regime devoted most of its efforts to implementing its Bantustan ideology. The purpose of this ideology was to suppress African resistance and to control the African workforce by concessions to the political aspirations of the oppressed black population. By allocating various ethnic groups of black South Africans to separate "homelands," this ideology not only enforced a total segregation of the black population, but also stripped black South Africans of their citizenship, which deprived them of

---

[53] Keyan G. Tomaselli, "Ideology and Censorship in South African Film," *Critical Arts – South-North Cultural and Media Studies Journal* 1.2 (2008): 1–15, at 9.
[54] For Coloured and Indian representation in the Directorate of Publication, see "Coloured Advisory Committee," and "Indian Advisory Committee," Government Gazette, Publication Act No.42 of 1974, Cape Town, 9 October 1974, No. 4426, 6–7.
[55] Jan-Ad Stemmet, "From nipples and nationalists to full frontal in the new South Africa: An abridged history of pornography and censorship in the old and new South Africa," *Communication: South African journal for communication theory and research* 31.2 (2005): 198–210.
[56] Rob Nixon, *Homelands, Harlem and Hollywood: South African Culture and the World Beyond* (London: Routledge, 1994), 43–45.
[57] Nixon, *Homelands, Harlem and Hollywood*, 46.

their few remaining political and civil rights in South Africa and declared them to be citizens of these homelands. The architects of apartheid, including Verwoerd, argued that television was dangerous because as a cultural agent it could potentially undermine the apartheid segregation program. However, the most outspoken opponent of television was the Minister of Posts and Telegraphs, Albert Hertzog, who viewed the television as an "evil black box" which would harm family life and morality. Nonetheless, in 1968, a window of opportunity emerged when Hertzog was removed from his role.[58]

After Verwoerd's assassination on 6 September 1966 in Cape Town, two terms began to appear in the Afrikaner lexicon, creating a rift in Afrikaner nationalism: "enlightened" (Verlig) and "Conservative" (Verkramp). The first referred to the stream of Afrikaner nationalism, which claimed openness towards the international arena and recognized the developments and changes that were taking place, while respecting the Christian-Calvinist Afrikaner tradition. The second, represented by Herzog and his followers, advocated closure, isolationism, and separation.[59] Ironically, the roots of this rift can be traced to the dizzying success of Afrikaner nationalism in consolidating political power and expanding its members' economic base. This was achieved through preference for Afrikaner-owned businesses and by providing employment to unskilled Afrikaners in the apartheid bureaucracy, while eroding the wages of black workers and exercising violent and relentless opposition to any black resistance.

The isolation that characterized Afrikaner nationalism in the early apartheid years led during the 1940s and 1950s to the creation of a powerful Afrikaner capitalist class. This change led to the intersection of the economic interests of Afrikaners with those of English speakers in the country, who perceived television as a commercial asset. In 1969 these developments led to fragmentation in the NP and to the establishment of the HNP. However, this new party soon became a relatively peripheral force in general and within the debate surrounding the introduction of television into the country.[60]

The last straw was the historic moment of the landing of the first man on the moon in July 1969, a moment people from the West watched from their living rooms, on live broadcasts on the small screen, while South Africans were forced to read about it in the newspapers. Shortly thereafter, the NP established a committee to examine the pros and cons of introducing the new medium into

---

58 Nixon, *Homelands, Harlem and Hollywood*, 71.
59 Nixon, *Homelands, Harlem and Hollywood*, 71.
60 Harrison Randall and Paul Ekman, "TV's Last Frontier," *Journal of Communication* 26.1 (1976): 102–109, 104; Nixon, *Homelands, Harlem and Hollywood*, 72.

the country.⁶¹ Its report, which compared the effects of television in fifteen countries, was submitted to the South African Cabinet, and in May 1971 the introduction of television to South Africa within four years was announced.

Experimental television broadcasts began in May 1975 in Johannesburg, and in July of that year in Cape Town and Durban, in the format of one-hour evening programming and a rerun at noon the next day. In October, the South African TV Broadcasting Corporation (SABC-TV) increased its broadcasting hours and on 5 January 1976, a five-hour evening schedule was initiated, and an additional weekend broadcast was dedicated to sports. Broadcasts were bilingual, and every evening shows were aired for two and a half hours in Afrikaans and for another two and a half hours in English. While SABC-TV was under total government control, it was established about a year after the Publication Act (1974) was enacted. The applicability of the Act to television broadcasts was therefore not clearly defined.

Holocaust on Television: *The World at War*

One of the first television programs to be screened by SABC-TV was the British documentary, *The World at War*, which included twenty-six episodes and appeared on screen in South Africa in January 1976. The series was produced by Jeremy Isaacs for the British commercial network *Thames TV* and focused on a global perspective of the Second World War, with each episode dedicated to a specific front.⁶² It gained global reception and was purchased by broadcasting companies over twenty years, reflecting growing global interest in the war and the Holocaust in the western world.⁶³

In South Africa, the documentary soon became a factor in promoting social cohesiveness, not only for Jews but for the entire white population. It brought the events of the Second World War into the living rooms of many homes in the country and became the talk of the day in the national press. For the Jewish community, the timing of the screening of the series was critical, as the first episode was screened only two months after the UN resolution equating Zionism with racism. As described in the *Jewish Herald*, "Our people were singled out as special victims

---

61 The committee included nine members of the Afrikaner brotherhood (Broederbond) and four members of the English-speaking community.
62 Patricia Aufderhedie, *Documentary Film: A Very Short Introduction* (Oxford: Oxford University Press, 2007), 97.
63 Jack C. Ellis and Betsy A. McLane, *A New History of Documentary Film* (London: Continuum,1995), 253.

of barbaric racism. This makes last November's United Nations' resolution equating Zionism with racism a depraved perversity."[64] While the *Jewish Herald* was a Jewish newspaper that endorsed the community's imperative not to forget the traumatic history of the Holocaust, it also aimed at shaping public opinion on Zionism and Judaism nation-wide. Indeed, public discourse concerning the series went far beyond the community's borders.

The most prominent public debate centered on episode 20, entitled "Genocide," which focused on the death camps. This episode was produced by Michael Darlow based on a screenplay by Charles Bloomberg and research by Drora Katz (Kass) and Susan McConachy. It included interviews with three former SS officers and five Holocaust survivors, accompanied by photos from the death camps, and described the Nazis systematic killing of the Jews in detail. The episode opens with Lawrence Olivier, a British actor, director and producer who served as the documentary narrator, facing the camera and warning viewers of the difficult sights they were likely to see and emphasizing the importance of watching because "these things happened in reality and must never happen again."[65]

In Britain, this episode was aired on 27 March 1974 at 9 pm in full, without commercial breaks, and was accompanied by a content advisory to viewers. Responses to the episode in the UK were divided: there was agreement that the sights were unbearable; however, while some thought that it should not have been broadcast, others argued that it was precisely because of its atrocity that the episode should be watched for all to remember and never forget.[66]

In South Africa too, the public was divided over the question of whether to ban or air the episode. Those in favor of banning the episode for its violent and horrific content were concerned that it would undermine German-Jewish relations in the country, thus making it undesirable in accordance with the categories of the 1974 Publication Act. Baroness Esther von Reibnitz, a prominent member of the Johannesburg German community, told the *Sunday Times*: "it is history – horrible history and is best left alone [. . .] a lot of people, not only Jews, lost relatives and friends in the concentration camps. My brother-in-law was one of them. I do not want that terrible period of my life revived."[67]

While German individuals voiced these concerns the spokesman for SABC-TV forcefully argued that the episode would be screened on 18 May as planned

---

[64] "6,000,000," *Jewish Herald*, 4 April 1976, File 520.2A: Holocaust Commemoration 1970–1979, Rochlin Archive, Johannesburg.
[65] Taylor Downing, *The World at War* (London: Palgrave Macmillan, 2012), 136–142.
[66] Downing, *The World at War*, 136–142.
[67] Patrick Taylor, *Sunday Times*, 9 May 1976, Press Items of Jewish Interest No. 10, Rochlin Archive, Johannesburg.

and that, because of the episode's explicit and often horrifying detail, the normal viewing time would be moved from 8:30 pm to nearly 10 pm. "It happened, and we will show the episode. There is no chance of our breaking the series," he stated.[68] The *Natal Witness* editorial from 10 May also addressed German concerns; however, it reassured its viewers, "SATV, wisely in our view, has decided to show the episode. The wholesale murder of Jews, but not only of Jews, happened. It happened in the mid-twentieth century in the world's most highly civilized continent and in probably the most cultured and most highly educated community in that continent." The editorial then turned to the German people in South Africa and stated:

> If the *World at War* teaches anything, it teaches that the dark curse of Hitler fell as harshly on his own people as on the rest of humanity. It is important that the younger generations, which escaped the war, should be given the opportunity to learn something of the terrible consequences that are liable to follow, perhaps anywhere, when half-crazed demoniac demagogues are able to exploit real and imaginary grievances and seize the apparatus of an efficient modern state for their own evil purposes.[69]

Events took an unexpected turn when SABC-TV announced three days before the expected screening that the genocide episode would not be shown after all. In a laconic announcement the director general of SABC-TV, J. Swanepoel, said: "because of the great deal of publicity given to the concentration camps issue, it was felt that the programme might be hurtful to some people."[70]

It is important to note that the documentary first became a controversial subject in South Africa when the Directorate of Publications unceremoniously banned it in early 1975 due to claims of violent content. Ironically, the SAZF was the one to submit the series for examination by the relevant committee of the Directorate, hoping to get it to approve the documentary for screening in public meetings. However, as mentioned earlier, the ban order focused on the cinematic medium, and as the 1974 Act was enacted prior to the introduction of television in South Africa, the Directorate of Publications decision did not apply to the small screen.

Nevertheless, by deciding not to screen the episode, SABC-TV selectively adopted the Directorate of Publication's decision as valid for television. While

---

68 "*Die Afrikaner* and Mr. Diamond," 24 June 1976, Press Items of Jewish Interest No. 13, Rochlin Archive, Johannesburg.
69 "Wise Decision," *Natal Witness*, 10 May 1976, Press Items of Jewish Interest No. 10, Rochlin Archive, Johannesburg.
70 "World at War – Genocide," *Sunday Express*, 16 May 1976, Press Items of Jewish Interest No. 12, Rochlin Archive, Johannesburg.

the Directorate of Publications had banned the entire series from being screened in the South African cinema, based on claims of an excessive degree of violence, SABC-TV had chosen to ban only the genocide episode and did not make its decisions based on degree of violence per se. The announcement focused instead on "the great deal of publicity given to the concentration camps" and mentioned the possibility that the episode would "be hurtful to some people," alluding to two of the six categories for undesirable material from the 1963 Act: Article 11(a), which addresses offensive or harmful materials to public morals, and Article 11(c), which refers to material that brings any segment of the Republic into ridicule or contempt. While the identity of these people was not explicit, due to the public discourse on the matter, it is safe to assume that the latter referred to the German community in the country.

The decision was followed by thousands of phone calls made by angry viewers to newspaper offices and to the SABC-TV headquarters in Auckland Park. Among them were Holocaust survivors who claimed that the banning added insult to injury.[71] The Jewish institutions also responded immediately to what it perceived as "completely specious" decision.[72] Piet Muller, Pretoria representative of *Die Beeld*, wrote in his column that regret had been expressed at the SABC's initial decision not to screen the genocide episode: "Even in peaceful Pretoria, there are a few people who carry a latent antisemitism under their skins like a wriggling red ant. Such a transmission could only have done them good."[73] *The Star* claimed that the handling of the issue by SABC-TV has shown the South African public how far the corporation would go to defer to the sensibilities of "a small, influential clique who call the tune at Auckland Park." It stated,

> SABC was willing to bow to this pressure, knowing that cancellation would be a slap on the face to South Africa's Jewish community, and indeed to several hundred thousand non-Jewish viewers who wished to exercise their option to see the programme [. . .] The SABC was distorting historical perspective, virtually dismissing the horror of the gas chambers as a non-event.[74]

While most of the local papers similarly condemned SABC-TV's decision, two particularly interesting responses came from the Afrikaans language paper, *Die*

---

[71] "World at War – Genocide," *Sunday Express*, 16 May 1976, Press Items of Jewish Interest No. 12, Rochlin Archive, Johannesburg.
[72] "World at War – Genocide," *Sunday Express*, 16 May 1976, Press Items of Jewish Interest No. 12, Rochlin Archive, Johannesburg.
[73] Piet Muller, *Beeld*, 17 May 1976, Press Items of Jewish Interest, No. 11, Rochlin Archive, Johannesburg (a translated collection).
[74] *The Star*, 17 May 1976, Press Items of Jewish Interest, No. 11, Rochlin Archive, Johannesburg.

Hoofstad, and from the English paper, *Cape Times*. Acknowledging the centrality of narratives of suffering and trauma to Afrikaner national identity, *Die Hoofstad* reported: "The whole handling by the SABC of this matter makes one wonder what the approach would be if a documentary television film concerning certain aspects of South African history, such as the Anglo-Boer war, were in the course of time to be considered."[75] In the *Cape Times*, on the other hand, TV correspondent Brian Barrow addressed the relevance of the ban to current race relations in South Africa and critically noted: "who would have been offended for instance by the harrowing concentration camp episode? The Jews? The Germans? Our children? Or was there a fear that Blacks would see that white man can commit barbarities unheard of even in Darkest Africa?"[76]

Eventually, after three stormy days and due to massive public pressure, the ban was lifted, and the episode was shown on 18 May as originally scheduled. The producer of the documentary, Jeremy Isaacs, who was in Johannesburg on the night of the screening, told the *Rand Daily Mail* that the genocide episode considers what one idea – the notion that one race is superior to another – can lead to. Ironically, he failed to see the relevance of his own wording to the racialist reality of apartheid South Africa. Concerning the public debate on the banning of the episode, he said: "I thought it [the genocide episode] was too important to leave out – not just because I am a Jew, but because what happened, and what still happens, concerns all mankind."[77]

According to South African press estimations, almost two million viewers gathered at 10 pm before some 450,000 TV sets to see how Jews and others had died in German concentration and death camps.[78] "Horrifying pictures of Hitler's total war on the Jews in last night's television screening of 'Genocide' prompted clashing reactions among the Jewish and German communities," reported the *Daily News*; the genocide episode "moved some people to tears," while others found it "as shocking as they expected it to be," stated the *Rand Daily Mail*;[79] and printed interviews with a number of people who watched the

---

75 *Hoofstad*, 17 May 1976, Items of Jewish Interest, No. 11, Rochlin Archive, Johannesburg (a translated collection).
76 *Cape Times*, 17 May 1976, Items of Jewish Interest, No. 11, Rochlin Archive, Johannesburg.
77 "Ban Reversed," *Rand Daily Mail*, 18 May 1976, Press Items of Jewish Interest, No 11, Rochlin Archive, Johannesburg.
78 "Ban Reversed," *Die Transvaler*, 18 May 1976, Press Items of Jewish Inerest, No. 11, Rochlin Archive, Johannesburg (a translated collection).
79 *Rand Daily Mail*, 19 May 1976, Press Items of Jewish Interest, No. 11, Rochlin Archive, Johannesburg.

episode, including several Holocaust survivors who recalled some of their own experiences, featured in *The Star*.[80]

The screening of the genocide episode also evoked arguments tainted with Holocaust denial. Letters published in the national press dwelled on the question of the objectivity of the documentary, while many of the writers based their arguments on information from Richard Harwood's booklet entitled 'Did Six Million Really Die?', an imported Holocaust denial text to be discussed at length over the next part of this chapter.[81] Furthermore, the *Daily News* reported the morning after the screening that the chairman of the Durban German Club, H. Haptman, insisted that the whole episode reflected Jewish propaganda against the Germans and that the killing of six million Jews by Germany never happened.[82] Nevertheless, members of the German community in Durban condemned Haptman's statement, and the West Germany vice-consul, M. A. Reinhardt, stated, "The film showing the suffering of Europe's Jewry during the Hitler regime must be appreciated as a lesson to strengthen world opinion against any repetition of such a tragedy."[83]

A particularly orchestrated attack came from *Die Afrikaner*, which dedicated several long editorials to the Second World War under the title "The Unnecessary War." The last five dealt with the Holocaust, which the editor, Beaumont Schoeman claimed was a complete fabrication by the Jews. Three days after the episode was screened, Schoeman wrote: "The SABC made a mockery of an earlier assurance that it would present facts objectively [. . .] The alleged 'slaughter' of six million Jews is based on falsification, lies and fraud." Schoeman reminded his readers of the banning of screening of the series by the Directorate of Publications two years earlier because of the potential of its content to disturb race relations in the country, and because it might give offense to one demographic within the population – the Germans.[84]

The second commentary published by *Die Afrikaner* appeared on 28 May, when the paper reported on a letter sent by Denis Diamond, Executive Director of the SAJBD, to SABC-TV management, an alleged proof of Jewish influence on

---

80 *The Star*, 19 May 1976, Press Items of Jewish Interest, No. 11, Rochlin Archive, Johannesburg.
81 "Letters," *Friend*, 18 May 1976; *Sunday Tribune*, 20 May 1976, Press Items of Jewish Interest, No. 11, Rochlin Archive, Johannesburg.
82 *Daily News*, 19 May 1976, Press Items of Jewish Interest, No. 11, Rochlin Archive, Johannesburg.
83 *The Star*, 20 May 1976, Press Items of Jewish Interest, No. 11, Rochlin Archive, Johannesburg.
84 "Flagrant Lies," *Die Afrikaner*, 21 May 1976, Press Items of Jewish Interest, No. 11, Rochlin Archive, Johannesburg (a translated collection).

national television.[85] In a front-page article published a week later, the paper reported on a meeting held on 12 April of that year, more than a month before the genocide episode was shown, between Diamond and the head of TV programs at SABC-TV, Jan Schutte. While Schoeman stated that the reasons for the meeting were unknown, he asserted, "obviously the deputation of the Jewish Board of Deputies wanted to make certain long before the time that the film would indeed be shown."[86]

The *Rand Daily Mail* devoted an extensive article to the varied responses to *Die Afrikaner's* reports with a subleader stating: "should any attention be paid to *Die Afrikaner,* the organ of the Herstigte Nasionale Party, when it dismisses as fabrication what was presented in the genocide episode of the World at War series?" It published Diamond's statement that the Jewish community "naturally took a stand against a completely unjustified incursion into the rights of the South African viewing public to see a perfectly legitimate film in an exceptionally popular series." The paper also presented the response of the leader of the HNP, Albert Hertzog, who argued that Schoeman's opinions were based on evidence. The *Rand Daily Mail* concluded that the opposition to the screening of the genocide episode by *Die Afrikaner* and the party it represented revealed the naked racism behind their worldview.[87]

As expected, a similar attack came from the *South African Observer* in its June 1976 issue, where Brown wrote a seven-page article on the subject, referring to the decision to show the episode as a world Zionist conspiracy to promote anti-German sentiment worldwide. He wrote, "With the capitulation of the Vorster Government to the forces of world Zionism, it was inevitable that a Zionist halter would be clamped firmly round the neck of the South African Broadcasting Corporation, and that it would become a regular transmission belt for unrestricted Zionist and anti-German propaganda."[88]

Brown argued that while the series was presented by the South African press as a 'straightforward documentary' of the Second World War, it had proved to be nothing more than a "history of the last war selected, compiled

---

85 "Further Attacks by *Die Afrikaner*," 28 May 1976, Press Items of Jewish Interest, No. 12, Rochlin Archive, Johannesburg (a translated collection).
86 "Further Attacks by *Die Afrikaner*," 4 June 1976, Press Items of Jewish Interest, No. 12, Rochlin Archive, Johannesburg.
87 "HNP and Genocide," *Rand Daily Mail*, 31 May 1976, Press Items of Jewish Interest, No. 12, Rochlin Archive, Johannesburg.
88 "The Six Million," *South African Observer*, June 1976, Press Items of Jewish Interest, No. 13, Rochlin Archive, Johannesburg.

and purveyed, not by qualified historians, but by two Zionist Jews, Jeremy Isaac and Charles Bloomberg."[89] He stated,

> For our part, if *The World at War* series [. . .] has one lesson for the people of South Africa, it is the pressing need for the whole question of Zionism, Judaism, the Talmud, 'anti-Semitism', the myth of the six million, and the whole matter of Jewish ethnocentrism to be opened up to free discussion and enquiry in just the same way that Western man's customs, his traditions, his racism, his nationalism and his Christian faith have since the end of the last war been subjected to the fierce and unremitting glare of public scrutiny by the Zionists themselves.[90]

The secretary of the SAJBD, Aleck Goldberg, dismissed Brown's claims as "ridiculous," arguing that "Brown's allegations are as much a myth as what he purports to be the truth. Every German of repute accepts the Nazi atrocities."[91]

In addition to the critical reception of the genocide episode from the radical right, an adverse reaction came from the left side of the political map in South Africa: Under the heading "Israeli Acts of Genocide," the *Muslim News* reported that during the years of occupation, Israeli rule had become increasingly repressive and was characterized by the complete absence of human rights. The article described the Palestinians' living conditions under occupation without freedom of expression, movement, demonstration, or association, and stated: "The genocide, an episode in the *World at War* series, portrays the Nazi evil which was of such a horrifying dimension that it still seems to be beyond the scope of ordinary comprehension. Six million Jews were put to death. Why then are the Israeli authorities completely ignoring human rights and repeating history?"[92]

The showing of the *World at War* in South Africa caused a public outcry during the months April to June 1976. For South African Jewry, who were in favor of screening the series, including the genocide episode, the weekly broadcast of the documentary soon became a cultural event. It was screened in Jewish schools, community centers, and in almost every house, becoming a major topic of interest for South African Jews. Moreover, it was featured in all national newspapers and became the talk of the day in various public circles. Vorster's

---

89 "The Six Million," *South African Observer*, June 1976, Press Items of Jewish Interest, No. 13, Rochlin Archive, Johannesburg.
90 "The Six Million," *South African Observer*, June 1976, Press Items of Jewish Interest, No. 13, Rochlin Archive, Johannesburg.
91 "Brown's article Dismissed," *Sunday Times*, 13 June 1976, Press Items of Jewish Interest, No. 13, Rochlin Archive, Johannesburg.
92 "Israeli acts of genocide," *Muslim News*, 28 May 1976, Press Items of Jewish Interest, No. 13, Rochlin Archive, Johannesburg.

visit to Israel in April 1976 and particularly his tour of Yad Vashem increased the legitimacy of the Jewish leadership's depicting of the Holocaust as the most traumatic event in Jewish history and the turmoil surrounding the genocide episode as another manifestation of antisemitism. The screening of the episode on national television was construed as part of the wider struggle against antisemitism and Holocaust denial in the country. Claims made by German individuals in South Africa, calling for the prevention of anti-German sentiments and protection within race relations between Jews and Germans, were rejected outright by the Jewish community.

Censoring Holocaust Denial under Apartheid

Immediately after the screening of the genocide episode, the nationalist newspaper *Die Afrikaner* published an Afrikaans translation of the English booklet titled "Did Six Million Really Die? The Truth at Last." The booklet was distributed to members of the defense force, the police, schools, and the public in city centers around the country.[93]

Written by Richard Verrall, one of the most notorious British Holocaust deniers, under the pseudonym Richard Harwood, this booklet belonged to a new type of Holocaust denial, emerging in the 1970s, which provided the link between conspiracy theories about Jews and virulent anti-Zionism. In many ways, the emergence of such publications preserved the atmosphere of siege and the fear of a second Holocaust, which characterized the period of the Six Day and Yom Kippur Wars in the Jewish world. As in other large Jewish communities, during the 1970s, the Holocaust and the State of Israel became a central part of the South African Jewish community's civil religion. The struggle against Holocaust denial was viewed as a struggle for Jewish survival, and the perception of the Holocaust as a unique and unprecedented event became the accepted perception in the Zionist world.[94]

Verrall himself was born in 1948 in England, and after a standard British education he obtained a history degree from Westfield College.[95] During the 1960s he was a member of the Conservative Party, though he left the party in the early 1970s to join the National Front (NF), a far-right, neo-Nazi political party. Verrall

---

[93] Diamond, "South Africa," 503–504.
[94] For further information on the emergence of Holocaust Uniqueness, see Novick, *The Holocaust in American Life*, 147–149.
[95] Deborah Lipstadt, *Denying the Holocaust: The Growing Assault on Truth and Memory* (New York: The Free Press, 1993), 104.

was also the editor of *Spearhead*, the NF magazine, and he produced a series of Holocaust denial works under the pseudonym Richard Harwood, beginning with the booklet in question, which first appeared in Britain in 1974.[96]

The booklet was published by the Historical Review Press in Brighton, owned by Robin Beauclair, a farmer with close affiliation to the NF and a friend of Anthony Hancock, the son of a Nazi sympathizer who was imprisoned during the Second World War.[97] At first, the publication was sent to all members of Parliament, leading journalists and scholars, as well as to prominent members of the British Jewish community. Soon, thousands of copies were printed in several languages, and the pamphlet was disseminated widely throughout Europe, the United States, and the Middle East.[98]

Verrall's text was the result of growing neo-fascist developments in Western Europe and particularly in England throughout that period.[99] Like many other Holocaust denial publications of that time, the booklet focused on refuting the central claims regarding the persecution and murder of European Jewry based on a selective review of German policy toward the Jews before and during the Second World War. It targeted various war crime trials, including the Nuremberg Trials, the Auschwitz Trials, and the Eichmann Trial, criticizing their legal integrity and the standards of evidence presented, as well as the judges' partiality. It also attempted to prove that it was statistically impossible for the Germans to kill six million Jews, arguing that the Jewish population in Nazi-controlled Europe never exceeded two and a half million.[100] Verrall claimed that the alleged exaggeration of the scale of the Holocaust by the Allies was meant to hide their guilt over their own human rights abuses, such as the dropping of atomic bombs on Japanese cities and the air raids of predominantly civilian towns such as Dresden in Germany. Moreover, he alleged that this exaggeration served as a pretext for the establishment of the state of Israel.[101]

The SAJBD struggle against the publication and distribution of Verrall's booklet serves as a fascinating case study for exploring the apartheid censorship

---

96 Stephan E. Atkins, *Holocaust Denial as an International Movement* (Westport, CT: Praeger, 2009), 117–118.
97 Michael Whine, "Holocaust Denial in the United Kingdom," in *Nationalist Myths and Modern Media: Contested Identities in the Age of Globalization*, ed. Jan Herman Brinks, Stella Rock, and Edward Timms (London: Tauris Academic Studies, 2005), 70.
98 Ray Hill and Andrew Bell, *The Other Face of Terror – Inside Europe's Neo-Nazi Network* (London: Grafton Books, 1988), 226–227.
99 To read more on global Holocaust denial during the 1960s and 1970s, see Lipstadt, *Denying the Holocaust*.
100 Atkins, *Holocaust Denial*, 118.
101 Hill and Bell, *The Other Face of Terror*, 226–227.

system, its insidious objectives, and thus its implications for the Jewish community. The monthly magazine *South African Observer* was keen to print parts of the booklet. This classic of Holocaust denial texts clearly suited the *Observer*'s conspiratorial worldview, which had been molded by its editor, Brown, well-known for his anti-Jewish views.[102] The publication of the notorious booklet in the *Observer* was supplemented to the aforementioned translation of parts of the booklet to Afrikaans, published in *Die Afrikaner*, also known for its promotion of antisemitic perspectives.

In June 1976 the SAJBD decided to appeal to the Publication Board regarding Verrall's booklet, arguing that it was "undesirable" according to section 10 (1)(a) of the 1974 Act, which refers to materials that are found to be "indecent or obscene or offensive or harmful to public morals."[103] The booklet was submitted to the relevant committee along with a letter from the Institute of Jewish Affairs located in London, an international Jewish research institute focusing on political, legal, and economic analysis of issues pertaining to Jewish life in the diaspora. The documents also included a press release from the British Jewish Board of Deputies that stated that the author of the booklet, Richard Harwood, did not exist and a letter from the University of London arguing that Harwood had never been attached to it.[104]

The SAJBD argued that the booklet's content was harmful and offensive for national public morals, thus attempting to define Holocaust denial as a national threat. However, the appointed committee which inspected the publication decided to ban the booklet on different grounds, arguing that it had no historical or scientific value, contained falsehoods, and was deeply insulting to sections of the population:

> The theme of the book is undesirable. It alleges that the stories regarding all that took place in the Jewish concentration camps during the last World War is in reality merely a plot to undermine all nationalism and a means for Israel to obtain money from Germany by bribery. The committee is of the opinion that the Jews in South Africa constitute a population group in terms of Article 47(2) (c) and (d).[105]

---

102 Shimoni, *Community and Conscience*, 72; Shain, "South Africa," 682.
103 "The Appeal That Failed – Special Report," *Jewish Affairs*, September 1977, 79–80, Jewish Studies Library and Research Resources, Kaplan Centre for Jewish Studies, University of Cape Town.
104 "Appeal – Banning of 'Did Six Million . . .'," *Citizen*, 23 June 1977, Press Items of Jewish Interest No. 13, Rochlin Archive, Johannesburg.
105 Attorneys for Appellant Couzyn, Herzof & Horak to the Clerk of Publications, "Appeal Board Regarding the Decisions of the Publication Act in the Appeal of: Helmuth Hansel (Appellant) and Committee of Publication (Respondent), Declaration," September 1976, 1, File 520.31, Rochlin Archive, Johannesburg.

The committee's decision not only reflected an acceptance of the Holocaust as a crucial part of Jewish collective memory and history. It also exemplified the perception of Jews under apartheid laws as a separate yet privileged ethnic, religious, and cultural group that must be protected through racial segregation.

The committee established that while "it might be argued that the figure of six million victims is too high," the booklet itself goes much further and denies that Nazi Germany perpetuated any planned violence against the Jews at all. "Such an argument endeavors to make liars of the whole of Jewry, including its representative organizations and the surviving family members of camp victims," stated the committee, condemning the booklet's content as blatantly antisemitic, which in addition made it undesirable in terms of Article 47(2)(e).[106] This Article refers to material that is prejudicial to the safety, the general welfare, or the peace and good order of the state. By defining the antisemitic message as a national threat, the committee marked an extraordinary achievement for South African Jewry – a clear declaration on the part of apartheid authorities that antisemitism was unacceptable. Again, through official national channels, the Jewish community publicly mediated the anti-antisemitic message of the Holocaust to local white communities as distinct from and completely irrelevant to local racism.

The committee also invoked Article 47(2)(c), which defined undesirable material as any such material that brings any section of the inhabitants of the Republic into ridicule or contempt, stating that "by alleging that Jews purposely spread false propaganda they are made to appear ludicrous and despicable." It also explained that "the real possibility that many South Africans will accept the book as the total truth and as a result thereof will bear ill will towards the Jewish community renders this book damaging of the relationship between the Jewish and the non-Jewish population groups of South Africa." Here, the committee invoked Article 47(2)(d), referring to the material's potential for being harmful to the relations between inhabitants of the Republic.[107]

---

106 Attorneys for Appellant Couzyn, Herzof & Horak to the Clerk of Publications, "Appeal Board Regarding the Decisions of the Publication Act in the Appeal of: Helmuth Hansel (Appellant) and Committee of Publication (Respondent), Declaration," September 1976, 1, File 520.31, Rochlin Archive, Johannesburg.
107 Attorneys for Appellant Couzyn, Herzof & Horak to the Clerk of Publications, "Appeal Board Regarding the Decisions of the Publication Act in the Appeal of: Helmuth Hansel (Appellant) and Committee of Publication (Respondent), Declaration," September 1976, 1–2, File 520.31, Rochlin Archive, Johannesburg.

The decision to ban the booklet appeared in many national newspapers.[108] While most reported positively on the banning decision, it was, unsurprisingly, condemned by others. *Die Afrikaner* reported:

> The latest episode in the six million legend was presented last week when the Publication Board banned a brochure entitled *Did Six Million Really Die?* as an undesirable publication and after this latest development it is obviously the South African Jewish Board of Deputies, which is having the most enjoyable laugh because it was especially that body which presented the strongest objection against the pressure in the press.[109]

It also stated that the booklet was a refutation of the lie of the Holocaust, exposed by irrefutable documentary proof.

The *Observer* printed a letter written by Brown in August 1976, addressed to the director of the Publication Board, demanding to know on what grounds the booklet was banned as "undesirable":

> We of the *South African Observer* find it strange that a booklet such as *Did Six Million Really Die?*, which clearly is an attempt to get to the facts of the matter – and written in the interests of historical truth, and for the sake of the future of western man – should be found by the Censor Board to be "undesirable," whereas the endless stream of blatant anti-German and anti-Western propaganda films flooding the country, month after month, year after year – thirty-one years after the end of World War II – are accepted as desirable by the same Board of Censors...[110]

In this letter, Brown announced: "we of the *South African Observer,* who have devoted time to research on the subject of the 'Six Million'," would appeal the ban to the Publications Appeal Board.[111]

Brown's letter also revealed the failed attempt by the British Jewish Board in 1974 to prosecute the author and the publishers of the booklet for "racial incitement" under the British Race Relations Act from 1965 and to have the booklet banned there. A report of the British Jewish Defence and Group Relations Committee meetings from the years 1973–1976 stated that a publication issued in July 1974 had been the subject of approaches to the Attorney General. The report mentioned that the booklet was published by the 'Historical Review

---

108 "Ban appeal postponed," *Rand Daily Mail*, 23 July 1976; "Twisoor publikasie na hof," ["Dispute over publication in court"] *Beeld*, 23 June 1977, File 520.31, Rochlin Archive, Johannesburg (translated by the author).
109 "Jewish Victory," *Die Afrikaner*, 30 July 1976, Press Items of Jewish Interest, No. 16, Rochlin Archive, Johannesburg (a translated collection).
110 "Letter from S.E.D. Brown," *South African Observer*, August 1976, Press Items of Jewish Interest, No. 17, Rochlin Archive, Johannesburg.
111 "Letter from S.E.D. Brown," *South African Observer*, August 1976, Press Items of Jewish Interest, No. 17, Rochlin Archive, Johannesburg.

Press' and written by Richard Harwood, a pseudonym for Robin Beauclair, who lived in Warwickshire and had NF connections. The report also argued that while Harwood claimed to have obtained his statistics from the Red Cross, the International Red Cross office in Geneva denied ever having given statistics of this kind.[112]

As stated in Brown's letter, the British Attorney General announced in July 1974 that the Jewish Board's request for persecution of the author and banning of the booklet was nonactionable under the Race Relations Acts.[113] But that was not the end of this fiasco in Britain. About two years later, the British *Observer* reported that thousands of copies of Verrall's booklet were being disseminated in British schools and being used in history lessons for 14-year-olds in a London girls' grammar school.[114]

A similar incident took place in Canada when in November 1983, Sabina Citron, then president of the Canadian Holocaust Remembrance Association, filed charges against Ernst Zundel in Toronto.[115] Zundel, a German immigrant and ardent Nazi, immigrated to Canada and settled in Montreal in 1958. He soon established links to the extremist Western Unity Movement and became an associate editor in the German magazine *Torontoer Zeitung*. Due to Zundel's low-scale distribution of neo-Nazi propaganda, he remained under the radar in Canada, which eventually allowed him to become the main disseminator of Holocaust denial material in the country in the late 1970s.[116]

The trail against Zundel opened in January 1985. The indictment focused on two separate charges involving the publication and distribution of two booklets: *The West, War and Islam* and *Did Six Million Really Die?* After thirty-eight days of proceedings, Zundel was convicted and sentenced to fifteen months in prison under Canada's Criminal Code for "publishing false news" and for "injury or mischief to a public interest" – in this case, to members of the Canadian

---

112 Board of Deputies of British Jews Annual Report 1972 and 1973–1976, Jewish Defence & Group Relations Committee, 32 Meetings Report, "Anti-Semitic Publications," 87, File 520.31, Rochlin Archive, Johannesburg.
113 Lionel Kochan and Miriam Kochan, "Western Europe–Great Britain," *American Jewish Yearbook* (1976): 287–302, at 300.
114 "World Jewish Congress Press Survey," 14 December 1976, File 520.31, Rochlin Archive, Johannesburg.
115 Alain Goldschlager, "The Trials of Ernst Zundel," in *Holocaust Denial: The Politics of Perfidy*, ed. Robert S. Wistrich (Berlin: De Gruyter, 2012), 111.
116 Ward Churchill, *A Little Matter of Genocide: Holocaust and Denial in the Americas 1492 to the Present* (San Francisco: City Lights Books, 1997), 23.

Jewish community who had survived the Holocaust or were relatives of the victims.[117]

Zundel won an appeal on procedural grounds but was charged again in 1988. He was again found guilty and sentenced to nine months in jail. He appealed to the Supreme Court, arguing that the Criminal Code infringed upon his freedom of expression, guaranteed under 5.2(b) of the Canadian Charter of Rights and Freedom. In 1992, the Canadian Supreme Court ruled that the section of the Criminal Code in question was indeed unconstitutional as it violated the right of freedom of expression. It stated that the code requires the expression to be violent, and the Court found the booklet to be nonviolent.[118]

In Germany, where publishing and distributing Holocaust denial literature was illegal, Zundel was convicted of inciting racial hatred for distributing "The Auschwitz Lie" video during a 1991 homeland visit and was ordered to pay a fine of approximately six thousand dollars.[119] He was finally deported to Germany in 2005 after the Canadian Federal Court ruled that he was a threat to national security. He was immediately arrested upon arrival in Germany.[120]

Back in South Africa, Brown and two other individuals, Helmuth Hansel, director of the League Against Anti-German Propaganda, and Dr. Hyacinth Josef Doussy, described in the press as a medical practitioner and director of companies, appealed the decision of the appointed committee to ban the booklet to the Publication Appeal Board. While the appeal itself was scheduled to take place on 27 June 1977, the appellants' attorneys submitted a written statement to the Clerk of Publications in Pretoria in September 1976. The first section of the statement focused on the reasons provided by the appointed committee for the banning order, presented in detail earlier. However, the second and main part of the statement included the appellants' arguments, which alleged that the committee's decision was groundless and incorrect.[121]

In their statement, the three argued that the booklet contained an academic, documented study, a "bona fide historical work," and accordingly fell

---

[117] E. Leonidas Hill, "The Trial of Ernst Zundel: Revisionism and the Law in Canada," *Simon Wiesenthal Annual* 6.7, Part 1, (1989).
[118] Nicholas j. Karolides and Margaret Vald, *Literature Suppressed on Political Grounds* (New York: Infobase Publishing, 2014), 149–150.
[119] Karolides and Vald, *Literature Suppressed on Political Grounds*, 149–150.
[120] CBC News, "Ernst Zundel Sentenced to 5 Years for Holocaust Denial," 15 February 2007, http://www.cbc.ca/news/world/ernst-zundel-sentenced-to-5-years-for-holocaust-denial-1.659372 [Accessed on 20 June 2017].
[121] Appeal Board Regarding the Decisions of the Publication Act in the Appeal of Helmuth Hansel (Appellant) and Committee of Publication (Respondent), September 1976, File 520.31, Rochlin Archive, Johannesburg.

outside the purview of the stated Articles. Therefore, they argued, the booklet should have been considered in terms of the definitions of Article 8(2)(b)(iii) of the Act, which focused on technical, scientific or professional publications.[122] They also rejected the committee's claim that Jews of South Africa constitute a population group as defined in Article 47(2)(c) and (d) of the Publication Act and stated, "if the Appeal Board finds that Jews in South Africa do constitute such a population group then the Appellant denies that such Jews are in any way implicated by the allegation of guilt [. . .] it is only the State of Israel and political Zionism which are affected."[123]

The appellants also argued that the additional documents submitted to the committee by the SAJBD together with the booklet itself were illegal in respect to case no. 6 – Brandwag Publications from April 1975 – in which the Appeal Board declared that letters from people in connection with a matter would not be admitted as evidence.[124] "It is submitted that the letter by the South African Jewish Board of Deputies, together with attached documents ought not to have been taken into account by the Respondent," the appellants posited, and suggested three other enclosed documents for the Appeal Board to explore in order to "better evaluate" the booklet, if the SAJBD's documents were in fact to be deemed permissible. Among the suggested reading materials, the appellants enclosed the notorious Holocaust denial essays, *The Drama of the European Jews* by Paul Rassinier; *The Hoax of the Twentieth Century* by Arthur Butz mentioned earlier in this chapter; and *The Auschwitz Lie* by Thies Christophersen.[125]

The appeal received support from different sections in white South African society. The South African Catholic Defence League published a statement of

---

[122] Appeal Board Regarding the Decisions of the Publication Act in the Appeal of Helmuth Hansel (Appellant) and Committee of Publication (Respondent), September 1976, 4, File 520.31, Rochlin Archive, Johannesburg.
[123] Appeal Board Regarding the Decisions of the Publication Act in the Appeal of Helmuth Hansel (Appellant) and Committee of Publication (Respondent), September 1976, 3–4, File 520.31, Rochlin Archive, Johannesburg.
[124] *Die Brandwag* became the first local magazine to be deemed undesirable by the new Appeal Board instated in 1974. The reason for the ban was the photograph of a women with exposed breasts on the cover; however, it is relevant to our case because it was in this context that the Publication Appeal Board established article 11(2)(b) declaring that an appointed committee shall without delay examine the publication without hearing any person directly related to the publication. To read more on *Die Brandwag* ban see Pieter B. Geldenhuÿs, *Pornografie, sensuur en reg [Pornography, Censorship and Law]* (Johannesburg: Lex Patria, 1977).
[125] Appeal Board Regarding the Decisions of the Publication Act in the Appeal of Helmuth Hansel (Appellant) and Committee of Publication (Respondent), September 1976, 4, File 520.31, Rochlin Archive, Johannesburg.

support to voice their objections against the banning of the booklet in the interest of historical truth and argued that "any action exposing the hoax of the 'Six Million' is necessary and highly welcome."[126] Another voice in support of the appeal came from members of the Soldiers of the Cross organization, which in a letter to the South African Board of Censors expressed their "utter disgust" at what they saw as the board's bowing to Jewish pressure in the case of banning the booklet.[127]

In December of that year, the appointed committee submitted its detailed response to the appellants' statement: "The one-sidedness of the publication, the contentious un-academic language and the doubtful academic qualification as historian of the writer renders the publication undeserving of the description 'Historical Factual Research.'"[128] Regarding the definition of the Jewish community within apartheid legislation, the committee made it clear that it perceived the Jews as a separate social, religious, and cultural group:

> On the one hand, Jewry is considered to be a racial group and on the other hand, it is considered as a religious group, or as a combination of both. In South Africa, they are certainly considered to be a population group whose own religious, educational, and cultural rights are recognized. In like manner, Christian, Afrikaners, and Xhosas are considered to be population groups.[129]

This perception of the Jewish community was followed by the recognition that numerous South African Jews had family members who were victims of Nazism. Jewish suffering during the Holocaust therefore was considered part of the South African Jews' cultural and historical background. The committee again defined the booklet as "exaggerated antisemitism, which is a danger to the State," and emphasized that some of its arguments were inconsistent with the truth and promoted hostility.

Referring to the appellants' claim of the illegality of the committee's decision due to its consideration of the letter from the SAJBD and the two attached documents, the committee proclaimed, "The documents were of benefit to the committee because inter alia they indicated (a) that the allegation [. . .] that the writer was attached to the University of London is untrue, and (b) that the

---

[126] "Support for Appeal," *South African Observer*, September 1976, Press Items of Jewish Interest, No. 19, Rochlin Archive, Johannesburg.
[127] A letter from Soldiers of the Cross to the South African Board of Censors, File 520.31, Rochlin Archive, Johannesburg.
[128] "In the Appeal Board for Publication – Response to Declaration," 1, File 520.31, Rochlin Archive, Johannesburg.
[129] "In the Appeal Board for Publication – Response to Declaration," 1–2, File 520.31, Rochlin Archive, Johannesburg.

allegation concerning the statistics of the Red Cross is untrue." Such documents enabled the committee to better evaluate the booklet and therefore were not considered the kind of letters to which the Brandwag Publication matter referred, it declared.[130]

On 27 June 1977, the proceedings came before the Publication Appeal Board. At the hearing, Judge Snyman, after listening to the appellants' counsel's claims of irregularities, ruled against the appeal but granted the appellants the right to turn to the Supreme Court for a review.[131] After receiving such a detailed report from the committee, it is not surprising that Judge Snyman did not second the committee's decision. However, by granting the appellants the right to appeal to the Supreme Court, Snyman bypassed the Publication Act of 1974, which abolished all judicial supervision in the establishment of the Appeal Board.

This action can be interpreted as Snyman's attempt to abdicate responsibility for ruling on the subject. While a committee, which was supposed to be professional, examined the booklet and found it to be undesirable according to the provisions of the Publication Act, and while Snyman himself ruled against the appeal on the committee's decision, the appellants were given another channel of action, one that should have been officially blocked according to the law – the Supreme Court.

As the appellants lodged an urgent appeal to the Supreme Court in Pretoria, the South African press began to engage with the upcoming trial. The *Sunday Express* printed an article on 4 September 1977, titled "Amazing Nazi Trial for Pretoria," which stated that "the most extraordinary trial of modern times will take place in Pretoria when a court is asked to adjudicate on whether the Nazis really did exterminate six million Jews or not." The newspaper defined the appeal as a possible "little Nuremberg trial" in Pretoria and stated that "the South African Jewish Board of Deputies sent a special emissary to Britain, Germany, Israel, and other countries to assist in compiling evidence to support the ban."[132]

Indeed, in preparing for the appeal hearing, the SAJBD decided that it would be essential to present certain evidence before the Court. Legally, the board had no *locus standi* at the hearing of the appeal, and the only accepted evidence in such proceedings was in the form of affidavits. To secure such evidence, the board appointed Arthur Suzman, who was for many years chairman of the Public

---

[130] "In the Appeal Board for Publication – Response to Declaration," File 520.31, Rochlin Archive, Johannesburg.
[131] "Appeal – Banning of 'Did Six Million . . .'," *Citizen*, 23 June 1977, Press Items of Jewish Interest No. 13, Rochlin Archive, Johannesburg.
[132] "Amazing Nazi Trial for Pretoria," *Sunday Express*, 4 September 1977, File 520.31, Rochlin Archive, Johannesburg.

Relations Committee of the SAJBD, and Denis Diamond, SAJBD executive director, as chief investigators. Their aim, as described in the September 1977 issue of *Jewish Affairs*, was "firstly, to expose the falsehoods and dishonest techniques employed by the author of the publication . . . and secondly, to place before the Appeal Board certain basic and authoritative facts relating to the Holocaust."[133]

Suzman and Diamond's journey began in Israel, where they interviewed various Holocaust survivors alongside prominent figures such as Gideon Hausner, who, as attorney general of Israel, was the prosecutor at the Eichmann Trial, and Brigadier General Yitzhak Arad, director-general of the World Holocaust Remembrance Center, Yad Vashem in Jerusalem. They also examined the records of the Eichmann Trial and made extensive use of the comprehensive library and archives on the Holocaust available at Yad Vashem.[134]

The two continued to England where they conducted interviews with Lord Elwyn-Jones, who was the Lord Chancellor from 1974 to 1979 and who had been one of the prosecutors at the Nuremberg Trials. Among other encounters, they took an affidavit from Hitler's Minister of Armaments Albert Speer, who had been sentenced to twenty years imprisonment at the Nuremberg Trials. The interviews and affidavits described above are only a small part of the extensive work done by Suzman and Diamond, which eventually found expression in the founding affidavit of the SAJBD.[135]

The appeal was due to be heard on 11 September 1977. However, on the eve of the hearing, the appellants withdrew their appeal, and the ban on the booklet remained in force.[136] After the withdrawal, Brown alleged that the State censors were influenced by Jewish pressure groups to ban the pro-Nazi publication. He told the *Sunday Express* that the appeal was withdrawn solely because he and the other two appellants did not have the financial resources to pursue the

---

[133] "The Appeal That Failed – Special Report," *Jewish Affairs*, September 1977, 83, Jewish Studies Library and Research Resources, Kaplan Centre for Jewish Studies, University of Cape Town.
[134] "The Appeal That Failed – Special Report," *Jewish Affairs*, September 1977, 83, Clippings Collection, Jewish Studies Library and Research Resources, Kaplan Centre for Jewish Studies, University of Cape Town.
[135] "The Appeal That Failed – Special Report," *Jewish Affairs*, September 1977, 81–83, Clippings Collection, Jewish Studies Library and Research Resources, Kaplan Centre for Jewish Studies, University of Cape Town.
[136] "The Appeal That Failed – Special Report," *Jewish Affairs*, September 1977, 80, Clippings Collection, Jewish Studies Library and Research Resources, Kaplan Centre for Jewish Studies, University of Cape Town.

case.[137] The *Sunday Times* reported that in an interview Doussy stated that he did not deny that six million Jews had died in Europe during the Second World War, but that he did not believe that this number had been killed by Germans in concentration camps. "One of the reasons why I appealed against the banning is that I do not believe scientific books should be banned," he argued.[138]

Since the legal proceedings were canceled, the SAJBD decided that the mass of evidence prepared to defend the banning of the booklet would be published in a 120-page publication entitled *Six Million Did Die: The Truth Shall Prevail*. On 18 September 1977, the *Sunday Express* reported, "Jewish bodies abroad, particularly in English-speaking countries, are keenly awaiting the book, which they hope to use to counter a wide front of pro-Nazi literature."[139] The book was launched by the Jewish Board in October of that year in a worldwide campaign aimed at discrediting extreme antisemitic organizations which were waging a propaganda battle against the facts of the Nazi genocide.[140]

By publishing the collected evidence as a book, the SAJBD aimed at refuting not only Verrall's booklet but all infamous attempts "on the part of some writers and small anti-Semitic movements to deny the guilt of the Nazis in the worst historical crime ever committed, with the annihilation of millions of Jews during the Hitler period."[141] The SAJBD publication called for a global effort to learn from past experiences of antisemitism that such manifestations of hatred have the capability to spread rapidly and to become a menace to all mankind.[142]

This case is yet another expression of the ways in which the rise of global antisemitism induced in South African Jews a deep need for specific forms of self-representation. The repressive apparatus of state censorship in South Africa formed one of the core pillars of the country's racial administration. Ironically, this system was used by the official Jewish community in South

---

[137] "Nazi death camps: Brown hits back," *Sunday Express*, 11 September 1977, File 520.31, Rochlin Archive, Johannesburg.
[138] "Nazi Backers drop Banned Book Appeal," *Sunday Times*, 4 September 1977, File 520.31, Rochlin Archive, Johannesburg.
[139] "Publication of Book," *Sunday Express*, 18 September 1977, File 520.31, Rochlin Archive, Johannesburg.
[140] "Board Publishes Rebuttal of 'Did Six Million . . .'" *Sunday Tribune*, 16 October 1977, File 520.31, Rochlin Archive, Johannesburg.
[141] Arthur Suzman and Denis Diamond, *Six Million Did Die: the truth shall prevail* (Johannesburg: SAJBD, 1977), xii.
[142] Suzman and Diamond, *Six Million Did Die: the truth shall prevail*, xii.

Africa for the purpose of countering the racism inherent in discourses of Holocaust denial as these circulated through the print media in South Africa.

Anne Frank: The Diary of a Young Girl in Afrikaans

In April 1977, when the appeal against the banning of Verrall's booklet was still unresolved, extreme right-wing circles declared *Anne Frank: The Diary of a Young Girl* a forgery, basing their claims on a sub-section entitled "Best-Seller-A Hoax," in Verrall's booklet. There he described *The Diary* as a worrying example of how myth is produced through propaganda.[143] The claims were made in response to the decision of the Performing Art Council of the Transvaal (PACT) to produce a play based on *The Diary* in Afrikaans.[144]

Despite the dazzling success of the English adaptation of *The Diary* in South Africa during the 1950s, described in chapter 2 of this book, it took almost two decades before *The Diary* was first translated into Afrikaans. In 1972 Fred Nel translated *The Diary* and adapted it for the stage, to be produced at Stellenbosch University in May-June of that year. During the Second World War, Stellenbosch University became fertile ground for anti-British, pro-Nazi and antisemitic expression. It had ties to the formulation of apartheid ideology and the formalization of Afrikaans as an academic language and was thus central to the cultivation of Afrikaner nationalism during the apartheid years. Therefore, the translation of *The Diary* into Afrikaans and its stage adaptation at Stellenbosch University can be interpreted as another expression of the withdrawal of Afrikaner nationalism from antisemitic positions and the recognition of the traumatic Jewish history of the Holocaust.

Another indication of a more inclusive approach towards Jewish history came five years later when, in 1977, the National Education Department decided to include *The Diary* in the recommended reading list in Afrikaner public high-schools in the Transvaal area.[145] At that time, Afrikaner national education provided a major agenda for South African theaters and for PACT, a government-funded body established in Pretoria in January 1963 with the aim of replacing the National Theatre Organization. Hans Horne from the

---

[143] Richard Harwood, "Best-Seller- A Hoax," in *Did Six Million Really Die? The Truth at Last* (London: Historical Review Press, 1974), 28.
[144] "Nastiness over Anne Frank Play," *Die Afrikaner*, 15 April 1977, Press Items of Jewish Interest, No. 9, Rochlin Archive, Johannesburg (a translated collection).
[145] Percy Baneshik, "Theatre," in *South African Jewry: A Contemporary Survey*, ed. Marcus Arkin (Cape Town: Oxford University Press, 1984), 91–92.

Department of Drama Studies at the University of Pretoria was commissioned by PACT to translate *The Diary* into Afrikaans in April 1977, and the Jewish director and producer, Leonard Schach, was invited to produce it for the stage. In his autobiographical account *The Flag is Flying* (1996), Schach recalled,

> I was invited by PACT to direct an Afrikaans-language production in the Transvaal. *The Diary* was actually a prescribed reading in Afrikaans-language Government schools and the production was to be toured through high schools all over the Transvaal. For these unusual circumstances I could not but accept, however personally harrowing it was going to be to work on this material for a second time. I gladly cancelled theatre work in Israel, where I was now living, in order to direct for my old associates at PACT.[146]

PACT was established to further the development and promotion of drama, ballet, music, and opera throughout the Transvaal area. It aimed at expressing the vitality of the country's artistic life and cultural ambitions in a way that largely reflected the Afrikaner nationalist agenda. PACT played a key institutional role in Afrikaner nationalism: an examination report from 1977 defined the theatre as central to the promotion of national education, national language, and national identity.[147]

It is worth noting that alongside the Afrikaner dominance at PACT there was considerable Jewish involvement in theater in general and in PACT in particular. Many South African Jews had been actively involved in local theaters as playwrights, actors, or producers, or in behind-the-scenes or administrative and fundraising roles.[148] Schach was one such figure in the theatre industry: a leading theatrical director and producer in the late 1940s who emigrated to Israel in 1965 to join the Cameri theater as a guest director. His English production of *The Diary* for South African audiences in 1957 broke every box-office and other theatre record at the time. Considering the Jewish involvement in the theatre world and in PACT in particular, as well as the governmental decision to include *The Diary* in the recommended reading list for public Afrikaner high schools in the Transvaal area, Schach was indeed the perfect choice for the task of staging the play in Afrikaans.[149]

---

[146] Leonard Schach, *The Flag is Flying: A Very Personal History of Theatre in the Old South Africa* (Cape Town,: Human Rousseau, 1996), 90–91.

[147] For more information on PACT see Loren Kruger, *The Drama of South Africa: Plays, Pageants and Publics Since 1910* (London: Routledge, 2005), 96–100.

[148] Baneshik, "Theatre," 160.

[149] Schach, *The Flag is Flying*, 91–92.

Verrall was not the first to spread the claim that *The Diary* was a forgery. The first allegations against the authenticity of *The Diary* appeared in Swedish and Danish newspapers in the late 1950s, where claims were made that the American journalist and novelist Meyer Levin was the real author of the diary. Similar allegations appeared in numerous publications on the matter emerging throughout the 1970s, including Verrall's notorious booklet.[150]

When Levin first read *The Diary* in its French edition in August 1950, he wrote to Otto Frank, asking if he could help arrange American publication rights for it. He also offered to translate *The Diary* and later expressed interest in adapting it for the stage and screen. Levin's draft of a stage adaptation was rejected by Otto Frank and the successful play that eventually opened on Broadway in 1955 was written by Frances Goodrich and Albert Hackett.

In 1952 Levin filed a lawsuit that was not settled until 1959. The bitter legal battle that ensued lasted no less than twenty-five years and ended only with the deaths of those involved. The disagreement between Levin and Frank had to do with the extent of Anna Frank's Jewish identity in the diary: while for Levin, Anne Frank symbolized the six million innocent Jews who were slaughtered solely because they were Jewish, for Otto Frank, a German assimilated Jew, Anne's story was not only a Jewish story but a universal one. He therefore preferred the universal message of Hackett and Goodrich's version, where less emphasis was placed on the horrors of the Holocaust. The conflict between Levin and Frank reached the press and was used by right-wing extremists to call the authenticity of the diary into question.[151]

In Pretoria, the condemnation of *The Diary* by local right-wing circles was widely reported in the national press. *Die Afrikaner* reported: "it is shocking that PACT resorted to a translated piece such as *The Diary of Anne Frank* [. . .] PACT was established and is kept in existence by taxpayers' money to promote Afrikaans theatre. Performances such as the one that is now being staged in Afrikaans make a mockery of the purpose for which PACT came into existence."[152] This statement not only defined Afrikaner nationalism but also excluded Jews from national resources aimed at investing in Afrikaner culture. *The Citizen, Die*

---
150 Dina Porat, "1958–1998, מערכה בת ארבעים שנה- יומנה של אנה פרנק ומכחישי השואה," ["A Forty-Year Struggle: Anne Frank's Diary and the Holocaust Deniers, 1958–1998,"] in ספר יובל ליהודה השואה: הייחודי והאוניברסלי, באואר, [*The Holocaust, History and Memory: Essays Presented in Honor of Yhuda Bauer*] ed. Shmuel Almog, David Bankier, Daniel Blatman, and Dalia Ofer (Jerusalem: The Hebrew University of Jerusalm Press, 2001), 176.
151 Porat, "מערכה בת ארבעים שנה" ["A Forty-Year Struggle,"] 160–183.
152 "Nastiness over Anne Frank Play," *Die Afrikaner*, 15 April 1977, Press Items of Jewish Interest No. 9, Rochlin Archive, Johannesburg (a translated collection).

Beeld, and *Die Hoofstad* further reported that the word "lies" and drawing of swastikas had been scrawled on posters advertising the play.[153]

Eghard van der Hoven, director of PACT, said, "the complaints are similar to those from the *World at War*," arguing that some people cannot accept that the Holocaust took place. "The play is a very heart-rending production, but it is sad to realize that humanity has not learnt its lesson. The same oppression and suppression are going on," he said. Van der Hoven told the press that while several phone calls had been received by PACT claiming that the diary was forged, he had no concerns about the intervention of the censors.[154]

The SAJBD published an official statement on the subject, expressing its amazement that a play based on *The Diary* could provoke such controversy, when it had gained world-wide acceptance, even in Germany. "Those who rely on the so-called forgery base themselves on a single American court case [. . .] They attach no importance to the authenticity of *The Diary* itself or any attempt by the Nazis to exterminate the entire Jewish community," it stated, while pressing the entire South African public to summarily reject such stands.[155] Nevertheless, Schach recalled, "the play aroused tremendous and sympathetic public interest wherever we played it in South Africa and its sad and tragic subject matter was able to attract large attendances."[156] Indeed, the translation of *The Diary* to Afrikaans, its inclusion in the recommended reading list for public Afrikaner high schools in the Transvaal area, and its dramatization by the Afrikaner national theatre provide yet another indication of the mainstream Afrikaner acceptance of the Jewish tragedy. However, while the Holocaust was foregrounded by the apartheid government, antisemitic sentiments persisted in some quarters of white society, preserving a limited discomfort for South African Jews.

---

153 Bill Edgson, "Afrikaans 'Anne' excels," Citizen, 25 April 1977; "Anne Frank bring begrip vir medemens," ["Anne Frank brings understanding to fellow human beings"] *Die Hoofstad*, 26 April 1977, File Anne Frank 199, Rochlin Archive, Johannesburg (translated by the author); *Beeld*, 26 April 1977, Press Items of Jewish Interest No. 9, Rochlin Archive, Johannesburg (a translated collection).

154 Bill Edgson, "Afrikaans 'Anne' excels," *Citizen*, 25 April 1977, File Anne Frank 199, Rochlin Archive, Johannesburg.

155 "Anne Frank bring begrip vir medemens," ["Anne Frank brings understanding to fellow human beings"] *Die Hoofstad*, 26 April 1977, File Anne Frank 199, Rochlin Archive, Johannesburg (translated by the author).

156 Schach, *The Flag is Flying*, 92.

Holocaust Miniseries in South Africa

In April 1978, the American network NBC televised the five-part miniseries *Holocaust: The Story of the Family Weiss*, directed by Robert Berger and based on Gerald Green's script. It dramatizes some of the main events of the Holocaust such as "Kristallnacht," ghettoization, and the concentration and death camps, through the experiences of two families – the German-Jewish Weiss family, and the German Dorf family – in which the father is a leading member of the SS who gradually becomes a ruthless war criminal.[157] NBC devoted much effort to promoting the series as a cultural event, including the launching of a massive advertising campaign to increase its ratings. The network also released one million copies of instructional leaflets to be distributed by educators as well as Christian and Jewish organizations, aimed at preparing American viewers for what was to be a national television event. Green, the screenwriter, also wrote a prose version of the series, a million copies of which were printed two weeks before the series aired. It is estimated that about a hundred and twenty million viewers watched the miniseries in the United States, about half of the country's population at the time.[158]

As mentioned briefly in the introductory chapter, most scholars focusing on Holocaust memory consider the broadcasting of the miniseries to be the beginning of the Americanization of the Holocaust. As described in *The New York Times* on 16 April 1978, the miniseries exposed the American audience to "the calculated brutality of the killers, the silent agony of the victims, and to the indifference of the outside world."[159] However, such images of the Holocaust, presented on commercial television, raised a stormy discussion among Holocaust survivors in America. Elie Wiesel argued: "Untrue, offensive, cheap: as a TV production, the film an insult to those who perished and to those who survived. [In] Spite of its name, this 'docu-drama' is not about what some of us remember as the Holocaust."[160] John O'Connor, *The New York Times* TV critic, added that the anomalous mixture of commercial breaks with historical tragedy contributed to a diminishment of the event. Frank Rich, a *Time* columnist, on the other hand, defended the miniseries for its educational implications and argued, "*Holocaust* does a lot to increase our comprehension of its unfathomable subject [. . .] it envelops the audience in grief and suffering, and long after the show has ended, the pain does not easily go away."[161]

---

157 Dreisbach, "Transatlantic Broadcasts," 76.
158 Dreisbach, "Transatlantic Broadcasts," 77–82.
159 Elie Wiesel, "TV View," *New York Times*, 16 April 1978.
160 Elie Wiesel, "TV View," *New York Times*, 16 April 1978.
161 Dreisbach, "Transatlantic Broadcasts," 84.

In Canada too, reactions to the miniseries ran the gamut from negative to extremely positive. Several Canadians of German descent felt the series did them an injustice and some Nazi supporters claimed that the events depicted in it were either grossly exaggerated or had never really happened. Others, among them several Holocaust survivors, felt that the events shown on television came nowhere near the actual horrors of the Holocaust. Criticism was levelled at several historical inaccuracies and the opinion was voiced that NBC should have consulted survivors in order to authenticate various details. By and large, however, the reaction was extremely positive. The Canadian National Holocaust Remembrance Committee received letters and phone calls from community leaders, teachers, rabbis, survivors, and people of all ages, commending the fact that the events of the Holocaust had finally been brought to the attention of the world. The miniseries had a profound effect on a large portion of the two and a half million Canadians who watched it.[162]

In South Africa, the miniseries made headlines even before it was first screened there. In April 1978, the *Pretoria News* reported, "America is turning its attention to antisemitism this week as 'Holocaust,' a harrowing and controversial dramatization of the extermination of the Jews by the Nazis, unfolds over four nights on national television."[163] A few months later, the Holocaust was once again placed under the magnifying glass of apartheid censorship system when Hymie Segal, director of the distribution company Premier Production, submitted the miniseries for examination by the Directorate of Publications, in order to attain the censors' approval for its release in South Africa on the home movie and video cassette markets.[164]

Cape Argus reported on 27 June 1978, "Holocaust, America's most widely viewed television show this year, has been passed by the South African censors with a two to 12 years age restriction and three minor cuts."[165] These cuts included a two-second full frontal of naked Jewish women on their way to being shot, and a short scene of naked women on their way to the gas chambers. A scene where three Jews are beaten by Nazis for refusing to disclose information was cut by half.

---

[162] The National Holocaust Remembrance Committee, The Canadian Jewish Congress, "NBCTV's Series Holocaust: a Canadian Reaction," 17 April 1978, Films Press Cuttings Collection, Rochlin Archive, Johannesburg.

[163] "Nazi Camp Horror for US Viewers," *Pretoria News*, 18 April 1978, Films Press Cuttings Collection, Rochlin Archive, Johannesburg.

[164] "Holocaust TV Series," *Cape Argus*, 27 June 1978, Films Press Cuttings Collection, Rochlin Archive, Johannesburg.

[165] "Holocaust TV Series," *Cape Argus*, 27 June 1978, Films Press Cuttings Collection, Rochlin Archive, Johannesburg.

Two weeks before the censors' decisions were published and after ascertaining that a commercial organization known as Premier Productions was distributing the film, *Die Afrikaner* wrongly reported that "the strange situation has now arisen in South Africa that the two Jewish organizations are actually acting as film distributors to show an anti-German propaganda film here." The paper called for a ban of the miniseries due to past experiences with similar films whose content was offensive to a section of the South African population and which, therefore, in terms of the stipulations of the Publications Act ought to be declared undesirable material. It criticized the Jewish leaders in South Africa for promoting anti-German propaganda and concluded that "The new film [. . .] is just a repetition of the favorite and already done-to-death theme of alleged 'Nazi atrocities' during the Second World War."[166]

The tabloid-style newspaper *The Citizen* reported on the miniseries from 3 July 1978, also criticizing the censors' decision and referring to *Holocaust* as "ethnic TV" which carried the potential to widen race rifts in the country. It compared the two canonical American series of the late 1970s, *Roots* and *Holocaust*, stating, "it all began with 'Roots', the TV phenomenon which raised black pride and made white Americans more guilt-ridden than ever before [. . .] The Americans, quick to catch on to the fact that money is to be made out of similar programmes, rapidly followed up with another ethnic series – 'Holocaust'."[167]

The *Roots* miniseries dealt with the chronicles of an African-American family from slavery to the early twentieth century and had significant impact on American society's awareness of African-American history and culture. It was produced as an eight-episode series that aired for eight days between 23 and 30 January 1977 on the ABC network and broke racial viewing patterns in America. *The Citizen* reported that the two series had earned the reputation of being the greatest series ever to be screened on television and that "people all over the world are being given the opportunity to relive the nightmare lives of the black slaves and of the Jews." In South Africa, however, viewers were not able to share in this world experience due to the SABC-TV decision not to purchase the miniseries, stated *The Citizen*, praising the Broadcasting corporation for its caution.[168]

Indeed, although the *Holocaust* miniseries was eventually approved for home use and public screenings by the South African censors, SABC-TV announced that

---

166 *Die Afrikaner*, 16 June 1978, Press Items of Jewish Interest No. 12, Rochlin Archive, Johannesburg (a translated collection).
167 "'Ethnic TV' Would Widen Race Rifts," *Citizen*, 3 July 1978, Films Press Cuttings Collection, Rochlin Archive, Johannesburg.
168 "'Ethnic TV' Would Widen Race Rifts," *Citizen*, 3 July 1978, Films Press Cuttings Collection, Rochlin Archive, Johannesburg.

it had no intention of screening the series on national television.[169] A week later, the *Jewish Herald* stated that SABC refused to buy the series "on the grounds of having a surplus of war films and documentaries."[170] However, it is safe to assume that the SABC-TV decision was directly related to the public debate surrounding the screening of the genocide episode of *The World at War* two years earlier.

Referring to *Holocaust* and *Roots*, *The Citizen* report noted that broadcasting such series would undoubtedly lead to unease among various racial groups in the country. However, the report made a clear distinction between the two above mentioned miniseries: while *Roots* was described as stereotypical – "The blacks were all portrayed as good and suffering, the whites as wicked and prosperous" – *Holocaust* was described as based on "more fact than fiction." Nonetheless, the paper stated that *Holocaust* should not be screened to people on a nationwide basis if there were any chance that it would incite racial fear and hatred. "While this possibility exists, the watching of *Holocaust* should be left to the free choice of individuals," concluded the report.[171] It is not surprising that the series dealing with black slavery in America was presented in the South African press as a distortion of history and as undesirable content. However, the exclusion of *Holocaust*, which focuses almost entirely on Jewish victimhood in Nazi Germany, prevented the representation of the lengthy narrative of the Holocaust to the white communities in South Africa.

Despite SABC-TV's decision not to broadcast the series on national television, public interest in *Holocaust* was considerable. The premiere was held at Johannesburg's President Hotel on 12 July and *The Star* reported that the first screening in South Africa was for charity.[172] Another public screening was held by the Natal Society of Arts at Natal University in Durban on two separate occasions in September;[173] and a closed-circuit screening of the whole miniseries over two nights was held at the Heerengracht Hotel in Cape Town.[174]

---

169 "Sensors sny Joodse skokprent," ["Sensors cut Jewish film"] *Beeld*, 27 June 1978, Films Press Cuttings Collection, Rochlin Archive, Johannesburg (translated by the author).
170 "South Africans can see 'Holocaust'," *Jewish Herald*, 4 July 1978, Films Press Cuttings Collection, Rochlin Archive, Johannesburg.
171 "South Africans can see 'Holocaust'," *Jewish Herald*, 4 July 1978, Films Press Cuttings Collection, Rochlin Archive, Johannesburg.
172 "Holocaust Helps Out," *The Star*, 30 June 1978, Films Press Cuttings Collection, Rochlin Archive, Johannesburg.
173 "Durban Showing for 'Holocaust,'" *Mercury*, 19 August 1978, Films Press Cuttings Collection, Rochlin Archive, Johannesburg.
174 "Extended," *Cape Times*, 4 August 1978, Films Press Cuttings Collection, Rochlin Archive, Johannesburg.

Cape Argus film critic Garth Verdal noted: "*Holocaust*, which cost about 4.3-million Rands, is emotionally pulverizing. It is also extremely well-acted with three dimensional, un-stereotyped performances, directed with realism and softened by melodramatic touch."[175] Nevertheless, for the Jewish community, the main discourse surrounding the miniseries concentrated on the criticism raised by American Holocaust survivors. The *Jewish Herald* reported that viewers agreed that the miniseries "merited the criticism many Jews – foremost among them Elie Wiesel – have levelled against it: that it is superficial, commercial, Hollywoodian in parts and that it can never be accepted as portraying the grim reality."[176] In a long commentary in the *Jewish Affairs* August 1978 issue, Diamond related to Wiesel's critique when he referred to the miniseries as "indecent and emotionally exploitative" and argued that it is "unforgivable that the TV mini-series *Holocaust* was ever put together." He claimed that "Melodrama is a legitimate art form, but not for all subjects," and concluded that "this film should never have been made."[177]

Diamond's response should be read in light of the turmoil that erupted following the advertising campaign launched in July 1978 by Premier Productions, which featured a photograph depicting the anguish of Jews captured by Nazis, captioned "Holocaust: With a cast of six million Jews." As reported in the *Sunday Express*, the campaign was condemned by many Rabbis, Jewish educators, and community leaders as tasteless and offensive. All agreed that the ad reflected private commercial enterprise, and Franz Auerbach, chairman of the South African National Yad Vashem Foundation and himself a Holocaust survivor, claimed that the wording of the advertisement was "offensive to all civilized people" and called for an apology. Rabbi Jonathan Mielke from the Reformed Temple Israel congregation in Hillbrow, Johannesburg also argued that it was "absolutely horrendous" and called for an appeal to be made to the censors to strike out its wording. "Imagine what the reaction from the Afrikaans community would be if one had to show a film about concentration camps in the Boer War and advertise the victims as the cast," he proclaimed.[178]

---

[175] "Holocaust: Pulverizing Experience," *Cape Argus*, 7 July 1978, Films Press Cuttings Collection, Rochlin Archive, Johannesburg.
[176] "Holocaust," *Jewish Herald*, 4 July 1978, Films Press Cuttings Collection, Rochlin Archive, Johannesburg.
[177] Denis Diamond, "Trivialising the Tragedy," *Jewish Affairs*, August 1978, 24–26, Clippings Collection, Jacob Gitlin Jewish Library, Cape Town.
[178] Clare Stern, "Insults Memory of Martyrs: Holocaust ad in Shocking Taste," *Sunday Express*, 30 July 1978, 12, Films Press Cuttings Collection, Rochlin Archive, Johannesburg.

Segal, head of marketing at Premiere Productions, told the newspaper that he would take immediate steps to have the offensive wording struck off. "Personally, I don't believe they [the ads] are offensive. The entire story revolves round those six million Jews who died in the Holocaust," he asserted. However, he denied that his company had hoped to increase their profit by sensationalizing the ad. "We have already had two premiere release shows of *Holocaust* and the tickets were sold exclusively for charity," he reminded, adding that the company also organized free screenings for the SAJBD and the SAZF.[179]

Interestingly, the miniseries was also screened for black political prisoners of the apartheid regime imprisoned on Robben Island, as evidenced in a letter written from prison by Ahmed Kathrada, the South African Indian youth leader and anti-apartheid activist whose life story is the focus of Chapter 7. Kathrada, who was imprisoned during the Rivonia Trial of 1964,[180] spent eighteen years on Robben Island, where he served as the librarian and head of the cultural committee from the late 1970s. As the prison's librarian, he ordered books and films for the use of the prisoners. In a letter written on 19 January 1980 to his friend Bob Vassen, a member of the ANC living at the time in exile in London, Kathrada told of the screening of the American miniseries on Robben Island, describing the emotions he felt while watching it:

> Many young people, especially those who were born after the war, find it hard to believe that *Holocaust* [the miniseries] was by and large based on historical fact. Indeed, I've read magazine articles which dismiss the happenings as propaganda. And this only after one generation! How can people have such short memories! This film, with all the reservations one may have, is a necessary reminder.[181]

Katrhada's testimony is a unique piece of evidence for the reception of the miniseries among communities outside the confines of the white public in South Africa. It invites further investigation into the ways in which the Holocaust was perceived and reflected upon by members of the black, Indian and Coloured communities. The next four chapters will tease out some of the engagements of black South African leaders with the traumatic memories of the Holocaust, on different levels and at various historical moments.

---

179 Clare Stern, "Insults Memory of Martyrs: Holocaust ad in Shocking Taste," *Sunday Express*, 30 July 1978, 12, Films Press Cuttings Collection, Rochlin Archive, Johannesburg.

180 The Rivonia Trial took place in Pretoria between 9 October 1963 and 12 June 1964. Ten leading opponents of apartheid were charged on two counts of sabotage and were sentenced to life imprisonment.

181 Robert D. Vassen, *Letters from Robben Island: A Selection of Ahmed Kathrada's Prison Correspondence 1964–1989* (Cape Town: Mayibuye Books, 1999), 118.

Chapter 5
Anne Frank in South Africa – Between the Communal and the National

The first democratic general elections in South Africa were held on 27 April 1994. Three months later, on 15 August, the newly elected President, Nelson Mandela, received the Anne Frank Medal for Human Rights and Tolerance at the opening of the exhibition *Anne Frank in the World, 1929–1945* (AFWE) in Johannesburg, held at Museum Africa.[1] As a joint project of the Anne Frank House (AFH) in Amsterdam, the SAJBD, and the Dutch Embassy in Pretoria, the traveling exhibition toured major city centers throughout the country between March 1994 and September 1995 and was visited by high school students as well as by the general public. As Gilbert argues,

> Though the 1994 exhibition was proposed originally by the Jewish community, it received high-profile government support, and publicity. It resonated with the nascent memorial culture of the early 1990s offering a powerful vehicle for promoting national unity, not least because Anne's story allowed for a generalized focus on human rights without requiring audiences to confront the difficulties of the country's past.[2]

A focus on the Jewish angle of this joint project allows for an exploration of the global and local events that led to the positioning of the AFWE as a pivotal event in the construction of post-apartheid Holocaust memory. By focusing on the SAJBD's decision-making during the planning stages of the exhibition, this chapter points to the tensions experienced by the Jewish community during the critical period of transition from apartheid to democracy. Moreover, it explores the ways in which Holocaust memory was mobilized by the Jewish community to secure its place of inclusion within the emerging new democratic administration, this time with leaders from the country's black majority.

Waiting: South African Jewry during the Transition to Democracy

In his book *Waiting: The Whites of South Africa* (1985), Vincent Carpanzano examines the effects of domination on the everyday lives of those who dominate,

---

[1] Address by President Nelson Mandela at the Johannesburg opening of the Anne Frank in the World exhibition, 15 August 1994, Anne Frank 199 File, Rochlin Archives in Johannesburg.
[2] Gilbert, "Anne Frank in South Africa," 378.

claiming that human beings privileged by power are themselves paradoxically victims of that power. He focuses on the experiences of white citizens in South Africa for whom, he argues, the present had become secondary to the future, from the 1980s onward. Carpanzano concludes, "It is my impression that South Africa today is caught in a deadened time of waiting. For most whites, waiting is compounded by fear."[3]

As demonstrated in the previous chapters, during the apartheid era the Jewish community was successfully integrated into the privileged white minority. However, the Jews were always also marked as a distinct religious, social, cultural, and racial group according to South African racial politics. During the 1980s, like the rest of the white population, Jews experienced "the deadened time of waiting" described by Carpenzano – a time fraught with anxieties and pressures, along with expectations for a better future. While these anxieties had to do mainly with its whiteness, the Jewish community had specific challenges and produced its own strategies to reinforce its ability to cope with the ongoing unstable and violent reality.

After the Soweto uprising of June 1976, international sanctions against apartheid intensified, leading to the imposition of an international embargo on arms to South Africa in 1977.[4] The frequent ANC guerrilla attacks from neighboring African countries, along with growing international protests, were accompanied by an increased industrialization of the South African economy in the late 1970s, which magnified the need for semi-skilled workers. Therefore segregation and apartheid, so essential in the early stages of South African industrial development, were no longer in line with local needs.[5]

In these circumstances, the new prime minister Peter William Botha, elected in 1978, sought to reassess his country's public image and political strategies and between 1979–1984 implemented the "Total Strategy." This reform focused on reorganizing South African society according to its new industrial needs while combining business interests with Botha's own political ambitions and with the interests of the State Security Forces.[6] Under Botha's reform, segregation was loosened in public facilities in an attempt to eradicate apartheid's external traits, while apartheid's "hard core" racial legislations remained in force.

In the South African constitution of 1983, Botha announced the Tricameral Parliament reform, which included separate representative houses for whites,

---

3 Vincent Crapanzano, *Waiting: The Whites of South Africa* (New York: Random House, 1985).
4 Alon Liel, צדק שחור: המהפך הדרום אפריקני [*Black Justice: The South African Upheaval*] (Tel Aviv: Hakibbutz Hameuchad, 1999), 15–16.
5 Shimoni, *Community and Conscience*, 123.
6 Worden, צמיחת המדינת החדשות באפריקה: התהוותה של דרום אפריקה המודרנית [*The Making of Modern South Africa*], 133.

Coloureds and Indians, with autonomy in education, health, and communal affairs, while leaving most of the political power in the hands of the whites.[7] In an attempt to create a semblance of collaborative power distribution, Botha sought to turn the Coloured and Indian communities into a recruited middle class that would balance the demographic inferiority of whites with that of the black majority. While this step was supported by many liberal whites, including many Jews, it was boycotted by most Indians and Coloureds for completely excluding the black majority from political representation.[8]

The black majority's staunch opposition to Botha's reforms led to the formation of a new anti-apartheid organization – the United Democratic Front (UDF) in 1983. Unlike the outlawed ANC, the UDF was a legal movement, which sought to establish a unified South African society under which apartheid would be eliminated. While the UDF promoted non-violent protest, the intensification of black resistance posed an existential challenge for the white minority and led to the radicalization of Botha's policy and a declared state of emergency in 1986.[9]

Alongside the ongoing repression, the apartheid government succeeded in stirring up an internal African conflict between the ANC and its rival organization, the *Inkatha ye Nkululeko* movement, an ethnic Zulu organization first formed in the 1920s. This movement was resurrected in KwaZulu Natal in 1975 by Chief Mangosuthu Buthelezi, once a member of the ANC Youth League, who later refused to accept the leadership of the ANC. In 1980 it became the largest (legal) African political organization in South Africa. Buthelezi criticized the ANC's support of the international sanctions, which he claimed would push South Africa into third world poverty. The violent conflict peaked in 1985 following the murder of Victoria Mkenge, a prominent UDF activist, claiming tens of thousands of lives. The apartheid government mobilized the conflict as evidence of the blacks' inability to govern.[10]

Botha's reforms also led to the expansion of the divisions within the NP support base. From the early 1980s, radical right-wing movements re-emerged in the public arena. Their common denominator was their support of Verwoerd's extremist positions and their strong opposition to Botha's reforms.[11] The two most prominent right-wing movements established during that period

---

7 Liel, צדק שחור [*Black Justice*], 16–17.
8 Worden, התהוותה של דרום אפריקה המודרנית [*The Making of Modern South Africa*], 134.
9 Liel, צדק שחור [*Black Justice*], 16–17.
10 Hermann Buhr Giliomee and Bernard Mbenga, *New History of South Africa* (Cape Town: Tafelberg, 2007), 243.
11 Davenport, *South Africa: A Modern History*, 413; Worden, *The Making of Modern South Africa*, 132.

were the Aksie Eie Toekoms (AET), formed by former members of the Afrikaner Broederbond; and the Afrikaner Weerstandsbeweging (AWB), a neo-Nazi movement that displayed much similarity to the *Grayshirt* movement from the 1930s and which sought to establish an Afrikaner-Boer Republic.[12] While these movements had political ambitions, most of their members eventually found a new political home in the Conservative Party (CP), founded in 1981.[13] The party was founded under the leadership of Andries Treurnicht and gained considerable popularity among the working class and the white and blue-collar populations.[14]

While these movements quickly disappeared from the parliamentary arena, right-wing parties such as the CP and the HNP frequently evinced antisemitic positions in the public sphere.[15] In September 1980, a crowd of about 1,000 extremists paraded the Vierkleur flag of the old Transvaal Republic at the eleventh Congress of the HNP. On the podium, the leader of the party, Jaap Marais, emphasized the struggle for the hearts of Afrikaner nationalists and "opened a bitter floodgate of recriminations against Nationalists, blacks and Jews."[16] A year later, in November 1981, copies of Hitler's *Mein Kampf* were on sale at a white protest rally organized by the HNP, together with the CP in Windhoek.[17]

Responding to these new radical developments from the right, the SAJBD concluded in 1981 that while the community should continue to provide an immediate communal reaction to every antisemitic manifestation, it should also focus on "positive" public relations by providing a positive image of Jews vis-à-vis gentiles through publications, meetings, and contact with other groups.[18] A Public Relations Committee was established, and three sub-committees were formed, including a committee for the defense of Jewish civic rights; a committee for protection against antisemitism and the promotion of the Board's profile and image; and a committee for building bridges between the Jewish community and other communities.[19]

---

[12] Gwyneth Williams and Brian Hackland, *The Dictionary of Contemporary Politics of Southern Africa* (New York: Routledge, 2015), 24; Davenport, *South Africa: A Modern History*, 412.
[13] Williams and Hackland, *The Dictionary of Contemporary Politics of Southern Africa*, 13.
[14] Giliomee, *The Afrikaner*, 606–607.
[15] "'Mein Kampf' At Windhoek Rally," *Sunday Times*, 1 November 1981, Press Items of Jewish Interest No. 21, Rochlin Archive, Johannesburg.
[16] "HNP and Anti-Semitism," *Sunday Tribune*, 28 September 1980, Press Items of Jewish Interest No. 18, Rochlin Archive, Johannesburg.
[17] "'Mein Kampf' At Windhoek Rally," *Sunday Times*, 1 November 1981, Press Items of Jewish Interest No. 21, Rochlin Archive, Johannesburg.
[18] "SAJBD Execution Council Minutes," 21 September 1981, Public Relations Session, 4, SAJBD Reports, Rochlin Archive, Johannesburg.
[19] "SAJBD Execution Council Minutes," 26 October 1981, Restructuring of Public Relations Committee, 3–4, SAJBD Reports, Rochlin Archive, Johannesburg.

When a group of survivors from New York decided to hold an international convention for Holocaust survivors at Yad Vashem in Jerusalem, the SAJBD worked together with the local Holocaust survivors organization *She'erith Hapleta* to encourage as many people as possible from South Africa to attend the world gathering.[20] The SAJBD perceived the World Gathering of Holocaust Survivors, which took place in Israel from 15 to 18 June 1981, as the ultimate opportunity to demonstrate solidarity with those who survived the Holocaust and also an act of homage and remembrance to the victims. However, as Mervyn Smith, then national chairman of the Board, stated at the 1980 World Jewish Congress Plenary Assembly, mass attendance of world Jewry at the gathering was also one of the methods of countering antisemitism worldwide.[21]

The World Gathering of June 1981 was a formative event in the development of what is known in Holocaust literature as "The Era of the Witness," briefly mentioned in the introductory chapter. In her book *Ethics of the Witness: History of a Problem* (2015), Michal Givoni offers a critical examination of the history of testimony and witnessing during the 20th century and its central role in the political field. Givoni points to the public debate that arose around the screening of the American television series *Holocaust* during the late 1970s, as a major catalyst for the establishment in 1979 of a grassroots organization called the Holocaust Survivors Film Project. This project videotaped Holocaust survivors and witnesses in New Haven, Connecticut, and in 1981 the original collection of testimonies was deposited at Yale University.[22] Similar projects began to appear throughout the Western world. In South Africa, too, the Student Holocaust Interviewing Project (SHIP) was inaugurated in 1983 to document testimonies of Holocaust survivors living in the country. The project was established following the participation of the South African Jewish students' delegation at the World Gathering of Holocaust survivors held in 1981.[23]

Another dominant mode of commemoration that was firmly established in South Africa during that period was Holocaust exhibitions. From 1975, the local community used exhibitions consisting of posters, photographs, and audiovisual programs as tools to raise Holocaust awareness in South Africa. Since the exhibitions were displayed in Jewish centers throughout the country, they

---

20 "Appeal to Holocaust Survivors in SA," *Zionist Record*, 18 April 1980; "SA Jews Urged: Go to Holocaust Gathering," *Zionist Record and SA Jewish Chronicle*, 10 October 1980, File 520.2A: Yom Hashoah 1980–1982, Rochlin Archive, Johannesburg.
21 "World Gathering of Jewish Holocaust Survivors," SAJBD Executive Council, 16 February 1981, Minutes, 2, SAJBD Reports, Rochlin Archive, Johannesburg.
22 Givoni. *Ethics of the Witness: History of a Problem*, 60–61, 127.
23 Piat-ka, "She'erith Hapletah," 194; Shain, "South Africa," 685.

were attended mainly by members of the Jewish community and therefore gained limited resonance among the general public.²⁴ To overcome this challenge, in 1982 a mobile exhibition was curated by the Giltlin Jewish Library in Cape Town. This exhibition aimed at Jewish and non-Jewish high school students and focused on the history of Nazism, the persecution of European Jews, "Kristallnacht," ghettoization, deportation, and the final solution.²⁵

While this exhibition marked a turning point as the first one to address Jewish and non-Jewish audiences alike, the important transformation took place in 1985 as part of local events marking the 40th anniversary of the liberation of the concentration camps. This development was initiated by Myra Osrin, then chair of the Western Cape SAZF Council, who would later orchestrate the arrival of the AFWE in South Africa in 1994 and thereafter the establishment of the first Holocaust permanent exhibition in Cape Town in 1999. In an interview I conducted with Osrin in August 2016, she recalled, "It [the 40th anniversary of the liberation of the concentration camps] was an opportunity possibly of going outside the Zionist Board or the Jewish day-schools, to find a public venue, to have something to nationally mark the occasion."²⁶

Indeed, Osrin turned to the management of the South African Cultural History Museum and proposed that some space be given to the community to mount a small exhibition. "He was very sympathetic," she said of her meeting with the museum director, "but immediately he said that unfortunately, according to their constitution, they were not able to do something general, but only something . . . directly relevant to South Africa." Osrin suggested that the exhibition could focus on the stories of South African survivors living in Cape Town. Her suggestion was accepted.²⁷

At that time, *She'erith Hapleta* was active in Cape Town. However, as Osrin testified,

> I actually didn't know there were about fifty survivors in those times living in Cape Town and I didn't know their stories [. .] working on the exhibition started a relationship with this amazing organization which in 1985 still kept to itself [. . .] we really had to work very hard with them for them to share some of their stories, but we had to keep their identities confidential.²⁸

---

24 "Correspondence between Gitlin Library and Barbara Meltz," 24 June 1985, ARCH 211, File 6: SAJBD Holocaust Exhibition April–May 1985, Rochlin Archive, Johannesburg.
25 "Holocaust Exhibition April-May 1985," Jacob Gitlin Library, 24 June 1985, ARCH 211, File 6: SAJBD Holocaust Exhibition April–May 1985, Rochlin Archive, Johannesburg; "Yom Hashoa Exhibition," *Jewish Herald*, 19 May 1981, Clippings Collection, Jacob Gitlin Jewish Library, Cape Town.
26 Personal Communication between Myra Osrin (MO) and Roni Mikel-Arieli, 23 August 2016.
27 MO, Personal Communication, 23 August 2016.
28 MO, Personal Communication, 23 August 2016.

The committee chose sixteen survivors living in Cape Town who possessed documentation and photographs and presented their stories in texts that accompanied the material exhibits. Wherever possible, when survivors had been helped by non-Jews this was emphasized and at the opening of the exhibition medals were awarded to such a helper dubbed "righteous among the nations"[29] from Cape Town and to a Dutch resistance fighter who helped to save Jews.[30] While the survivors' testimonies which emerged in the early 1980s focused on preserving the stories of local Holocaust survivors by their communities, the choice in this case to make these stories the focus of an exhibition displayed at the South African Cultural History Museum placed the witness-survivor at the center of the national stage. However, here too, as with other commemorative efforts made under the auspices of South African Jewish institutions during the apartheid years, the local context of racism and segregation remained absent.

Following the success of the 1985 exhibition, the SAJBD decided to set up the Holocaust Memorial Coordinating Committee, which included members of the Cape Town Jewish Board of Deputies, the SAZF, *She'erith Hapleta*, and the Gitlin Jewish Library, as well as school representatives from the Cape area. Similar committees were established in other community centers in the country: local exhibitions were installed in Durban in 1986, and in Johannesburg in 1987, and discussion of the possibility of establishing a permanent exhibition began. This, however, did not materialize until the late 1990s.[31]

When the 1985 exhibition was launched, the first official Jewish declaration against apartheid was formulated. While the SAJBD had been calling for significant social, economic, and political change in South Africa to prevent violence and bloodshed since 1980, its statements remained sporadic and did not reflect an overall stand against apartheid.[32] Only at the 33th Congress of the SAJBD held in 1985 did the official institution issue its first condemnation of South African government policy, which explicitly included the term 'apartheid': "Congress records its support and commitment to justice, equal opportunity and the removal of all provisions in the laws of South Africa which discriminate on

---

29 The Righteous Among the Nations are non-Jewish individuals who have been honored by Yad Vashem, Israel's Holocaust memorial, for risking their lives to aid Jews during the Holocaust.
30 "Correspondence between Gitlin Library and Barbara Meltz," 24 Jun 1985, ARCH 211, File 6: SAJBD Holocaust Exhibition April–May 1985, Rochlin Archive, Johannesburg.
31 "SA Jewish Board of Deputies – Holocaust Exhibition Committee," 30 October 1985; "SA Jewish Board of Deputies – Holocaust Exhibition Committee," 28 January 1986; "SA Jewish Board of Deputies – Holocaust Exhibition Committee," 3 September 1986, ARCH 211, File 6: SAJBD Holocaust Exhibition April–May 1985, Rochlin Archive, Johannesburg.
32 Shimoni, *Community and Conscience*, 137.

grounds of colour and race, and rejects apartheid."³³ This statement was expanded at the April 1987 Congress to include a call for more significant negotiations and reform in South Africa, alongside condemnation of apartheid as the main cause of political violence in the country and as a racist prejudice that stood in stark contrast to Jewish values.³⁴

This new stand taken by the SAJBD, however, overlooked the established economic and military links between Israel and South Africa that had emerged since the early 1970s.³⁵ The secret alliance between the two countries placed Israel in a dilemma regarding its strong ally in Pretoria at a time when voices calling for the isolation of South Africa were intensifying in the international arena. Ignoring the relationship between South Africa and Israel was possible because, although the military and economic collaborations remained solid on a rhetorical level, Israel had not expressed explicit support for apartheid but instead voiced its support for the establishment of a multi-racial society in South Africa.³⁶

In late 1986 the Israeli foreign ministry predicted that the end of apartheid was approaching and therefore formed an additional diplomatic communication channel with black leaders. Alon Liel, then foreign ministry spokesman, was appointed head of the African desk in the ministry and Shlomo Gur was sent to Pretoria. Although Gur was officially appointed deputy ambassador, he worked primarily with the UDF to pave the way for cooperation with the emerging black leadership.³⁷ These developments were kept confidential both from white South African officials (including members of the local Jewish community) and from Israeli Defense Ministry officials. Moreover, the Israeli Embassy in Pretoria secretly launched a project of Israeli leadership courses for black South Africans, providing them with tools based on Israel's national experiences since its inception: settlement, education, absorption, cooperation, volunteering, youth movements, etc.³⁸

In an interview with Liel in May 2018, he described the SAJBD's reaction to the new Israeli Foreign Ministry policy line on apartheid:

---

33 Quoted in Gideon Shimoni, "South African Jews and the Apartheid Crisis," *American Jewish Yearbook* 88 (1988): 3–58, at 30.
34 Shimoni, *Community and Conscience*, 138–139.
35 Azim Husain, "The West South Africa and Israel: Strategic Triangle," *Third World Quarterly* 4.1 (1982): 44–73, at 72.
36 Fachler, "The Jewish Factor in Israeli Foreign Policy," 84; Shimoni, "South African Jews and the Apartheid Crisis," 42.
37 Personal communication between Alon Liel (AL) and Roni Mike-Arieli, 11 May 2018.
38 Liel, צדק שחור [*Black Justice*], 25–26.

They (the SAJBD) were furious and argued that the black leaders are antisemitic, and pro-Palestinians, "don't waste your time on them," they said. I told them that we were determined and asked to meet with Joe Slovo. In response, they threatened that if I will meet Slovo, all donations to Israel would be stopped. They said, "All of these, black leaders are not Jews, but Slovo is a traitor to the whites because he supports Mandela, and he is also a traitor to Jews because he is a self-hating Jew, he is a communist and a terrorist – you will not meet him." I came back to Israel and reported to my superiors who said, "we cannot create a fracture with the South African Jewish community." We gave up.[39]

Liel's testimony expresses the dilemma that characterized Israeli diplomacy regarding apartheid South Africa and emphasizes the need to take into consideration local Jewish sentiments in Israel's foreign relations. However, it also reveals the rather narrow and murky conception of sections of the official Jewish leadership regarding the growing relations between Israel and the black leadership. The emerging black leaders were seen as largely antisemitic and pro-Palestinian, and Joe Slovo, the Jewish anti-apartheid activist who served as the military commander of the ANC, as well as other Jewish activists, were seen as traitors, even after the SAJBD officially condemned apartheid.

Despite the Jewish factor, on 18 March 1987, the Israeli government issued a statement officially condemning apartheid policy, reducing cooperation, and avoiding new joint initiatives with South African entities. The Israeli statement appeared a month before the release of an American report placing Israel at the head of six Western countries that provided military support to the apartheid regime. The sharp turn in Israeli policy stunned the South African government, but while in the 1950s and 1960s Israel's stand against apartheid had angered the white population in South Africa, the current change in attitude was mostly viewed as a result of American pressure on Israel.[40]

Between March and September of 1987, Liel served as secretary of the Israeli Committee for Review of Sanctions Against South Africa. He recalled: "We had taken the European model for sanctions and added a section declaring that we intend to conduct leadership courses for the black, Coloured and Indian population of South Africa."[41] On 16 September 1987 the second Israeli Cabinet meeting on South Africa approved the new sanctions package on apartheid.[42] In a confidential letter sent by Botha to then-Israeli Prime Minister Yitzhak

---

39 AL, Personal communication, 11 May 2018.
40 Shimoni, "South African Jews and the Apartheid Crisis," 42; Shimoni, *Community and Conscience*, 163; Liel, צדק שחור [*Black Justice*], 39.
41 AL, Personal communication, 11 May 2018.
42 Liel, צדק שחור [*Black Justice*], 42.

Shamir in 1987, he defined the change in Israeli policy towards the apartheid regime as a knife in the back. "How could you do this to us, after so many years of friendship and alliance?" asked Botha, emphasizing the favorable conditions his country provided to Israel in fields of investment and contributions from the Jewish community. He stated, "the South African government cannot accept the fact that the Israeli government is now funding education and training activities in Israel, restricted only for certain groups of the South African population."[43] While Botha's claims focused on what he perceived as discrimination against South African whites who were excluded from the Israeli leadership courses, both the SAJBD and SAZF declared their opposition to the whole sanctions package. Outwardly, the community institutions recognized that Israel's actions were intended to protect its national interests; however, they stressed that regarding relations with South Africa, Israel was under considerable pressure from the United States.[44]

In September 1989 Frederick Willem de Klerk of the NP won the general elections in South Africa.[45] He began by promoting reforms to abolish apartheid that, unlike Botha's strategies, included the black majority in power-sharing from the outset. In a historic speech in Parliament on 2 February 1990, De Klerk announced the abolition of the ban on the ANC and other opposition organizations, the release of political prisoners, and the opening of the negotiation process for a new and democratic future for all South Africans.[46] This was a result of a long domestic political process that included confidential negotiations between the Afrikaner political and intellectual leadership, the ANC leaders in exile, and with the imprisoned Nelson Mandela. But for most South African citizens – whites, blacks, Coloureds, and Indians – the period of transition to democracy that began in February 1990 and ended in the 27 April 1994 democratic elections was one of high hopes alongside enormous insecurity.[47]

De Klerk's declaration led to massive political activity that included rallies, protests, and strikes across South Africa following the release of Nelson Mandela from prison on 11 February 1990.[48] The CP's demonstration of power in the form of mass rallies, alongside the emergence of neo-Nazi movements, brought about a relative increase in antisemitism. Pigs' heads were placed at the entrance to

---

43 Amir Mizroch, "Late SA President P.W. Botha Felt Israel Hadd Betrayed Him," *Jerusalem Post*, 2 November 2006.
44 Shimoni, "South African Jews and the Apartheid Crisis," 47.
45 Shimoni, *Community and Conscience*, 245–246.
46 Davenport, *South Africa: A Modern History*, 444–445.
47 Shimoni, *Community and Conscience*, 242.
48 Giliomee and Mbenga, *New History of South Africa*, 396.

Jewish synagogues and public buildings and Jewish cemeteries were vandalized with antisemitic inscriptions.[49] Nevertheless, antisemitism was not a widespread phenomenon during those years, and condemnations of the sporadic events were voiced both in the political and the religious arenas.[50]

Jewish tensions were exacerbated when, in October 1989, Archbishop Desmond Tutu of Cape Town met with Palestinian Liberation Organization (PLO) leader Yasser Arafat in Cairo. At the meeting, the two discussed issues including the situation of Palestinians in Israeli occupied territories, the similarities between the plight of the Palestinians and that of black South Africans, and the recognition by Arafat and the PLO of Israel's right to exist.[51] Mandela too met with Arafat immediately after his release in February 1990. When asked at a press conference whether he risked alienating South Africa's influential Jewish community by meeting with the Palestinian leader in Lusaka and comparing his struggle to that of blacks in South Africa, Mandela answered: "if the truth alienates the powerful Jewish community in South Africa, that's too bad. I sincerely believe that there are many similarities between our struggle and that of the PLO. We live under a unique form of colonialism in South Africa, as well as in Israel, and a lot flows from that statement."[52]

In reaction to Mandela's remarks the SAJBD and the SAZF issued a joint statement: "Like Mr. Mandela and others, the SAJBD and SAZF are concerned with the establishment of a just, fair and equal dispensation for everyone living in South Africa. They believe that what is happening in other countries is not relevant to the situation here." As far as Israel was concerned, the statement asserted that "the society in that country is totally non-racial, with Arab members sitting in her Parliament. Unfortunately, she has as neighbours a number of nations such as Syria, Iraq and Iran, which are still in a state of war with her and openly committed to her destruction." It concluded that "although the PLO has recently referred to peace negotiations, it has still not renounced her covenant which is committed to the elimination of the Jewish state," and called for an open dialogue with Mandela.[53]

---

49 "Swastika Flags, Anti-Semitic Slogans at Protest March," *Sunday Times*, 11 February 1990; *Sunday Star*, 11 February 1990; *Citizen*, 30 March 1990, Press Items of Jewish Interest No. 3, Rochlin Archive, Johannesburg.
50 Shimoni, "South African Jews and the Apartheid Crisis," 47.
51 "Tutu Meets Arafat and Mubarak," *The Star*, 25 October 1989; *Business Day*, 24 October 1989; *Daily News*, 3 January 1990, Press Items of Jewish Interest No. 20, Rochlin Archive, Johannesburg.
52 "Mandela PLO and SA Jewish Community," *Citizen*, 1 March 1990; *Beeld*, 1 March 1990, Press Items of Jewish Interest No.4, Rochlin Archive, Johannesburg (a translated collection).
53 "Mandela PLO and SA Jewish Community," *Citizen*, 1 March 1990; *Beeld*, 1 March 1990, Press Items of Jewish Interest No.4, Rochlin Archive, Johannesburg (a translated collection).

The image of Mandela embracing Arafat appeared in all national newspapers, raising the question whether Mandela was in fact an antisemite.[54] While members of the Jewish community were disturbed by Mandela's point of view concerning Israel and the PLO, the official stance of the SAJBD was that Mandela's statement to the press was made spontaneously and not as part of a prepared speech and should therefore be viewed as a casual comment.[55]

Indeed, alongside the ANC's support for the Palestinian struggle, the organization made it clear that its positions were not antisemitic and was quick to eradicate sporadic antisemitic incidents that emerged in its ranks. In June 1990 Mandela met with Jewish leaders in Johannesburg and assured them that the ANC was not antisemitic.[56] Following this meeting, Mandela gave a number of public speeches at Jewish centers throughout the country, where he reiterated his claim that the ANC condemned Zionism insofar as the term connoted the Israeli State's right to occupy Palestinian lands and its refusal to deal with Arab leaders.[57]

At the time, Israel's ambassador in Pretoria, Zvi Gur-Ari, focused on relations with the white government and avoided forging visible and formal relations with the black majority leadership. However, when Alon Liel became the new ambassador in November 1992, a change in policy was announced.[58] This change was related to developments in the Middle East: In June of that year, Yitzhak Rabin became Prime Minister in Israel, paving the way for a peace agreement with the PLO. The first agreement was secretly signed in Oslo on 20 August 1993 by Shimon Peres and Mahmoud Abbas. Two weeks later, the White House in Washington held a solemn ceremony, attended by United States President Bill Clinton, Israeli Prime Minister Yitzhak Rabin, and PLO Prime Minister Yasser Arafat in order to sign a Declaration of Principles.[59]

When Liel first met Mandela on 4 December 1992, the Oslo Accords were not yet signed but reports on the ongoing negotiation between the Israelis and the Palestinians had already appeared in the world media. The South African coverage of the peace process was essentially positive and frequently invoked

---

54 "Mandela not Antisemitic," *Sunday Star*, 1 April 1990, Press Items of Jewish Interest No. 6, Rochlin Archive, Johannesburg.
55 Gavin Evans, "Jewish leaders and antisemitism," *Weekly Mail*, 30 March to 4 April 1990, Press Items of Jewish Interest No. 6, Rochlin Archive, Johannesburg.
56 "Jews and Mandela," *The Star*, 11 June 1990, Press Items of Jewish Interest No. 11, Rochlin Archive, Johannesburg.
57 "Mandela," *Citizen*, 11 September 1990, Press Items of Jewish Interest No. 16, Rochlin Archive, Johannesburg.
58 Liel, צדק שחור [*Black Justice*], 54.
59 For more information on the Oslo Accords see Petter Bauck and Mohammed Omer, *The Oslo Accords: A Critical Assessment, 1993–2013* (Cairo: American University in Cairo Press, 2013).

analogies to local processes of transformation from apartheid to democracy.[60] At the meeting, Mandela emphasized: "We have never questioned the State of Israel and its right to exist [. . .] Our disagreements with Israel on the Middle East issue evolves from our belief that the Palestinians are entitled to self-determination."[61]

De Klerk also communicated his acceptance of the change in Israeli policy towards South Africa to the new ambassador, stating: "We understand your new direction, we also have regular talks with Mandela and strive together for peace. However, you must not forget that we [the whites] are not disappearing, and we won't disappear in new South Africa either." In this atmosphere, Liel was greeted with sympathy by the leadership of the SAJBD, which also anticipated change in the South African political map. The SAZF, however, strongly opposed the Israeli change in policy towards the ANC, which it perceived as a terrorist organization, a major supporter of the PLO and an enemy of Zionism and Israel.[62]

In March 1992, some of the international economic sanctions imposed on South Africa during apartheid were lifted. At the local level, however, the social atmosphere remained tense. In the face of severe violence and a widespread economic crisis, the ANC and De Klerk's government negotiated the end of what was on the verge of developing into a civil war. It was in this complex reality that the plans for a joint project to bring the traveling exhibition focusing on the Jewish iconic victim of the Holocaust – Anne Frank – to South Africa took shape.

From Amsterdam via London en route to South Africa

As mentioned in Chapter 2, following the Broadway production of the diary in 1955 and its 1958 Hollywood film version, Anne Frank became an international symbol of Jewish children who perished during the Holocaust. When the diary became famous, people from all over the world flocked to visit the Secret Annex in Amsterdam.

AFH in Amsterdam opened to the public on 3 May 1960. However, at that point, it was not yet clear what the purpose of the building would be. The vision of Anne Frank's father, Otto Frank, was to turn the AFH into an international

---

60 "The Peace Process in Israel," Press Items of Jewish Interest No. 50 (September 1993), Rochlin Archive, Johannesburg.
61 AL, Personal communication, 11 May 2018.
62 Liel, צדק שחור [Black Justice], 57–80.

youth center to serve as a meeting place for young people, a site that would embody the lessons of the past and focus on the future. This vision was realized on 4 May 1961 and the adjacent building was designated for holding meetings, group visits, and special exhibitions, paving the way for the AFH International Youth Conferences of 1963.[63]

From 1963 onward, young people from all over the world came to the AFH annually for international summer conferences on emancipation, religion, and human rights. While the conferences mainly focused on Holocaust-related subjects, toward the end of the 1960s their scope widened to include more general social criticism. The AFH soon became a global hub for exhibitions, gatherings, and dialogue groups dedicated to contemporary injustices and human rights violations such as the Vietnam War, the United States' civil rights struggle, South American exploitation networks, South African apartheid, and even the Israel-Palestine conflict. According to the House's line of thought, the lessons of the Holocaust were relevant for understanding and meeting current global challenges.[64]

In 1985, the AFH curated the AFWE with the aim of presenting Anne Frank's story against the backdrop of events in occupied Europe, while increasing visitors' awareness of antisemitism, racism, and other forms of discrimination and prejudice.[65] The exhibition was designed to travel around the world and in each venue local sponsors were invited to suggest additional lectures, films, publications, and other displays reflecting local contexts to accompany the exhibition. At the time there were three versions of the traveling exhibition – those in Amsterdam, the United States, and West Germany. However, soon after the exhibition in Amsterdam was opened in 1985 it was declared a financial failure and in September of that year the Executive Committee announced that forty years after the war the public's interest in the Holocaust was limited and that the exhibition was to be closed.[66]

Jan Erik Dubbelman, who worked at the International Department of the AFH at the time, decisively resisted the decision to cancel the exhibition's tour. "I thought it was mismanaged," he stated, when describing his decision to take

---

[63] Jos Van Der Lans en Herman Vuijsje, *Het Anne Frank Huis- Een Biografie* [*The Anne Frank House - A Biography*] (Basel: Anne Frank Fonds, 2010), 99–110.
[64] "From Hiding Place to Museum – the History of the Anne Frank House," Anne Frank House website, http://www.annefrank.org/en/Museum/From-hiding-place-to-museum/International-Youth-Centre/ [Accessed 26 November 2017].
[65] Gilbert, "Anne Frank in South Africa," 378.
[66] Personal Communication between Jan Erik Dubbelman (JED) and Roni Mike-Arieli, 28 January 2017.

a road trip to London, where he received the help of some local friends in promoting the exhibition there.⁶⁷ The first call he made when arriving in London was to an exiled South African friend, Amin Cajee. Cajee was one of the first Indian South Africans to be sent out of the country for training as part of the ANC's new policy of armed resistance, established in 1962. He was trained in Czechoslovakia and spent several years in a military camp in Tanzania, founded by the ANC and SACP as part of the anti-apartheid movement's armed wing, *uMkhonto weSizwe* (MK). Cajee was accused of treason as part of an inter-factional struggle in the organization and fled to London in 1967.⁶⁸ There he met his wife, Pat Shanks, at the time Assistant General Secretary of the Student Christian Movement of Great Britain and Ireland. Shanks had close links with Pat Herbert, the head of the African Education Trust, which supported exiled students from Southern Africa. Shanks helped Cajee to secure a student grant, and the two later married.

The late 1970s witnessed an exacerbation of violent attacks by NF supporters on ethnic minorities in London and northern cities such as Birmingham. The 1978 Brick Lane attack, clashes in the summer of 1980, and the 1981 Brixton "Riots" made race relations a matter of political concern and motivated a parliamentary investigation into the matter. The Scarman Report was published in 1981 to inquire into the Brixton riots, and although police violence was not condemned, the report did admit a disproportionate targeting of black youth and pointed to discriminatory conditions for immigrant and ethnic minority communities.⁶⁹

During that period, the Greater London Council (GLC), headed by Labour Party member Ken Livingstone, advocated measures to improve the lives of disadvantaged minorities within London. In 1982, Livingstone founded the Ethnic Minorities Unit (EMU) to meet the needs of local ethnic minority groups. During 1983, the EMU met to discuss plans and funding schemes for communities in Bangladesh and Pakistan and in China, as well as for the British Jewish community.⁷⁰ Cajee was a member of the EMU when he launched the successful London against Racism campaign of 1984, which culminated in hosting the AFWE at various sites in and around London in 1986.⁷¹

---

67 JED, Personal Communication, 28 January 2017.
68 Amin Cajee, *Fordsburg Fighter: The Journey of a MK Volunteer* (London: Cover2Cover Books, 2016).
69 For further reading on racism in Britain during the 1970s and 1980s, see Paul Gilroy, *There Ain't No Black in the Union Jack* (New York: Routledge, 2013).
70 Gilroy, *There Ain't No Black in the Union Jack*, 190.
71 Cajee, *Fordsburg Fighter*, 172.

The arrival of the exhibition in London was particularly striking because it exposed the tangled axis of left-wing Holocaust memory and racial politics in contemporary Britain. Livingstone's position on Zionism corresponded with UN resolution 3379 from 1975, which determined Zionism to be a form of racism. Moreover, the Israeli invasion of Lebanon in 1982 whipped the anti-Zionism of the British left into a fever pitch. In May 1982, the Labour Party's National Executive Committee, which at that point had already supported the PLO's cause, passed a motion criticizing Israeli policies on the West Bank and the bombing of Lebanon. By then, anti-Zionism had become a standard item on the agendas of many members of the Labour Party.[72] It is not surprising therefore that the British Jewish Board of Deputies decided to boycott the opening event of the AFWE organized by Livingston's administration.[73]

This matrix of events reveals how constructs of suffering during the Holocaust and under apartheid served as tropes for the discussion of domestic racism in London.[74] As London became the home for many exiled South Africans and the base for the international anti-apartheid movement, events in South Africa informed the way anti-racist activists in Britain thought about racial politics. Therefore Cajee saw the importance of hosting a Jewish project under the auspices of the GLC's new anti-racism campaign. As Dubbelman recalled, Cajee identified Anna Frank as a Jewish victim and dedicated the AFWE to the local Jewish community in London. However, he also viewed the exhibition as part of a broader anti-racism campaign and Anne Frank's life story as one that "deals primarily with human beings."[75]

In many ways, the London 1985 exhibition illustrates Levy and Szneider's approach, which conceives Holocaust memory as a cross-border cosmopolitan memory on the eve of the end of the Cold War.[76] Moreover, it most certainly anticipates the role played by the AFWE six years later in South Africa, where Anne Frank's image "provided an ideal medium through which South Africans could be encouraged to build a common future in a spirit of hope and reconciliation."[77]

---

72 Ken Livingstone, *You Can't Say That: Memoirs* (London: Faber & Faber, 2011), 219–223.
73 For the reception of the exhibition by the British Jewish community in London, see "Anne Frank at the Mall," *Jewish Chronicle*, 31 January 1986, 21; Simon Rocker, "Anne Frank Exhibition Daubed," *Jewish Chronicle*, 25 April 1986, 36; "Anne Frank Comes to Leeds," *Jewish Chronicle*, 28 November 1986, 10; "Anne Frank Display," *Jewish Chronicle*, 14 February 1986, 40, The Jewish Chronicle Archive.
74 This section is part of a joint ongoing research project conducted by Tal Zalmanovich together with the author, focusing on Holocaust memory and anti-racism in London during the 1980s.
75 JED, Personal Communication, 28 January 2017.
76 Levy and Szneider, "Memory Unbound," 87–106.
77 Gilbert, "Anne Frank in South Africa," 383.

"Anne Frank in the World Exhibition" in South Africa

At a private visit to London in 1992, Osrin was contacted by Gillian Walnes, the founder of the Anne Frank Trust UK, who at that time worked closely with Jan Erik Dubbelman from the AFH. Osrin recalled: "we knew that the AFH was very involved in the struggle against apartheid. We also knew that they had a very successful traveling exhibition touring the US, Britain, and other Western countries, and that in principle they did not agree that it would be exhibited in South Africa. However, in 1992, they saw what was about to happen."[78]

The anti-apartheid position of the AFH underpinned the reservations regarding a South African tour of the exhibition on the part of both the Dutch and the South Africans. When Dubbelman came to South Africa in 1993 to meet with the national chair of the SAJBD, Mervin Smith, he was received with ambivalence. "They [the Jewish community] felt that the AFH had poor priorities, and particularly mentioned an exhibition hosted by the institute in the 1970s comparing the Holocaust to apartheid," Dubbelman recalled.[79]

As Gilbert demonstrates, the AFH's firm stand against apartheid during the 1970s included providing a home for several critical exhibitions on the matter. The first exhibition was curated in 1971 by Pluto, a group of Afrikaner students in Amsterdam led by Brand Schuiteme. It was designed at the request of AFH's then-CEO, the theologian Hans van Houte, who hoped to inspire Dutch religious groups to take a stand against apartheid by highlighting similarities between the Nuremberg laws and apartheid regulations.[80] In 1972, Schuiteme began working as an archivist at the AFH and during that summer he organized another exhibition focusing on international investment in apartheid, which included a life-size puppet of the then South African prime minister Vorster holding a swastika. A third exhibition was curated in 1973. The South African press reported on the critical exhibition as a hate campaign against South African government policy under the auspices of the Dutch AFH.[81]

The issue of comparing the Holocaust to apartheid was central to the community's reservations regarding working together with the AFH. This issue was also well reflected in the early discussions of the SAJBD on the traveling exhibition.

---

[78] MO, Personal Communication, 23 August 2016.
[79] JED, Personal Communication, 28 January 2017.
[80] The 1971 exhibition was one of the first public activities of the Dutch Anti-Apartheid Movement (Anti-Apartheid Beweging Nederland – AABN) established in 1971, and its location the tourist site of the AFH led to its public exposure. For more information about the exhibition see Gilbert, "Anne Frank in South Africa," 374–375.
[81] Gilbert, "Anne Frank in South Africa," 374–375.

As a national project, the exhibition was directed at the general community in South Africa, and first and foremost at "Junior High, High school and University students of all races."[82] Following Osrin's first presentation of the exhibition project to the SAJBD National Executive Council in August 1992, Chief Rabbi Cyril Harris emphasized "that the Anne Frank Exhibition was vital for the general community but totally unnecessary for the Jewish community" and called on the Board to clarify the reasons for bringing the exhibition to South Africa.[83] A similar claim was made by Marlene Bethlehem, the Chair of the Transvaal SAJBD, who thought that the exhibition was the best outreach program that the Board could ever hope to embark upon and that it could be "successful in answering other organizations' questions of how Anne's story related to the events in South Africa today."[84] In their remarks, Rabbi Harris and Bethlehem called the Board finally to embrace the opportunity to think about the possible links between the tragic Jewish history of the Holocaust and the very recent past of South African apartheid.

Nevertheless, at a Board meeting of December 1993 Osrin emphasized: "it was important that people knew that the exhibition was not comparing what happened during the Holocaust with today's South Africa. No parallels could or would be drawn."[85] This stance was also expressed at a meeting of the National Education Committee held on 25 August 1993 where concerns were raised about "the imbalance in the scale and nature of oppression in each case." The committee stressed the need to focus on "the non-violent aspect of the Anne Frank Diary." To avoid blatant comparison, it concluded, "the focus should fall not so much on what happened but on how it happened, so that it would never happen again [. . .] the focus should also fall on the positive and human rights."[86]

The subject of parallels between the Holocaust and apartheid was particularly emphasized in relation to the exhibition entitled "Apartheid and Resistance," curated by the Mayibuye Centre for History and Culture in South Africa to accompany

---

[82] "Summary of Proposal for a National Tour of the 'Anne Frank in the World 1929–1945' Exhibition," Minutes of Meetings of the National Committee of the Anne Frank in the World Exhibition, Box C-SA-I, Anne Frank House Archive, Amsterdam.
[83] "Presentation by Mrs. Osrin- Anne Frank Exhibition," SAJBD National Executive Council, 30 August 1992, 10, SAJBD Reports, Rochlin Archive, Johannesburg.
[84] "Presentation by Mrs. Osrin- Anne Frank Exhibition," SAJBD National Executive Council, 30 August 1992, 9, SAJBD Reports, Rochlin Archive, Johannesburg.
[85] "Report on Anne Frank Exhibition," SAJBD National Executive Council, 5 December 1993, 8–9, SAJBD Reports, Rochlin Archive, Johannesburg.
[86] "Minutes of the National Education Committee Meeting Held in the Annex of the SA National Gallery at 15:30 on Wednesday 25 August 1993," 4.3 Parallels, Minutes of Meetings of the National Committee of the Anne Frank in the World Exhibition, Box C-SA-I, Anne Frank House Archive, Amsterdam.

the AFWE. Established in 1992 at the University of the Western Cape under the leadership of Andre Odendaal, the Mayibuye Centre aimed "to help recover areas of South African history which were neglected in the past and to create space for cultural creativity and expression in a way that helps along the process of change and reconstruction in a democratic South Africa."[87] The ancillary exhibition was designed following the request of the AFH to provide the local context of racial discrimination and apartheid and to show that antisemitism and other forms of racism still exist. It contained sixteen panels and was the only ancillary content to accompany the AFWE throughout its entire national itinerary.[88]

The first panel presented the visitor with the exhibition's central objective "to help people to understand the Anne Frank experience within a South African context." The text further stated that "while it is not correct to equate the Holocaust with apartheid, there are parallels which need to be remembered."[89] The appropriateness of comparisons between the Holocaust and apartheid had to be addressed from the planning stages. Gordon Metz, a representative of the Mayibuye Centre, explained the motivations behind the pairing of the two exhibitions in an article in *On Campus*, the University of Western Cape newsletter: "South Africans have lived under their own system of oppression. We can't equate the Holocaust with apartheid, but there are many parallels, and lessons to be learnt [. . .] we have tried to ensure that our component of the exhibition has a wide focus, an important point that comes through is that ordinary people make history."[90]

While the issue of comparisons stood at the heart of the Jewish discourse during the planning stage, another major issue emerged from the work of the SAJBD with the Mayibuye Centre around the issue of Israel's ties with the apartheid regime. The first sketch of the ancillary exhibition placed emphasis on Israel's close trade relations with South Africa during the apartheid years. The SAJBD felt that the statement was unbalanced and argued that if Israel was

---

87 Cited from: "Apartheid and Resistance" Exhibition, Panel 1, Mayibuye Centre for History and Culture in South Africa, University of Western Cape, South Africa. One distinct collection donated to the Centre was composed of the material collected by the International Defence and Aid Fund (IDAF), which was banned in 1966 and continued its work in London until 1991. For more information on the establishment of the Mayibuye Centre see Coombes, *History After Apartheid*, 60.
88 "Prospectus for 'Anne Frank in the World' Exhibition Tour of South Africa," Minutes of Meetings of the National Committee of the Anne Frank in the World Exhibition, Box C-SA-I, Anne Frank House Archive, Amsterdam.
89 The exhibition is on permanent display at the Mayibuye Centre for History and Culture in South Africa, University of Western Cape, and I would like thank Sarika Talve-Goodman, who photographed the panels for me in April 2017.
90 Quoted in Coombes, *History After Apartheid*, 84.

mentioned, all other countries that had relations with South Africa during the apartheid years should also be mentioned.[91] However, the Maybuye Centre rejected what it perceived as an attempt to censor their exhibition, thus posing a dilemma for the strongly Zionist community.

The SAJBD knew that the involvement of the Mayibuye Centre was crucial for reaching the target audiences. Moreover, they acknowledged that in the present situation, if the Mayibuye Centre were to pull out of the exhibition, the whole event would collapse. Therefore, when, following the intervention of the Dutch Ambassador, the Centre eventually amended the statement to "the government of Israel and other countries such as Taiwan and Chile had close links with South Africa and supplied and exchanged military expertise and equipment with the apartheid government despite an international arms embargo," the Board agreed to conclude the matter.[92]

While the ancillary exhibition was critical of Israel's ties with the apartheid government, the central exhibition concluded by addressing contemporary issues such as neo-Nazism, Holocaust denial, antisemitism, anti-Zionism, and contemporary racism. Anti-Zionism was described in the exhibition catalogue as a position that "rejects the state of Israel as a Jewish state, which is not the same as criticizing certain policies of the Israeli government." It further stated that "when the Israeli government takes action, not only the government is judged but all Jews everywhere are held responsible. In this way criticism of the state of Israel is used as justification for antisemitism."[93]

This was not the first time that the AFH had to address the issue of criticism directed against Israel. While in its early years the AFH expressed strong support for the young Jewish state, the outbreak of the Six-Day War in June 1967 marked a change in its attitude toward Israel following the Israeli-Palestinian conflict.[94] A delegation of the Israeli Knesset to Amsterdam that visited the AFH in 1973 expressed its dismay that the AFH is now highlighting the Palestinian war as a freedom struggle, and perceives Israel, which was established to prevent the Holocaust that Anne Frank and her people perished in, as a suppressor of freedom and rights.[95] Indeed,

---

91 MO, Personal Communication, 23 August 2016.
92 SAJBD National Executive Council, 20 March 1994, 12, SAJBD Reports, Rochlin Archive, Johannesburg.
93 *Anne Frank in the World, 1929–1945* (Amsterdam: Anne Frank Stichting, 1985), 56.
94 Van Der Lans and Vuijsje, *Het Anne Frank Huis Een Biografie* [*The Anne Frank House - A Biography*], 142–143.
95 "משלחת הכנסת מתרעמת על אופי 'בית אנה פרנק'," ["The Knesset Delegation Resents the Anne Frank House"] *Davar*, 24 March 1973, Historical Jewish Press, The National Library of Israel and Tel-Aviv University.

during the early 1970s the AFH hosted a number of exhibitions on the Israel-Palestine conflict. Following these events, in 1976 Otto Frank insisted on adding a clear statement to the AFH's constitution confirming that the Holocaust must be regarded as a partial but direct cause of the establishment of the State of Israel and that, therefore, the organization supported the Jewish people's right to a national home in Israel, without, however, identifying itself with all Israeli actions.[96]

The above statement reflects the spirit of Otto Frank's efforts from 1976: Frank viewed anti-Zionism as undermining the legitimacy of Israel's right to exist and placed it alongside phenomena such as Holocaust denial, antisemitism, and other forms of racism. While the AFWE statement referring to anti-Zionism was not composed especially for the South African tour, the fact that it was placed at a spot in the exhibition just before the visitor moves to the ancillary exhibition on apartheid, which criticizes Israel, prepared the visitor for the upcoming positions. The statement was crucial for South African Jewry at a time when anti-Zionist and anti-Israeli stands from the left side of the political map were frequently voiced.

The placing of the AFWE alongside the ancillary exhibition on apartheid and resistance received significant leverage when it became known that a copy of *The Diary of Anna Frank* had reached the hands of senior political prisoners during their imprisonment on Robben Island, as will be described in detail in Chapter 7. The first to testify to the *Diary*'s unique influence on political prisoners was Govan Mbeki, one of the activists sentenced to life imprisonment during the Rivonia Trial. Speaking shortly after the transition to democracy in South Africa, at the grand opening of the AFWE at the Feather Market Hall in Port Elizabeth on 18 May 1994, Mbeki stated:

> One first became familiar with Anne Frank's diary in circumstances similar to the conditions in which she lived. It was on Robben Island while serving a life sentence for opposing racism that one first read Anne Frank's diary. The Rivonia Group of prisoners lived in a separate section, away from the other political prisoners, and it was there that Anne Frank's diary landed into our hands. How it came is a matter I cannot explain, but it was passed from person to person to be read only in the evenings after we had been locked up. The pages had already fallen apart.[97]

Mbeki testified that besides the Bible, the only other book he read during his time on Robben Island was *The Diary of Anne Frank*. He emphasized that the circumstances under which the diary had been written were startlingly similar to those in which he and his one thousand fellow ANC prisoners found themselves.

---

96 Van Der Lans and Vuijsje, *Het Anne Frank Huis Een Biografie* [*The Anne Frank House - A Biography*], 142–143.
97 Address by Govan Mbeki at the Port Elizabeth opening of the Anne Frank in the World exhibition, May 18, 1994, Box C-SA-II, Anne Frank House Archive, Amsterdam.

Mbeki mentioned that he, Nelson Mandela (who "was one cell away"), and Walter Sisulu were not allowed to speak to each other: "We had to live in official silence, like Anne Frank. If I wanted to communicate with Nelson, I could not speak to him – I wrote a note on a piece of paper, and we contrived to pass it between cells." Upon reading the *Diary*, Mbeki realized that it was a book all political prisoners should read: "It had to be shared, and the frustration was that you couldn't tell your friends what the book meant to you. So, we wrote it out – using those of us who had small handwriting – and it was soon read by all prisoners in all seven sections."[98]

President Nelson Mandela made a similar reflection at the opening of the AFWE in Johannesburg, held at Museum Africa on 15 August 1994,

> During the many years my comrades and I spent in prison, we derived inspiration from the courage and tenacity of those who challenge injustice even under the most difficult circumstances. As my colleague Govan Mbeki indicated at the Port Elizabeth exhibition, some of us read Anne Frank's diary on Robben Island and derived much encouragement from it. Combined with news of the heroic struggles of the people, led by the ANC, as well as the support of the international community, the tales of heroes and heroines of Anne's caliber kept our spirits high and reinforced our confidence in the invincibility of the cause of freedom and justice.[99]

The addresses by Mbeki and Mandela served as testimonies to the early analogies drawn between apartheid and the Holocaust on Robben Island. Moreover, by pointing to parallels between Nazi Germany and apartheid South Africa at national events organized by the Jewish community, the ANC leaders legitimized the Nazism-apartheid analogy, which up to that point had been considered taboo.

The participation of ANC leaders in the events of the exhibition nationwide can also be interpreted as an effort by the ANC leadership to emphasize its stand against antisemitism. While Mandela had constantly reassured South African Jewry that the ANC was not antisemitic and that its criticism was of the Israeli policy of occupation of Palestinian lands, the attendance of ANC comrades at the main events of an exhibition focusing on the Holocaust and organized by the Jewish community was meant to demonstrate publicly the adoption of the anti-antisemitic message by the new leaders of the country.[100] Furthermore, the involvement of ANC comrades at the exhibition events was perceived

---

[98] "Mbeki Moved by Diary," *Evening Post*, 4 March 1994, 263–264, Anne Frank 199 File, Rochlin Archive, Johannesburg.
[99] Address by President Nelson Mandela at the Johannesburg opening of the Anne Frank in the World exhibition, 15 August 1994, Anne Frank 199 File, Rochlin Archives, Johannesburg.
[100] "Mandela," *Citizen*, 11 September 1990, Press Items of Jewish Interest No. 16, Rochlin Archive, Johannesburg.

by many Jewish leaders as an opportunity to rehabilitate the perception of Jews as a communal entity among the black public.

In its effort to accommodate the emerging black leadership, the community had to account for its implicit position as a direct beneficiary of whiteness under apartheid. An exploration of the National Board's meetings from the years 1991–1993 reveals how central this issue was in communal discussions. At the SAJBD National Executive Council meeting of 14 June 1992, for example, Selwyn Zwick of the Pretoria Council told the National Board that "the Jews were perceived as influential and as having done nothing much to redress the evils of apartheid" and stressed the importance of correcting this perception.[101] John Moshal of the KwaZulu-Natal Council said, on the other hand, that one needed to consider the climate of fear "regarding the Security Police in bugging and over involvement" when criticizing the Board for its silence during the apartheid years. "The Board had always successfully trod the very thin line between involvement and activities which could endanger the community," he claimed.[102] All agreed that the community was currently privileged, and a call was made for the Board to help develop organizational awareness of problems in South African society and to educate the Jewish community "that a concrete contribution could be made without relinquishing Jewish identity."[103]

If so, during that period the Jewish community was trapped between its desire to defend both Holocaust uniqueness and Israel, on the one hand, and its need for accommodation with the new leaders, who were critical of the community's silence during the apartheid years and of Israel's past ties with the apartheid regime and who openly supported the PLO, on the other. This dilemma was reflected in the official exhibition objectives, as presented by Osrin to the members of the SAJBD in December 1993: "To educate the general public; to heighten public acknowledge of prejudice; to show that antisemitism still exists; to encourage racial tolerance; to foster understanding and knowledge of the Jews and their history; to highlight the importance of Israel as a haven and home for Jews."[104] The last two objectives, which highlight the connection between the Holocaust and the rebirth of Israel,

---

[101] SAJBD National Executive Council, 14 June 1992, 8, SAJBD Reports, Rochlin Archive, Johannesburg.
[102] SAJBD National Executive Council, 14 June 1992, 8, SAJBD Reports, Rochlin Archive, Johannesburg.
[103] SAJBD National Executive Council, 14 June 1992, 9, SAJBD Reports, Rochlin Archive, Johannesburg.
[104] SAJBD National Executive Council, 5 December 1993, 8–9, SAJBD Reports, Rochlin Archive, Johannesburg.

were defined by Osrin as "the hidden agenda," reflecting the concerns that accompanied the Jewish community throughout the project's planning process.

Comparing the objectives defined by the SAJBD in December 1993 to those that appeared in the initial contract formulated by the AFH in March of that year reveals that while the first four objectives were similar in nature, the last two were not included in the AFH contract at all. In fact, there was no mention of Israel or an emphasis on Jewish history in the contract. It is safe to assume that these two additional objectives were formulated by the SAJBD as part of their adaptation of the exhibition to the national tour in South Africa.[105]

The addition of these "hidden" objectives by the SAJBD is not surprising considering its strong community ties with Israel. During a period when the close links between Israel and the apartheid regime occupied the public discourse, and in light of the ANC leaders' repeated expressions of support for the Palestinian struggle, Jewish fears of a government led by the ANC, which would not only embrace the PLO but would also serve as a propaganda tool for delegitimizing Israel, were pervasive. It reveals the conception of the exhibition as an opportunity to restore the image of Zionism and of Israel for the entire South African public by establishing the connection between the Holocaust and the subsequent rebirth of Israel as a national home for the Jewish people.

The national project was ambitious in many respects, mainly due to the critical moment in which it was launched. Osrin said,

> When they (AFH) asked me whom I would be working with, I replied that I would ideally apply to the education department but in 1992 it was very complicated – with what department – of blacks? Of Coloureds? Of the Indians? Because I had experience with educators following the small exhibitions we set up (since 1985), I knew it would not work in 1992.[106]

Due to the apartheid "separate development" policy, until the early 1990s nineteen separate education departments operated in South Africa, each with its own curricula and textbooks. While the process of integration of the national education system began in 1990, it was only completed after the first democratic elections of 1994, when the nineteen departments were merged, the previous curricula cancelled, and a uniform national curriculum developed for the entire population.[107] Therefore, the first steps taken by Osrin after she was appointed by the SAJBD as chair of the National Organizing Committee of the exhibition in 1992 was to hold a round table with the various representatives of the educational departments. Osrin recalled,

---

[105] Rental Agreement for the Exhibition, Prospects for "Anne Frank in the World" Exhibition Tour of South Africa, article 4, Box C-SA-I, Anne Frank House Archive, Amsterdam.
[106] MO, Personal Communication, 23 August 2016.
[107] Petersen, "Politics, Policy and Holocaust Education in South Africa," 1, 8.

> We were having to set up an education committee and we invited all the schools in the area and all three of the boards of education departments to join. They came sitting around the table to discuss the exhibition program- this was the first time that they were sitting with their counterparts, and so, before we were getting to the agenda, they were already talking about other issues – that was quite extraordinary.[108]

It was at that roundtable meeting that Holocaust memory became a primary cultural resource for all sections of South African society.

Alongside the decision to involve all the education departments in the exhibition planning process, the SAJBD knew that in order to turn to the general public, they would have to host the exhibition in 'non-Jewish' venues. Indeed, the national itinerary included venues such as the South African National Gallery in Cape Town, the King George Gallery in Port Elizabeth, the National Art Festival in Grahamstown, the Boet Troskie Hall at the Technion in Bloemfontein, Africana Museum in Johannesburg, Pretoria Art Museum, the Natal Museum in Pietermaritzburg, and the Urban Art Gallery in Durban.[109]

As mentioned earlier, the SAJBD began to invest in mediating exhibition projects focusing on presenting the Holocaust to non-Jewish audiences in the early 1980s. Past experience had taught them of the importance of location in branding exhibitions as national, as evident in the successful exhibition held in 1985 at the Museum of South African Cultural History in Cape Town, which paved the way for bringing the AFWE to South Africa. However, as mentioned earlier, the unprecedented nature of the AFWE in South Africa did not lie in the mounting of an exhibition focusing on the Holocaust on South African soil, nor was it AFWE's national itinerary that stood out. It was the existence of a permanent ancillary exhibition focusing on apartheid, which institutionalized the analogies between the Holocaust and very recent local trauma that made this event distinctive.

The exhibition patrons also reflect the efforts made to provide the project a national character from its inception. The list included, among others, prominent South African clerics who were part of the leadership of the South African Council of Churches (SACC) – an affiliate of the World Council of Churches which represented all major Christian churches in South Africa, apart from the Dutch Reformed Church and the Catholic Church.[110] From the late 1970s onward, the SACC became a strong force in the revival of mass action against apartheid.

---

108 MO, Personal Communication, 23 August 2016.
109 SAJBD, "Anne Frank in the World Exhibition" – Update Report June-November 1993, 10, SAJBD Reports, Rochlin Archive, Johannesburg.
110 Hendrik J.C. Pieterse, "Introduction," in *Desmond Tutu's Message: A Qualitative Analysis*, ed. Hendrik J.C. Piererse and Peer Scheepers (Leiden: Brill, 2001), 11. For more scholarship on the World Council of Churches and its role in the anti-apartheid struggle, see Tal Zalmanovich,

The first patron was Dr. Rev Frank Chikane, who served as secretary general of the SACC since 1987 and was a member of the ANC, but whose entry into the South African public arena was associated with his work as secretary of the UDF.[111] While Rev Chikane was known for his critical views of Zionism and Israel, his position became more moderate after his visit to Israel in 1989. Addressing the SAJBD National Executive Council IN on 25 August 1991, he stressed that prior to his visit he equated Zionism with racism, but subsequent to visiting Israel he became aware of the complexities of the issues and saw Zionism and racism as "two totally different things."[112] The second patron was Cardinal Wilfred Napier, who served as Archbishop of Durban and as President of the South African Catholic Bishops Conference. During the transition from apartheid to democracy, Napier was also involved, along with other leaders, in negotiations between the National leadership and the ANC and even attended the signing of the National Peace Agreement in September 1991.[113] The third patron was Archbishop Desmond Tutu of Cape Town, on whom I will elaborate in the concluding chapter. Tutu was known for his critical views of the Israeli occupation and for his tendency to mobilize the Nazism-apartheid analogy in political speeches against apartheid. However, following the Oslo Accords, his relationship with the Jewish community and Israel reached a temporary highpoint; therefore his nomination as patron of the AFWE is not at all surprising.

Exhibition patrons also included Professor Pieter Cornelius Potgieter of the Department of Christian Ethics at the University of Pretoria, who served as chair of the Dutch Reformed Church Council of South Africa from 1990–2002. Potgieter was known for his public confession before Archbishop Tutu on behalf of his church. The confession, made in 1990 at the Rustenburg Conference, acknowledged the church's responsibility for political, social, economic, and structural wrongs done against black South Africans during the apartheid era and included a call for reconciliation between all people and all churches.[114]

"'What Is Needed Is an Ecumenical Act of Solidarity': The World Council of Churches, the 1969 Notting Hill Consultation on Racism, and the Anti-Apartheid Struggle," *Safundi: The Journal of South African and American Studies* 20.2 (2019): 174–193.
111 Tzippi Hoffman and Alan Fischer, *The Jews of South Africa: What Future?* (Johannesburg: Southern Book Publishers, 1988), 20–23.
112 SAJBD National Executive Council, 25 August 1991, 5, SAJBD Reports, Rochlin Archive, Johannesburg.
113 John Allen, *Conclave: The Politics, Personalities, and Process of the Next Papal Election* (Doubleday, 2002); Harris M. Lentz, *Popes and Cardinals of the 20th Century: A Biographical Dictionary* (London: McFarland, 2009).
114 Frits Gaum, "From *Church and Society* (1986) to Rustenburg (1990): Developments within the Dutch Reformed Church," in *Reformed Churches in South Africa and the Struggle for Justice:*

The chief rabbi of the Union of Orthodox Congregation in South Africa, Cyril Harris, was also among the patrons. Harris's appointment in 1988 reflected the change in the position of the SAJBD on apartheid. From his first day in office, Harris had identified in the name of Judaism with the struggle against apartheid and called for active Jewish support in the transition to democracy. He argued: "The essence of Judaism is that you are not allowed to ignore the world around you. You cannot live on an island [. . .] in some area called religion, where you just have your prayers, rituals and ceremonies."[115]

Another Jewish patron was the Honorary Justice Richard Goldstone, a South African jurist who served at that time as a Constitutional Court judge. Since his appointment as a judge in 1980, Goldstone had delivered several landmark judgements in the field of human rights.[116] In 1990 he chaired the commission of inquiry into the Sebokeng shootings, in which 18 people were killed in March 1990, exposing the involvement of the police in the violent outcome. Following the publication of his report, the South African government established the Goldstone Commission to investigate human rights abuses committed by the country's various political factions.[117] In many ways, his work paved the way for the establishment of the Truth and Reconciliation Commission (TRC). On the day of the opening of the AFWE in Johannesburg, Goldstone was nominated the first chief prosecutor of the United Nations International Criminal Tribunal for the former Yugoslavia and for Rwanda from August 1994 to September 1996.[118]

Remembering 1960–1990, ed. Marry-Anne Plaatjies-Van Huffel and Robert Vosloo (Stellenbosch: Sun Press, 2013), 67–74, at 72–73.
115 Shimoni, *Community and Conscience*, 248–249.
116 Shimoni, *Community and Conscience*, 189.
117 Shimoni, *Community and Conscience*, 190; Alan Hart, *Zionism: Conflict without end?* (Atlanta: Clarity Press, 2010), 350.
118 Godstone became a controversial persona in Israel and the Zionist world sixteen years later when in 2009 he was appointed as head of the UN Fact Finding Mission on the Gaza Conflict, also known as the Goldstone Report. Goldstone's team was founded as an independent international fact-finding mission "to investigate violations of international human rights law and international humanitarian law by the occupying power, against the Palestinian people throughout the Occupied Palestinian Territory." The Goldstone Report accused both the Israel Defense Forces and the Palestinian militants of war crimes and possible crimes against humanity. It recommended that each side openly investigate its own conduct and advised bringing the allegations to the International Criminal Court if they failed to do so. However, the Israeli government rejected the report as prejudiced. For the 2009 report see "Human Rights in Palestine and Other Occupied Arab Territories: Report of the United Nations Fact Finding Mission on the Gaza Conflict," September 15, 2009, Human Rights Council, Twelfth session, Agenda item 7, A/HRC/12/48.

Among the overwhelmingly male list of patrons, the only woman appointed was the South African Jewish anti-apartheid activist and politician Helen Suzman. Of her thirty-six years in parliament as the PP's only MP, Suzman spent thirteen as the lone voice against apartheid inside the chamber. She became a symbol of white liberal opposition to the apartheid regime, mainly due to her vigorous action on behalf of political prisoners.[119] In 1989 Suzman retired from political life, only five years before the profound transformation of the South African political system.[120] In 1994 she was appointed by Mandela to the first Independent Electoral Commission (IEC), which oversaw South Africa's first democratic elections.[121]

In this diverse list of patrons, which included African, Afrikaner, and Jewish public figures and which ostensibly represented the complexity of South African society, the absence of Coloured and Indian representation stood out. One can interpret this as an indication of the alliance established between the Jewish community and the new leaders of the country. This alliance reflects Jewish efforts to atone for their involvement and silence during the apartheid era and to establish a relationship of cooperation with the black majority. The distinct black representation among the patrons, as well as the active participation of the ANC's most prominent leaders at the opening events, were a demonstration of a new positioning of Holocaust memory in South Africa: because the Holocaust was perceived as the archetype of human rights violations, Anne Frank's story was a means for the black leadership to validate its commitment to human rights and thus establish South Africa's new image in the international arena.[122]

Despite the challenges, dilemmas, and concerns that accompanied the planning of the national project from start to finish, the feedback from visitors, as reflected in the local press coverage of the exhibition, testify to its success. As Richard Freedman, who at the time served as principal of the Jewish Herzlia Weizmann School in Cape Town, stated: "For the first time most South Africans who saw the exhibition were exposed to the concept that racism is not a black/white issue alone but is rooted in prejudices experienced across the globe."[123] On 5 March 1994, the *Cape Times* reported on the reactions of high school students from Manenberg

---

[119] "Power under the Bonnet," *Jewish Chronicle*, 15 October 1993, Press Items of Jewish Interest No. 51, Rochlin Archive, Johannesburg.
[120] Shimoni, *Community and Conscience*, 59–60.
[121] Robin Renwick, *Helen Suzman: Bright Star in a Dark Chamber, the Biography* (London: Biteback Publishing, 2014).
[122] Gilbert, "Anne Frank in South Africa," 379.
[123] Richard Freedman, "Engaging with Holocaust Education in Post-apartheid South Africa," in *Holocaust Education in a Global Context*, ed. Karel Francapane and Matthias Hass (Paris: UNESCO, 2014) 134–143.

township, which was established by the apartheid government in 1966 to house low-income Coloured community members as part of the notorious Group Area Act. The pupils testified that "they had never heard of Anne Frank but were aware of the atrocities committed by Hitler's Third Reich." Many were moved by the courageous story and expressed their astonishment at Anne Frank's strong confidence in human nature, despite the great suffering she experienced.[124]

When the exhibition opened in Johannesburg in August 1994, it included a reconstruction of Anne Frank's hideaway bedroom. In an interview with the *Mail & Guardian*, a 9th grade pupil from the township Sebokeng, Soweto, stated after seeing the reconstruction: "That girl should have come to stay with us in Sebokeng. Four of us to a room this size." However, she added, "It's terrible what happened to the Jews. It's just like what happened to us blacks in this country." The article also reported that the Soweto pupils were particularly moved by the "Apartheid and Resistance" exhibition as it displayed the iconic photograph of a youth carrying the body of Hector Pietersen, the first victim of the 1976 Soweto uprising.[125] Most exhibition visitors were not only exposed to the history of the Holocaust for the first time, but also to iconic images of the anti-apartheid struggle all over the world, which had been until then banned by the apartheid regime.

As expected, high school pupils who attended the exhibition repeatedly and movingly emphasized the parallels between Anne Frank's story and the local context of apartheid. A pupil from Lereko High School for blacks in Bloemfontein wrote, "to my point of view, I see this tragedy of Jewish people the same as of black people of South Africa;" and a pupil from Lenasia South High School in the Indian township of Southern Soweto testified: "considering the racial discrimination in South Africa and the Jewish massacre, people should learn to accept people of different culture and to be accepted in society."[126]

However, there were also some less sympathetic reactions, mainly from Afrikaner pupils. The *Mail & Guardian* reported that most of the pupils from Kempton Park Afrikaner High School near Johannesburg felt that the exhibition was one-sided and questioned the content of the ancillary exhibition: "what about all the bad things the ANC has done? Why isn't that up there?" In response to the Afrikaner reactions, the report suggested that the Mayibuye Centre has missed a golden opportunity:

---

124 "City Pupils moved by the Anne Frank exhibition," *Cape Times*, 5 March 1994, Press Items of Jewish Interest No. 55, Rochlin Archive, Johannesburg.
125 Mark Gevisser, "Anne Frank through a Prism of the Present," *Mail & Guardian*, 19 August 1994, Press Items of Jewish Interest No. 60, Rochlin Archive, Johannesburg.
126 "Anne Frank in the World in South Africa: an International Exhibition to Promote Tolerance and Understanding: Report of National Tour March 1994 to May 1995," 10–11, Box C-SA-I, Anne Frank House Archive, Amsterdam.

"instead of engaging viewers in the history of apartheid it has mounted didactic and heavy-handed collages. Struggle posters, in fact, that distance the viewer by not allowing personal points of entry."[127] A similar criticism can be detected in Osrin's interview, where she stated, "It wasn't so graphic, it was like a book on the wall." While the ancillary exhibition failed precisely where the AFWE succeeded, Osrin still insisted on its importance to the success of the national project.[128]

During the apartheid years, the Holocaust was presented by the official Jewish community as a unique event whose implications were relevant primarily to Jews, as a means to prevent antisemitism and Holocaust denial and as leverage for the Jews in their integration into the white society. By foregrounding these elements, the lessons that could have been drawn from the Holocaust for the local context of segregation and apartheid were suppressed, and any comparison made between the Holocaust and apartheid was perceived as taboo. However, during the period of transition from apartheid to democracy, the universal lessons of the Holocaust were mobilized in the framework of this national project. The Holocaust was instated as the paradigm of a traumatic historical past while the traumas of apartheid were still being enacted in the present. This positioning invited an awareness of the historical similarities between two distinct events, the Holocaust and apartheid, whose imagined juxtaposition held potential not only for alienation but also for mutual understanding and empathy.

Alongside concerns about the implications of drawing parallels between the Holocaust and apartheid, the SAJBD's role in planning the exhibition forced the community to confront many demons from its past, such as its silence during apartheid, as well as Israel's economic and military relations with the apartheid government. These key issues reveal the ongoing uncertainty of the Jewish community even during the hopeful period of transition from apartheid to democracy. As the Jewish community sought to secure its status in the newly emerging administration, a shift in the local discourse on the Holocaust occurred – from one focusing on the particularity of the destruction of European Jews to a discourse dealing with issues of human rights. The exhibition was the first platform to underline publicly the parallels between apartheid and Nazism within a national framework, to highlight the devastating circumstances of racism, discrimination, and prejudice, and to stress the consequent importance of protecting human rights. However, as the next section of the book will demonstrate, the use of these parallels existed long before this critical period within the anti-apartheid struggle.

---

[127] Mark Gevisser, "Anne Frank through a Prism of the Present," *Mail & Guardian*, 19 August 1994, Press Items of Jewish Interest No. 60, Rochlin Archive, Johannesburg.
[128] MO, Personal Communication, 23 August 2016.

Chapter 6
Holocaust Memory in the Lexicon of the Anti-Apartheid Movement

Adopted on 9 December 1948 against the background of the extermination of the European Jews by the Nazis, the United Nations Convention on the Prevention and Punishment of the Crime of Genocide aimed at preventing further genocides and at prosecuting genocide perpetrators. Six months earlier, on 23 May 1948, the South African NP parliamentary election had introduced apartheid. Given the right-wing Afrikaner pro-Nazism displayed during the 1930s and 1940s, described in length in Chapter 1, including the direct influence of Nazism on the ideology of apartheid, it is not surprising that apartheid opponents regularly invoked connections between the apartheid policy and Nazism.

In the immediate post-war period, anti-apartheid rhetoric positioned itself as "the most important moral battle in the world since the defeat of Nazism,"[1] focusing on anti-fascist and anti-Nazi rhetoric. However, on the eve of the Sharpeville Massacre in March 1960, the Jewish genocide also seeped into the anti-apartheid lexicon, positioning Jewish suffering during the Holocaust as a point of comparison to the reality of black South Africans under apartheid. The following paragraphs will provide an overview of the use of the Nazi analogy in anti-apartheid activism from the 1940s through to the 1980s as a way to explore the strategies employed by anti-apartheid activists in South Africa and abroad.

Early Post-War Analogical Connections (1945–1960)

The Second World War and its legacies have been, in Shula Marks' words, "important factor[s] in releasing left and liberal energies" in South Africa.[2] South African participation in the war introduced and disseminated anti-Nazi and anti-fascist rhetoric among the general public, offered thousands of South Africans to fight fascism actively on several military fronts, ignited hopes for deep

---
[1] Mark Gevisser, *Thabo Mbeki: The Dream Deferred* (Johannesburg: Jonathan Ball, 2007), 397.
[2] Shula Marks, "Afterword: Worlds of Impossibilities?" in *South Africa's 1940s: Worlds of Possibilities,* ed. Saul Dubow and Alan Jeeves (Lannsdowne: Double Storey, 2005), 267.

Note: Parts of this sub-chapter are based on an article co-written by Asher Lubotzky and the author, entitled "'The Great Trek Towards Nazism': Anti-Fascism and the Radical Left in South Africa During the Early Apartheid Era," *South African Historical Journal* (2021): 1–25.

progressive reforms within the country, and raised the popularity and membership of the previously marginal, local communist party. As demonstrated in Chapter 1, for many South Africans fascism also had a local, familiar manifestation, inasmuch as since the early 1930s Afrikaner ultra-nationalist groups adopted proto-fascist, pro-Nazi, and antisemitic stances and gained in political importance.[3]

During the post-war period, the direct and analogical connections between right wing Afrikaners and Nazi and fascist ideologies drove many activists who opposed the racist segregation policies of the Union to point to parallel policies of racial discrimination between the South African and Nazi regimes.[4] Their anti-fascist language combined global concepts – heavily borrowed from the struggle against fascism and Nazism in Europe in the 1930s and 1940s – with the colonial and racialist realities in South Africa. By doing so, activists contested the alleged uniqueness of conditions in South Africa – conditions that justified, according to Afrikaner Nationalists, the need for apartheid policies. At the same time, they gave anti-Nazism new meaning and drew practical lessons from it, adjusted to specific South African conditions.

In its June 1945 "Declaration of the Nations of the World," the Non-European Unity Movement invoked an extended comparison between the lives of blacks, Indians, and Coloureds in South Africa and the lives of Jews in Nazi Germany.[5] Over the years, such parallels were further elaborated by anti-apartheid activists in exile, such as Brian Bunting in his book *The Rise of the South African Reich* (1964), which systematically compared the Nuremberg Laws and apartheid legislation.[6]

Similar positions also emerged among the Indian population in South Africa, following the internal public discourse on local segregation policy in the 1930s and 1940s. Several observers of mid-century South Africa have noted that its anti-Indian atmosphere echoed core tropes of antisemitism, evident in claims that "the Indian was, according to a common saying, the Jew of Africa."[7] The historian Jon Soske argues that "the Nazi Genocide served as a powerful point of comparison and rendered the situation of the Indian diaspora legible in terms of international discussions over human rights, minorities, and the cause of the Second World War."[8]

---

[3] Furlong, *Between Crown and Swastika*, 3–4.
[4] Gilbert, "Jews and Racial State," 34.
[5] Gilbert, "Jews and Racial State," 39; Shain, "South Africa," 680.
[6] Bunting, *The Rise of the South African Reich*.
[7] Jon Soske, *Internal Frontiers: African Nationalism and the Indian Diaspora in Twentieth-Century South Africa* (Athens: Ohio University Press, 2018), 43.
[8] Soske, *Internal Frontiers*, 85–86.

Such a comparison was invoked in 1946 when the South African Indian Congress (SAIC) Passive Resistance Movement launched a campaign against the Asiatic Land Tenure and Indian Representation Act, also known as the "Ghetto Act," to protest both the limited political representation afforded to Indian South Africans and the restriction of their living areas. The use of the term 'ghetto' in this context was undoubtedly imbued with the resonance of its use by the Nazi regime. In fact, this campaign frequently invoked the Nazi analogy, drawing connections between local legislation repressing Indians and elements of Hitler's policy toward the Jews.[9]

While many of the NP politicians who became the architects of the apartheid state in 1948 were influenced by Nazi and fascist ideologies, these attitudes were mostly neglected during the post-war years and the NP made considerable effort to distance itself from associating with Nazism or fascism.[10] This development was a direct result of the new global order dictated by the Cold War: Since many of the opposition voices against segregation, and later apartheid, came from local communist movements, the apartheid government targeted communism as a dangerous evil. Thus in 1950 the CPSA, which had stood alongside the government in its fight against fascism during the war, was outlawed under the Suppression of Communism Act, and communism was framed as the new enemy of the country.[11] As Jonathan Hyslop argues,

> South African Communists of that generation, whose formative experiences had been those of the Popular Front and World War, naturally tended to view Nazi Germany as the paradigmatic case of fascism. Their interpretation of apartheid drew on the definition of fascism constructed by the Comintern in the mid-1930s, to present the Nationalist regime as a terrorist dictatorship of the most reactionary section of the ruling class, in which legality was abandoned, and in which real power lay in the hands of monopoly capital.[12]

Inkululeko (Freedom), the press organ of the CPSA, frequently referred to the government's new Act against communists as "Nazi tactics;" "the tactics of Goebbels;" or "Gestapo methods,"[13] pointing to ideological similarities between Afrikaner nationalism and Nazism.

Anti-fascism and anti-Nazism provided ideological justification for forming broad cross-class and multiracial coalitions, most prominently between communists

---

9 Gilbert, "Jews and the Racial State," 39.
10 Furlong, *Between Crown and Swastika*, 3.
11 Drew, *South Africa's Radical Tradition*, 34–35.
12 Jonathan Hyslop, "A Prussian Path to Apartheid? Germany as Comparative Perspective in Critical Analysis of South African Society," *SA Sociological Review* 3.1 (1990), 33–55, at 35.
13 *The Guardian*, 24 June 1948, 1; *The Guardian*, 15 July 1948, 1; *The Guardian*, 5 August 1948, 1; *Inkululeko*, 12 March 1949, 1; *Inkululeko*, 1 June 1950, Press Cutting Collection, South African National Library, Cape Town.

and African nationalists. Therefore, while during the 1940s many members of the ANC, including Nelson Mandela and Oliver Tambo, opposed cooperation with the Communist Party,[14] with the coming to power of the NP in 1948, a change in attitude towards communism emerged in the ANC. During the first decade of apartheid, the ANC and its Youth League, while a composite of different regional political cultures, aimed at joint action with the left and with all races. The government's struggle against communism only stimulated wider unity. As Thomas Karis argues, "when the Communist Party was banned, African Communists who were members of the ANC redirected their energies to this still-legal movement, and Communists of other races sought close cooperation with them."[15]

Thus, it is not surprising that in an address by Mandela at the Annual Conference of the ANCYL from December 1951, he described the political situation in South Africa as one that "is developing [in] the direction of an openly fascist state," using a somewhat communist rhetoric. According to Mandela, Afrikaner nationalism might be

> [T]he centre of the fascist ideology in this country, but like other things, it is itself merely an instrument of the ruling circles which are to be found in all white parties. The commandos are the nucleus of a future Gestapo. The acts passed by the government, in particular the Suppression of Communism Amendment Act and the Group Areas Act, provide the readymade framework for the establishment of the fascist state. True to the pattern depicted for the rest of the imperialist world, South African capitalism has developed [into] monopolism and is now reaching the final stage of monopoly capitalism gone mad, namely, fascism.[16]

A similar rhetoric was also prominent in the ANC's magazine, *Liberation*.[17] Between 1953 and 1957, *Liberation* dedicated twenty-five articles to delineating the parallels between racial discrimination policies implemented by the apartheid and Nazi regimes. For instance, South African Pass Laws were likened to

---

14 Thomas G. Karis, "South African liberation: the communist factor," *Foreign Affairs* 65.2 (1986): 267–287, at 273.
15 Karis, "South African Liberation: The Communist Factor," 274.
16 Address by Nelson Mandela at Annual Conference of the African National Congress Youth League, December 1951, *Speeches and messages by Nelson Rolihlahla Mandela*, Nelson Mandela Foundation.
17 *Liberation: A Journal of Democratic Discussion* was founded in Johannesburg to focus on issues of concern to blacks in South Africa. It was published in English between February 1953 and December 1959 and aimed to promote the new multiracial leadership of what was soon to become the Congress Alliance. Among its contributors were Mandela, Joe Slovo, Duma Nokwe, Helen Joseph, Govan Mbeki, and other prominent critics of apartheid.

the Jewish Yellow Star, while the Group Areas Act was compared to Hitler's *Lebensraum* and the Nazi ghettos.[18]

In April 1953, for example, the magazine editorial stated the NP had "made their aim as clear as daylight: it is to abolish every vestige of democratic freedom in South Africa and to establish a total, terroristic dictatorship of the sort which they so much admired in Germany between 1934 and 1944."[19] Furthermore, in his criticism of the 1953 Bantu Education Act, which brought African education under complete control of the government and extended apartheid to black schools, Mandela referred to the Act as "the Specter of Belsen and Buchenwald is haunting South Africa;"[20] and in 1957, within discussions about expanding the Bantu Education Act to universities, he claimed: "The Nationalist Government have frequently denied that they are a fascist Government inspired by the theories of the National-Socialist Party of Hitlerite Germany. Yet the declaration they make, the laws they pass and the entire policy they pursue clearly confirm this point."[21]

As Chapter 7 will demonstrate through a close exploration of Holocaust memory in the struggle of the Indian South African Ahmed Kathrada against apartheid, in the first decade after the Second World War South African radical thinkers had increasingly reevaluated the links between fascism, Nazism, and colonial racialism. Adopting anti-fascist and anti-Nazi perspective, sometimes via Marxist-inspired interpretations, helped anti-apartheid activists analyze their local realities and identify structural oppression and its enablers.

The Jewish Genocide in the Anti-Apartheid Lexicon (1960s–1980s)

The Genocide Convention came into effect in 1951, a time when European policy toward colonial Africa was on the cusp of a dramatic change. The Bandung

---

[18] Walter Sisulu, "The Extension of the Pass Laws," *Liberation – A Journal of Democratic Discussion*, No. 17, March 1956, 12–14, at 13; Wallace Mlingesi, "Organise to Defeat 'Group Areas'," *Liberation – A Journal of Democratic Discussion*, No. 21, September 1956, 14–16, at 15, African National Congress, Historical Documents Archive, South Africa.
[19] "Epitaph for a Parliament," *Liberation – A Journal of Democratic Discussion*, No. 2. April 1953, 1–6, at 3, African National Congress, Historical Documents Archive, South Africa.
[20] Nelson Mandela, "The Specter of Belsen and Buchenwald," *Liberation – A Journal of Democratic Discussion*, No. 14, October 1955, 22–24, at 24, African National Congress, Historical Documents Archive, South Africa.
[21] Nelson Mandela, "Bantu Education Goes to University," *Liberation – A Journal of Democratic Discussion*, No. 25, June 1957, 7–10, at 7, African National Congress, Historical Documents Archive, South Africa.

Conference of 1955, mentioned in Chapter 3, was the first public international move toward a "Asian-African" regional alliance.[22] Three years later, most African colonies had become independent states, and in 1958 they collectively established the African Group to coordinate all matters of common concern to the African states at the UN.[23] As Leo Kuper, a South African Sociologist and Liberal Party member who was exiled to Los Angeles in 1961, stated in a lecture delivered at Indiana University in 18 April 1980: "with the entry of many African states into the United Nations, and the more vigorous prosecution of the campaign against apartheid, there begins to appear in United Nations documents an identification of apartheid with Nazism and with genocide."[24]

There were two important local factors for the growing interest in apartheid at the UN forums. The first was the ban of the ANC in 1960 by the apartheid government, which drove most of its members underground, into exile, or into apartheid prisons. The total suppression of internal resistance to the apartheid regime, including the incarceration of Nelson Mandela and other ANC leaders and activists following the Treason Trial (1958–1962) and the Rivonia Trial (1963–1964), provided the conditions for the emergence of anti-apartheid movements worldwide during the 1960s, creating space for the development of what is defined by Rob Skinner as "a new transnational political culture," linked to the process of decolonization.[25] These movements were major factors in pushing the anti-apartheid issue in UN forums and in communications such as resolutions, seminars, special committees, and official investigations. The second factor is the Sharpeville massacre of 21 March 1960, which evoked widespread dismay and fueled anti-apartheid sentiments worldwide.

Apartheid was annually condemned by the General Assembly as contrary to Articles 55 and 56 of the Charter of the United Nations from 1952 until 1990 and was regularly condemned by the Security Council after the Sharpsville Massacre in 1960. An examination of UN resolutions from the years 1948 to 1973 reveals recurring charges against apartheid as a crime related to the crime of genocide.[26] Until 1966, the UN General Assembly condemned apartheid as violating the

---

[22] Irwin, *Gordian Knot: Apartheid and the Unmaking of the Liberal World Order*, 3–6.
[23] Paul Taylor and A. J. R. Groom, *United Nations at the Millennium: The Principal Organs* (London: Continuum, 2000), 237.
[24] Leo Kuper, "South Africa: Human Rights and Genocide" (Eleventh Annual Hans Wolff Memorial Lecture, African Studies Program, Indiana University, Bloomington, IN, 1980).
[25] Skinner, *The Foundations of Anti-Apartheid*, 5–6.
[26] For example, UNGA Resolution 2438, from December 19, 1968, dealt with measures to be taken against Nazism and racial intolerance. The resolution explicitly stated that racism, Nazism, and apartheid are incompatible with the objectives of the Convention on the Prevention and Punishment of the Crime of Genocide.

principles and spirit of the Charter of the UN and the Universal Declaration of Human Rights, as well as addressing the danger posed to international peace and security due to the tensions this policy created in South Africa.[27] The 16 December 1966 condemnation of apartheid as a crime against humanity by the UN General Assembly was a turning point in the international struggle against apartheid.[28] Moreover, an ad hoc group of experts appointed by the UN Commission on Human Rights in 1967 to investigate the torture and ill treatment of prisoners in South Africa extended its mandate into a preliminary examination of the South African government on charges of genocide.[29] Although UN institutions officially moved away from associating apartheid with genocide, this investigation ultimately led to the 1973 International Convention on the Suppression and Punishment of the Crime of Apartheid, fashioned after and referencing the Genocide Convention.[30]

This rhetoric was not restricted to UN forums and frequently appeared in public speeches of anti-apartheid activists worldwide. Delivering a statement at a press conference in Addis Ababa on 11 July 1973, the president of the ANC, Oliver Tambo, stated,

> South Africa is in violation of the United Nations Convention on Genocide . . . The vicious racism preached and practiced by the ruling minority, the indoctrination of children in schools, the youth and grown-up men and women in every walk of life is breeding hatred, suspicion and fear. The massive and relentless dispossession of peoples, coupled with the denial of elementary rights on the grounds of race, has established all the preconditions of genocide . . . Is it genocide only when one starts to put children in gas ovens? Is it not equally extermination if you deliberately create conditions in which more than 50 per cent of African children in one reserve in South Africa die before reaching the age of five?[31]

This kind of discursive performance of Holocaust memory in the lexicon of the anti-apartheid struggle, which evolved since the early 1960s onward, was

---

[27] Alschech, "The Apartheid Paradigm: History, Politics and Strategy," 168.
[28] UN General Assembly, The policies of apartheid of the Government of the Republic of South Africa, 13 December 1967, A/RES/2307.
[29] Commission on Human Rights Report on the Twenty-Fourth Session, 5 February to 12 March 1968, Economic and Social Council Official Records: Forty-Fourth Session, Supplement No. 4, United Nations, "Report of the ad hoc Working Group of Experts on the treatment of political prisoners in the Republic of South Africa," 2 (XXIV).
[30] International Convention on the Suppression and Punishment of the Crime of Apartheid, 30 November 1973, UNGA, Resolution 3068 (XXVII).
[31] Statement by Oliver Tambo at a press conference in Addis Ababa, 11 July 1973, Speeches by ANC Leaders, African National Congress, Historical Documents Archive.

multifaced and varied. By focusing on the individual experiences of the political prisoner Ahmed Kathrada, Chapter 7 will provide a glimpse into the effect of Holocaust memory on black prisoners of the apartheid regime on Robben Island; and the concluding chapter of this book will provide one case study of the performance of an analogical lexicon as a rhetorical weapon in his struggles for justice, focusing on the struggle of Archbishop Desmond Tutu against apartheid.

Chapter 7
Holocaust Memory in Ahmed Kathrada's Struggle against Apartheid

In Gilbert's article about Anne Frank's image in South Africa she describes how Ahmed Kathrada – an anti-apartheid activist imprisoned for eighteen years on Robben Island – secretly recorded in his prison notebooks inspiring quotations from *The Diary of Anne Frank,* among other quotations from smuggled books and newspapers.[1] On November 2014, I visited the University of Western Cape – Robben Island MayiBuye Archives and located Kathrada's seven secret prison notebooks. Notebook number three contains thirteen entries from *The Diary*, carefully chosen by Kathrada when he read the diary in prison in the late 1960s.

However, it soon became clear to me that Kathrada's interest in the Jewish genocide did not begin with the reading of *The Diary* on Robben Island. In his memoirs, written in 2004, he dedicated a chapter to a formative visit he made to the Auschwitz death camp and to the Warsaw ghetto in Poland in 1951, where he witnessed first-hand the destructive effects of the Second World War. In his writing, Kathrada contemplated the similarities between his struggle and the Warsaw ghetto uprising, invoking a productive interaction between Holocaust memory and his own experiences in apartheid South Africa.

In June 2016, two months before my third visit to South Africa, I came across a Facebook post by the Johannesburg Holocaust & Genocide Centre about an event they had organized marking World Refugee Day. They had invited a special key speaker – Ahmed Kathrada. I saw the opportunity and asked Tali Nates, the Centre director, to put me in touch with Kathrada, and on Friday morning, 11 August 2016, I met Kathrada in his apartment in Johannesburg. He received me with open arms and was keen to share his fascinating and inspiring life story. Kathrada died six months after our interview, on 28 March 2017, at the age of 87. This chapter is dedicated to his memory with the hope that the

---

1 Gilbert, "Anne Frank in South Africa," 366.

Note: This chapter is based on two articles published by the author of this book in 2019: "Reading the Diary of Anne Frank on Robben Island: On the role of Holocaust Memory in Ahmed Kathrada's Struggle against Apartheid," *Journal of Jewish Identities* 12.2 (2019): 175–195; "Ahmed Kathrada in Post-War Europe: Holocaust Memory and Apartheid South Africa (1951–1952)," *African Identities* 17.1 (2019): 1–17. The later was funded with the support of the European Union's Seventh Framework Programme (FP/2007–2013) / ERC Grant Agreement no. 615564.

https://doi.org/10.1515/9783110715545-008

principles which he embodied in his life and writings will continue to enrich the categories through which we imagine social change.

Becoming Communist

Kathrada was born on 21 August 1929 in Schweizer-Reneke, a small, rural, Afrikaner-dominated town about 240 miles from Johannesburg into a religious Muslim family of Indian descent.[2] Most Indians arrived in South Africa between 1860 and 1911 under labor contracts, to serve employers according to stipulated conditions for five years. At the end of their contract period, they were entitled to go back to India or to settle in a small area of Natal.[3] However, a minority of traders, mostly Muslims, who, like Kathrada's father, had come to South Africa independently, opened small shops.[4]

Stereotypes of the Indian merchant as dishonest, crafty, and exploitative were prevalent in South African society from the very inception of Indian settlement in the country. As Soske argues, "The Indian was not just ethnically foreign, but embodied the increasing power of an alien mode of calculating and distributing wealth."[5] Although anti-Indian legislation had been imposed at regular intervals from the late 19th century, the rise of right-wing, proto-fascist Afrikaner organizations over the 1930s and 1940s provoked violent anti-Indian demonstrations across the country.[6] The spread of extreme right-wing movements that nurtured the myth of Indian shopkeepers as exploitative, was closely tied to the Great Depression of 1929 and the resultant white poverty.[7] Such movements advocated displacing Indians from their position of economic privilege.[8]

---

[2] Ahmad Kathrada, *A Simple Freedom: The Strong Mind pf Robben Island Prisoner, No. 468/64 Ahmed Kathrada* (Johannesburg: Wild dog Press, 2009), 20.
[3] Leonard Thompson, *A History of South Africa* (New Haven: Yale University Press, 2001), 99; Christoph Marx, *Oxwagon Sentinel: Radical Afrikaner Nationalism and the History of the 'Ossewabrandwag'* (Münster: LIT Verlag, 2009), 249.
[4] Thompson, *A History of South Africa, Third Edition*, 171; Ahmed Kathrada, *Memoirs* (Cape Town: Zebra Press, 2004), 20.
[5] Soske, *Internal Frontiers*, 42.
[6] John Higginson, *Collective Violence and the Agrarian Origins of South African Apartheid, 1900–1948* (New York: Cambridge University Press, 2014), 25.
[7] Shain, *A Perfect Storm*, 86.
[8] John Hyslop, "White Working-Class Women and the Invention of Apartheid: 'Purified' Afrikaner Nationalist Agitation for Legislation against 'Mixed' Marriages, 1934–9," *The Journal of African History* 36.1 (1995): 57–81, at 70.

While Kathrada describes his childhood in Schweizer-Reneke as "smooth, marked by the joy of major celebrations, and the warmth and friendship, the sense of community, of small-town life," he had distinct memories of the impact of segregation laws on race relations in the town. He singled out, for instance, the ringing of the 9 pm curfew bell "signaling the hour after which Africans required a special pass to be on the streets." He also recalled that during the 1930s his father acquired another house. Given the restrictions on land ownership by Indians, "the properties were [. . .] acquired in the name of a 'Cape Malay' friend, whose 'race group' had not been disqualified from owning residential premises or business sites."[9] Here, Kathrada refers to the Transvaal Asiatic Land Tenure Act of 1932 and its subsequent amendments in 1934, 1935, and 1937, which limited Indian trading by preventing Indians from acquiring property outside of designated areas.[10]

Local laws of segregation also enforced separate schools for separate races. In Schweizer-Reneke there was a school for black South Africans and a school for whites, but as an Indian, Kathrada could not attend either.[11] This political reality forced him to migrate to Johannesburg without his parents when he was only eight years old. As he memorably put it: "politics dispatched me to the city and that is where I learned my politics at a very early age."[12]

In 1937, while Kathrada was a pupil at Newtown Indian Primary in downtown Johannesburg, Strijdom, then the Transvaal provincial leader of the NP, eliminated Jewish membership in his party while adopting antisemitic and anti-Indian ideas from local proto-fascist propaganda.[13] These right-wing nationalistic trends gained greater prominence after the 1938 "Great Trek" commemoration. As John Higginson argues, "In the wake of the centennial commemoration of the Great Trek, a trail of anti-African, anti-Indian, and anti-Semitic flashpoints, usually carried out by younger members and 'cheerleaders' of the *Ossewa Brandwag* and South African *Greyshirts*, shadowed the ceremonial ox-wagons once they arrived in the western Transvaal and Pretoria."[14]

When the South African parliament decided to enter the Second World War on the side of the Allies, it also introduced the Asian Land Tenure and Trading Act, placing further restrictions on Indian residence. This resulted in a new

---

9 Kathrada, *Memoirs*, 21–22.
10 Anthony K. Appiah and Henry L. Gates, *Africana: The Encyclopedia of the African and African American Experience* (Oxford: Oxford University Press, 2005), 293.
11 Kathrada, *A Simple Freedom*, 21.
12 Kathrada, *Memoirs*, 21.
13 Higginson, *Collective Violence*, 326.
14 Higginson, *Collective Violence*, 25.

Indian leadership evolving from the left, which was influenced by the CPSA.[15] The Indian South African activist Yusuf Dadoo was one of the first Indian leaders to join the Communist Party in early 1939. In his *Memoirs*, Kathrada refers to him as "a pivotal and revolutionary leader in South Africa" and recalls how he and his Johannesburg friends distributed political pamphlets and hung posters with anti-war messages on his behalf.[16]

Following Dadoo, Kathrada joined the Young Communist League (YCL) when he was just twelve.[17] In his memoirs, he stated that he had joined the YCL "not out of any intellectual appreciation of Marxism-Leninism, or any intelligent understanding of its politics on South Africa . . . [but out of] the broad struggle against injustice and inequality, and for democracy and non-racialism."[18] This statement is crucial for an understanding of Kathrada's complex political identity, which was not limited to communism *per se* but which included diverse ideas drawn from various ideologies and traditions.

By the mid-1940s, however, Kathrada was already well-versed in communism and was admitted into the CPSA, which at that time followed the example of the British Communist Party and actively embraced culture as its main tool for mobilization and education.[19] As Kathrada noted in our interview, it was at the Party meetings that he acquired deeper knowledge of Nazi Germany and the ongoing tragedy of European Jewry:

> The Communist Party had such schools. Their speakers were not confined to South Africa. It was very internationalist. So, I learned at a young age, not to be confined just to South Africa. So that was really useful [. . .] I became conscious of the world outside of South Africa, and that's how one learned of Nazism and later on of course, of the Holocaust, all the things out there, the ghettos, you know?[20]

Kathrada's account is compatible with scholarly historiography of the CPSA's position on the war. Until June 1941 the CPSA opposed the war, claiming that it was an inter-imperialist conflict, and focused on building a united front against

---

[15] Soske, *Internal Frontiers*, 81.
[16] Kathrada, *Memoir*, 21, 31.
[17] Mac Maharaj, *Reflections in Prison: Voices from the South African Liberation Struggle* (Cape Town: Zebra Press, 2001), 91.
[18] Kathrada, *Memoir*, 34.
[19] Corinne Sandwith, "'Yours for Socialism': Communist Cultural Discourse in Early Apartheid South Africa," *Safundi: The Journal of South African and American Studies* 14 (2013): 5–6.
[20] Personal communication between Ahmed Kathrada (AK) and Roni Mikel Arieli, 11 August 2016, Johannesburg.

the war which included the white and black working class.[21] The *Molotov-Ribbentrop* Pact signed by the Soviets and the Germans in 1939 helped reinforce this stance. However, immediately after Germany's invasion of the Soviet Union on 21 June 1941, the Party shifted position and became a staunch defender of human liberty in the face of Nazi terror.[22] As mentioned in Chapter 1, although South Africa had joined the war against Nazi Germany in September 1939, opposition to the war was prominent in Afrikaner nationalist circles.[23] Indeed, Kathrada testified that the Communist Party's anti-fascist message had a great impact on him, especially in light of right-wing Afrikaner support for Nazism at that time. Moreover, he asserted that the sights of war he witnessed ten years later, during his European odyssey, reinforced his anti-fascist tendencies.[24]

Kathrada soon became prominent as a youth leader. Over the mid-1940s, he worked fulltime in the offices of the Transvaal Passive Resistance Council. In his memoirs he states: "A mere twelve months after the Second World War ended, there was widespread expectation of a future in which freedom, equality and peace would flourish, and colonialism, racism and armed conflict would be no more."[25] The South African political circumstances of the mid-1940s, however, witnessed increasing segregation. The Sauer Commission, appointed by the NP in 1946 to prepare its policy statement on the racial problem, treated Indians as "an alien, unassimilable element in South Africa," while simultaneously recommending "the rigorous segregation of the Coloured People, the consolidation of the African reserves, the removal of missionary control of African education, and the abolition of the Natives Representative Council and the representation of Africans in Parliament."[26]

These circumstances had a tremendous impact on Kathrada's political development. In 1946, he was one of the organizers of the South African Indian Congress (SAIC) Passive Resistance Movement against the Asiatic Land Tenure and Indian Representation Act, also known as the "Ghetto Act," in protest of the restricted political representation afforded Indian South Africans and their confined living areas.[27] As discussed in the previous chapter, the use of the

---

21 Allison Drew, *South Africa's Radical Tradition: A Documentary History, Volume One 1907–1950* (Cape Town: University of Capte Town Press, 1996), 34.
22 Sandwith, "'Yours for Socialism,'" 5; Drew, *South African's Radical Tradition*, 35.
23 Shain, *A Perfect Storm*, 232.
24 AK, Personal communication, 11 August 2016.
25 Kathrada, *Memoir*, 41.
26 Thompson, *A History of South Africa, Third Edition*, 185.
27 Kathrada, *Memoir*, 43–44.

term 'ghetto' in this context was undoubtedly charged with resonances of its use by the Nazi regime.[28]

The general election in 1948 marked the beginning of a new era in South Africa. The Nationalists' election slogan was "apartheid," marking the radicalization of race-based laws. Kathrada recalls: "The legislation that followed might have been taken straight from Hitler's Third Reich. After all, some of the most prominent members of the NP had unashamedly supported Nazi Germany."[29] In 1950, when the apartheid government introduced some of its most repressive acts such as the Suppression of Communism Act, the Immorality Act, and the Group Areas Act, Kathrada enrolled at the University of Witwatersrand for a Bachelor of Arts degree. At that point, he had already learned about the atrocities of the Second World War through books, films, and YCL lectures. However, in his memoirs he stated, "it is another thing entirely to enter the belly of the dead beast yourself and be surrounded by the voiceless bones of those it has devoured," referring to his visit to post-War Europe in 1951.[30]

Reflecting on Apartheid in Post-War Europe

On 14 June 1951, Kathrada left South Africa and travelled through Zambia, Kenya, Sudan, and Greece to Italy, England, Czechoslovakia, and Hungary, where he finally settled at the World Federation of Democratic Youth (WFDY) headquarters as the head of the African desk.

While in Europe, Kathrada was exposed to lingering evidence of war-time destruction. In his memoir, he mentions his visit to Prague, where he first learned of the village of Lidice, which was destroyed by Nazi forces in reprisal for the assassination of Reich Protector Reinhard Heydrich in the late spring of 1942 – an assassination carried out on behalf of the Czechoslovak government in exile.

> Thoughts of the bloody and cruel retribution exacted by his [Heydrich's] henchmen darkened the edge of my consciousness as I walked the city streets . . . Surveying the scene of such merciless destruction, I recalled how bravely Julius Fucik had continued to write his last words, almost up to the very moment of his execution. Fucik symbolized resistance to Nazism, and his words, published as *Notes from the Gallows*, took their place in a body of literature that would inspire future generations.[31]

---

28 Kathrada, *Memoir*, 85–86.
29 Kathrada, *Memoir*, 60.
30 Kathrada, *Memoir*, 88.
31 Kathrada, *Memoir*, 90.

The Nazis in Berlin eventually executed Fucik, an active member of the Communist Party of Czechoslovakia and at the forefront of the anti-Nazi resistance, in September 1943. His book, *Notes from the Gallows*, written during his imprisonment in Prague, was smuggled out of prison and published after the war. Fucik became an icon of the Communist Party after 1948, when the communists used his text as evidence of their heroic resistance to Nazism.[32] Though he did not explicitly recall this, it is possible that Kathrada was first introduced to Fucik's book during his participation in the cultural activities of the South African YCL during the late 1940s, in the context of the construction of the communist narrative of the Second World War as a war against fascism.

As mentioned in Chapter 3, in the international arena, after the war, perceptions of the role of the battle for Stalingrad and of resistance to Nazism in Western Europe and the USSR were intertwined.[33] Thomas C. Fox (2004) argues that during the early post-War period, the communist narrative of the Holocaust was part of the master narrative of Marxism. Within this framework, antisemitism or any other ethnically or racially based form of oppression was construed as the product of efforts by the ruling classes "to divert the attention of the oppressed from their oppressors."[34] Fox demonstrates how the Soviet definition of fascism, which viewed fascism as an extreme form of capitalism, excluded the specificity of the Jewish victims. Even when the Soviets did mention the Nazi murder of Jews, this was usually viewed as part of the catastrophe of the Great Patriotic War that derived from fascist racism.[35] Within this narrative, communists were classified as 'Fighters against Fascism,' whereas Jews were classified as 'Victims of Fascism.'

Kathrada's adoption of this communist narrative, as we have seen with reference to his reflections on the Lidice massacre, was especially pertinent for his description of sites of war atrocities that were not tied to Jews in particular. This is also evident in Kathrada's recollections of his visit to the German city of Dresden. Dresden came under massive attack by the Allies during four aerial bombing raids between 12 to 15 February 1945, resulting in what was described as a 'German catastrophe,' with approximately 380,000 civilian victims.[36] During the first years after the war, the bombing was presented by the Allies as a

---

[32] Arnold Suppan and Maximilian Graf, *From the Austrian Empire to Communist East Central Europe* (Berlin: LIT Verlag, 2010), 184.
[33] Kotek, *Students and the Cold War*, 62–63.
[34] Thomas C. Fox. "The Holocaust under Communism," in *The Historiography of the Holocaust*, ed. Dan Stone (New York: Palgrave McMillan, 2004), 420–439, at 420.
[35] Fox, "The Holocaust under Communism," 421.
[36] Benda-Beckmann, *German Catastrophe?*, 11.

consequence of failed air protection and as a response to the aggressive war of the Nazi State. However, after 1948, on the eve of the Cold War, the Soviet bloc portrayed the bombing of Dresden as an act of terror and a war crime committed by the Western Allies against innocent German citizens. By emphasizing that the Red Army had been the only true liberator of Germany from Hitler's fascism, the Soviet Union used the Dresden bombing to demonstrate American aggression against the German population and as evidence of American imperialism.[37]

The sight of the ruined city made a huge impact on Kathrada. In his memoirs, he states, "for many years afterwards, the ruined town became synonymous in my mind with District Six, Sophiatown and other areas razed to the ground in the name of ideology."[38] As Kathrada testifies, this insight was made retrospectively. The Group Areas Act was passed in 1950, creating the legal framework for the government to establish segregated neighborhoods where only people of a particular race were able to reside.[39] However, the Sophiatown forced removals took place only on 9 February 1955, when two thousand police officers forcefully moved the black families of Sophiatown to Meadowlands, Soweto. Moreover, the destruction of District Six, also under the Group Areas Act, would only be implemented in 1969, when the Indian, black, and Coloured members of the neighborhood were forcibly moved and their homes and businesses destroyed.[40] Sixty-three years after his visit, the suffering of the South Africans who were evacuated from their homes merges with the suffering of the German citizens of Dresden for Kathrada. These reflections resonate with the Soviet narrative that frames the bombing of Dresden as an Anglo-American imperialist war crime. Despite their anachronism, Kathrada's reflections can be read as a general critique of inhumane acts performed "in the name of ideology," namely imperialism, colonialism, and totalitarianism.

Kathrada's anti-imperialist and anti-colonialist tendencies were formed during his membership in the South African YCL, and it is safe to assume that they were well maintained during his European odyssey and especially during his tenure as head of the African desk at the WFDY headquarters. WFDY was founded in London in November 1945 as the broadest possible international organization of the younger generation. Its chief objective was to prevent a resurgence of fascism and to outlaw war forever, thus reflecting the intertwined post-war anti-fascist perceptions between East and West.[41] Kathrada was also involved with the International

---

[37] Benda-Beckmann, *A German Catastrophe?*, 35–36.
[38] Kathrada, *Memoir*, 91.
[39] Thompson, *A History of South Africa, Third Edition*, 194.
[40] Thompson, *A History of South Africa, Third Edition*, 194.
[41] Kotek, *Students and the Cold War*, 62–63.

Union of Students (IUS), established in August 1946 in Prague to enlist students world-wide to confront political questions and in particular the problem of defending peace and freedom.[42]

These two youth organizations were responsible for launching the World Festivals for Youth and Students as early as 1947. At the time of their establishment, the World Festivals were seen as important international cultural events that included a variety of cultural performances, including dance groups, choirs, dance and song soloists, sketches, and so on, showcasing the national traditions and aspirations of young people from around the world.[43] Although South Africa never sent an official delegation to these festivals, local youth organizations sent a handful of representatives during the late 1940s and early 1950s. South African representation, however, was mostly comprised of South African students studying abroad. On the preparation of the South African delegation to the East Berlin World Festival for Youth and Students in 1951, Kathrada recounted in our interview:

> In the South African delegation, we were sixty members, most of whom were based outside of South Africa because there was a question of passports. I had a passport issued when the United Party was still in power in South Africa and it was a five-year passport, so when I went to Europe it was still valid. When the Nats [the Nationalists] came into power, passports became almost impossible, and we had to smuggle people out and all that. So fortunately, I had a passport, and as I mentioned there was sizeable number of South Africans, black and white students, that came to the Festival from London. Quite a few of them were already politically conscious, and they became more conscious at the Berlin festival.[44]

A report of the International Committee of the Festival meeting in Berlin from May 1951 reveals the presence of South African organizations such as the Transvaal Indian Youth Congress, the Union of African Youth, the Federation of Free Students, the Peace Committee, and the South African Indian Congress, on the festival committee.[45] South African involvement in organizing the festival was also reflected in its official objectives, which were to provide "[a] broad basis for the rallying of youth. Neither the color of skin, nor the difference of opinions or

---

42 Kotek, *Students and the Cold War*, 86–87.
43 Third World Festival of Youth and Students for Peace, Berlin 5–19 August 1951 [Brochure], 1, World Youth Festival Collection- WYFC (File Berlin, 1951), International Institute for Social History- IISH, Amsterdam.
44 AK, Personal communication, 11 August 2016.
45 "International Committee of the 3rd World Festival of Youth and Students for Peace, Meeting in Berlin, May 19th-20th, 1951," Box 1st – 7th Festivals 1941–1955, folder 3rd Festival Berlin, 1951, 12, World Youth Festival Collection, International Institute for Social History, Amsterdam.

religions represent an obstacle or a condition for the participation at the Festival. Black, white and colored from South Africa, Negroes and white in the United States, prepare in common their trip to Berlin."[46]

The festival opened on 5 August 1951 and lasted until 19 August, with one-and-a-half million young Germans and more than 25,000 delegates from 104 countries attending.[47] The South African cultural program included a mixed black and white South African choir, which sang "the songs of the English and Boer population, as well as the beautiful songs of the Africans" in an attempt to reflect South African society as a whole.[48] This utopian representation can be perceived either as highly ironic in light of the cultural segregation intrinsic to apartheid rule or perhaps, more positively, as a performance expressing hope for a more egalitarian society.

The festival was framed as a non-political, primarily cultural and social event. In practice, however, it was clearly communist.[49] Communist states subsidized the attendance of young people from Africa and Asia, in addition to providing special trains and translating newspapers and magazines into up to eight languages, in an effort to promote an idyllic vision of socialism aimed at participants from the West, as well as the participants from the emerging postcolonial nations.[50] Kathrada recalls,

> There were some moving events that I shall never forget, social gatherings where young people met and talked, sang, danced, ate, drank, kissed, embraced and pledged everlasting friendship. Thus, Vietnamese met the French, Koreans talked to Americans, and Israelis consorted with Germans. In a gesture of solidarity, delegates sent postcards to Paul Robeson and Jomo Kenyatta, who personified the fight against racism and all forms of discrimination.[51]

Seen through Kathrada's eyes, the festival was a unique opportunity for intercultural interaction, where participants from the Global South were able to criticize their colonizers, and Israeli Jewish survivors were able to confront their German executioners. This depiction of colonized people and of Holocaust

---

[46] "International Committee of the 3_{rd} World Festival of Youth and Students for Peace, Meeting in Berlin, May 19_{th}-20_{th}, 1951," Box 1_{st} – 7_{th} Festivals 1941–1955, folder 3rd Festival Berlin, 1951, 5, World Youth Festival Collection, International Institute for Social History, Amsterdam.
[47] Kotek, *Students and the Cold War*, 23–25.
[48] "International Committee of the 3_{rd} World Festival of Youth and Students for Peace, Meeting in Berlin, May 19_{th}-20_{th}, 1951," Box 1_{st} – 7_{th} Festivals 1941–1955, folder 3rd Festival Berlin, 1951, 21, World Youth Festival Collection, International Institute for Social History, Amsterdam.
[49] Kotek, *Students and the Cold War*, 189.
[50] Kotek, *Students and the Cold War*, 190.
[51] Kathrada, *Memoir*, 191.

survivors as victims of the destructive forces of racism provides a glimpse into the ways in which Kathrada wove disparate traumatic histories into the broad struggle against injustice and inequality. This reflection on the festival gathering alludes to Kathrada's later adoption of the idiosyncratic Jewish suffering, as we shall see in his contemplation on the sites of Jewish suffering such as the Warsaw ghetto and the Auschwitz death camp. It reflects a marked departure from the Soviet narrative described above, which argued that people died during the Holocaust not because of their race, but because they were opposed to fascism.

Kathrada's departure from the Soviet narrative of the Holocaust is reinforced in his narration of his visit to Poland, after the East Berlin festival was over. He was invited to participate in the Warsaw meeting of the IUS, held from 31 August to 6 September 1951, and travelled through the city and its surroundings in the weeks prior to the event.[52] It was during that short period that he visited the Warsaw ghetto and Auschwitz death camp. He reflected on the enormous impact of the sights he had witnessed:

> When we went to what had been the Warsaw Ghetto, I was reminded of the Nazi atrocities in Czechoslovakia. The Jews who rose up in Warsaw had been crushed as ruthlessly as the villagers of Lidice. Confined to an area of the city behind a wall eighteen kilometers long and almost three meters high, the beleaguered Jews had been warned by one of the rare escapees from Treblinka that extermination waited at the end of a nightmarish rail journey in closed cattle cars. Led by Mordecai Anielewicz, the young and the brave rose up against their captors on 19 April 1943. By 8 May, the uprising had been crushed, and rather than be taken prisoner, Anielewicz and others took their own lives . . . When I visited the site of this blot on humanity, only a modest monument marked the murder of tens of thousands of Jews and paid tribute to the handful who fought back and died.[53]

Kathrada's encounter with the remains of the Warsaw ghetto in 1951 and his detailed description of the Jewish uprising points to his perception of the Jewish tragedy in Europe as a source of inspiration. While Kathrada's memoirs specifically describe the Warsaw ghetto victims as Jews, he also acknowledged the non-Jewish victims of Nazi atrocities, including the inhabitants of the Czechoslovakian village of Lidice, who are central to his recollection of his visit to Prague. Kathrada points to similarities between the story of the crushed resistance of the Warsaw ghetto Jews and the story of the persecution and massacre of the inhabitants of Lidice. By recognizing the specifically Jewish identity of the victims of the Warsaw ghetto, while at the same time placing their heroic resistance and tragic death alongside those of the victims of Lidice, Kathrada

---

52 Kathrada, *Memoir*, 91.
53 Kathrada, *Memoir*, 92.

retains some elements of the Soviet narrative of the war, but abandons others, in order to reflect on the struggle in South Africa.

Kathrada testified that his visit to the Auschwitz death camp made an indelible impression on him. In 1947, the Polish government declared Auschwitz-Birkenau a memorial site at which "Poles and citizens of other nationalities fought and died a martyr's death."[54] The International Auschwitz Committee, comprised of survivors and relatives of victims, was dominated by veterans of the largely Communist Auschwitz underground. This committee decided to turn over the barracks in the original work camp area to twenty countries for use as 'national pavilions.' One of these structures became a 'Jewish pavilion' which was usually locked and opened only on special occasions.[55] Auschwitz was conceived as a site of Nazi terror and international martyrdom.[56] It was "squarely Polish from its inception, but the national narrative was told in the Socialist mode and according to Socialist parameters."[57] As the Jewish killing was forced into the background, the extent of Polish suffering, as well as the role of the heroic liberating Red Army, was foregrounded.[58]

Kathrada writes of Auschwitz: "I could never obliterate the sight of the trench in which dogs mauled and savaged people to death; the gas chambers and incinerators; the lampshades made of human skin, the pillows stuffed with human hair."[59] He found the death camp to be a "poignant reminder to mankind of the evils of racism," and was overcome with emotion "as [he] walked on the fragments of human bones littering the street near the incinerators."[60] In his interview, Kathrada mentioned a friend named John who accompanied him on the Auschwitz visit. He could not recall John's last name, though he remembered that he was an Afrikaner studying at one of London's universities.

> His parents were Nationalists, and Nationalists were pro-Hitler. The boy had broken away from that because he was a student in London, where he became politically aware. Outside of South Africa, his whole attitude had changed, and of course when he went to Europe and experienced firsthand what racism meant. It was a lesson for him, and of course, Auschwitz was a lesson for all of us.[61]

---

54 Michael C. Steinlauf, *Bonding to the Dead: Poland and the Memory of the Holocaust* (Syracuse, NY: Syracuse University Press, 1997), 69.
55 Steinlauf, *Bonding to the Dead*, 70.
56 Steinlauf, *Bonding to the Dead*, 161.
57 Genevieve Zubrzycki, *The Cross of Auschwitz: Nationalism and Religion in Post-Communist Poland* (Chicago: The University of Chicago Press, 2006), 103.
58 Zubrzycki, *The Cross of Auschwitz*, 105.
59 Kathrada, *Memoir*, 92.
60 Kathrada, *Memoir*, 92.
61 AK, Personal communication, 11 August 2016.

Kathrada believed that the Jewish genocide constituted an important lesson for humanity and bore particular relevance for his own country. Thus he "carefully collected a handful of bone fragments," bringing them back to South Africa to serve as stark reminders of racism's consequences.[62] Moreover, it appears that, although the Auschwitz memorial site was constructed to reflect the communist narrative of the war, Kathrada's feelings about the camp were more consistent with the Jewish narrative with its emphasis on Jewish suffering, persecution, and murder.

The Road to Robben Island

Kathrada returned to South Africa in May 1952, determined to participate actively in the struggle against apartheid. He immediately became involved in organizing the 1952 Defiance Campaign against six apartheid laws and was one of twenty defendants, including Nelson Mandela and Walter Sisulu, sentenced to a nine-month suspended sentence.[63]

On a winter morning in September 1952, Kathrada stood on the podium at the Trades Hall in Johannesburg, holding the bottle full of human bones he had collected in Auschwitz, and addressed the audience of the ANC Youth League. He stated, "People are fighting for freedom in the whole world. I was in Europe a few months ago and there saw numbers of human bones lying about the country, bones of Jews that Hitler killed because he accused them of being communists. They were not communists; Malan is now following the example of Hitler by arresting our leaders."[64]

This speech, delivered only a few months after Kathrada's return from Europe, provides an accurate and contemporaneous indication of his perception of the Holocaust. On the one hand, he specifically refers to the Jews as Hitler's victims. Simultaneously, however, in noting that Hitler accused the Jews of being communist, Kathrada departs from the Jewish narrative of the Holocaust and implies that Nazi ideology was motivated by anti-communism and not solely by antisemitism, a position more compatible with the Soviet narrative of the war. As we shall see below in other addresses from the 1950s, this position

---

62 Kathrada, *Memoir*, 92.
63 Kathrada, *A Simple Freedom*, 21.
64 Kathrada, A. 28 September 1952, Restrictions: Ahmed Mohamed Kathrada, South African Police reports on Kathrrada, A. public addresses, File 1.1.1952–1954, South African Police Profile AMK, The Ahmed Kathrada Foundation Archive, Lenasia.

enabled Kathrada to draw parallels between Hitler and Malan's policy of invoking the struggle against communism in order to suppress opposition.

At his address to the Anti-Permit Committee on 18 November 1956, Kathrada continued to draw connections between Hitler and Malan's anti-Communist agenda: "I said to you before that Dr. Malan tried to imprison our leaders under the Suppression of Communism Act. In 1933 Hitler also had the Suppression of Communism Act in Germany. It was an Act to suppress communism. It was an Act which killed millions and millions of innocent people who fought for freedom!"[65]

In this address. Kathrada neglects to designate the victims' Jewish identity, and therefore obscures the racial dimension of the Nazi killing. However, his comparison between the Nazi Enabling Act of March 1933, which allowed the Nazis to effectively determine who constituted an opponent, and the apartheid Suppression of Communism Act of 1950, is not inaccurate. According to statistics held by the Nazis, the most common form of opposition derived from those ideologically opposed to the Nazis, primarily the communists and socialists. As in the South African case, once one was labelled an opponent of the government, arrest was inevitable.

Later in the same address, Kathrada makes a comparison between Hitler's *Lebensraum* Policy and the Ghettoization of the Jews in Europe with Malan's Group Areas Act, referring specifically to the suffering of Hitler's Jewish victims. He states:

> Dr. Malan has given you the Group Areas Act. Hitler also had the Group Areas Act for the Jewish people. He also said that the Jews must stay on one side; and when the Jews were put on one side, what did Hitler do? I remind you of the Warsaw Ghetto. In the Warsaw Ghetto Hitler sacrificed two square miles of land where the Jews had to live; A wall [was constructed] all-round the ghetto and all round that wall he placed electricity – live electricity – electric wires! and the Jews who wanted to leave those ghettos, the Jews who wanted to get into those ghettos had to get a pass like our people had to get passes in this country![66]

This description of Jewish life in the Warsaw ghetto is far more specific and draws attention to the similarities between the racially based restrictions imposed on Jews by the Nazis and those imposed on Indian, black, and Coloured South Africans by the apartheid government. Kathrada enlists the memory of the racial persecution of European Jews in order to reflect on his own struggle against racist

---

[65] Police Memorandum, South African Police reports on Kathrrada, A. public addresses, 60. File 1.6–23 January 1949 to 4 July 1966-South African Police records, AMK letters, speeches, public meetings, The Ahmed Kathrada Foundation Archive, Lenasia.
[66] Police Memorandum, South African Police reports on Kathrrada, A. public addresses, 60. File 1.6 -23 January 1949 to 4 July 1966-South African Police records, AMK letters, speeches, public meetings, The Ahmed Kathrada Foundation Archive, Lenasia.

apartheid policies. The rhetorical value of this comparison for him is important here. As a youth leader, Kathrada hoped that the memory of an event that was comparatively recent would be an asset for mobilizing his listeners to action. Most of them had lived through the war and had been subject to dual propaganda from those opposing it and those supporting it. Moreover, most of the youth Kathrada addressed in his speeches were politically involved in various organizations and were probably familiar with the frequent analogy made between apartheid and Nazism within the publications of the anti-apartheid movement.

In December 1956, Kathrada was among the one hundred fifty-six activists and leaders charged with high treason.[67] Although he and the others were granted bail soon after being apprehended, the trial continued for five years.[68] The massacre at Sharpeville occurred while Chief Luthuli was testifying for the defense. Kathrada recalls this day: "The entire court listened with rapt attention as the ANC's highly respected president slowly and clearly spelt out every aspect of the organization's policy and goals [. . .] little did we know that not two hours' drive from the courtroom, a tragedy was unfolding that would have an irrevocable impact on South Africa's history."[69] A state of emergency was declared, and the trialists were arrested anew.[70] A year after the Sharpeville events, on 29 March 1961, judgment was passed, and the accused were acquitted. However, as Kathrada argues, "the shootings jolted us into realizing that the ANC's declared policy of non-violence had become an anachronism."[71]

During the 1950s and early 1960s, security police repeatedly placed Kathrada under restrictions. However, he continued to address young activists publicly, frequently invoking the sights of destruction he had witnessed while visiting post-war Europe, in particular the sights of Jewish suffering under the Nazi regime. During those years, he became closer to the leadership of the ANC and was a member of a small committee in charge of facilitating Mandela's day to day activities.[72] When Mandela was arrested again in August 1962, Kathrada

---

67 Kathrada, *Memoirs*, 120.
68 Alan Wieder, "The Treason Trial and Underground Action," in *Ruth First and Joe Slovo in the War Against Apartheid* (New York: Monthly Review Press, 2013), 90–111; Kathrada, *Memoirs*, 122.
69 Kathrada, *Memoirs*, 126.
70 Kathrada, *Memoirs*, 122.
71 Kathrada, *Memoirs*, 127.
72 Kathrada, *Memoirs*, 137–138.

was appointed secretary of the Free Mandela Committee, and while Mandela was awaiting trial he saw him several times.[73]

On 11 July 1963, the police descended on Liliesleaf Farm in the Johannesburg suburb of Rivonia, purchased by the Jewish South African anti-apartheid activist Arthur Goldreich on behalf of the South African Communist Party. During the raid, Kathrada, Walter Sisulu, Govan Mbeki, Raymond Mhlaba, Lionel Bernstein, and Bob Hepple were arrested. Arthur Goldreich, Andrew Mlangeni, James Kantor, Dennis Goldberg, Harold Wolpe and Elias Motsoaledi were arrested shortly after the raid.[74]

These arrests led to the infamous Rivonia Trial, held on 11 June 1964, in which eight defendants were each charged with two counts of sabotage and sentenced to life imprisonment with hard labor.[75] The trial was a pivotal moment in South African history, and along with Mandela, Sisulu, Mbeki, and others, Kathrada was a major actor in this national drama. On 13 June 1964, the black prisoners landed on Robben Island to begin their life sentences.[76] For Kathrada, it would be almost twenty-seven years before he would finally be free.[77]

Reading Cultures on Robben Island

Robben Island has always figured in South African history as the ultimate place of exclusion – used over its history as an asylum hospital; a facility for imprisoning slaves, traditional leaders, and chiefs who resisted British colonial authorities; a place of incarceration for lepers; and finally, a prison for political prisoners of the apartheid regime.[78] In *A Long Walk to Freedom*, Nelson Mandela terms Robben Island "another country."[79] Indeed, during apartheid rule the Island figured both as a foreign place so radically cut off from South Africa as to be almost unknowable, and as a repetition or mirror of South Africa where

---

[73] Kathrada recalls in his memoirs that Joe Slovo, who was Mandela's lawyer, informed the prison authorities that he needed Kathrada to be present during consultations, as he would probably be called as a witness. See Kathrada, *Memoirs*, 150.
[74] Kathrada, *A Simple Freedom*, 26.
[75] Maharaji, *Reflections in Prison*, 96; Sahm Venter, *A Free Mind: Ahmed Kathrada's Notebook from Robben Island* (Johannesburg: Jacana Media, 2005), 10–11.
[76] Venter, *A Free Mind*, 194.
[77] Kathrada, *A Simple Freedom*, 32.
[78] Barbara Hutton, *Robben Island: Symbol of Resistance* (Johannesburg: SACHED Books, 1997), 9–10. The author would like to thank Dr. Karin Berkman for her insights on the history of Robben Island.
[79] Nelson Mandela, *A Long Walk to Freedom* (New York: Little, Brown & Co., 1995), 227.

the restrictions of apartheid were replicated.[80] One replication of apartheid restriction on the Island was manifested through the censorship of the reading materials that inmates could receive from the outside world. Books and letters were censored, and prisoners were not allowed to have newspapers until 1980.[81] However, as Archie L. Dick relates, because apartheid censorship frequently banned books and condemned political activists to imprisonment for having such material in their possession, prisoners smuggled books into prison "to subvert the worst designs of incarceration and censorship."[82]

In her book *Robben Island and Prisoner Resistance to Apartheid* (2003), Fran Buntman describes how Robben Island became the principal site for apartheid's incarceration of political prisoners. Because the Island held the largest concentration of political prisoners during apartheid rule, it soon became a pivotal component of the evolution of anti-apartheid politics.[83] Buntman describes the ways in which political prisoners transformed Robben Island into a site of resistance. For most of the men on the Island, surviving imprisonment was their own way to contribute to the liberation struggle, and they frequently challenged prison conditions to secure both their physical and mental survival.[84]

The Rivonia Trialists were held with thirty to forty other prisoners in a single-cell courtyard – officially designated Section B but known to prisoners as the "leadership section" – cut off from the general population.[85] This division was intended to separate the prisoners and prevent communication between them; however, with time, prison conditions slowly improved, and the degree of separation likewise diminished over the years. The need for communication between the different sections, as well as with the outside world, drove the prisoners to establish the communication committee, led by Kathrada. This committee focused both on facilitating effective means of communication among prisoners and on establishing a smuggling system for banned material. Kathrada explained its workings during our interview:

> About twenty-five of us were completely isolated from the rest of the prison community with Mandela and others; the others were in the communal cells, so our experiences were different. And we had to do a lot of smuggling, which took place mainly in the communal

---

[80] Fran Lisa Buntman, *Robben Island and Prisoner Resistance to Apartheid* (Cambridge: Cambridge University Press, 2003), 3.
[81] Hutton, *Robben Island*, 75.
[82] Archie L. Dick, *The Hidden History of South African Books and Reading Cultures* (Toronto: University of Toronto Press, 2013), 124–125.
[83] Buntman, *Robben Island and Prisoner Resistance to Apartheid*, 3–4.
[84] Buntman, *Robben Island and Prisoner Resistance to Apartheid*, 33–34.
[85] Buntman, *Robben Island and Prisoner Resistance to Apartheid*, 39.

cells, where there were hundreds of prisoners and some of them worked in the warders' houses. We were not allowed to have newspapers for fourteen years, so we kept ourselves informed, and our colleagues working at the warders' houses just took newspapers from there and then copied items of interest and smuggled them into us.[86]

While outside news was a top priority for the Island smuggling network, books too became coveted objects for smuggling since they were not readily available and often censored by the prison authorities.[87] Prison regulation number 109(3) in 1965 required the establishment and maintenance of a properly organized library for all prisoners, including those imprisoned on Robben Island, "containing literature of constructive and educational value."[88] However, while the library in the General Section of the Robben Island prison became operational at the end of 1965, the library in B section, where Kathrada, Mandela, Sisulu, and other senior political prisoners were held, received a restricted number of books from the 1960s through the 1970s.[89]

Apart from smuggling, another way to get books into prison was by enrolling in academic education or correspondence-based learning at the University of South Africa (UNISA) and other institutions with long-distance study programs. Studies became a way of maintaining one's morale in prison. Though only few prisoners registered in such educational programs, their studies had an enormous effect on the prison community as a whole thanks to an attempt to educate all Islanders, even the illiterate.[90] During the period of his imprisonment Kathrada completed three degrees:

> I was never interested in studies. I thought it was a waste of my time. But I saw that one advantage of formal education is that it gets books, because in jail you couldn't just order books as you like [. . .] Robben Island had a whole office full of censors for our letters and books and so forth, and fortunately for us they were not really advanced enough to know what is what. Therefore, many books came in.[91]

When asked why *The Diary of Anne Frank* was forbidden on Robben Island, Kathrada recalled:

---

86 AK, Personal communication, 11 August 2016.
87 David Schalkwyk, *Hamlet's Dreams: The Robben Island Shakespeare* (London: The Arden Shakespeare, 2012), 15–16.
88 Dick, *Hidden History*, 129–130.
89 Only in early 1978 was Kathrada allowed by the prison authorities to establish a tiny library in his section, where he could use his B.A. degree in Library Studies to justify his new role. For further reading see Dick, *The Hidden History of South African Books and Reading Cultures*, 130.
90 Buntman, *Robben Island and Prisoner Resistance to Apartheid*, 62–64.
91 AK, Personal Communication, 11 August 2016.

We had to smuggle it in because the wardens would not allow it. Not because they were aware of Anne Frank – they were completely ignorant—it is just that they ruled that they only allow books that are directly connected to our studies, so things like *Anne Frank* and quite a few books we had to smuggle in. And we succeeded in it, and of course, the younger people were really interested, so we circulated this book [. . .] There was a sizable number of prisoners who were also internationalists and who knew of Nazism, so when we were smuggling in *The Diary of Anne Frank* and other books, they copied parts of the books so that it could be circulated much more. What happened with *Anne Frank* in particular was that some of the prisoners copied the whole diary and circulated it among us prisoners; I copied only chosen parts to my private notebooks.[92]

Anne Frank: The Diary of a Young Girl was first issued in Dutch in 1947 and was translated into English in 1950. It was published in the United States and Great Britain in 1952, soon becoming a best seller.[93] When *The Diary* was smuggled onto Robben Island, Anne Frank was already the most iconic victim of the Holocaust, mainly due to the dramatic adaptations of her text on Broadway and on film in 1955 and 1959 respectively.[94] However, as Sidra Ezrahi argues, while the adaptation of Frank's text "brought the Holocaust to the forefront of mass consciousness, [it] did not really seek to dispel the curiously functional 'amnesia' toward the events themselves."[95] This 'amnesia' had to do with the consolidation of a homogenous Western identity during the 1950s and 1960s. In the shadow of the Cold War, adaptations of *The Diary* were made to conform to constructs of universalized suffering palatable to an American audience: the overall message was of the virtues of American democracy, with universalism the principal vehicle of this ideological agenda. In the process, some of Anne Frank's musings about Jewish suffering were omitted altogether, while others were transformed into declarations about the universal nature of suffering.[96]

While the adapted versions were not circulated on Robben Island, *The Diary* in its original form served as an important source of inspiration for the prisoners. Gilbert describes the significance of *The Diary* for some of the most prominent political prisoners.[97] However, she argues that it was only after their release from prison, during the transition to democracy, that the former political prisoners

---

92 AK, Personal Communication, 11 August 2016.
93 Jeffrey Shandler, "From Diary to Book: Text, Object, Structure," in *Anne Frank Unbound: Media, Imagination, Memory*, ed. Barbara Kirshenblatt-Gimblett and Jeffrey Shandler (Bloomington: Indiana University Press 2012), 25–58.
94 Alvin H. Rosenfeld, *The End of the Holocaust* (Bloomington: Indiana University Press, 2011), 105.
95 Sidra DeKoven Ezrahi, *By Words Alone: The Holocaust in Literature* (Chicago: The University of Chicago Press, 2008), 202.
96 Nahshon, "Anne Frank from Page to Stage," 66.
97 Gilbert, "Anne Frank in South Africa," 372.

incorporated the book into what she refers to as "consensual memory in the New South Africa," casting Anne Frank as a universal victim of discrimination.[98] As discussed in Chapter 5, during the period of transition from apartheid to democracy, the AFH in Amsterdam, in collaboration with the SAJBD and the Netherlands Royal Embassy in Pretoria, presented a traveling exhibition entitled "Anne Frank in the World: 1929–1945" (AFWE) in several South African cities. Given the national itinerary of the exhibition and its symbolic importance, the former political prisoners, now national leaders, were among the key speakers at the various events launching the exhibition.

The addresses made by Govan Mbeki at the opening of the exhibition in Port Elizabeth, and by Nelson Mandela in Johannesburg, serves as testimonies to the early analogical connections drawn between apartheid and the Holocaust on Robben Island. While their spoken testimonies of their reading of *The Diary* on Robben Island were made in retrospect, and as Gilbert argues paved the way for the memory of the Holocaust to become part of the new South Africa's consensual memory, Kathrada's entries in his prison notebook are the only available written evidence of the smuggling of *The Diary* into the prison and its frequent circulation among the prisoners at the time. The next section will focus on Kathrada's individual reading of *The Diary* through a textual examination of the thirteen direct quotations found in his prison notebook. This notebook, which served as his "diary of diaries" during the late 1960s, provides a glimpse into his individual reading of *The Diary* as a mirror of his own experiences, insights, and beliefs.

Reading *The Diary of Anne Frank* on Robben Island

Rothberg argues that "there is no shortage of cross-referencing between the legacies of the Holocaust and colonialism, but many of those moments of contact occur in marginalized texts or in marginal moments of well-known texts."[99] However, an examination of Kathrada's entries from *The Diary* in his secret notebooks will allow us to trace consequences of this act of reading that are not marginal at all.

Most of the quotations from *The Diary* that appear in Kathrada's notebooks can be interpreted as forging imaginative links between his experience of political imprisonment while isolated on Robben Island and the experiences of a

---

98 Gilbert, "Anne Frank in South Africa," 376, 379.
99 Rothberg, *Multidirectional Memory*, 18.

Jewish girl hiding in Nazi-occupied Amsterdam. In his interview with Tim Couzens in 2008, Kathrada states, "In some ways, her [Anne Frank's] situation was similar to ours. But, of course, hers was much worse."[100] This is crucial evidence of the relevance of Rothberg's paradigm to a reading of Kathadra's notebooks. Multidirectional memory "takes dissimilarity for granted, since no two events are ever alike, and then focuses its intellectual energy on investigating what it means to invoke connections nonetheless."[101]

Anne Frank's endurance while in hiding and her emphasis on the importance of remaining optimistic even under the worst circumstances appear as recurring themes in Kathrada's recorded entries. The entries invite us to reconsider the importation of the term 'annex' – specific to Frank's experience – into the context of apartheid and more specifically that of Kathrada's experience of imprisonment in the Robben Island cells. A clear example of these insights is evident in a passage from *The Diary* recorded in Kathrada's notebook and dated 20 November 1942:

> Yet we shall still have our jokes and tease each other, when these horrors have faded a bit in our minds. It won't do us any good, or help those outside, to go on being as gloomy as we are at the moment. And what would be the object of making our "Secret Annex" into a "Secret Annex of Gloom"?[102]

As mentioned earlier, for political prisoners on Robben Island, the mere ability to survive prison was an act of defiance in the face of attempts by the apartheid government to suppress the struggle. Prisoners had to remain optimistic and conduct a "normal" social and cultural life inside the prison walls. In line with this, the entries from Anne Frank's diary recorded in Kathrada's notebook emphasize her optimistic spirit alongside her longing for everyday things – listening to a familiar song, reading an interesting book, even getting a clear look at the stars in the sky – deprivations similar to those suffered in many contexts of captivity and imprisonment.

On 12 February 1944, Anne Frank wrote, "The sun is shining, the sky is a deep blue, there is a lovely breeze and I'm longing – so longing – for everything. To talk, for freedom, for friends, to be alone."[103] This entry particularly resonated

---

100 Kathrada, *A Simple Freedom*, 91.
101 Rothberg, *Multidirectional Memory*, 18.
102 Quotations from *Anne Frank: The Diary of a Young Girl* (1952), MCH42-Box file 12, 12.3-Notebook 3, 65–66, Ahmed Kathrada Collection, Robben Island Museum Mayibuye Archive, University of Western Cape.
103 Quotations from *Anne Frank: The Diary of a Young Girl* (1952), MCH42-Box file 12, 12.3-Notebook 3, 64, Ahmed Kathrada Collection, Robben Island Museum Mayibuye Archive, University of Western Cape.

with prisoners enduring the harsh conditions on Robben Island through the mid-1960s. Years later, Kathrada similarly contemplated prison hardships, "Nor could I possibly have realized that it would be two decades before I would see a child again, or that we would have to adapt to living with grown men in conditions where I could never see the stars in the night sky or know the joy of celebrating birthdays, Diwali, Eid, or Christmas with family and friends."[104] The entries reflect not only Kathrada's identification with the conditions of Frank's incarceration and with her enduring optimism: they reveal a particular identification with Jewish suffering during the Holocaust.

On 22 May 1944, Frank wrote of tensions in the attic arising from news about Jews who revealed secrets to the Germans and about the fate of Christians who had hidden Jews: "Is discord going to show itself while we are still fighting, is the Jew once again worth less than another? Oh, it is sad, very sad, that once more, for the umpteenth time, the old truth is confirmed: 'What one Christian does is his own responsibility, what one Jew does is thrown back at all Jews.'"[105]

In her description of Jewish suffering as the outcome of racial prejudice, Frank seeks to criticize the perception of Jews as a determinant racial category. She points to the essentialism driving antisemitism, which assumes that any individual partakes, by virtue of birth, of the presumed attributes of the group to which he belongs. Kathrada's choice of passages from *The Diary* that reflect on German antisemitism indicates that he is keenly aware of the parallels between Nazi racial stratification and the racist separatism that underlies apartheid policies.[106]

Moreover, as mentioned earlier, the right-wing Afrikaner pro-Nazism that Kathrada encountered as a child during the war years, and the direct influence of Nazism on apartheid's ideology, did not escape his recollections. In his interview he recalled, "They [the Nationalists] were direct disciples of Hitler. I mean, they made it clear. Their policy was taken from the Third Reich."[107] As mentioned earlier, most of the proto-fascist organizations of that period focused not only on the "Jewish question" but also targeted Indians as a threat to society. To be sure, Kathrada was only nine years old at the time; however, his childhood recollections described above, as well as his later involvement in the

---

[104] Kathrada, *Memoirs*, 197.
[105] Quotations from *Anne Frank: The Diary of a Young Girl* (1952), MCH42-Box file 12, 12.3-Notebook 3, 253, Ahmed Kathrada Collection, Robben Island Museum Mayibuye Archive, University of Western Cape.
[106] AMK letters, speeches, public meetings, a police report of the Communist Party meeting in Johannesburg on February 26, 1950, File 1.6, 23 January 1949 to 4 July 1966-South African Police records, Ahmed Kathrada Foundation Archive, Lenasia.
[107] AK, Personal communication, 11 August 2016.

Passive Resistance Campaign against the 'Ghetto Act' of 1946, reveal his awareness of these developments. By choosing Anne Frank's musing on antisemitism, Kathrada not only drew analogous connections between antisemitism and other forms of racism but also revealed the direct connections between Afrikaner Nationalism and Nazi Germany as the basis of this analogy.

In another entry from *The Diary* captured in Kathrada's notebook – this one dated 11 April 1944 – Frank looks forward to a time when she and her family will be defined by their shared humanity.

> We have been pointedly reminded that we are in hiding, that we are Jews in chains, chained to one spot, without any rights, but with a thousand duties. Surely, the time will come when we are people again, and not just Jews. Who has inflicted this upon us? Who has made us Jews different from all other people? Who has allowed us to suffer so terribly up till now? [. . .] We can never become just Netherlanders, or just English, or representatives of any country for that matter, we will always remain Jews, but we want to, too [. . .] During that night I really felt that I had to die, I waited for the police, I was prepared, as the soldier is on the battlefield. I was eager to lay down my life for the country, but now, I've been saved again, now my first wish after the war is that I may become Dutch! I love the Dutch, I love this country, I love the language, and want to work here.[108]

Significantly, this entry was elided in the American stage adaptation of *The Diary* in the belief that it was too specifically Jewish for general American audiences.[109] In the play, Frank's reflections above are transformed into a declaration about the universal nature of suffering, avoiding any specific reference to Jewish suffering: "We're not the only people that've had to suffer. There've always been people that've had to [. . .] sometimes one race [. . .] sometimes another [. . .] I still believe, in spite of everything, that people are really good at heart."[110] Yet for his part, in choosing to record this quotation from the book, Kathrada provides evidence that he was drawn to the particularly Jewish characteristics of Anne Frank's exhortation.

This musing by Frank serves as yet another demonstration of her criticism of the antisemitic trope of Jewish identity as innate. In her account, unlike people who practice other religions, Jews will never be regarded simply as ordinary citizens in a particular country; they will always remain Jews – and therefore inferior to the rest of the citizens, who are blinded by antisemitic stereotypes.

---

108 Quotations from *Anne Frank: The Diary of a Young Girl* (1952), MCH42-Box file 12, 12.3-Notebook 3, 221–222, Ahmed Kathrada Collection, Robben Island Museum Mayibuye Archive, University of Western Cape.
109 Nahshon, "Anne Frank from Page to Stage," 66.
110 Frances Goodrich and Albert Hackett, *The Diary of Anne Frank* (New York: Random House, 1955), 168.

Blindness resulting from stereotypes was a familiar theme in Kathrada's political consciousness. More than a decade before reading *The Diary* on Robben Island, at a meeting of the ANC held in Germiston on 19 September 1954, Kathrada spoke of the racial stereotyping inherent in apartheid. He protested: "A white uniformed police officer rapes an African woman and is sentenced to six months and sometimes discharged. An African man is invited to the room of a white girl and gets a death sentence."[111]

The entry from *The Diary* dated 15 July 1944 in Kathrada's notebook is the only entry to be included in a volume of Kathrada's collected writings.[112] This passage epitomizes Frank's idealism:

> It's really a wonder that I haven't dropped all my ideals, because they seem so absurd and impossible to carry out. Yet I keep them, because in spite of everything I still believe that people are really good at heart. I simply can't build up my hopes on a foundation consisting of confusion, misery, and death. I see the world gradually being turned into a wilderness, I hear the ever-approaching thunder, which will destroy us too, I can feel the suffering of millions and yet, if I look up into the heavens, I think that it will all come right, that this cruelty too will end, and that peace and tranquility will return again. In the meantime, I must uphold my ideas, for perhaps the time will come when I shall be able to carry them out.[113]

The phrase "in spite of everything I still believe that people are really good at heart" is the most cited entry from *The Diary*, and has long been considered to convey the essence of Anne Frank's philosophy and to constitute her epitaph.[114] This constituted the closing line of the American stage adaptation and was frequently invoked in speeches, movies, and book reviews.[115] However, Kathrada did not record this short phrase in isolation but rather reproduced the surrounding passage, a choice that indicates a different kind of reading and identification.

---

111 AMK letters, speeches, public meetings, "Police Memorandum," section 55, Ahmed Kathrada's address at the African National Congress meeting, 19 September 1954, File 1.6, 23 January 1949 to 4 July 1966 South African Police records, Ahmed Kathrada Foundation Archive, Lenasia.
112 Kathrada, *A Simple Freedom*, 133.
113 Quotations from *Anne Frank: The Diary of a Young Girl* (1952), MCH42-Box file 12, 12.3-Notebook 3, 278–279, Ahmed Kathrada Collection, Robben Island Museum Mayibuye Archive, University of Western Cape.
114 Alex Sagan, "An Optimistic Icon: Anne Frank's Canonization in Postwar Culture," *German Politics & Society* 13.3 (1995): 95–107, at 96.
115 Alvin H. Rosenfeld, "Popularization and Memory: The Case of Anne Frank," in *Lessons and Legacies: The Meaning of the Holocaust in a Changing World*, ed. Peter Hayes (Evanston, IL: Northwestern University Press, 1991), 261.

Anne Frank refers to the suffering of millions without mentioning the victims' Jewish identity; however, it is clear that her description alludes to the suffering of Jews under the Nazis. The passage is a significant expression of Frank's own identity as a Jew and it movingly expresses her optimism as a means of enduring the misery and suffering she experienced. For Kathrada, this optimism served as the main point of identification with *The Diary*.

In his introduction to the film *A Simple Freedom*, Kathrada stresses that Anne Frank and her family "were given refuge by a Dutch family, at great risk to themselves, as happened here." He argues, "Madiba was given refuge when he was underground by a number of white families who took great risks [. . .] So those were the similarities." However, he also emphasizes, "we must stress that the condition under which Anne Frank, the little child, lived, was much, much worse than ours. But, yet, you can't escape the similarities."[116] Moreover, in his memories Kathrada frequently mentions the names of people who helped him when he went underground. He specifically mentions his relations with some famous activists such as Ruth First and Joe Slovo, emphasizing their communist tendencies and the sacrifice to the struggle they made by endangering themselves as white activists.[117]

While the apparent disproportion of Jewish names in the list of the accused at the Treason Trial and the Rivonia Trial made news in the national press in English and Afrikaans,[118] Kathrada himself never referred to his comrades' Jewish identity. We can surmise that the reason behind this has to do with the fact that he did not think that this racial category should be significant. However, another reason could be that most of the Jewish activists defined themselves as atheists and were not observant. While most immigrated from Lithuania and brought with them socialist ideas along with their Jewish traditions and values, their identity as Jews was not critical to their role in the struggle.[119] As Kathrada mentioned, just like the Dutch individuals who helped Jews in occupied Holland, "our white comrades were our brothers for the struggle, and they risked their lives for the just cause of all non-whites in this country. This was the most unselfish act of all."[120]

---

[116] This was taken from Tom Couzens' recorded interview with Ahmed Kathrada, "The courage of young women," in the DVD accompanying the book *A Simple Freedom: The Strong Mind of Robben Island Prisoner, No. 468/64 Ahmed Kathrada* (Johannesburg: Wild Dog Press, 2008).
[117] Kathrada, *Memoirs*, 34–35, 92, 149.
[118] Shimoni, *Community and Conscience*, 62.
[119] For more information about Jewish activists against apartheid see Suttner, *Cutting Through the Mountain*, 1–7.
[120] AK, Personal communication, 11 August 2016.

Among all Kathrada's statements on *The Diary* after his release from prison, his awareness of the Jewish identity of Anne Frank and of the particular and unique circumstances of the Jewish Holocaust is clearly visible. His repeated emphasis on the significant differences between his own historical circumstances and Frank's is important in marking the particularity of the Holocaust. This points to a contextual understanding of Jewishness on Kathrada's part, which nevertheless is put into real engagement with an overarching need to oppose racism in its South African form.

The unusual story of an Indian South African political prisoner reading *The Diary of Anne Frank* on Robben Island allows us to apprehend a deep examination of his selected entries as a mirror of his own insights, experiences, and identity, revealing its multidirectional dynamics. The Jewish-oriented entries from *The Diary*, together with Kathrada's past and retrospective statements on the Jewish Holocaust, reveal the similarities he draws between European Jewish subjects in Nazi Germany and Indian, black, and Coloured subjects in apartheid South Africa in terms of exclusion and racism. Kathrada used Anne Frank as an analogy; but while drawing similarities between Frank's and his own situations and struggles, he constantly emphasized that each situation is distinct and that each identity and history has its own path.

Conclusion: On the Role of Analogies

Keith Feldman argues that an analogy is never perfect, because two given events are never identical.[1] Nonetheless, he continues, "the 'likeness' or 'parallel' [. . .] juxtapose[s] unique historical formations, ideological concepts, or geographies – relations not objects – which are then linked together via the radically unstable 'like' or 'as.'"[2] Feldman recognizes that at the core of the analogy lies a difference "always on the verge of collapse into identity, socially produced under contextually specific conditions that are always on the verge of conflation." However, it is these permanent conditions that "holds an analogy together and produce its rhetorical effectivity."[3]

The AFWE, the focus of Chapter 5, was the first official national effort to legitimize analogical connections between apartheid and the Holocaust. Nevertheless, as I have demonstrated throughout this book, during the apartheid years, the relationship between these two entangled histories was not always a productive one. Connections between the suffering of Jews during the Holocaust and the suffering of blacks under apartheid were frequently drawn by anti-apartheid activists, usually acknowledging the differences between the two traumatic histories before pointing to their actual and analogical similarities. However, during the apartheid years, the leadership of South African Jewry avoided engaging analogical or actual connections between the Holocaust and apartheid, and instead focused its efforts on mediating the Holocaust to the white communities in the country as an unprecedented event in human history and as a pillar of the Jewish community's collective identity. The anti-antisemitic message mediated by the Jewish community was often confronted by local memories of suffering, mainly invoked by Afrikaner individuals and movements, evoking the form of competition in a zero-sum struggle. The Jews were accused of claiming ownership of human suffering and of overshadowing other local traumatic sufferings. These responses reflect the white communities' ambivalent attitudes toward Jewish

---

1 Keith Feldman, *A Shadow over Palestine: The Imperial Life of Race in America* (Minneapolis: University of Minnesota Press, 2015), 70.
2 Feldman, *A Shadow over Palestine*, 71.
3 Feldman, *A Shadow over Palestine*, 71.

Note: Extensive parts of this chapter are based on an article published by the author of this book in 2019: "Between Apartheid, the Holocaust and the Nakba: Archbishop Desmond Tutu's Pilgrimage to Israel-Palestine (1989) and the Emergence of an Analogical Lexicon," *Journal of Genocide Research* 22.3 (2020): 334–353. This article was funded with the support of the European Union's Seventh Framework Programme (FP/2007–2013) / ERC Grant Agreement no. 615564.

whiteness in South Africa as a direct expression of the race politics of the apartheid regime.

As demonstrated throughout this book, as a minority within the privileged white minority, the Jewish community was vulnerable, but it was also economically integrated. This privilege enabled the community to play its part in both supporting Israel and fighting against local and global antisemitism by mobilizing the lessons of the Holocaust as a bulwark thrust into the white public arena. Nevertheless, during the apartheid years, the community adopted a policy of non-involvement in politics except where Jewish interests were implicated. Therefore the lessons of the Holocaust were perceived by the official community's institutions as particular to themselves and not universal enough to stand for anti-racism in the apartheid context. Holocaust uniqueness allowed for Holocaust memory to present South African Jews with a unique narrative of suffering that simultaneously kept the community within the borders of white South Africa while denying its guilt in accommodating apartheid.

In his recent book, *The Implicated Subject* (2019), Michael Rothberg introduces a new subject position that differs from the ideal types of victims, perpetrators, and bystanders. He argues, "implicated subjects are morally compromised and most definitely attached [. . .] to consequential political and economic dynamics."[4] Drawing on Rothberg's new notion and based on this book's interventions within the study of apartheid-era Jewish commemorations of the Holocaust, this concluding chapter seeks to address the role of analogies in the South African context and to shed light on the complex nexus of South African Jewry's implicated status as a direct beneficiary of whiteness under apartheid.

The chapter explores the role of analogies in the South African context by tracing the history of different sets of interlocking analogies in the thought of the anti-apartheid activist and Nobel Peace Prize laureate Desmond Tutu.[5] Beginning in the late 1970s, Tutu would draw analogical connections between the Final Solution of the Nazi regime and the apartheid regime. From the early 1980s, Tutu would also allude to the historical connections between Afrikaner nationalism in South Africa and Nazi Germany in order to condemn Israel's close ties with the apartheid government. Here Tutu would address South African Jewry's implication as main supporters of Israel, as direct beneficiaries of apartheid, and as a community that upheld the anti-antisemitic message while refraining from condemning the apartheid racist regime until 1985. During the 1980s, Tutu's associations

---

4 Rothberg, *The Implicated Subject*, 33.
5 For additional scholarship on the Israel-apartheid analogy, see Jon Soske and Sean Jacobs, *Apartheid Israel: The Politics of an Analogy* (Chicago: Haymarket Books, 2015).

between apartheid and Nazism evolved into a comparison between Jewish asylum-seeking during the Holocaust and in its aftermath and the Palestinian plight following the 1948 Nakba ("The Catastrophe" in Arabic), eventually leading Tutu to posit to a fully-fledged analogy between Israel and the apartheid regime.

Tutu's analogical lexicon was a rhetorical weapon in his struggle for justice. Like many other anti-apartheid activists of his time, Tutu perceived apartheid, and later the Nakba, as direct expressions of the destruction brought about by colonialism. This perception is well reflected in Maier's writing on the entangled histories of the Holocaust and post-colonialism mentioned in the Introduction to this book. Maier points out that the Holocaust narrative was adopted as a benchmark for human rights mainly by liberal democratic countries, while these same countries were the ones responsible for colonial violence and human rights violations.[6] As this chapter will demonstrate, in a similar vein, Tutu offers innovative, imaginative links in his emphasis on the illegitimacy of the alliances between Jerusalem and Pretoria which strengthened apartheid, and of those between Zionism and the West which led to the Palestinian Nakba.

Apartheid South Africa constituted an unstable and frequently changing historical context in which Tutu's analogical lexicon evolved throughout his years of opposition to the regime. At the same time, it is important to realize that his lexicon was also shaped by what Louise Bethlehem has termed the "restlessness" of apartheid as a political signifier. As mentioned in my Introduction, through charting what she names the "global itinerary" of the term apartheid, as well as the diffusion of anti-apartheid expressive culture beyond South Africa, Bethlehem interprets apartheid as a heuristic through which struggles over race and social justice might be interpreted in a transnational setting.[7] Building on such efforts, this chapter poses a Christmas pilgrimage Tutu made to Israel and the occupied territories in December 1989 – neglected thus far in the critical literature – as a milestone in his thinking. While the chapter offers a critical analysis of yet another performance of the Israel-apartheid analogy in the political struggle against the Israeli occupation, its emphasis is on the genesis of the analogy in Tutu's ongoing engagement with the suffering of Jews during the Holocaust and on the South African Jewish reactions to it.

---

6 Maier, "Consigning the Twentieth Century to History," 826–827.
7 Bethlehem, "Apartheid: The Global Itinerary."

Desmond Tutu and the Evolution of an Analogical Lexicon

Born on 7 October 1931 in Klerksdorp, a town in the southwestern Transvaal province, Tutu emerged from an impoverished childhood to become one of the leading Anglican figures in South Africa.[8] He was drawn to Anglican theology after moving to Johannesburg with his family at the age of twelve. Under the guidance of the British Anglican priest, Trevor Huddleston, who arrived in South Africa in 1943 to become a leading anti-apartheid activist, Tutu's awareness of the damaging impact of apartheid on blacks was sharpened.[9]

The apartheid government enacted many oppressive measures during the early 1950s, including the destruction of Sophiatown under the Group Areas Act (1950) and the establishment of a new public school system of downgraded education for Africans under the Bantu Education Act (1953). In protest, Tutu, who had trained as a teacher, decided to resign and turned to theology. Although the subsequent period in Tutu's life was devoted to studying theology in England, he was always attentive to developments in his homeland.[10]

Tutu spent most of the 1950s and 1960s outside of South Africa, not playing an active role in the emerging anti-apartheid movement at this stage.[11] His theological orientation was further developed in the late 1960s and early 1970s when the Anglican Church established the University Christian Movement, a Christian student movement which eventually became the vehicle of the Black Consciousness Movement in South Africa.[12] Tutu, who believed that the context of apartheid required a specific type of theology, saw Christianity as "a religion of liberation" and argued that "Christians of all races needed to speak for the weak and meek, to expose evil and seek to end it."[13] For him, the Bible was perceived as "on the side of the black struggle for liberation and life in South Africa,"[14] and he constantly called for the commitment of whites and blacks alike to the liberation movement, stating "you (whites) will never be free until we blacks are free."[15]

---

8 Steven Gish, *Desmond Tutu: A Biography* (Westport, CT: Greenwood Press, 2004), 4.
9 Gish, *Desmond Tutu*, 88.
10 Gish, *Desmond Tutu*, 19–22.
11 Samuel W. Crompton, *Desmond Tutu: Fighting Apartheid* (New York: Chelsea House, 2007), 30.
12 Gerald West, "The Legacy of Liberation Theologies in South Africa, with an Emphasis on Biblical Hermeneutics," *Studia Historiae Ecclesiasticae* 36 (2010): 157–183.
13 Gish, *Desmond Tutu*, 46.
14 Desmond Tutu, *Hope and Suffering: Sermons and Speeches* (Johannesburg: Skotaville, 1983), 124–129.
15 Deane W. Ferm, *Third World Liberation Theologies: An Introductory Survey* (Eugene, OR: Wipf & Stock, 2004), 66.

This brief reflection on the theological impulses underpinning Tutu's thought is crucial for an understanding of the evolving patterns of his analogical lexicon. Such patterns began to appear soon after Tutu's appointment in March 1978 to the position of General Secretary of the SACC, a position that brought him to prominence in the context of the anti-apartheid struggle.[16] As mentioned in Chapter 5, as an affiliate of the WCC the SACC represented all major Christian churches in South Africa apart from the Dutch Reformed Church and the Catholic Church.[17] Under Tutu's leadership, the SACC became a strong force in the revival of mass action against apartheid. Moreover, it was in this position that Tutu first used the analogy with Nazism to articulate his opposition to apartheid.

In 1979, Tutu issued a statement protesting the enactment of the new Group Areas Act, an amendment of the original law passed in 1950 authorizing the government to remove Africans from urban areas and to relocate them to desolate and unproductive tribal areas. He described African life in the squatter camps as "the government's final solution to the African problem" and argued that the policy of Peter William Botha's administration "was deliberately designed to have the Africans starve to death, not because there was no food, but because it was the policy the government had defined and was now pursuing."[18] As demonstrated throughout this book, Tutu was not the first to use the Nazi analogy in the struggle against apartheid. These parallels were strengthened by the actual connections between Afrikaner Nationalists and the Nazis during the 1930s and the 1940s, a historical legacy that would inform the evolution of Tutu's thought.

As discussed in Chapter 1, the South African United Government's decision to join the war on the Allies' side was met with an increase in right-wing and proto-fascist pronouncements within the Afrikaner community.[19] As Patrick Jonathan Furlong points out, in the Transvaal province where Tutu grew up, the impact of such extreme right-wing thought, derived from Nazism abroad, was particularly evident.[20] David Brock Katz suggests, "the ANC traditional chiefs, and church groups saw the war as an opportunity for blacks to gain equal rights and ease racial policies by squeezing concessions from the government during wartime," drawing many black youngsters to join the United Defence Front.[21] In his biography, Tutu,

---

16 Crompton, *Desmond Tutu*, 164, 167.
17 Pieterse, *Desmond Tutu's Message*, 11.
18 Dickson A. Mungazi, *In the Footsteps of the Masters: Desmond M. Tutu and Abel T. Muzorewa* (Westport, CT,: Praeger, 2000), 92.
19 Shain, *A Perfect Storm*, 236–237.
20 Furlong, *Between Crown and Swastika*, 101–102.
21 David Brock Katz, *South Africans versus Rommel: The Untold Story of the Desert War in World War II* (Guilford, CT: Stackpole Books, 2017), 17.

who was only an eight-year-old child at the outbreak of the war, nostalgically recalls waving goodbye to the soldiers who were on their way to the front.[22]

During the war years, the black communities in South Africa mostly supported the war efforts, and in the post-war period the emergent anti-apartheid movement used anti-fascist and anti-Nazi rhetoric to emphasize the urgency of the struggle against segregation and, later, apartheid.[23] Indeed, the systematic killing conducted by the Nazis had no equivalent in South Africa. However, as Tutu argued, what distinguished the Nazi final solution from apartheid were merely the means employed to achieve the goal of genocide. While "the one was not a carbon copy of the other," there were substantial similarities.[24]

It is important to position Tutu's 'final solution' analogy from the late 1970s onward within the context of a wider international debate on the definition of genocide. As mentioned in Chapter 6, the 1948 Genocide Convention, established against the background of the Holocaust, and the 1973 Apartheid Convention, established within the context of the ongoing implementation of apartheid in South Africa, created general definitions for two distinct atrocities, providing a framework for discussions concerning apartheid's genocidal characteristics on the one hand, and the characteristics of apartheid that might emerge outside of South Africa on the other.

Tutu's frequent use of the Nazi analogy in his public statements fueled a media campaign against him in the national press. A report in the South African newspaper *The Citizen* on 4 July 1984 stated:

> The use of the South African-Nazi analogy has become almost standard practice by the SACC and its officials, especially its general secretary, Bishop Desmond Tutu [. . .] After referring to the scale of Hitler's crime – the elimination of 6-million Jews, he said: "South Africa is almost halfway there. Three-and-a-half million already disposed of by resettlement and another 2-million to go – half a million short of Hitler's total."[25]

The article concluded critically: "although we do not agree with relocation and resettlements, forced or otherwise, that cause great suffering to those who are moved, we cannot see how anyone can suggest that this is like the extermination of 6-million Jews by Nazi Germany."[26] This argument, which appeared in a

---

[22] John Allen, *Rabble Rouser for Peace: The Authorized Biography of Desmond Tutu* (New York, London, Toronto and Sydney: Free Press, 2006), 24.
[23] Gilbert, "Anne Frank in South Africa," 366–393.
[24] Kader Asmal, Louise Asmal and Ronald Suresh Roberts, *Reconciliation Through Truth* (Cape Town: David Philip Publications, 1997), 132–133.
[25] "Nazi Analogy," *Citizen*, 4 July 1984, Press Items of Jewish Interest No. 13, Rochlin Archive, Johannesburg.
[26] "Nazi Analogy," *Citizen*, 4 July 1984, Press Items of Jewish Interest No. 13, Rochlin Archive, Johannesburg.

local conservative English language paper, expresses the effective mediation of the idea of Holocaust uniqueness by South African Jewry to the white minority communities. As demonstrated throughout the book, through commemorative efforts, official statements, various publications, and other mnemonic practices, the Jewish community transmitted their universal anti-antisemitic message to those who wielded hegemony within South African society, as a distinct form of racism, which is completely irrelevant to local racial segregation.

Despite such criticism, Tutu continued to raise similar arguments in international forums. In an interview on the US television network ABC on 16 October 1984, Tutu argued,

> I believe that apartheid has reached a stage in its development where one can speak about the final solution when they are stripping us of our South African citizenship and turning us into aliens in the land of our birth and uprooting stable communities, destroying them to satisfy a racist ideology. They are doing nothing less than what the Nazis did and if you say, where are the gas chambers, I would say, I mean, that the gas chambers are probably more efficient and more clean, because if you put children in places where you know they are going to starve, you are as guilty as those who filled up the gas chambers.[27]

Notably, Tutu reiterated these claims during his Nobel lecture delivered on 11 December 1984, stating: "Blacks are systematically being stripped of their South African citizenship and being turned into aliens in the land of their birth. This is apartheid's final solution, just as Nazism had its final solution for the Jews in Hitler's Aryan madness."[28]

Needless to say, the South African national press criticized Tutu's speech, arguing that it was a result of "political megalomania brought on by the award" and stressing that "whatever one might think of the relocation [. . .] the policy cannot be equated with the annihilation of the Nazis of six-million Jews."[29] The South African Minister of Foreign Affairs at the time, Pik Botha, also condemned Tutu's analogy, asserting that "to compare us with the Nazis is an insult to the more than 100,000 South African of Jewish origins who came to this country,

---

[27] The interview was conducted by Peter Jennings on the day Tutu was awarded the Nobel Peace Prize. An extract from the interview was published in the January 1985 issue of the magazine of the Conservative Party of South Africa, *Die Patriot*. See "South Africa compared to Nazi Germany," *Die Patriot*, January 1985, Press Items of Jewish Interest No. 1, Rochlin Archive, Johannesburg (a translated collection).
[28] "Desmond Tutu: Nobel Lecture," 11 December 1984, *The Nobel Prize*, https://www.nobelprize.org/prizes/peace/1984/tutu/lecture/ [Accessed 17 May 2019].
[29] "Comment," *Citizen*, 4 January 1985, Press Items of Jewish Interest No. 1, Rochlin Archive, Johannesburg.

and to our forefathers who fought with the Allied powers against Nazi Germany;"[30] thus Botha also alluded to the taboo of Holocaust uniqueness.

The South African Jewish community perceived Tutu's 'final solution' analogy in a similar vein. *The Jewish Herald* newspaper stated,

> The Bishop was deliberately exploiting an emotive memory to evoke international horror in simple, or ignorant, minds which will equate South Africa's policies with Hitler's systematic mass murder of six million Jews. The government of Mr. P. W. Botha has not drawn up any plans for the final extermination of the black population. There are no Dachaus, Auschwitzes, Treblinkas or Maideneks in South Africa. There are no gas ovens. Soweto, Kwazulu and Lebowa are not the Warsaw ghetto.[31]

The reaction of the Jewish community is indicative of their adherence to the principle of Holocaust uniqueness mentioned throughout this book, which was well represented in South Africa, where Zionism and the state of Israel were integral to the Jewish community's ethnic identity.[32]

The strongly Zionist South African Jewish community tracked Tutu's actions and statements attentively, and with anxiety. In addition to his frequent use of the Nazi analogy, Tutu repeatedly voiced criticism of Israel's close ties with the apartheid regime, speaking mainly in American Jewish circles. In a speech at the Jewish Theological Seminary of America in New York in 1984, Tutu declared: "we cannot understand how Jews can cooperate with a government, many of whose members were sympathetic to Hitler and the Nazis and who for a long time refused Jews membership in their political party because they were Jews."[33] Here Tutu was alluding to the direct connections between Afrikaner Nationalism and Nazi Germany while acknowledging the centrality of the memory of the Holocaust as a core memory of the Jewish-Zionist world and of Israeli nationalism, in order to criticize the Israeli state for its relations with the apartheid government.

Furthermore, in an interview Tutu gave in 1987 he was asked how he thinks black South Africans view the local Jewish community. He stated that while there was no doubt that many Jews played a central role in the struggle against apartheid, the Israeli government had ties to the apartheid regime and the support of members of the Jewish community given to the NP had damaged the reputation of the local Jewish community among blacks. In his interview, Tutu

---

30 Botha's statement was given in the course of a discussion with Tutu, which was televised on News Focus on SATV and later reported in *The Star*. See "Pik and Tutu Clash on SATV," *The Star*, 19 March 1985, Press Items of Jewish Interest No. 4, Rochlin Archive, Johannesburg.
31 "Jewish Herald Responds," *The Star*, 2 January 1985, Press Items of Jewish Interest No. 1, Rochlin Archive, Johannesburg.
32 Shimoni, *Community and Conscience*, 4.
33 Desmond Tutu and John Allen, *God Is Not A Christian* (London: Rider, 2011), 87.

acknowledged the uncertain position of South African Jewry during the apartheid years, stating that "there are many that are feeling that it is probably better for their own survival not to be too open." Nevertheless, regarding the community's collective responsibility, he argued: "[A]t present time [. . .] South Africa's involvement with Israel, with no apparent disapproval being expressed by the Jewish community here as well as Israeli collaboration with the South African government, is something that we [blacks] find unacceptable."[34]

Tutu's statements above reflect what Rothberg defines as "Complex Implication," where "subjects implicated in histories of perpetration also possess genealogical connections to or postmemories of victimization."[35] The Jewish history of victimization and persecution was invoked by Tutu, together with the implication that Jews were white and privileged citizens under apartheid racial order. By pointing out this complex position of the Jews, Tutu sought to awaken the Jewish community from its silence and into action against apartheid.

As discussed at length in Chapter 4, the Six-Day War, and subsequently the Yom Kippur War, proved to be turning points in restoring good diplomatic relations between Israel and South Africa after two decades of instability.[36] As Sasha Polakow-Suransky argues: "As an uneasy peace settled over the Middle East in November 1973, Israeli and South African defense officials quietly began to lay the foundations for a lucrative and far-reaching alliance."[37] This alliance became a source for criticism in anti-apartheid circles and served as a strong base for public discussion about the similarities between the two countries' racial policies, especially following the affirmation of the UN 1973 Apartheid Convention and of Resolution 3379 in November 1975.

It is not surprising, then, that from the mid-1980s, in addition to his critique of Jerusalem-Pretoria ties, Tutu became very critical of Israel's treatment of the Palestinian people. At the same 1984 speech to the New York Jewish Theological Seminary mentioned above, Tutu also declared, "I am myself sad that Israel, with the kind of history and traditions her people have experienced, should make refugees of others. It is totally inconsistent with who she is as a people."[38] For the first time, Tutu directly addresses the Nakba, the Palestinian deportation from Palestine, and the loss of their homeland in the 1948 War. Yet again he turns to the traumatic experience of the Holocaust, focusing on the result of

---

34 Hoffman and Fischer, *The Jews of South Africa*, 11–12.
35 Rothberg, *The Implicated Subject*, 24.
36 Shimoni, *Community and Conscience*, 154–156.
37 Polakow-Suransky, *The Unspoken Alliance*, 73.
38 "Nobel Prize Winner Praises Jewish People As 'a Light into the Nations' but is Also Sharply Critical," *Jewish Telegraphic Agency*, 28 November 1984.

Jewish statelessness in order to restore empathy in American Jewish circles for the plight of the Palestinian refugees.

Here we can observe a shift at work, as Tutu reorients his focus on Jewish suffering during the Holocaust as an analogy for black suffering in apartheid South Africa to concentrate instead on how Jewish statelessness during the Holocaust and in its aftermath resembled the Palestinian plight following the 1948 Nakba. This shift invites a deeper reflection on two contested narratives – the Holocaust for Jews and the Nakba for Palestinians – as two national narratives of suffering and victimization.[39] Bashir Bashir and Amos Goldberg have recently argued that "these two narratives collide head-on when it comes to Palestine/Israel, as the Palestinian national narrative is constructed within the larger framework of the anticolonial metanarrative."[40] On the one hand, the Palestinians perceive the Nakba as the last crime of European settler colonialism. On the other, the Jewish Zionist narrative focuses on the destruction of European Jewry by the Nazis as an unparalleled event in human history and as the ultimate reason for Jewish nation-building in Israel.[41]

Tutu was aware of the two contested narratives of suffering and victimization, and he consciously draw parallels between them in order to create a space for the construction of commonality between the two peoples. Nonetheless, such parallels were perceived as a blatant anti-Jewish manifestation in both American and South African circles. The *Business Day* newspaper reported: "invited to address a faculty of students of the Jewish Theological Seminary in New York, he [Tutu] exploited the opportunity to condemn Jews for not being what the Bible requires of them: 'A light unto the nations.'"[42] In an interview published in the *Sunday Star* Tutu was confronted with allegations of antisemitism. He responded by saying, "Rubbish; after all, the Jews put us in business," but also added, "you know, most blacks in South Africa have a problem with Israel. We cannot understand how a country of people with such a history of persecution themselves can collaborate with this Government to support apartheid."[43]

These antisemitic allegations did not deter Tutu, and by the end of the 1980s he had drawn a direct equation between Israel and apartheid, thus bringing two existing discursive configurations into intersection. When asked for his definition

---

39 Bashir and Goldberg, *The Holocaust and the Nakba*, 2.
40 Bashir and Goldberg, *The Holocaust and the Nakba*, 4.
41 Bashir and Goldberg, *The Holocaust and the Nakba*, 5.
42 "Tutu- Baiting," *Business Day*, 3 December 1985, Press Items of Jewish Interest No. 1, Rochlin Archive, Johannesburg.
43 "Bishop Tutu," *Sunday Star*, 10 November 1985, Press Items of Jewish Interest No. 20, Rochlin Archive, Johannesburg.

of Zionism, Tutu stated: "where you exclude people on ethnic grounds, or other grounds, over which they, in a sense, have no control, and you penalise them. I mean, it's always to their exclusion. Apartheid is also the politics of exclusion."[44] This analogy, linking Zionism with apartheid, was also drawn by Tutu on a visit to New York in January 1989, in an address to an audience at the Stephen Wise Free Synagogue, where he received the Reform congregation's George Brussel Jr. Award for his struggle against apartheid in South Africa. He stated: "I am a black South African, and if you changed the names, the description of what is happening in the Gaza Strip and the West Bank could be a description of what is happening in South Africa."[45] This statement implies similarities between the Palestinian Intifada and traumatic events in South Africa such as the Sharpeville Massacre (1960) and the Soweto riots (1976), where black demonstrators were violently dispersed by government forces. These remarks were followed by Tutu's repeated condemnation of Israel for collaborating with South Africa's leaders on security and nuclear matters. "We blacks cannot understand how people with your kind of history (can) allow the government of Israel, as distinct from its people, to have the kind of relationship" it has with South Africa, Tutu said.[46]

Tutu's statement caused a stir in New York Jewish circles, as reports in both the South African and the American Press recorded.[47] Tensions were further exacerbated when, in October 1989, Tutu met with Arafat, the PLO leader, in Cairo, where they pointed to similarities between the plight of the Palestinians and that of black South Africans.[48] Tutu's critique equating the Israeli occupation with apartheid unsettled large segments of the Jewish world, and his repeated acknowledgment of Israel's right to exist did not rehabilitate his image among the Jewish communities in South Africa, the US, and Israel, where he was frequently accused of anti-Jewish inclinations.[49] The news of his upcoming visit to the Holy Land was thus received with predictable ambivalence by the Israeli authorities.

---

44 Hoffman and Fischer, *The Jews of South Africa*, 16.
45 Allen, *Rabble Rouser for Peace*, 384–385.
46 Andrew Sllow Carroll, "Tutu Says He and Elie Wiesel can 'Mediate' Mideast Peace," *Jewish Telegraphic Agency*, 31 January 1989.
47 "Tutu on Link Between South Africa and Israel," *Sowetan*, 8 February 1989, Press Items of Jewish Interest No. 3, Rochlin Archive, Johannesburg.
48 "Tutu meets Arafat and Mubarak," *The Star*, 25 October 1989; *Business Day*, 24 October 1989, Press Items of Jewish Interest No. 20, Rochlin Archive, Johannesburg.
49 Feld *Nations Divided*, 125.

Desmond Tutu's Pilgrimage to Israel-Palestine (Christmas, 1989)

On 4 December 1989, the Israeli Government Press Office Director Yossi Olmert wrote to a variety of government representatives:

> Archbishop Desmond Tutu is about to visit Israel and the occupied territories [. . .] The Archbishop is, to put it mildly, not a friend of Israel and the Jewish people [. . .] His visit [. . .] which coincides with Christmas and with the second anniversary of the Intifada [. . .] is likely to become a media event on a global scale that can seriously damage the image of the state of Israel. The South African connection bears a special sensitivity, precisely now, following the Prime Minister's visit to the US.[50]

The special sensitivity Olmert refers to here alludes to the ambivalence of Israeli policy toward the apartheid regime at the time. On the rhetorical front, the sanctions package approved by the Israeli cabinet and adopted on 16 September 1987 outlawed all new investments in South Africa and officially allied Israel with international sanctions against apartheid. However, the sanctions had had hardly any impact on the flourishing trade between the two countries, especially in the defense sector, where contracts signed before 1987 remained in effect.[51] Prime Minister Yitzchak Shamir, who since 1987 had assured the US administration in Washington of his pro-sanctions position, was actually playing a double game. By 1989, the Americans were already pushing him into a corner, given Israel's ongoing aid to the South African missile program.[52]

Yigal Antebi, then director of the African department of the Israeli Foreign Ministry, prepared a thorough report, which included a brief paragraph on Tutu's biography, his views on the Israeli-Palestinian conflict, Jews, and Zionism, information on relations between Israel and South Africa, and a list of questions whose goal, in Antebi's words, was "to attack the guest when necessary."[53] Based on these reports, Olmert called for the establishment of an ad-hoc committee to prepare an appropriate Israeli response to the "unwanted" upcoming visitor. While

---

50 "סוף חודש דצמבר – ביקור הארכיבישוף דזמונד טוטו בישראל," ["Archbishop Desmond Tutu Visit in Israel- End of December"] a Letter from Yossi Olmert, Director of the Israeli Government Press Office to the Prime Minister Office, 4 December 1989, file ISA-PMO-GPO-000hkin, Israel State Archives, Jerusalem.

51 Polakow-Suransky, *The Unspoken Alliance*, 204.

52 Polakow-Suransky, *The Unspoken Alliance*, 206–218.

53 "22–26.12.89, ביקור הארכיבישוף דזמונד טוטו בישראל," ["Archbishop Desmond Tutu visit in Israel December 22–26, 1989"] 21 December 1989, a letter from Yigal Antebi, director of the African department at the Israeli Foreign Ministry to the Prime Minister Communication Advisor, 2, file ISA-PMO-GPO-000hkin, Israeli State Archives, Jerusalem.

the Israeli administration predicted that the visit might trigger "a spectacular anti-Israeli blitz in the world media," it acknowledged Tutu's international status and offered to "strangle him with love" by creating convenient moments for positive media coverage of the upcoming visit.[54]

The committee's proposals included meetings of Tutu with a delegation of Jewish Ethiopian immigrants; with the then mayor of Jerusalem Teddy Kollek; with the interfaith committee operating in Jerusalem; and with members of the Anglican Church who were sympathetic to Israel. The committee also suggested a scheduled visit to the Yad Vashem Holocaust memorial in Jerusalem.[55] However, in practice, Tutu, who was hosted by the Anglican Archbishop of Jerusalem, Samir Kafity, declared in response that his visit was private and religious in nature.[56] He refused to participate in most of the proposed meetings from the Israeli side and spent most of his time in East Jerusalem, Bethlehem, and Beit Sahour.[57]

Tutu's visit began with a round of visits to Christian, Jewish, and Muslim holy places. At the compound surrounding the Al-Aqsa Mosque, Islam's third holiest shrine, Tutu told senior Muslim clergymen and Palestinian nationalists: "We support your struggle for justice, peace, statehood and independence." While he emphasized that he "bears no animosity to the Jewish people," he stated: "We call into question the policies of the Israeli government."[58] During a visit to the Roman Catholic Patriarchate, Tutu similarly declared: "We say that the Palestinians have right on their side when they say they want an independent state. In the same breath we affirm the right of Israel to its independence and territorial integrity."[59]

---

54 "סוף חודש דצמבר – ביקור הארכיבישוף דזמונד טוטו בישראל," ["Archbishop Desmond Tutu Visit in Israel- End of December"] a Letter from Yossi Olmert, Director of the Israeli Government Press Office to the Prime Minister Office, 4 December 1989, file ISA-PMO-GPO-000hkin, Israel State Archives, Jerusalem.

55 "ביקור טוטו," ["Tutu's Visit"] a Letter from Yossi Olmert, Director of the Israeli Government Press Office to the Prime Minister Office, 13 December 1989, file ISA-PMO-GPO-000hkin, Israel State Archives, Jerusalem.

56 "דזמונד טוטו יבוא לישראל לתפילות חג המולד," ["Desmond Tutu will arrive in Israel for Christmas services"] *Maariv*, 20 December 1989, 2.

57 David Landau, "Tutu Speaks of Israeli Repression but his Rhetoric is taken in Stride," *Jewish Telegraphic Agency*, 25 December 1989.

58 Alan Cowell, "Tutu, Visiting Jerusalem, Backs Palestinian Statehood," *New York Times*, 24 December 1989.

59 Alan Cowell, "Tutu, Visiting Jerusalem, Backs Palestinian Statehood," *New York Times*, 24 December 1989.

Tutu spent Christmas Eve at a carol service at the chapel of the Shepherd's Field, outside the village of Beit Sahour near Bethlehem.[60] Beit Sahour, a mostly Christian village under constant siege by the Israeli army, played a key role in the First Intifada, with local activists pioneering nonviolence resistance practices.[61] It became known for its community's acts of civil disobedience during the summer of 1989, which manifested as a tax revolt in protest of Israeli occupation under the slogan "No taxation without representation."[62] Tutu's attendance turned the service into a major political event as thousands of Palestinians gathered outside the Church and demonstrated in support of the PLO and the ANC.[63]

Tutu opened his sermon with a reflection on the Christian belief that shepherds tending their flocks were the first to receive word of the birth of Jesus. He stated, "Our people in South Africa love that story because it says shepherds are actually more important than the world thinks [. . .] Or even more wonderfully, the story says that God has a special caring for those whom the world thinks are not important [. . .] that God sides with those whom the world oppresses."[64] In his statement, Tutu again asserted his support for Palestinian nationhood, but added, "the Jews have a right to their independent state as well."[65] This particular event at which Tutu spoke was a traditional Christmas service, but the substance was notably political and the tone defiant. It positioned the "two-state solution" as the Palestinians' blueprint for resolving their conflict with Israel and mapped the South African context onto the Israeli occupied territories.

On his last evening spent at St. George's Cathedral in East Jerusalem, Tutu met Israeli and Palestinian journalists and talked about the two-year uprising by Palestinians protesting the Israeli occupation of the West Bank and Gaza Strip. He compared Israel to South Africa stating: "'In the methods of resistance used by Palestinians, and in the ways the Israeli government deals with resistance, we experience an extraordinary sense of being at home."[66] Of the Israeli criticism of his statements, he said: "I'm saddened because I like to be liked. But I will certainly not change one iota when I say I believe something is wrong."[67] When asked by an Israeli reporter to say whether his condemnation of violence included

---

60 Tutu and Allen, *God is not a Christian*, 92.
61 Noah Berlatsky, *The Arab-Israeli Conflict* (Detroit: Greenhaven Press, 2012), 186.
62 Georg Martin and James Manney, "Report from the Beit Sahour: Tax Strike for Justice – Building Autonomy," *Commonweal*, 26 January 1990, 36–38.
63 Berlatsky, *The Arab-Israeli Conflict*, 186.
64 Tutu and Allen, *God is not a Christian*, 92–93.
65 Allen, *Rabble Rouser for Peace*, 386.
66 Alan Cowell, "Tutu Cool to Pretoria Offer to Join Talks," *New York Times*, 26 December 1989.
67 Alan Cowell, "Tutu Cool to Pretoria Offer to Join Talks," *New York Times*, 26 December 1989.

the violence of Palestinians throwing stones at Israeli soldiers in the occupied territories, he answered, "Except for David and Goliath, I have not heard that a stone killed a soldier. I condemned all violence, but if we condemn then we have to condemn those who break bones and who use bullets."[68]

Tutu's statements above reflect his attitude toward non-violent struggle in his own country. As General Secretary of the SACC, Tutu's position demonstrates the line taken by the SACC towards violence, which combined "an understanding of the reasons for taking up arms with a blanket condemnation of all violence, from whatever side it came."[69] This line of policy evolved directly from the WCC's changing position towards the turn to an armed struggle in South Africa by the ANC. As Tal Zalmanovich argues, from the early 1960s, "although some of the members of the WCC were still struggling with how to react to the inherent violence of racism, many called for an active response to the suffering endured by those living in racial domination."[70] Zalmanovich demonstrates the ways in which this shift in WCC policies facilitated "the South African regime's capacity to limit the activity of the WCC in the country, accusing it of supporting violence" on the one hand, and forced the South African churches, and the SACC in particular, "to clarify their positions and to commit to their stand against apartheid" on the other.[71] This shift is clearly discernible in Tutu's statement of 1989. Here he stated, "Apartheid is in and of itself violent. Apartheid is in and of itself evil, totally and completely. There is no way in which you can use nice methods. It has, *ipso facto*, to use methods that are consistent with its nature."[72]

The only Israeli official to meet Tutu during his visit was the then Minister of Religious Affairs, Zevulun Hammer, who was from the religious Mafdal Party, which of all the Israeli political parties most resembled the South African NP in its core ideology. At the meeting, the Minister confronted Tutu on his criticism of Israel's treatment of the Palestinians, arguing that Tutu showed "a simple lack of understanding toward the problems of the Middle East."[73] He stated,

---

68 Alan Cowell, "Tutu Cool to Pretoria Offer to Join Talks," *New York Times*, 26 December 1989.
69 Allen, *Rabble Rouser for Peace*, 172.
70 Zalmanovich, "What Is Needed Is an Ecumenical Act of Solidarity," 185.
71 Zalmanovich, "What Is Needed Is an Ecumenical Act of Solidarity," 186–187.
72 Archbishop Desmond Tutu quoted in Asmal and Roberts, *Reconciliation Through Truth*, 42.
73 "Tutu Defends Criticism of Israeli Policy: Middle East: South African prelate is assailed for condemning treatment of Palestinians in visit to area. He calls nation's former leaders terrorists," *Los Angeles Times*, 26 December 1989.

> We [the Jewish people] were never received by the Arabs as people returning home [. . .] we returned home to the homes of our forefathers that we had prayed for 2,000 years, and you [Tutu] have to see this if you want to contribute to peace.[74]

Tutu responded, "I still feel that some of the things that I have seen on the occupied West Bank are things that I have seen at home."[75] He further explained, "when I find injustice and oppression anywhere in the world, whoever perpetrates it must know that I will condemn it. If I am accused, as I am often accused, of being antisemitic, tough luck." However, at the same time, he stressed that he understood the anxieties and fears of the Jewish people:

> I have articulated that time and time again, saying that it is important for the Arabs, the Palestinians, to recognize Israel's right to a sovereign statehood; but equally, I would hope that the Israelis would hear the anguish and the cry of the Palestinians to equal recognition of their aspirations for sovereign statehood.[76]

On the last day of his visit, Tutu was taken to the Yad Vashem memorial in Jerusalem. That Israeli official memorial to the victims of the Holocaust was established in 1953 on the western slope of Mount Herzl in Jerusalem, in accordance with the Holocaust and Heroism Remembrance Law.[77] Under the Israeli legal protocol, visits to Yad Vashem were (and still are) mandatory for all diplomats visiting Israel for the first time, since in the words of a Foreign Ministry document of protocol, "you cannot understand Israel [. . .] without visiting the Holocaust."[78] As Idith Zertal argued, the law "made the crucial, exclusive link between Holocaust memory and the State of Israel, between the Holocaust and Jerusalem, the only place that could house this memory, according to the official Israeli narrative."[79] Presumably, the proposal for an official visit by Tutu to Yad Vashem was related to the fact that he was already considered an influential figure in the Christian world and in the international arena in general. Since the Israeli internal reports on Tutu's visit present the many concerns held by the organizers thereof on the Israeli side regarding possible anti-Zionist and pro-Palestinian statements by Tutu, it is safe to assume that the visit to Yad Vashem, which clearly links the Holocaust to the rebirth of Israel, was meant to soften Tutu's views.

---

[74] Ann Peters, "Tutu Visit Jerusalem Holocaust Memorial," *United Press International*, 27 December 1989.
[75] Tutu and Allen, *God is not Christian*, 95.
[76] Tutu and Allen, *God is not Christian*, 95.
[77] The Martyrs' and Heroes' Remembrance (Yad Vashem) Law 5713–1953, *The Statute Book*, no. 132, 8 Elul 5713, 19 August 1953.
[78] Sara McDowell and Maire Broniff, *Commemoration as Conflict: Space, Memory, and Identity in Peace Processes* (London: Palgrave MacMillan, 2014), 111–112.
[79] Zertal, *Israel's Holocaust and the Politics of Nationhood*, 86.

Some members of the Anglican church in East Jerusalem tried to talk Tutu out of visiting the Yad Vashem memorial, arguing, "the Holocaust is not the other side of the story. We [the Palestinians] were not responsible for the Holocaust."[80] Nonetheless, Tutu was not dissuaded from his plans. In his personal account of his experience at the Yad Vashem memorial, Tutu recalls,

> I visited the Holy Land over Christmas 1989 and had the privilege during that visit of going to Yad Vashem, the Holocaust museum in Jerusalem. When the media asked me for my impressions, I told them it was a shattering experience. I added that the Lord whom I served, who was himself a Jew, would have asked, 'But what about forgiveness?' That remark set the cat among the pigeons. I was roundly condemned. I had also expressed my dismay at the treatment meted out to the Palestinians, which was in my view quite at variance with what the Jewish prophets taught and what the Jewish rabbi that we Christians followed demanded from his followers.[81]

In Israel, Tutu's Yad Vashem statement was interpreted as another manifestation of pro-Palestinian leanings. He was again accused of antisemitism and graffiti appeared on the walls of St. George's Anglican Cathedral in Jerusalem with the slogan: "Tutu is a black Nazi pig."[82] Zvi Gur-Ari, the Israeli Ambassador to South Africa, published an official statement on Tutu's visit to the South African press, referring selectively to Tutu's pro-Palestinian sympathies and to his repeated comparison between Israel and apartheid, without mentioning the Yad Vashem statement.[83]

The incident met, however, with outrage on the part of the official representatives of American Jewry. The New York Community Relations Council, as well as the National Jewish Community Relations Advisory Council, the American Jewish Congress, and the anti-Defamation League of B'nai B'rith issued statements criticizing Tutu's remarks at Yad Vashem as profoundly insensitive.[84] Elie Wiesel, the renowned 1986 Nobel Peace Prize recipient and Holocaust survivor stated: "No one has the right to forgive except the dead themselves, and the dead were killed and silenced by their murderers. For anyone in Jerusalem, at Yad Vashem, to speak about forgiveness would be, in my view, a disturbing lack

---

80 Allen, *Rabble Rouser for Peace*, 387.
81 Tutu, *No Future Without Forgiveness*, 203–204.
82 Tutu, *No Future Without Forgiveness*, 204.
83 "Israel Ambassador on Archbishop Tutu," *Cape Times*, 6 February 1990, Press Items of Jewish Interest No. 3, Rochlin Archive, Johannesburg.
84 Allison Kaplan, "Behind the Headlines: Jews Disagree Whether to Protest Tutu's Appearance at Inauguration," *Jewish Telegraphic Agency*, 28 December 1989.

of sensitivity toward the Jewish victims and their survivors. I hope that was not the intention of Bishop Tutu."[85]

A stronger reaction came from Rabbi Marvin Hier, dean of the Los Angeles-based Simon Wiesenthal Center, then the largest Holocaust study institution in the United States. He saw Tutu's call for prayer and the forgiveness of those responsible for the Nazi genocide as "a gratuitous insult to the Jews and victims of Nazism everywhere. Bishop Tutu showed the arrogance of an ancient crusader who had come to Yad Vashem with a bag full of Christian morality. The bishop surely knows where that Christian conscience was when millions of Jews and others suffered at the hands of the Nazis."[86]

When Tutu arrived again in the US in January 1990 to participate in the inauguration ceremony of David Dinkins as New York's first black mayor, he was the target of a water-bomb tossed at him by Jewish protesters; and in May of that year, he received hostile reception from Jewish activists protesting in Pasadena, California, against his recent statements made in Israel declaring his support for the right of the Palestinians. The protesters shouted: "why do you hate Jews?" as he left the All Saints Episcopal Church in Pasadena.[87] The protestors' actions were deplored by a group of American Jewish leaders, who issued a joint statement after meeting with Tutu in Cincinnati. However, while distancing themselves from allegations leveled against Tutu for antisemitism, they expressed their belief that his criticism of Israel was asymmetrical, stating: "Jewish community leaders and Archbishop Tutu differed on whether comparisons could be drawn between the policies of the South African and Israeli governments."[88]

In South Africa, too, the Jewish community was troubled by Tutu's statements throughout his visit to Israel, albeit without specifically addressing Tutu's controversial call for forgiveness. At the Cape Committee meeting of the SAJBD held in January 1990, Rabbi Arthur Seltzer, chairman of the South African Association of Progressive Rabbis, said that he had been very disturbed by the recent pronouncements made by Tutu. He argued that any leader who uses Jews and Israel to "push" his own political power should be stopped and called on the

---

85 David Landau, "Tutu Speaks of Israeli Repression but his Rhetoric is taken in Stride," *Jewish Telegraphic Agency*, 25 December 1989.
86 David Landau, "Tutu Speaks of Israeli Repression but his Rhetoric is taken in Stride," *Jewish Telegraphic Agency*, 25 December 1989.
87 "Hostile Reception for Tutu in US," *Sowetan*, 23 May 1990, Press Items of Jewish Interest No. 10, Rochlin Archive, Johannesburg.
88 "Hostile Reception for Tutu in US," *Sowetan*, 23 May 1990; "Archbishop Tutu," *Daily News*, 31 May 1990, Press Items of Jewish Interest No. 10, Rochlin Archive, Johannesburg.

Board to issue a clear and vigorous statement to that effect.[89] Moreover, in an article in the *Sunday Times* from 14 January 1990, Rabbi David Hoffman of Cape Town wrote, "Respecting the real suffering of the victims and appreciating the burdens borne by the survivors becomes difficult when blurring over the historical uniqueness of the Holocaust and equating the suffering of its victims with the suffering caused by other situations."[90] Hoffman referred specifically to Tutu's visit to Jerusalem's Yad Vashem Holocaust Memorial, stating:

> Admittedly biased toward a certain simplistic concept of how peace in the Middle East might be attained when he entered, the Archbishop would not allow his encounter with Yad Vashem to deter him from his mission or his message. To do so would have meant to challenge himself at the very core of conviction and being, to really consider the way that Jews everywhere bear witness to the Holocaust and to allow that testimony to challenge his own Holocaust theology and the gaps in his knowledge.[91]

While Tutu's statement was critically received in the Jewish-Zionist world, the arguments of his critics reflect insufficient consideration of his eclectic theological orientation which drew upon elements of African spirituality, black liberation theology, and Anglican humanism, all informed by the anti-apartheid struggle in South Africa. Tutu's goal was liberation from apartheid, and throughout his struggle he repeatedly declared to the Jewish-Zionist world, "[opposition to apartheid] is not a political issue, it is our faith and it has very deep roots in your history, your tradition."[92] Tutu here draws on the concept of *Ubuntu*, the Southern African word for humanness often used to encapsulate sub-Saharan moral ideals and which he defines as meaning "my humanity is caught up, is inextricably bound up, in yours, [..] a person is a person through other persons."[93] He states, "if social harmony is for us the summon bonum – the greatest good – then the primary aim when dealing with wrongdoing [. . .] should be to establish harmonious relationships between wrongdoers and victims."[94]

This convention, which was clearly echoed in Tutu's controversial call at Yad Vashem, was also used as a yardstick to evaluate South African society during the transition from apartheid to democracy. Tutu maintained that, through

---

89 SAJBD, Cape Committee Activities report, November 1989 to January 1990, 7–8, SAJBD Reports, Rochlin Archive, Johannesburg.
90 "Blurs Historical Uniqueness," *Sunday Times*, 14 January 1990, Press Items of Jewish Interest No. 1, Rochlin Archive, Johannesburg.
91 "Blurs Historical Uniqueness," *Sunday Times*, 14 January 1990, Press Items of Jewish Interest No. 1, Rochlin Archive, Johannesburg.
92 Feld, *Nations Divided*, 125.
93 Tutu, *No Future Without Forgiveness*, 31.
94 Tutu, *No Future Without Forgiveness*, 31.

Ubuntu, democratic South Africa should deal with apartheid-era political crimes by seeking reconciliation or restorative justice. In his address to the first gathering of the TRC on 16 December 1995, Tutu stated,

> We are privileged to be on this Commission to assist our land, our people to come to terms with our dark past once and for all. They say that those who suffer from amnesia, those who forget the past, are doomed to repeat it. It is not dealing with the past to say facilely, let bygones be bygones, for then they won't be bygones.[95]

From this perspective, Tutu's call for Jews to forgive the Nazi perpetrators was not a call for a Jewish amnesia or for a general amnesty, but rather a call for the Jewish nation to rise above its historical tragedy in order to empathize with and prevent the suffering of others. Viewed retrospectively, the position adopted by Tutu in Jerusalem in 1989 is consistent with his approach to transitional justice in South Africa six years later, which aimed at helping South Africans come to terms with their past and which laid the foundation for reconciliation and for social cohesion.[96]

Holocaust Memory in Post-Apartheid South Africa

An exploration of Tutu's analogical lexicon reveals the gradual evolution of different sets of analogies from the late 1970s onwards. The focus on Tutu's various public statements and their reception in these years invites us to shed light on the complex nexus of South African Jewry's position as a direct beneficiary of whiteness under apartheid and the limitations of the idea of Holocaust uniqueness in this context. It also allows us to reposition Tutu's religious visit to Israel-Palestine as a prominent political event in his ongoing struggle against apartheid, and as one that was formative for the emergence of his using the Israel-apartheid analogy and his articulation of a parallel struggle: that of the Palestinians against the Israeli Occupation. However, as mentioned above, Tutu's lexicon should also be interpreted as a pretext for the processes of reconciliation that would be consolidated in South Africa following the first democratic elections of 27 April 1994.

---

95 Desmond Tutu, "Archbishop Desmond Tutu's Address to the First Gathering of the Truth and Reconciliation Commission," 16 December 1995, TRC press release.
96 Ziyad Motala, "The Promotion of National Unity and Reconciliation Act, the Constitution and International Law," *The Comparative and International Law Journal of Southern Africa* 28.3 (1995): 338–362, at 338.

The establishment of the ANC-led Government of National Unity, headed by Nelson Mandela, led to the formation of the TRC under the Promotion of National Unity and Reconciliation Act (no. 34) of 1995. As part of the Commission's discussions, which were broadcast in the local media, South African society was exposed to the terrible suffering experienced by black, Indian, and Coloured communities during the apartheid era. Through victims' testimonies, the public histories of the not-so-distant traumatic past were shaped. The committee was the cornerstone of the national project of the new South Africa, which formed the personal traumas of individuals into a uniform narrative framed in terms of the collective memory of a new nation.[97]

In his book *No Future Without Forgiveness* (1999), Tutu explains the decision to pursue the path of truth commissions in South Africa, rather than Nuremberg style criminal trials. He states: "In World War II the Allies defeated the Nazis and their allies comprehensively and were thus able to impose what has been described as 'victor's justice.'"[98] However, the situation in South Africa, he argues, was different, as there was no decisive military victory in the struggle against apartheid. More importantly, he emphasizes, "[w]hile the Allies could pack up and go home after Nuremberg, we in South Africa had to live with one another."[99] Therefore, Tutu saw it as imperative not to seek "revenge against the perpetrators but a healing for their traumatized and divided nation."[100]

Tutu's politics of comparison can contribute to the understanding of a recent debate on analogies and, more particularly, on the limitation of Holocaust uniqueness. On 17 June 2019, Democrat representative Alexandria Ocasio-Cortez described migrant detention facilities at the southern US border as concentration camps during an Instagram live stream.[101] Following up on Twitter, she repeated the "concentration camp" analogy, describing the facilities conditions as dehumanizing. Two days later, a post on the Yad Vashem Twitter account encouraged Ocasio-Cortez to educate herself about concentration camps,[102] and not long after, the US Holocaust Memorial Museum (USHMM) joined Yad Vashem's denunciation and

---

97 Heidi Grunebaum-Ralph, "Re-Placing Pasts, Forgetting Presents: Narrative, Place, and Memory in the Time of the Truth and Reconciliation Commission," *Research in African Literature* 32.3 (2001): 198–212.
98 Tutu, *No Future Without Forgiveness*, 22.
99 Tutu, *No Future Without Forgiveness*, 23.
100 Tutu, *No Future Without Forgiveness*, 37.
101 Sheryl Gay Stolberg, "Ocasio-Cortez Calls Migrant Detention Centers 'Concentration Camps,' Electing Backlash," *New York Times*, 18 June 2019.
102 "Yad Vashem tells Alexandria Ocasio-Cortez to 'learn about concentration camps,'" *Jewish Telegraphic Agency*, 20 June 2019.

issued a statement rejecting "efforts to create analogies between the Holocaust and other events, whether historical or contemporary."[103]

An open letter to the Director of the USHMM, Sara J. Bloomfield, was delivered on 1 July by three hundred and seventy-five scholars from around the world, stating:

> By "unequivocally rejecting efforts to create analogies between the Holocaust and other events, whether historical or contemporary," the United States Holocaust Memorial Museum is taking a radical position that is far removed from mainstream scholarship on the Holocaust and genocide. And it makes learning from the past almost impossible.[104]

A similar claim was made by Tutu's spokesman in an official statement to the press in November 1989:

> The Holocaust is always the one supreme example the archbishop uses in talking about massive atrocities and evil things that governments do to people. If they say one might not refer to the Holocaust as an illustrative point, then by the same standard one should not refer to Idi Amin's massacres in Uganda and the massacres inflicted on Cambodians by the Pol Pot regime. This would severely hamper a preacher's ability to illustrate a sermon with examples of evil.[105]

The critical reception of Tutu's analogical lexicon within the Jewish-Zionist world serves as another manifestation of discourses rooted in the perception of Holocaust uniqueness. It is yet another indication that the use of the Holocaust as an analogy for other genocides, mass atrocities, and human rights violations is long-standing, even if it remains highly controversial. When analogies become illegitimate, the question that remains is: How can we learn from the past if we are prevented from reflecting on its relevance for the present?

To answer this prevailing question, one must turn to the place of Holocaust memory in post-apartheid South Africa. As demonstrated throughout this book, until 1994, Holocaust memory was mainly confined to South African Jewry. However, during the post-apartheid era, a growing interest in the Jewish genocide can be detected and the Holocaust became crucial for the project of nation-building within the new democratic South Africa. Following the success of the AFWE tour in the country in 1994–1995, described in detail in Chapter 5, a permanent Holocaust exhibition was curated, and a first Holocaust center in the African continent

---

[103] "Statement Regarding the Museum's Position on Holocaust Analogies," 24 June 2019, Press Releases, USHMM.
[104] "An Open Letter to the Director of the US Holocaust Memorial Museum," *New York Review Daily*, 1 July 2019.
[105] "Response from Archbishop's Office to Letter," *Sunday Tribune*, 19 November 1989, Press Items of Jewish Interest No. 23, Rochlin Archive, Johannesburg.

was opened in Cape Town in 1999.[106] While the center was established in newly constructed premises on the first floor of the Albow Bros. Centre in the city, it was situated near the Jewish Museum and the Great Synagogue and was defined as an independent organization within the framework of Cape Town's Jewish community.[107] Its mission was defined "to serve as a memorial to the 6 million Jews who were killed in the Holocaust and all victims of Nazi Germany."[108] Nevertheless, its main objective was to provide an educational hub with a permanent exhibition focusing on the history of apartheid alongside the history of the Holocaust.

In 2007, in response to a decision by the National Department of Education to include the history of the Holocaust in the national curriculum of both grades 9 and 11, the South African Holocaust & Genocide Foundation (SAHGF) was formed as an umbrella organization to provide a national home for the field of Holocaust and genocide education.[109] As Tali Nates, director of the Johannesburg Holocaust & Genocide Centre and present chairperson of the SAHGF, argues, "the inclusion of the Holocaust in the national curriculum represents commitment to protecting and educating about human rights . . . through learning about the Holocaust first and then Apartheid, the hope is that students will be better equipped to make connections to current issues, including human rights abuses in South Africa and throughout the African continent."[110]

Two additional Holocaust centers were established in 2008 in Durban and in Johannesburg to provide training in Holocaust education nationwide. The Durban Centre was located at the Durban Jewish Club and focused on public education about the Holocaust and human rights and hosted a small permanent exhibition. Like the Cape Town Centre, its mission was to serve as a place of remembrance for the six million Jews who died in the Holocaust and all other victims of Nazism, and to engage in public outreach programs about contemporary human rights abuses and genocide.[111] The Johannesburg Centre was

---

106 Tali Nates, "The Presence of the Past: Creating a New Holocaust and Genocide Centre of Education and Memory in Post-Apartheid South Africa," in *Remembering the Holocaust in Educational Settings*, ed. Andy Pearce (London: Routledge, 2018), 205–220.
107 Minutes of a Special Meeting of the Cape Town Holocaust Memorial Council held on the 20th January 1997 at 5:00 pm in the Goldschmidt Board Room, LEEUSIG BLDG, Cape Town, 1, Holocaust Memorial Council 1991–1998 folder, Cape Town Holocaust Centre Archive, Cape Town.
108 Nates, "The Presence of the Past," 211.
109 National Curriculum Statement (NCS), "Curriculum and Assessment Policy Statement, Senior Phase Grades 7–9, Social Sciences" the Department of Basic Education, Republic of South Africa, 2011.
110 Nates, "The Presence of the Past," 209.
111 "In the Beginning," The Durban Holocaust & Genocide Centre Website, https://dbnholocaust.co.za/about-us-2/ [Accessed 27 September 2021].

first situated at a temporary office with no permanent exhibition and focused mainly on facilitating educational programs in the area. Only in 2016 did the Centre move to its permanent location at a new building in the heart of Johannesburg.[112] From its inception, the Johannesburg Centre differed from its two sister Centres in many ways: it was defined as the Johannesburg Holocaust & Genocide Centre; its new building was established on municipal land and it was thus defined as a public-private partnership with the City of Johannesburg; and its permanent exhibition, officially opened to the public in March 2019, focused on the history of two case studies: the Holocaust and the 1994 genocide in Rwanda.[113] In 2018 the two sister Centres followed suit. In February of that year, Richard Freedman, then director of the Cape Town Holocaust Centre and chair of the SAHGF, informed the public of the official renaming of the Cape Town and Durban Centres as Holocaust & Genocide Centres. He stated, "it is imbedded in our mission to widen our focus to understand how other genocides were possible. Thus, it makes sense to reflect in our name more accurately our activities."[114]

If so, while Holocaust memory was presented during the apartheid years as a unique event whose implications were relevant primarily to the South African Jewish community, it became a subject of national relevance in the post-apartheid era. South Africa continues to face its traumatic past and as it is forced to confront many issues relating to racism in the present, the three Holocaust & Genocide Centres serve as key national actors in the promotion of anti-racialism, human rights, and peace through Holocaust and genocide education. Almost three decades after the end of apartheid, the historical similarities between two different events, the Holocaust and apartheid, are mobilized not for alienation but for the promotion of human rights, mutual understanding, and empathy.

---

[112] Nates, "The Presence of the Past," 2012.
[113] "About the Johannesburg Holocaust & Genocide Centre," Johannesburg Holocaust & Genocide Centre Website, https://www.jhbholocaust.co.za/about/ [Accessed 27 September 2021].
[114] Cape Town Holocaust & Genocide Centre, Facebook Page, 19/2/2018, https://www.facebook.com/CTHGCpage/photos/a.296659157120452.68098.296257723827262/1473325446120478/?type=3&theater [Accessed 15 April 2018].

Archives

African National Congress, Historical Documents Archive, South Africa
Liberation Magazine, 1953–1959

Ahmed Kathrada Foundation Archive, Lenasia, South Africa
South African Police reports on Ahmed Kathrrada Public Addresses, File 1.1
Ahmed Kathrada Letters, Speeches, Public Meetings, File 1.6

Anne Frank House Archives, Amsterdam, Holland
The Anne Frank in the World Exhibition in South Africa, Box C-SA-I.
The Anne Frank in the World Exhibition in South Africa, Box C-SA-II.

Cape Town Holocaust & Genocide Centre Archive
Cape Town Holocaust Centre Planning Committee, 1999
Holocaust Memorial Council, 1991–1998
Holocaust Remembrance Collection
In Sacred Memory Collection
She'erith Hapletah Collection

Durban Holocaust & Genocide Centre Archive
Museum Opening and Planning Collection
HASHALOM newspaper, 1940s-1980s

Historical Papers Research Archive, University of The Witwatersrand, Johannesburg
Jewish Community, 1937–1965 Collection, 131
Jewish Community, 1952–1975 Collection, 131.1
Censorship 1974, AD1912 59.2
Reddy Biographical Collection, Ahmed Kathrada, A 2094-EL

International Institute of Social History, Amsterdam, Holland
World Youth Festival Collection, File Berlin, 1951.
World Youth Festival Collection, Box 1st – 7th Festivals, 1941–1955.

Israel State Archives, Jerusalem, Israel
Israel-South Africa Relations 1961–1967, ISA-PMO-StateDocumentsDep-0012tfj
Desmond Tutu 1989–1990, ISA-PMO-GPO-000hkin
The Eichmann Affair, Correspondence and Echoes, ISA/RG 93.43/MFA/293/13
Stenograms of Government meetings, 1960, ISA-PMO-GovernmentMeeting-0002eel

Kaplan Centre Library, University of Cape Town, South Africa
South African Jewish Chronicle, 1939–1965
South African Zionist Record, 1958–1964
Jewish Affairs, 1945–1949; 1953–1984
Press Items of Jewish Interest Collection, 1957–1986
Reports to South African Jewry, South African Jewish Board of Deputies, 1962–1976

Nelson Mandela Foundation Archive, South Africa
Speeches and messages by Nelson Rolihlahla Mandela

Oral Records Centre, The Avraham Harman Institute of Contemporary Jewry, Hebrew University of Jerusalem, Israel
Interview with Gus Saron by Simon Herman and Geoffrey Wigoder, 4–5 August 1961

Robben Island Mayibuye Archives, University of Western Cape, South Africa
Israel-South Africa, 1977–1989 Collection
Israel-South Africa, 1990–1992 Collection
Oral History and Sound Collection
Roskam Collection, MCH177
Ahmed Kathrada Collection, MCH42

Rochlin Archive, South African Jewish Board of Deputies, Johannesburg, South Africa
Holocaust Commemoration 1940s-2000s, 520.2
Memorials, 1947–1952
SAJBD Holocaust Exhibition, April-May 1985, ARCH 211
Holocaust Survivors Recollections, 520.3
Jewish Affairs, 1942–1943
Mauritius Collection, 130A
Ungar Biographical Collection
Society of Jews and Christians Collection, 607.7–8
Wald Herman 199 Collection
South African National Yad Vashem Memorial Foundation Collection
Press Items of Jewish Interest Collection, 1977–1983
South African Jewish Board of Deputies National Executive Council Reports, 1947; 1953–1957; 1981; 1983–1995
Press Digest Collection 1940s; 1950s; 1980s; 1990s
Eichmann A. 1961 Collection, 527
Anne Frank 199

Films Press Cuttings Collection
Holocaust Denial and False Statements, 520.31

South African Broadcasting Corporation Radio Archive, Johannesburg, South Africa
Interviews with Holocaust Survivors in South Africa, T 87/252; T 87/253

South Africa History Archive – SAHA, Johannesburg, South Africa
Press Statements, AL. 254, E. 6.4.8
The Objector, AL. 2547, E. 6.4.5
Speeches, Statements, Press Releases, H. 5.8.2
Jews for Justice Collection O. 7.2.1; O. 7.2.2; O. 7.2.3
The TRC Collection AL3110-A2.3.32

South Africa History Online
African National Congress Collection
Oliver Reginald Kaizana Tambo Collection

South African National Library, Cape Town, South Africa
Press Cutting Collection, 1970s-1980s
Press Cutting Collection, 1990s
Press Cutting Collection, 2000s

US Holocaust Memorial Museum Archive, Washington DC, USA
Austrian and Polish Jewish Relief Fund 1938–1941, SAJBD Archive, Holocaust-Related Records, ARCH 216.1
South African Jewish Board of Deputies Reports – Reel 1
South African Boycott of German Products – Reel 3
Jewish Refugee Camp in Mauritius, ARCH 210.1

Bibliography

Abulof, Uriel. *The Mortality and Morality of Nations: Jews, Afrikaners, and French-Canadians*. New York: Cambridge University Press, 2015.

Alexander, Jeffrey C. "On the Social Construction of Moral Universals: the Holocaust from War Crime to Trauma Drama." *European Journal of Social Theory* 5.1 (2002): 5–85.

Alexander, Jeffrey C. *Remembering the Holocaust: A Debate*. New York: Oxford University Press, 2009.

Allen, John. *Conclave: The Politics, Personalities, and Process of the Next Papal Election*. New York: Doubleday, 2002.

Allen, John. *Rabble Rouser for Peace: The Authorized Biography of Desmond Tutu*. New York: Free Press, 2006.

Almog, Oz. *The Sabra: The Creation of the New Jew*. Berkeley: University of California Press, 2000.

Anne Frank in the World, 1929–1945. Amsterdam: Anne Frank Stichting, 1985.

Alschech, Jonathan. "פרדיגמת האפרטהייד: היסטוריה, פוליטיקה ואסטרטגיה" ["The Apartheid Paradigm: History, Politics and Strategy"]. In *Law, Minority and National Conflict*, edited by Raif Zarik and Ilan Saban, 151–184. Tel Aviv: Tel Aviv University Press, 2017.

Appelfeld, Aharon. *The Story of a Life*. Schocken, 2006.

Appiah, Anthony and Henry L. Gates. *Africana: The Encyclopaedia of the African and African American Experience*. Oxford: Oxford University Press, 2005.

Atkins, Stephan E. *Holocaust Denial as an International Movement*. Westport, CT: Praeger, 2009.

Arieli-Horowitz, Dana. "The Politics of Culture in Nazi Germany: Between Degeneration and Volkism." *The European Legacy* 6.6 (2001): 751–762.

Arieli-Horowitz, Dana. אמנות ורודנות: אוואנגרד ואמנות מגויסת במשטרים טוטליטריים [*Creators and Dictators: Avantgarde and Mobilized Art in Totalitarian Regimes*]. Tel Aviv: Tel Aviv University Press, 2008.

Arkin, Marcus. *South African Jewry: A Contemporary Survey*. Cape Town: Oxford University Press, 1984.

Asmal, Kader, Louise Asmal, and Suresh Ronald Roberts. *Reconciliation Through Truth*. Cape Town: David Philip Publications, 1997.

Assmann, Jan. "Collective Memory and Cultural Identity." *New German Critique* 65 (1995): 125–133.

Assmann, Jan. *Cultural Memory and Early Civilization*. Cambridge: Cambridge University Press, 2011.

Aufderhedie, Patricia. *Documentary Film: A Very Short Introduction*. Oxford: Oxford University Press, 2007.

Baade, W. Hans. "The Eichmann Trial: Some Legal Aspects." *World Law* (1961): 400–421.

Bae, Sangim. "The right to life vs. the state's ultimate sanction: abolition of capital punishment in post-apartheid." *The International Journal of Human Rights* 9.1 (2005): 49–68.

Baneshik, Percy. "Theatre." In *South African Jewry: A Contemporary Survey*, edited by Marcus Arkin, 160–163. Cape Town: Oxford University Press, 1984.

Barker, Brian J., Paul Bell, Allan Duggan, Vivien Horler, Vincent Leroux, Portia Maurice, Cecile Reynierse, and Peter Schafer. *Illustrated History of South Africa: The Real Story*. Cape Town: The Reader's Digest Association of South Africa, 1988.

Bashir, Bashir and Amos Goldberg. *The Holocaust and the Nakba: A New Syntax of History, Memory, and Political Thought*. New York: Colombia University Press, 2019.

Bauck, Petter and Mohammed Omer. *The Oslo Accords: A Critical Assessment, 1993–2013*. Cairo: American University in Cairo Press, 2013.

Bellah, Robert N. "Bibical Religion and Civil Religion in America," *Daedalus, Journal of the American Academy of Arts and Sciences*, 96.1 (1967): 1–21.

Belling, Veronica. "Yiddish." In *The Social and Political History of Southern Africa's Languages*, edited by Tomasz Kamusella and Finex Ndhlovu, 331–339. London: Palgrave Macmillan, 2018.

Benda-Beckmann, Bas Von. *A German Catastrophe? German Histories and the Allied Bombing, 1945–2010*. Amsterdam: Amsterdam University Press, 2010.

Berlatsky, Noah. *The Arab-Israeli Conflict*. Detroit: Greenhaven Press, 2012.

Bethlehem, Louise. "Apartheid: The Global Itinerary: South African Cultural Formations in Transnational Circulation 1948–1990." ERC research proposal, 2013.

Bethlehem, Louise. "Restless Itineraries: Anti-Apartheid Expressive Culture and Transnational Historiography." *Social Text* 36.3 (2018): 47–69.

Bethlehem, Louise. "Stenographic fictions: Mary Benson's *At the Still Point* and the South African political trial." *Safundi* 20.2 (2019): 193–212.

Blatman, Daniel. "Holocaust Scholarship: towards a post-uniqueness era." *Journal of Genocide Research* 17.1 (2015): 21–43.

Bloxham, Donald. *Genocide on Trial: War Crimes Trials and the Formation of Holocaust History and Memory*. Oxford: Oxford University Press, 2001.

Bradlow, Edna. "J. H. Hofmeyr, 'Liberalism and Jewish Immigration.'" *South African Historical Journal* 40.1 (1999): 114–129.

Braude, B. Claudia. *Contemporary Jewish Writing in South Africa*. Lincoln: University of Nebraska Press, 2001.

Breines, Paul. *Tough Jews: Political Fantasies and the Moral Dilemma of American Jewry*. New York: Basic Books, 1990.

Brog, Mooli. "Victims and Victors: Holocaust and Military Commemoration in Israel Collective Memory." *Israel Studies* 8.3 (2003): 69–99.

Brown, Julian. *The Road to Soweto: Resistance and the Uprising of 16 June 1976*. Johannesburg: Jacana, 2016.

Bunting, Brian. *The Rise of the South African Reich*. Harmondsworth: Penguin Books, 1964.

Buntman, Fran L. *Robben Island and Prisoner Resistance to Apartheid*. Cambridge: Cambridge University Press, 2003.

Cajee, Amin. *Fordsburg Fighter: The Journey of a MK Volunteer*. London: Cover2Cover Books, 2016.

Cesarani, David. "How Post-war Britain Reflected on the Nazi Persecution and Mass Murder of Europe's Jews: A Reassessment of Early Responses." *Jewish Culture and History* 12.1–2 (2010): 95–130.

Cesarani, David and Eric J. Sundquist. *After the Holocaust: Challenging the Myth of Silence*. London: Routledge, 2012.

Chazan, Naomi. "The Fallacies of Pragmatism: Israeli Foreign Policy towards South Africa." *African Affairs* 82.327 (1983): 169–199.

Christoph, Marx. *Oxwagon Sentinel: Radical Afrikaner Nationalism and the History of the 'Ossewabrandwag.'* Münster: LIT Verlag, 2009.

Churchill, Ward. *A Little Matter of Genocide: Holocaust and Denial in the Americas 1492 to the Present.* San Francisco: City Lights Books, 1997.

Consonni, Manuela. 1945–1985 רזיסטנציה או שואה : זיכרון הגירוש וההשמדה באיטליה [*Resistance or Holocaust: The Memory of the Deportation and the Extermination in Italy, 1945–1985*]. Jerusalem: Magness Press, 2010.

Confino, Alon. *Foundational Pasts: The Holocaust as Historical Understanding.* Cambridge: Cambridge University Press, 2012.

Coombes, Annie, E. *History After Apartheid: Visual Culture and Public Memory in a Democratic South Africa.* Durham, NC: Duke University Press, 2003.

Crapanzano, Vincent. *Waiting: The Whites of South Africa.* New York: Random House, 1985.

Crompton, Samuel W. *Desmond Tutu: Fighting Apartheid.* New York: Chelsea House, 2007.

Davenport, Rodney H. *South Africa: A Modern History.* London: MacMillan Press LTD, 1991.

De Gruchy, John W. *The Church Struggle in South Africa.* Minneapolis: Fortress Press, 2005.

De Lange, Margreet. *The Muzzled Muse: Literature and Censorship in South Africa.* Amsterdam: John Benjamin's Publishing Co., 1997.

Diamond, Denis. "South Africa." *American Jewish Yearbook* 78 (1978): 500–516.

Dick, Archie L. *The Hidden History of South African Books and Reading Cultures.* Toronto: University of Toronto Press, 2013.

Diner, Hasia R. *We remember with reverence and love: American Jews and the myth of silence after the Holocaust 1945–1962.* New York: New York University Press, 2010.

Doneson, Judith E. "The American history of Anne Frank's diary." *Holocaust and Genocide Studies* 2, 1 (1987): 149–160.

Downing, Taylor. *The World at War.* London: Palgrave Macmillan, 2012.

Downing, L. Frederick. *Eli Wiesel: A Religious Biography.* Macon, GA: Mercer University Press, 2008.

Dreisbach, Tom. "Transatlantic Broadcasts: Holocaust in America and West Germany." *Penn History Review* 16.2 (2009): 76–97.

Drew, Allison. *South Africa's Radical Tradition: A Documentary History.* Volume One 1907–1950. Cape Town: University of Cape Town Press, 1996.

Dubow, Saul. *Apartheid 1948–1994.* Oxford: Oxford University Press, 2014.

Nahshon, Edna. "Anne Frank from Page to Stage." In *Anne Frank Unbound: Media, Imagination, Memory*, edited by Barbara Kirshenblatt-Gimblett and Jeffrey Shandler, 59–92. Bloomington: Indiana University Press, 2012.

Nates, Tali. "The Presence of the Past: Creating a New Holocaust and Genocide Centre of Education and Memory in Post-Apartheid South Africa." In *Remembering the Holocaust in Educational Settings*, edited by Andy Pearce, 205–220, London: Routledge, 2018.

Elazar, Judah D., and Peter Medding. *Jewish Communities in Frontier Societies: Argentina, Australia, and South Africa.* New York: Holmes & Meier, 1983.

Ellis, Jack C., and Betsy A. McLane. *A New History of Documentary Film.* London: Continuum, 1995.

Elphick, Richard and Hermann B. Giliomee. *The Shaping of South African Society.* Cape Town: Maskew Miller Longman, 1989.

Ezrahi, Sidra D. *By Words Alone: The Holocaust in Literature.* Chicago: The University of Chicago Press, 2008.

Fachler, David. "The Jewish Factor in Israeli Foreign Policy: The Case of South Africa (1948–1994)." Master's Thesis, The Hebrew University of Jerusalem, Israel, 2012.

Feld, N. Marjorie. *Nations Divided: American Jews and the Struggle over Apartheid*. New York: Palgrave Macmillan, 2014.

Feldman, Keith. *A Shadow over Palestine: The Imperial Life of Race in America*. Minneapolis: University of Minnesota Press, 2015.

Ferm, W. Deane. *Third World Liberation Theologies: An Introductory Survey*. Eugene, OR: Wipf & Stock, 2004.

Fox, Thomas C. "The Holocaust under Communism." In *The Historiography of the Holocaust*, edited by Dan Stone, 420–439. New York: Palgrave McMillan, 2004.

Frank, Anne. *Anne Frank: The Diary of a Young Girl*. New York: Doubleday, 1952.

Frankel, Jonathan. *Prophecy and Politics: Socialism, Nationalism & the Russian Jews, 1862–1917*. Cambridge: Cambridge University Press, 1984.

Freedman, Richard. "Engaging with Holocaust Education in Post-apartheid South Africa." In *Holocaust Education in a Global Context*, edited by Karel Francapane and Matthias Hass, 134–143. Paris: UNESCO, 2014.

Friedlander, Shaul. "Opening Lecture: The Shoah between Memory and History." *Jewish Studies* 30 (1990): 11–20.

Frits, Gaum. "From Church and Society (1986) to Rustenburg (1990): Developments within the Dutch Reformed Church." In *Reformed Churches in South Africa and the Struggle for Justice: Remembering 1960–1990*, edited by Marry-Anne Plaatjies-Van Huffel and Robert Vosloo, 67–74. Stellenbosch: Sun Press, 2013.

Furlong, Patrick J. *Between Crown and Swastika: The Impact of the Radical Right on the Afrikaner Nationalist Movement in the Fascist Era*. Johannesburg: Witwatersrand University Press, 1991.

Gagarin, Yuri. *Soviet Man in Space*. Honolulu, HI: University Press of the Pacific, 2001.

Geldenhuÿs, Pieter B. *Pornografie, sensuur en reg* [*Pornography, Censorship and Law*]. Johannesburg: Lex Patria, 1977.

Giladi, Rotem. "Negotiating Identity: Israel, Apartheid, and the United Nations, 1949–1952." *The English Historical Review* 132.559 (2017): 1440–1472.

Gilbert, Shirli. "Jews and Racial State: Legacies of the Holocaust in Apartheid South Africa." *Jewish Social Studies* 16.3 (2010): 32–64.

Gilbert, Shirli. "Anne Frank in South Africa: Remembering the Holocaust During and After the Apartheid." *Holocaust and Genocide Studies* 26.3 (2012): 366–393.

Gilbert, Shirli. "Remembering the Racial State: Holocaust Memory in Post-Apartheid South Africa." In *Holocaust Memory in a Globalizing World*, edited by J. S. Eder, P. Gassert, and A. Steinweis, 199–214. Göttingen: Wallstein Verlag: 2016.

Gilbert, Shirli, and Alba Avril. *Holocaust Memory and Racism in the Post-War World*. Detroit: Wayne State University Press, 2019.

Gilbert, Shirli. "Nazism and Racism in South African Textbooks." In *Holocaust Memory and Racism in the Post-War World*, edited by Shirli Gilbert and Avril Alba, 350–385. Detroit: Wayne State University Press, 2019.

Gilbert, Shirli. *From things Lost: Forgotten Letters and the Legacy of the Holocaust*. Detroit: Wayne State University Press, 2017.

Giliomee, Hermann. *The Afrikaner: Biography of a People*. London: Hurst & Company, 2003.

Giliomee, Hermann and Bernard Mbenga. *New History of South Africa*. Cape Town: Tafelberg, 2007.

Gilroy, Paul. *There Ain't No Black in the Union Jack*. New York: Routledge, 2013.
Gish, Steven. *Desmond Tutu: A Biography*. Westport, CT: Greenwood Press, 2004.
Givoni, Michal. אתיקת העדות -היסטוריה של עדיה [*The Ethics of Witnessing: A History of a Problem*]. Jerusalem: Van Leer Institute Press, 2015.
Goldberg, Amos, and Hazan Haim. *Marking Evil: Holocaust Memory in the Global Age*. New York: Berghahn, 2015.
Goldschlager, Alain. "The Trials of Ernst Zundel." In *Holocaust Denial: The Politics of Perfidy*, edited by Robert S. Wistrich, 109–136. Berlin: De Gruyter, 2012.
Goodrich, Frances, and Albert Hackett. *The Diary of Anne Frank*. New York: Random House, 1955.
Green, Michael A. "South African Jewish Responses to the Holocaust, 1941–1948." Master's thesis, University of South Africa, Pretoria, 1987.
Grunebaum-Ralph, Heidi. "Re-Placing Pasts, Forgetting Presents: Narrative, Place, and Memory in the Time of the Truth and Reconciliation Commission." *Research in African Literature* 32.3 (2001): 198–212.
Halbwachs, Maurice. *The Collective Memory*. Chicago: The University of Chicago Press, 1992.
Haron, Muhammed. "The Muslim News (1960–1986): Expression of an Islamic identity in South Africa." In *Muslim Identity and Social Change in Sub-Saharan Africa*, edited by Louis Brenner, 210–226. London: Hurst, 1993.
Hart, Alan. *Zionism: Conflict without end?* Atlanta: Clarity Press, 2010.
Harwood, Richard. *Did Six Million Really Die? The Truth at Last*. London: Historical Review Press, 1974.
Hellig, Jocelyn. "The Jewish Community in South Africa." In *Living Faiths in South Africa*, edited by Martin Prozesky and John de Gruchy, 155–176. New York: St. Martin's Press and Hurt & Co., 1995.
Hellig, Jocelyn. *Anti-Semitism in South Africa Today*. Tel Aviv: Tel Aviv University Press, 1996.
Henry, Kenny. *Architect of Apartheid: H. F. Verwoerd, an Appraisal*. Johannesburg: John Ball, 1980.
Herf, Jeffrey. *Divided Memory: The Nazi Past in the Two Germanys*. Cambridge, MA: Harvard University Press, 1997.
Hexham, Irvin, and Karla Poewe. "The Spread of Christianity among Whites and Blacks in Transorangia." In *Christianity in South Africa: A Political, Social, and Cultural History*, edited by Richard Elphick and Rodney Davenport, 121–134. Berkeley: University of California Press, 1997.
Higginson, John. *Collective Violence and the Agrarian Origins of South African Apartheid, 1900–1948*. Cambridge: Cambridge University Press, 2014.
Hill, Leonidas E. "The Trial of Ernst Zundel: Revisionism and the Law in Canada." *Simon Wiesenthal Annual* 6 (1989): 165–219.
Hill, Ray, and Andrew Bell. *The Other Face of Terror- Inside Europe's Neo-Nazi Network*. London: Grafton Books, 1988.
Hoffman, Tzippi, and Alan Fischer. *The Jews of South Africa: What Future?* Johannesburg: Southern Book Publishers, 1988.
Hofmeyr, Jan Hendrik. *The Open Horizon: Speeches and Addresses Delivered by Jan H. Hofmeyr Administrator of the Transvaal Province, 1924–1929*. Johannesburg: Central News Agency, 1929.
Hope, Marjorie, and James Young. *The South African Churches in a Revolutionary Situation*. Maryknoll, NY: Orbis Books, 1981.

Huener, Jonathan. *Auschwitz, Poland, and the politics of commemoration, 1945–1979*. Athens: Ohio University Press, 2003.
Husain, Azim. "The West South Africa and Israel: Strategic Triangle." *Third World Quarterly* 4.1 (1982): 44–73.
Hutton, Barbara. *Robben Island: Symbol of Resistance*. Johannesburg: SACHED Books, 1997.
Hyslop, Jonathan. "A Prussian Path to Apartheid? Germany as Comparative Perspective in Critical Analysis of South African Society." *SA Sociological Review* 3.1 (1990): 33–55.
Hyslop, Jonathan. "White Working-Class Women and the Invention of Apartheid: 'Purified' Afrikaner Nationalist Agitation for Legislation against 'Mixed' Marriages, 1934–9." *The Journal of African History* 36.1 (1995): 57–81.
Irwin, M. Ryan. *Gordian Knot: Apartheid and the Unmaking of the Liberal World Order*. Oxford: Oxford University Press, 2012.
Johns, Sheridan. "The Comintern, South Africa and the Black Diaspora," *The Review of Politics* 37.2 (1975): 200–234.
Jones, Derek. *Censorship: A World Encyclopedia*. London: Routledge, 2001.
Joseph, Helen. *If this be Treason: Helen Joseph's Dramatic Account of the Treason Trial, the Longest in South Africa's History and One of the Strangest Trials of the 20th Century*. Johannesburg: Quagga Publishers, 1963.
Kathrada, Ahmed. *Memoirs*. Cape Town: Zebra Press, 2004.
Kathrada, Ahmed. *A Simple Freedom: The Strong Mind of Robben Island Prisoner, No. 468/64 Ahmed Kathrada*. Johannesburg: Wild dog Press, 2008.
Katz, Brock David. *South Africans versus Rommel: The Untold Story of the Desert War in World War II*. Guilford, CT: Stackpole Books, 2017.
Kaplan, Mendel. *Jewish Roots in the South African Economy*. Cape Town: C. Struik Publishers, 1986.
Karis, G. Thomas. "South African liberation: the communist factor." *Foreign Affairs* 65.2 (1986): 267–287.
Karolides, Nicholas J., and Margaret Vald. *Literature Suppressed on Political Grounds*. New York: Infobase Publishing, 2014.
Klaaren, Jonathan. "Early practices of regulating mobility." In *From Prohibited Immigration to Citizens- The origins of citizenship and nationality in South Africa*, 14–46. Cape Town: University of Cape Town Press, 2017.
Kochan, Lionel, and Kochan, Miriam. "Western Europe-Great Britain." *American Jewish Yearbook* 76 (1976): 287–302.
Kotek, Joel. *Students and the Cold War*. London: Macmillan, 1996.
Kruger, Loren. *The Drama of South Africa: Plays, Pageants and Publics Since 1910*. London: Routledge, 2005.
Krut, M. Riva. "Building a Home and a Community: Jews in Johannesburg, 1886–1914." PhD dissertation, University of London, England, 1985.
Kucia, Marek. "Holocaust Memorials in Central and Eastern Europe: Communist Legacies, Transnational Influences and National Developments." *Remembrance and Solidarity* 5 (2016): 159–184.
Kuper, Leo. "South Africa: Human Rights and Genocide." Eleventh Annual Hans Wolff Memorial Lecture, African Studies Program, Indiana University, Bloomington, IN, 1980.
Lagrou, Pieter. "Victims of Genocide and National Memory: Belgium, France and the Netherlands, 1945–1966." *Past and Present* 154 (1997): 181–222.

Lagrou, Pieter. *The Legacy of Nazi Occupation. Patriotic Memory and National Recovery in Western Europe, 1945–1965*. Cambridge: Cambridge University Press, 2000.

Lentz, Harris M. *Popes and Cardinals of the 20th Century: A Biographical Dictionary*. London: McFarland, 2009.

Levy, Daniel, and Natan Sznaider. "Memory Unbound: The Holocaust and the Formation of Cosmopolitan Memory." *European Journal of Social History* 5.1 (2002): 87–106.

Levy, Daniel, and Natan Sznaider. *The Holocaust and Memory in the Global Age*. Philadelphia: Temple University Press, 2006.

Liel, Alon. צדק שחור: המהפך הדרום אפריקני [*Black Justice: The South African Upheaval*]. Tel Aviv: Hakibbutz Hameuchad, 1999.

Lipstadt, Deborah E. *The Eichmann Trial*. New York: Schocken Books, 2011.

Lipstadt, Deborah E. *Denying the Holocaust: The Growing Assault on Truth and Memory*. New York: The Free Press, 1993.

Lipstadt, Deborah E. "Holocaust-Denial and the Compelling Force of Reason." *Patterns of Prejudice* 26.1/2 (1992): 64–76.

Livingstone, Ken. *You Can't Say That: Memoirs*. London: Faber & Faber, 2011.

Lubotzky, Asher, and Roni Mikel Arieli. "'The Great Trek Towards Nazism': Anti-Fascism and the Radical Left in South Africa During the Early Apartheid Era." *South African Historical Journal* (2021): 1–25.

MacDonald, David B. *Identity Politics in the Age of Genocide: The Holocaust and Historical Representation*. London: Routledge, 2008.

Maharaj, Mac. *Reflections in Prison: Voices from the South African Liberation Struggle*. Cape Town: Zebra Press, 2001.

Maier, Charles S. "Consigning the Twentieth Century to History: Alternative Narratives for the Modern Era." *American Historical Review* 165.3 (2000): 807–830.

Malamat, Abraham, and Hayim Tadmor. *A History of the Jewish People*. Cambridge, MA: Harvard University Press, 1976.

Mandela, Nelson. *A Long Walk to Freedom*. New York: Little, Brown & Co., 1995.

Marks, Shula. "Afterword: Worlds of Impossibilities?" In *South Africa's 1940s: Worlds of Possibilities*, edited by Saul Dubow and Alan Jeeves, 267–282, Lannsdowne: Double Storey, 2005.

McDonald, Peter D. *The Literature Police: Apartheid Censorship and its Cultural Consequences*. Oxford: Oxford University Press, 2010.

McDowell, Sara, and Maire Broniff. *Commemoration as Conflict: Space, Memory and Identity in Peace Processes*. London: Palgrave MacMillan, 2014.

Mendelsohn, Richard. "The Boar War, The Great War, and the Shaping of South African Jewish Loyalties." In *Memories, Realities and Dreams: Aspects of the South African Jewish Experience*, edited by Milton Shain and Richard Mendelsohn, 50–59. Johannesburg: Jonathan Ball Publications, 2002.

Mendelson, Richard, and Milton Shain. *The Jews in South Africa: An Illustrated History*. Johannesburg: Jonathan Ball Publishers, 2008.

Midgley, James. "Public Opinion and the Death Penalty in South Africa." *The British Journal of Criminology* 14.4 (1974): 345–358.

Miller, Judith. *One, By One, By One: Facing the Holocaust*. New York: Simon & Schuster, 1991.

Miller, Roberta Balstad. "Science and Society in the Early Career of H. F. Verwoerd." *Journal of Southern African Studies* 19.4 (1993): 634–661.

Mikel Arieli, Roni. "Between Apartheid, the Holocaust and the Nakba: Archbishop Desmond Tutu's Pilgrimage to Israel-Palestine (1989) and the Emergence of an Analogical Lexicon." *Journal of Genocide Research* 22.3 (2020): 334–353.

Mikel Arieli, Roni. "Reading the Diary of Anne Frank on Robben Island: On the role of Holocaust Memory in Ahmed Kathrada's Struggle against Apartheid." *Journal of Jewish Identities* 12.2 (2019): 175–195.

Mikel Arieli, Roni. "Ahmed Kathrada in Post-War Europe: Holocaust Memory and Apartheid South Africa (1951–1952)." *African Identities* 17.1 (2019): 1–17.

Monama, Fankie L. "South African Propaganda Agencies and the Battle for Public Opinion during the Second World War, 1939–1940." *Scientia Militaria* 44.1 (2016): 145–167.

Moodie, Dunbar. *The Rise of Afrikanerdom: Power, Apartheid, and the Afrikaner Civil Religion.* Berkeley: University of California Press, 1975.

Mouton, Alex F. "'Fascist or opportunist?:' The political career of Oswald Pirow, 1915–1943." *Historia* 63.2 (2018): 93–111.

Mungazi, Dickson A. *In the Footsteps of the Masters: Desmond M. Tutu and Abel T. Muzorewa.* Westport, CT: Praeger, 2000.

Naor, Mordechai. *The Twentieth Century in Eretz Israel: A Pictorial History.* Cologne: Könemann, 1998.

Nates, Tali. "'But, apartheid was also genocide . . . What about our suffering?' Teaching the Holocaust in South Africa: opportunities and challenges." *Intercultural Education* 21.S1 (2010): 17–26.

Neubauer, Hans-Joachim. *The Rumour: A Cultural History.* London: Free Association Books, 1999.

Nixon, Rob. *Homelands, Harlem and Hollywood: South African Culture and the World Beyond.* New York, London: Routledge, 1994.

Novick, Peter. *The Holocaust in American Life.* New York: Houghton Mifflin Company, 1999.

Ofer, Dalia. "השיח הישראלי על השואה," ["The Israeli Discourse on the Holocaust."] In Holocaust in Jewish History, edited by Dan Michman, 328–393. Jerusalem: Yad Vashem, 2005.

Ofer, Dalia. "The Strength of Remembrance: Commemorating the Holocaust during the First Decade of Israel." *Jewish Social Studies* 14.1 (2009): 1–35.

Ofer, Dalia. "We Israelis Remember, But How? The Memory of the Holocaust and the Israeli Experience." *Israel Studies* 18.2 (2014): 70–85.

Pearce, Andy. *Holocaust Consciousness in Contemporary Britain.* London: Routledge, 2014.

Peires, Juliette. *Ruling by Race: Nazi Germany and Apartheid South Africa.* Cape Town: Century City, 2008.

Peterson, Tracey. "Politics, Policy and Holocaust Education in South Africa,. *Policy and Practice: Pedagogy about the Holocaust and Genocide Papers* 11 (2013).

Piat-ka, Xavier. "She'erith Hapletah." In *In Sacred Memory: Recollections of the Holocaust by Survivors Living in Cape Town*, edited by Gwynne Schrire Robins, 194–198. Cape Town: Holocaust Memorial Council, 1995.

Pieterse, J. C. Hendrik. "Introduction." In *Desmond Tutu's Message: A Qualitative Analysis*, edited by Hendrik J.C. Piererse and Peer Scheepers, 9–14. Leiden: Brill, 2001.

Pietrzykowski, Szymon. "Holocaust, Israeli Statehood and Jewish Identity: International Reception of the Eichmann Trial (1961–1962)." *Pisma Humanistyczne* XIV (2016): 117–157.

Pitot, Geneviève. *The Mauritian Shekel: The Story of the Jewish Detainees in Mauritius 1940–1945.* Lanham, MD: Rowman & Littlefield, 1998.

Polakow-Suransky, Sasha. *The Unspoken Alliance: Israel's Secret Relationship with Apartheid South Africa*. New York: Random House, 2010.

Porat, Dina. "1958–1998, השואה ומכחישי פרנק אנה של יומנה -שנה ארבעים בת מערכה" ["A Forty-Year Struggle- Anne Frank's Diary and the Holocaust Deniers, 1958–1998"]. In *The Holocaust, History and Memory: Essays Presented in Honor of Yhuda Bauer*, edited by Shmuel Almog, David Bankier, Daniel Blatman, and Dalia Ofer, 160–184. Jerusalem: The Hebrew University of Jerusalem Press, 2001.

Harrison, Randall, and Paul Ekman. "TV's Last Frontier: South Africa." *Journal of Communication* 26.1 (1976): 102–109.

Renwick, Robin. *Helen Suzman: Bright Star in a Drack Chamber, the Biography*. Biteback Publishing, 2014.

Robins, Steven. *Letters of Stone: From Nazi Germany to South Africa*, Cape Town: Penguin Books, 2016.

Rothberg, Michael. *Multidirectional Memory: Remembering the Holocaust in the Age of Decolonialization*. Stanford: Stanford University Press, 2009.

Rothberg, Michael "Multidirectional Memory and the Implicated Subject: On Sebald and Kentridge." In *Performing Memory in Art and Popular Culture*, edited by Liedeke Plate and Anneke Smelik, 38–59. London: Routledge, 2013.

Rothberg, Michael. *The Implicated Subject: Beyond Victims and Perpetrators*. Stanford: Stanford University Press, 2019.

Rosenberg, Alan. "Was the Holocaust Unique?: A Peculiar Question?" In *Genocide and the Modern Age*, edited by Isidor Wallimann and Michael N. Dobkowoski, 145–161. Syracuse, NY: Syracuse University Press, 2000.

Rosenfeld, Alvin H. "Popularization and Memory: The Case of Anne Frank." In *Lessons and Legacies: The Meaning of the Holocaust in a Changing World*, edited by Peter Hayes, 243–278. Evanston, IL: Northwestern University Press, 1991.

Rosenfeld, Alvin H. *The End of the Holocaust*. Bloomington, IN: Indiana University Press 2011.

Sagan, Alex. "An Optimistic Icon: Anne Frank's Canonization in Postwar Culture." *German Politics & Society* 13.3 (1995): 95–107.

Sandwith, Corinne. "'Yours for Socialism': Communist Cultural Discourse in Early Apartheid South Africa." *Safundi: The Journal of South African and American Studies* 14 (2013): 1–24.

Saron, Gustav, and Louis Hotz. *The Jews of South Africa: A History*. Oxford: Oxford University Press, 1955.

Saron, Gustav. *The South African Jewish Board of Deputies, its role and development: an analytical review on its 70th anniversary*. Johannesburg: The South African Jewish Board of Deputies, 1973.

Schach, Leonard. *The Flag is Flying: A Very Personal History of Theatre in the Old South Africa*. Cape Town: Human Roussean, 1996.

Schaller, J. Dominik, and Jürgen Zimmerer. *The Origins of Genocide: Raphael Lemkin as a Historian of Mass Violence*. London: Routledge, 2009.

Schmidt, W. David. *Partners Together in This Great Enterprise: The Role of Christian Zionism in the Foreign Polices of Britain and American in the 20th Century*. Jerusalem: Xulon Press, 2011.

Scott, M. Thomas. *The Diplomacy of Liberation: The Foreign Relations of the ANC Since 1960*. London: Tauris Academic Studies, 1995.

Segev, Tom. *The Seventh Million: The Israeli and the Holocaust*. New York: Picador, 2000.

Shain, Milton. *The Roots of Anti-Semitism in South Africa*. Charlottesville: University Press of Virginia, 1994.

Shain, Milton. "South Africa." In *The World Reacts to the Holocaust*, edited by David S. Wyman and Charles H. Rosenzveig, 670–689. Maryland: The Johns Hopkins University Press, 1996.

Shain, Milton. "Ambivalence, Antipathy, and Accommodation: Christianity and the Jews." In *Christianity in South Africa: A Political, Social, and Cultural History*, edited by Richard Elphick and Rodney H. Davenport, 278–285. Berkeley: University of California Press, 1997.

Shain, Milton, and Margo Bastos. "Muslim Antisemitism and Anti-Zionism in Postwar South Africa." In *Holocaust Denial*, edited by Robert S. Wistrich, 137–156, Berlin: De Gruyter, 2012.

Shain, Milton. *A Perfect Storm: Antisemitism in South Africa 1930–1948*. Johannesburg: Jonathan Ball Publishers, 2015.

Shain, Milton. "From Undesirable to Unassimilable: The Racialization of the 'Jew' in South Africa." In *Holocaust Memory and Racism in the Postwar World*, edited by Shirli Gilbert and Avril Alba, 72–90. Detroit: Wayne State University Press, 2019.

Shandler, Jeffrey. "From Diary to Book: Text, Object, Structure." In *Anne Frank Unbound: Media, Imagination, Memory*, edited by Barbara Kirshenblatt-Gimblett and Jeffrey Shandler, 25–58. Bloomington, IN: Indiana University Press, 2012.

Shapira, Anita. יהודים חדשים, יהודים ישנים [*Yehudim Hadashim, Yehudim Yeshanim*]. Tel Aviv: Am Oved, 1997.

Shimoni, Gideon. "The Jewish Community and the Zionist Movement in South African Society (1910–1948)." PhD dissertation, The Hebrew University of Jerusalem, Israel, 1974.

Shimoni, Gideon. *Jews and Zionism: The South African Experience (1910–1967)*. Cape Town: Oxford University Press, 1980.

Shimoni, Gideon. "South African Jews and the Apartheid Crisis." *American Jewish Yearbook* 88 (1988): 3–58.

Shimoni, Gideon. *Community and Conscience: The Jews in Apartheid South Africa*. Waltham, MA: Brandeis University Press, 2003.

Skinner, Rob. *The Foundations of Anti-Apartheid: Liberal Humanitarians and Transnational Activists in Britain and the United States, c. 1919–64*. New York: Palgrave Macmillan, 2010.

South African Jewish Board of Deputies. *The Anti-Jewish Movements in South Africa: The Need for Action*. Johannesburg: SAJBD, 1936.

South African Jewish Board of Deputies. *South African Jews in World War II*. Johannesburg: SAJBD, 1950.

Soske, Jon. *Internal Frontiers: African Nationalism and the Indian Diaspora in Twentieth-Century South Africa*. Athens: Ohio University Press, 2018.

Soske, Jon, and Sean Jacobs. *Apartheid Israel: The Politics of an Analogy*. Chicago: Haymarket Books, 2015.

Stauber, Roni. *The Holocaust in Israeli Public Debate in the 1950s: Ideology and Memory*. Edgware, UK: Vallentine Mitchell, 2007.

Steinlauf, C. Michael. *Bonding to the Dead: Poland and the Memory of the Holocaust*. Syracuse, NY: Syracuse University Press, 1997.

Stier, Baruch O. "South Africa's Jewish Complex." *Jewish Social Studies* 10.3 (2004): 123–142.

Stemmet, Jan-Ad. "From nipples and nationalists to full frontal in the new South Africa: An abridged history of pornography and censorship in the old and new South Africa."

Communication: South African journal for communication theory and research 31.2 (2005): 198–210.

Stoler, Laura Ann, and Carole McGranahan. "Refiguring Imperial Terrains." In *Imperial Formations*, edited by Ann Laura Stoler, Carole McGranahan, and Peter Perdue, 3–42. Santa Fe, NM: School of American research, 2007.

Stone, M. Lotte. "Seeking asylum: German Jewish refugees in South Africa, 1933–1948." PhD dissertation, Clark University, Worcester, Massachusetts, 2010.

Suppan, Arnold, and Maximilian Graf. *From the Austrian Empire to Communist East Central Europe*. Berlin: LIT Verlag, 2010.

Suttner, Immanuel. *Cutting Through the Mountain: Interviews with South African Jewish Activists*. New York: VIKING, 1997.

Suzman, Arthur, and Denis Diamond. *Six Million Did Die: the truth shall prevail*. Johannesburg: SAJBD, 1977.

Taffy, Adler. "Lithuania's Diaspora: The Johannesburg Jewish Workers' Club, 1928–1948." *Journal of Southern African Studies* 6.1 (1979): 70–92.

Taylor, Paul, and A. J. R Groom. *United Nations at the Millennium: The Principal Organs*. London: Continuum, 2000.

Tayob, Abdulkader. *Islamic Resurgence in South Africa*. Cape Town: University of Cape Town Press, 1995.

Thompson, Leonard. *A History of South Africa, Third Edition*. New Haven: Yale University Press, 2001.

Tomaselli, Keyan G. "Ideology and Censorship in South African Film." *Critical Arts – South-North Cultural and Media Studies Journal* 1.2 (2008): 1–15.

Tutu, Desmond, and John Allen. *God is not a Christian*. London: Rider, 2011.

Tutu, Desmond. *Hope and Suffering: Sermons and Speeches*. Johannesburg: Skotaville, 1983.

Turrell, Robert. *White Mercy. A Study of the Death Penalty in South Africa*. Westport, CT: Praeger, 2004.

Van der Lans, Jos, and Herman Vuijsje. *Het Anne Frank Huis Een Biografie [Anne Frank House – A Biography]*. Basel: Anne Frank Fonds, 2010.

Vassen, Robert D. *Letters from Robben Island: A Selection of Ahmed Kathrada's Prison Correspondence 1964–1989*. Cape Town: Mayibuye Books, 1999.

Venter, Sahm. *A Free Mind: Ahmed Kathrada's Notebook from Robben Island*. Johannesburg: Jacana Media, 2005.

Wald, Herman. *Craved Thoughts*. Johannesburg: unpublished, 1944.

Weaver-Hightower, Rebecca. "This is the Place Salt Lake City, Utah and the Voortrekker Monument Pretoria: monuments to settler constructions of history, race, and religion." *Safundi: The Journal of South African and American Studies* 22.2 (2021): 105–129.

Weinberg, Leonard, and Peter H. Merkl. *The Revival of Right-Wing Extremism in the Nineties*. New York: Routledge, 2014.

Weitz, Yehiam. "Changing Conceptions of the Holocaust: The Kasztner Case." In *Reshaping the Past: Jewish History and the Historians*, edited by Jonathan Frankel, 211–230. Oxford: Oxford University Press, 1994.

West, Gerald. "The Legacy of Liberation Theologies in South Africa, with an Emphasis on Bibical Hermeneutics." *Studia Historiae Ecclesiasticae* 36 (2010): 157–183.

Whine, Michael. "Holocaust Denial in the United Kingdom." In *Nationalist Myths and Modern Media: Contested Identities in the Age of Globalization*, edited by Jan Herman Brinks, Stella Rock, and Edward Timms, 69–82. London: Tauris Academic Studies, 2005.

Wieder, Alan. "The Treason Trial and Underground Action." In *Ruth First and Joe Slovo in the War Against Apartheid*, 90–111. New York: Monthly Review Press, 2013.

Wiesel, Elie. *A Jew Today*. New York: Random House, 1978.

Williams, Gwyneth and Hackland, Brian. *The Dictionary of Contemporary Politics of Southern Africa*. New York: Routledge, 2015.

Wistrich, Robert. S. "Introduction: Lying about the Holocaust." In *Holocaust Denial: The Politics of Perfidy*, edited by Robert S. Wistrich, 1–26. Berlin: De Gruyter, 2012.

Worden, Nigel. צמיחת המדינות החדשות באפריקה: התהוותה של דרום אפריקה המודרנית [*The Making of Modern South Africa*]. Tel Aviv: The Open University Press, 2002.

Wyman, David S. *The World Reacts to the Holocaust*. Baltimore: The Johns Hopkins University Press, 1996.

Yablonka, Hanna. *The State of Israel Vs. Adolf Eichmann*. Schocken Books, 2004.

Young, James E. "The Biography of a Memorial Icon: Nathan Rapoport's Warsaw Ghetto Monument." *Representations* 26 (1989): 69–106.

Zalmanovich, Tal. "'What Is Needed Is an Ecumenical Act of Solidarity': The World Council of Churches, the 1969 Notting Hill Consultation on Racism, and the Anti-Apartheid Struggle." *Safundi* 20.2 (2019): 174–193.

Zertal, Idith. *Israel's Holocaust and the Politics of Nationhood*. Cambridge: Cambridge University Press, 2005.

Zimmermann, Moshe. "Muscle Jews versus Nervous Jews." In *Emancipation Through Muscles: Jews and Sports in Europe*, edited by Michael Brenner and Gideon Reuveni, 13–26. Lincoln: University of Nebraska Press, 2006.

Zubrzycki, Genevieve. *The Cross of Auschwitz: Nationalism and Religion in Post-Communist Poland*. Chicago: The University of Chicago Press, 2009.

Zuckerman, Moshe. שואה בחדר האטום: ה"שואה" בעיתונות הישראלית בתקופת מלחמת המפרץ [*Shoah in the Sealed Room: The "Holocaust" in the Israeli Press during the Gulf War*]. Tel Aviv: Hotzaat HaMehaber, 1993.

Index

Abbas, Mahmoud 154
Addleson, Abraham 92
Allon, Yigal 106
Anielewicz, Mordecai 46, 191
Antebi, Yigal 218
Arad, Yitzhak 131
Arafat, Yasser 153–154, 217
Arnon, Michael 94
Auerbach, Franz 141

Bar-Kokhba, Simeon 45
Barrow, Brian 117
Beauclair, Robin 122, 126
Ben-Gurion, David 9, 41, 75–76, 79, 94, 96
Benson, Mary 93–94
Ben-Zvi, Izhak 94
Bergmann, Hugo 95
Bernstein, Edgar 49–50, 73–74
Bernstein, Lionel 196
Bethlehem, Marlene 160
Bloomfield, J. Sara 228
Bloomberg, Charles 114, 120
Botha, Pik 213–214
Botha, William, Peter 101, 144–145, 151–152, 211, 214
Brown, E. D. Sydney 107, 119–120, 123, 125–127, 131–132
Buber, Martin 95
Bunting, Brian 1, 90, 174
Bunting, Sonia 90
Buthelezi, Mangosuthu 145

Cajee, Amin 157–158
Chikane, Frank 168
Clinton, Bill 154
Coertze, L. I. 96
Comay, Michael 75
Couzens, Tim 201, 205

Dadoo, Yusuf 184
Darlow, Michael 114
De Klerk, Willem, Frederick 152, 155
Diamond, Denis 102, 115, 118–119, 121, 131–132, 141

Dinur, Yehiel 84
Doussy, J. Hyacinth 127, 132
Dubbelman, Jean-Eric 156, 158–159

East, Sidney 77
Eichmann, Adolf 9–12, 68–98, 122, 131
Erasmus, Louis 98
Ernst Simon, Akiva 95
Ettlinger, Bernard Arthur 36–37

Feit, Leo 48, 51
First, Ruth 90, 205
Frank, Anne 1, 7, 13–14, 55, 98, 133–137, 143– 172, 181, 198–206
Frank, Otto 135, 155, 163
Freedman, Richard 170, 230
Fucik, Julius 186–187

Gagarin, Yuri 87–90
Goldberg, Aleck 120
Goldberg, Dennis 196
Goldreich, Arthur 196
Goldstone, Richard 169
Goodrich, Frances 55, 135, 203
Gottein, David Edward 41
Grobler, Jan 75–76
Gur, Shlomo 150
Gur-Ari, Zvi 154, 223

Hackett, Albert 55, 135, 203
Hammer, Zevulun 221
Hanock, Anton 43
Hansel, Helmuth 123–124, 127–128
Haptman, H. 118
Harris, Cyril 160, 169
Harwood (Verrall), Richard 13, 118, 121–123, 126, 132, 135
Hausner, Gideon 131
Havemann, Chris 25
Hepple, Bob 196
Herbert, Pat 157
Hersov, Jack 57
Hertzog, Albert 102, 112, 119
Hertzog, James Barry Munnik 29

Heydrich, Reinhard 186
Hier, Marvin 224
Hitler, Adolf 8, 24–25, 33, 35–36, 54, 61, 67, 71, 89, 96, 115, 117–118, 131–132, 146, 171, 175, 177, 186, 188, 192–194, 202, 212–214
Hoffman, David 225
Hofmeyr, Jan Hendrik 26–28
Huddleston, Trevor 210
Hurwitz, Harry 101

Isaacs, Jeremy 113, 117

Kafity, Samir 219
Kantor, James 196
Kathrada, Ahmed 17–18, 142, 177, 180–206
Katz, David Brock 211
Katz, Drora 114
Kenyatta, Jomo 190
Kollek, Teddy 219
Kruger, Paul 88
Kuper, Leo 178

Lanzmann, Claude 13
Levavi, Arieh 82
Levin, Mayer 135
Liel, Alon 150–151, 154–155
Livingstone, Ken 157–158
Louw, Eric 76–77
Luthuli, Albert 195

Maisels, Israel 57, 72
Malan, François Daniel 27, 30, 39–41, 108, 193–194
Mandela, Nelson 143, 151–155, 164, 170, 176–178, 193, 195–200, 227
Marais, Jaap 146
Mbeki, Govan 90, 163–164, 173, 176, 196, 200
McConachy, Susan 114
Metz, Gordon 161
Meyer, A. L. 59
Mhlaba, Raymond 196
Mielke, Jonathan 141
Millin, Sarah Gertrude 49
Mkenge, Victoria 145

Mlangeni, Andrew 196
Moerdijk, Gerard 52
Motsoaledi, Elias 196
Muller, Hilgard 106
Muller, Piet 116

Napier, Wilfred 168
Nates, Tali 7, 181, 229–230
Nel, Fred 133
Nordau, Max 45
Nurock, Mordechai 66

Ocasio-Cortez, Alexandria 227
Odendaal, Andre 161
Olivier, Lawrence 114
Olmert, Yossi 218–219
Osrin, Myra 148, 159–160, 165–166, 172

Paton, Alan 110
Peres, Shimon 106, 154
Pietersen, Hector 171
Pirow, Oswald 72
Postma, Dirk 88
Potgieter, Cornelius, Pieter 168

Rabin, Yitzhak 106, 154
Rapoport, Nathan 36–38, 46
Reinhardt, M. A. 118
Rev C. H. S. Runge 28
Rich, Frank 137
Robeson, Paul 190
Rosenne, Shabtai 94
Rotenstreich, Mathan 95
Roy, Simon 50

Saron, Gustav 6, 24, 32, 57, 71–72
Schach, Leonard 55, 134, 136
Schauder, Adolph 24, 57
Schneier, Minna 55
Schoeman, Johan 91–92
Schuiteme, Brand 159
Segal, Hymie 138, 142
Shaban, Abel 56–57, 59–60
Shamir, Yitzchak 152, 218
Shanks, Pat 157
Shertok, Moshe 37

Sisulu, Walter 164, 177, 193, 196, 198
Slovo, Joe 151, 176, 195–196, 205
Smith, Mervyn 147, 159
Smuts, Jan Christian 24, 29–30, 34–35, 37, 39, 41, 74
Snyman, Lammie 110–111, 130
Speer, Albert 131
Strijdom, Johannes Gerhardus 68, 183
Suzin, Leon 38
Suzman, Arthur 130–131
Suzman, Helen 69, 110, 170

Tambo, Oliver 176, 179
Tutu, Desmond 17–18, 153, 167– 168, 180, 208–228

Ungar, Andre 70–71

van der Hoven, Eghard 136
Vassen, Bob 142
Verdal, Garth 141

Verwoerd, Frensch Hendrik 66, 68–70, 76–78, 111–112, 145
Visser, J. H. 96
Vorster, Balthazar Johannes 30, 97–99, 105–107, 119–120, 159

Wald, Herman 43–67
Wald, Jacob 43
Wald, Marcus 44
Wald, Pearl 44
Walnes, Gillian 159
Weichardt, Louis 24
Weiler, Cyrus Moses 46
Wessels, Manie 24
Wiesel, Elie 100, 137, 141, 223
Wilson, Boris 69
Wolpe, Harold 196

Yaméogo, Maurice 75
Yellin, Solly 87

Zundel, Ernst 126–127

www.ingramcontent.com/pod-product-compliance
Lightning Source LLC
Chambersburg PA
CBHW020226170426
43201CB00007B/334